Table of Contents

Vancouver Island
Region 1

Fishing Mapbooks

"With their guides you will be an expert on the lake even before you get there"

~ **Fishing4Fools.com**

"…Mussio Ventures gets a big two thumbs up from this angler!"

~ **Richard A. Cuffe**

"Tells you anything and everything you could possibly want to know about fishing…"

~ **Vancouver Sun**

come see us at
www.backroadmapbooks.com

British Columbia
Total Area... 944 735 km²
Population...4 113 487
Capital...Victoria
Largest City...Vancouver
Highest Point...Mount Fairweather
4 663 meters (15 299 ft)
Tourism info...1.800.HELLO.BC
www.hellobc.com

Acknowledgements

Published by:

Mussio Ventures Ltd.
Unit 106- 1500 Hartley Ave,
Coquitlam, BC, V3K 7A1
P. (604) 521-6277   F. (604) 521-6260
E-mail: info@backroadmapbooks.com
www.backroadmapbooks.com

Backroad Mapbooks

DIRECTORS
Russell Mussio
Wesley Mussio
Penny Stainton-Mussio

ASSOCIATE DIRECTOR
Jason Marleau

VICE PRESIDENT
Chris Taylor

COVER DESIGN & LAYOUT
Farnaz Faghihi

COVER PHOTO
David Lambroughton

CREATIVE CONTENT
Russell Mussio
Wesley Mussio

PROJECT MANAGER
Farnaz Faghihi

PRODUCTION
Rhianna Beauchamp,
Shaun Filipenko
Oliver Herz, Justin Quesnel
Dale Tober

SALES / MARKETING
Joshua Desnoyers
Chris Taylor

WRITER
Trent Ernst

Library and Archives Canada Cataloguing in Publication

Ernst, Trent
Vancouver Island BC fishing mapbook [cartographic material] /
Trent Ernst.

(Fishing mapbooks)
ISBN 978-1-897225-01-1

1. Fishing--British Columbia--Vancouver Island--Maps. 2.
Fishing--British Columbia--Vancouver Island--Guidebooks. 3.
Vancouver Island (B.C.)--Bathymetric maps. 4. Vancouver
Island (B.C.)--Guidebooks. I. Title. II. Series.

G1172.V3E63E76 2008   799.1'1097112   C2008-902177-0

Acknowledgement

We would like to thank everyone for their support and encouragement to resurrect the Fishir
Mapbook series. This book is a collaboration of many organizations and people and is intende
to be a resource that can and will be used by all anglers on Vancouver Island. First off, this is
big thank you to the Freshwater Fisheries Society of BC, in particular Brian Chan. They helpe
us refine our lake list and gave us many helpful pointers along the way. Then there is Trent Erns
He took over the writing and research of the lakes and streams and has really learned to fish o
impressive information. Of course we can not forget the helpful team of mappers, editors ar
graphics people at Backroad Mapbooks. These are the people who pieced everything together
such a convenient, yet comprehensive package. Thank you Andrew Allen, Rhianna Beaucham
Joshua Desnoyers, Farnaz Faghihi, Shaun Filipenko, Oliver Herz, Justin Quesnel, Chris Taylc
and Dale Tober.

When doing our research, we had to consult numerous people who live and play on the Islan
Again, we would like to thank the fine folks at the Freshwater Fisheries Society of BC who he
keep the fish stocked in so many Island lakes; without them, the fishing wouldn't be anywhe
near as good as it is. Then there is Bill Shaw at the Department of Fisheries and Oceans wh
gave us the skinny on salmon stocks around the various Island streams, while Scott Silvestri at th
BC Conservation Foundation kept us up to date on how steelhead returns were doing.

Getting back to the lakes, Randy Dolighan with Fisheries provided us with information on mar
of the lakes. Lyle Bond at the Sooke Hatchery gave us the lowdown on how things are doir
on the southern Island. Jack Toomer, with the Island Waters Fly Fishing Association answere
a bunch of questions for us, as did folks at a variety of outdoor stores. These include Les
Timberland Sport Centre, Jim and Nita at Jim's Hardy Sport, Andrew at Screaming Fish ar
Fly, everybody at River Sportsman Outdoor Store and the various Gone Fishing Shop as well
Roger and crew at Tyee Marine Sports.

Figuring out road access is a real challenge these days. However, people like Richard Blier ar
Richard Powell were very helpful and helped to provide a whole whack of feedback about curre
road conditions and access.

Finally, to all those people we talked to and forgot to mention, thank you. It is our forgetfulnes
not our ingratitude that precludes us mentioning you specifically.

The maps and charts are courtesy of Backroad Mapbooks. However, they had to source B
Fisheries for the templates for the Lake Depth Chart Maps as well as Geogratis and the Minist
of Sustainable Resources for the source data for the overview maps.

Finally we would like to thank Allison, Devon, Jasper, Nancy, Madison and Penny Mussio for the
continued support of the Mapbook Series. As our family grows, it is becoming more and mor
challenging to break away from it all to explore our beautiful country.

Sincerely,

Russell and Wesley Mussio

Distributed by
Gordon Soules Book Publishers Ltd.
1359 Ambleside Lane,
West Vancouver, BC, Canada V7T 2Y9
604-922-6588 | books@gordonsoules.com
Fax: 604-922-6574 | www.gordonsoules.com

Disclaimer

The lake charts contained in this book are not intended for navigational purposes. Uncharted rock
and shoals may exist. Mussio Ventures Ltd. does not warrant that the information contained in th
guide is correct. Therefore, please be careful when using this or any source to plan and carry out you
outdoor recreation activity. Also note that travelling on logging roads, trails and waterways is inherentl
dangerous, and you may encounter poor road conditions, unexpected traffic, poor visibility, and lo
or no road/trail maintenance. Please use extreme caution when travelling logging roads, trails an
waterways.

Please refer to the British Columbia Freshwater Fishing Regulations for closures and restriction
Salmon and steelhead anglers should also visit www.gov.bc.ca/fw/ or www.pac.dfo-mpo.gc.ca/rec
fish/default_e.htm before heading out. It is your responsibility to know when and where closures an
restrictions apply.

Help Us Help You

A comprehensive resource such as Fishing Mapbooks for Vancouver Island BC could not be
put together without a great deal of help and support. Despite our best efforts to ensure tha
everything is accurate, errors do occur. If you see any errors or omissions, please continue to
let us know.

All updates will be posted on our web site: www.backroadmapbooks.com

Please contact us at:
Mussio Ventures Ltd.
Unit 106- 1500 Hartley Ave,
Coquitlam, BC, V3K 7A1

Email: updates@backroadmapbooks.com
P: 604-521-6277 toll free 1-877-520-5670
F: 604-521-6260 , www.backroadmapbooks.com

Welcome

Vancouver Island
Region 1

Welcome to the Second Edition of Fishing Vancouver Island Mapbook. This book is an evolution of the former Fishing BC title for the Island, but has been expanded to include the lakes found on the north, as well as the popular rivers around the Island.

Vancouver Island is a land set apart from the rest of the province. While its towering mountain peaks and thick rainforest unite it with the rest of the province, there is something palpably different about the place. Maybe it's the fact that it is surrounded on all sides by water, making it one of the most moderate climates in the country. Maybe it is the fact that it is so sparsely populated. Or maybe it is just the attitude of the people you meet, who live life on island time. Whatever it is, a visit to Vancouver Island is a magical experience.

The Island is home to some of the most storied, and some of the most famous fishing to be found anywhere. An impressive number of salmon and steelhead bearing rivers attract thousands of anglers annually. Combine the remote fishing with world-class steelhead, salmon and resident trout and you see why Island rivers make such an excellent year round fishery.

Steelhead remains the fish of choice for Vancouver Island river anglers, but most rivers also support a resident population of trout, be it cutthroat, rainbow, or less often, brown or brook. And, at the right time of year, all manner of spawning salmon—Chinook, Coho, chum, pink and sockeye can be found.

The fish that inhabit the Island's lakes are one of the best-kept secrets of local anglers. As saltwater and river fishing draws the lion's share of angling attention, the various species of trout, kokanee and bass that inhabit these waters have not seen the same pressure as the sea-run species. And, since these fish spend all their time in freshwater, they don't have the same issues as anadromous species. They don't have to deal with mackerel and sea lions and other predators as they make their way out to sea. They don't have to deal with ever-changing government policies and regulations, or any of a thousand other issues that salmon and steelhead have to deal with.

Unfortunately, timber companies like TimberWest hold much of the land of southern Vancouver Island privately. Historically, these companies have allowed anglers and others onto their land, but in the last few years, gates have been springing up, barring access to these areas. These companies have adopted a no public access policy. The lake list that is being cut off by TimberWest is shocking and is a very concerning issue that really affects people's ability to get out and play.

Even with loss of access to the more remote southern lakes, there are still lots of lakes that the avid angler can access. There are big lakes and small, urban lakes and wilderness, high elevation and low. Some lakes are easily accessible, found alongside major highways, while other lakes require the better part of a day to hike in. Some are found on the wet west coast of the island, where the phenomenal amount of rainfall washes the nutrients out of the lake, making the fish small but hungry. Some are found in the rain shadow on the Island's east side, where they grow big and lazy.

Getting to many of these lakes require long trips on a maze of backroads, and knowing where you are going is essential. It is highly recommended to bring along a copy of the Vancouver Island Backroad Mapbook along with a GPS to help guide you on your journey.

The Fishing Mapbook Series is designed to show you where and how to fish any given area. To help you have a successful trip, we have provided fishing tips, breakdowns of each species, fly hatches and information on individual lakes and streams throughout the area. To help you find your way, there are inset maps, as well as depth charts for the popular lakes and bar or hot spot maps of the main rivers in the area.

No other source combines such detailed information on how and where to fish the Island as this. If you are new to the area, or just looking for a new place to fish, we are certain you will find the Fishing Mapbook an excellent guide.

History

The Fishing Mapbook Series evolved from research done when creating the Backroad Mapbook Series. The authors and researchers really enjoy exploring and fishing new lakes but didn't always know where to start. After stumbling across the depth charts for a few lakes, they learned how to read a lake a lot quicker and have been able to fish that much more effectively.

In their travels, they get a chance to explore a lot of new lakes and streams. The visual information provided in the depth charts and river maps help the researchers find the best place to fish time and time again. They figured if they found these charts that useful, other anglers would too.

Mussio Ventures Ltd. was not the first company to see the value of depth charts. Other companies were producing individual lake charts and selling them for a premium. In typical entrepreneurial fashion, Russell and Wesley Mussio took it one step further. Rather than selling individual charts, they put several lakes in a single book and added valuable information on everything from directions and facilities to fishing tips and stocking information. They also priced the book reasonably.

Today, the series have evolved into even bigger books and now cover the more popular streams in the area. Working with key people in the industry has also helped gain more valuable insight into fishing the various lakes and rivers covered in each book.

Russell & Wesley Mussio - Founders of Backroad Mapbooks

3

Regional Boundaries

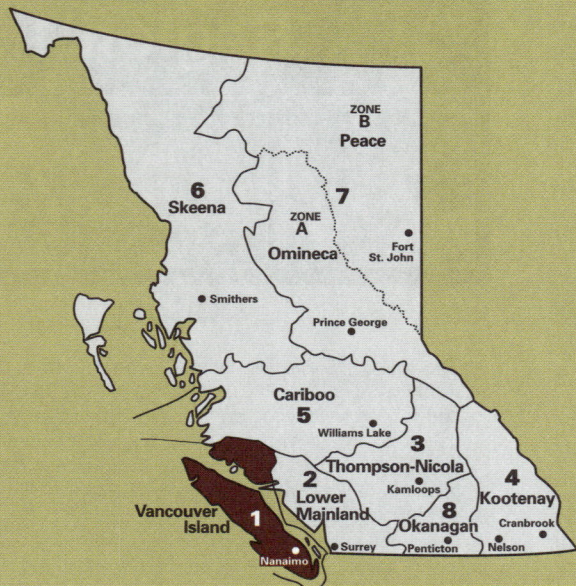

Lake Chart Classifications:

⧾⧾	Rocks		Sandbar
🦆	Swamp / Marsh		Provincial Park
→	Stream		Lake
=======	Highway	————	Side Road
≡≡≡≡	Main Road	- - - - -	Old Road/Trail
┼─┼─┼	Railways	———	Management Zones

Recreational Activities and Miscellaneous

♿ Wheelchair	🚶 Hiking	▱ Dock/Wharf	⚓ Anchorage
P Parking	🏊 Boat Launch	Beacons	Viewpoint
Swimming	🚴 Biking	Waterfall	View
Paddling	Picnic Area	Lodge / B&B	● Community
Float Plane Access		Resort	= Dam
5 Highway, Primary		★ Point of Interest	
Highway, Secondary		A Truck Only Campground	
Highway, Trans-Canada		A Trail or Water Access Campsite	
		Trailer and Tent Campground	

For Salmon Information Only Fisheries and Oceans Canada District Offices (DFO)

Duncan:	250-746-6221
Campbell River:	250-850-5701
Comox:	250-339-2031
Nanaimo:	250-754-0230
Port Alberni:	250-720-4440
Port Hardy:	250-949-6422
Tofino:	250-725-3500
Victoria:	250-363-3252
Shellfish Information Line	1-866-431-3474

Region 1- Vancouver Island:
Fish and Wildlife Regional Office

Nanaimo: 2080A Labieux Rd, V9T 6J9, 250-751-3100
Conservation Officer Service District Offices
Please call one of the numbers below for recorded information or to make an appointment:
Campbell River: 250-286-7630   Duncan: 250-746-1236
Nanaimo: 250-751-3190   Port Alberni: 250-724-9290
Port Hardy: 250-949-2800   Victoria: 250-391-2225
Vancouver Island Trout Hatchery
Duncan: 250-746-5180

4

Top 5 Hot Spot Rivers

1. Campbell/Quinsam Rivers
2. Cowichan River
3. Gold River
4. Salmon River
5. Stamp-Somas River

Top 20 Hot Spot Lakes

1. Alice Lake
2. Beavertail Lake
3. Comox Lake
4. Croteau & Lady Lakes
5. Elk & Beaver Lakes
6. Flora Lake
7. Fuller Lake
8. Gracie Lake
9. Kathleen Lake
10. Kemp Lake
11. Loon Lake
12. Maple Lake
13. McCreight Lakes
14. Nahwitti Lake
15. Quennell Lake
16. Roberts Lake
17. Shawnigan Lake
18. Spider Lake
19. Thetis Lakes
20. Westwood Lake

Fish Species

The book begins with a rather elaborate section on the main sportfish species in the region. In it we give pointers on how to identify and fish for these sometimes elusive fish. These tips should not be overlooked, as they are an accumulation of many years of personal experience and research. Of course there are many anglers out there that know a lot more than we do, but few sources put it all together in such a convenient, compact package. Whether you are new to the area or new to fishing or have fished these holes for years, we guarantee that following these tips will help you find more fish.

The Lakes (Bathometric Charts)

The lake fishing section of this book features all of the favourites as well as some of those lesser know lakes that can produce that lifetime fishing memory. With so many lakes to choose from, the task was indeed a challenge to try to get that right mix in our book.

Similar to this book's predecessors, Fishing BC Southern Vancouver Island, we have highlighted many of the better lakes with depth charts. These charts, if read properly will help you pinpoint the likely areas on a lake to start fishing. These charts show the contours of the lake and help readers figure out where the shoals, drop-offs, hidden islands or basically any sort of water structure that will likely hold fish is located. Reviewing these charts before visiting the lake for the first time could reveal where to find the fish. At the very least, they will help you know where to start fishing.

We have also included the fish species and whether they are stocked or not for each listing. In some cases we even tell you how and what to fish with. If there are no fishing tips included under the individual listing, you can refer to the front or back of the book to refresh yourself on tactics and fly patterns of the prominent species in that lake. Of course, when you get to the lake and there are other anglers there do not be shy to ask where to fish and what to use. Most people are more than willing to help out.

Rivers & Streams

The river or streams section is new to the series, but follows the similar pattern of including fish tips, access and facilities for each stream that is highlighted. Of course, the river maps are a popular feature that include fishing pools and popular access points where possible.

Fishing Tips & Techniques

Near the back of the book this is another excellent resource to refer to. In this section, we give pointers on how to fish using the various lake and stream fishing techniques, as well as some useful fishing tips. Constant referral to this section will help anglers new and old to the sport.

Overview Map and Index

There are also handy planning tools such as the Overview Map and an Index. If you know the waterbody you are planning on visiting, you simply turn to the lakes or river section and find the listing you are interested in. Alternatively, you can look it up in the index to see what page it is listed on.

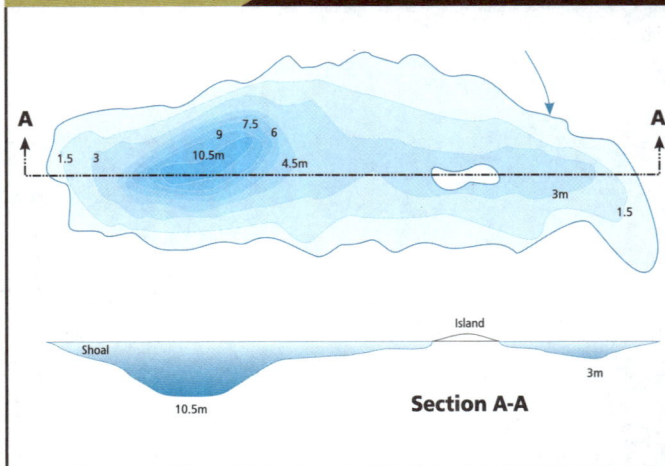

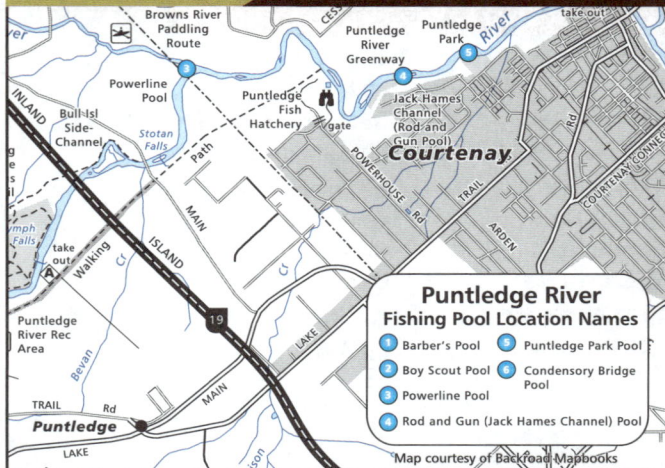

Fish Species

The breadth and variety of fish species on Vancouver Island is a testament to how good the fishing can be here. At any given time, there is quality fishing for one sport fish or another. We have listed the main sport fish found on the Island along with tips on how and when to fish each species.

Bass (Smallmouth) are found in many of the low elevation lakes on southern Vancouver Island. They spawn in May to June, at which time they become an aggressive fish that is very easy to catch. The fishery branch has now made most lakes catch and release during spawning season to help preserve the growing bass fishery.

In the summer months the bass fishery really heats up. Smallmouth bass will strike most well presented bait that resemble the chironomids, small baitfish, leeches and tadpoles that they feed on. Fly fishers should use attractor type patterns such as a Woolly Bugger or Werner shrimp. If spincasting, there are many different plugs such as Rapalas. Other tackle to try includes spinner blades, spoons, buzzy baits, orange Flatfish, top-water plugs or plastic worms.

Bass hang around cover such as a sunken log, lily pad or weed bed or even man-made structures such as docks. The fish do not move much from their hiding place so you have to get your plug or fly right in close to these types of cover. Larger fish tend to hold in deeper water and rarely come out during the day.

Brown Trout are considered one of the wiliest species of trout. There are only a few lakes and rivers on Vancouver Island that have brown trout. The Cowichan River is one of the best known brown trout rivers in the country. The brown trout is more adaptable to warmer water conditions and can often be found cruising shorelines near stream mouths. Brown trout are generally less than 1 kg (2 lbs), but fish as large as 4.5 kg (10 lbs), have been caught in the Cowichan. Stream browns are best caught on the fly, while lake browns are caught mainly by trolling with spoons or spinners.

Chinook are the largest of the Pacific Salmon, getting up to 27 kg (60 lbs) on occasion. They are recognized by their black mouths and spots on their back.

On big rivers, the traditional set-up is a 10-foot or longer rod, a level wind reel with at least 30-pound test. Cast into about 2 m (4 to 8 ft) of water with the current slow enough that the rig will hold up. Your rig should consist of a barrel swivel 30 cm (12-16 in) above the weight. The main line should hold the large lead weight with a wire standoff. The lure is often a #8 red Spin-N-Glo suspended just off the bottom. Don't forget a rod-holder, bell and lawn chair.

In smaller rivers, cast or drift fish with cured roe into deep holes. If trout are cleaning the hook of bait, switch to lures, wool (white, red or pink) or flies. Lures of choice include a Kitimat spoon or Spin-N-Glos.

The fly angler will need heavy gear and fast sinking lines with short strong tippet to get down to the deep holes. Shooting heads allow increased line control and help maintain a drag-free drift. Patterns mixing bright and dark colours seem to be most effective. Woolly Buggers, Egg Sucking Leeches or Marabou Eggs dead drifted are equally good.

Chum salmon can be found in most rivers from late September until late November. Often referred to as dog salmon, they prefer fast, shallow water and colour quickly when they enter fresh water. They are the second largest Pacific Salmon, averaging 5-9 kg (12-20 lbs).

Flies such as a '52 Buick (a small, green shrimp imitation) work well. However, many anglers prefer big Marabou flies (green, pink or orange) with size 2 hooks. Bead heads help vary the presentation. Fly-fishing works best by leaving the fly dead or by a slow steady retrieve. You will need heavy gear to fish these strong, acrobatic fish. Alternatively, float fishing with pink worms or bottom bouncing wool or lures with pink in them can also be very effective.

Coho are the most prized of all river run salmon. These silver fish are identified by their white mouths and spots on their tail, and their acrobatic nature makes them a joy to catch. They average 2-5 kg (5-10 lbs). On most rivers, you can use lighter line (10 lb main with 8 lb test). Smaller floats and lighter weights are essential

SMALLMOUTH BASS

Jaw extends to about middle of eye

Three short spines on anal fin

BROWN TROUT

Black or brown spots, many with light halos

Adipose fin with spots

Tail with few or no spots

CHINOOK

Black mouth, black gums

Round spots on both lobes of tail

CHUM SALMON

Purple streaks or bars in fresh water

No spots

COHO

Black mouth, white gums, black tongue

A few round spots on upper lobe only

since Coho are easily spooked. Look for them to run quickly from the deep pools and structure when the water raises and clarity of the river is reduced.

Coho can be caught by drift fishing wool or bait (salmon eggs or roe). Spincasters should try size 4 or 5 spinners (Blue Fox or Mepps) cast upstream and worked through slower edges of pools. Spoons such as Gibbs Ironhead, Pen Tac's BC Steel and a Little Cleo with 2/0 hook are other popular spincasting gear.

In slack water, fly anglers use a slow sinking line, while in faster water a faster sinking line is needed. Flies vary in colour and size. They can be as small as size 8 in clear water or as big as size 1 in murky streams. Coho will only chase moving flies – Rolled Muddlers and Harrison Fiords are local favourites. Working with a size 4 to 8 gold or silver Muddler Minnow, Mickey Finn or beaded Woolly Bugger can also be dynamite. Try olive colours on bright days and brighter colours on darker days.

When fishing for salmon and steelhead, it is essential to know the current regulations since they change often.

Visit www.env.gov.bc.ca/fw/
and www.pac.dfo-mpo.gc.ca/recfish/default_e.htm before fishing.

CUTTHROAT TROUT

Teeth in throat at back of tongue

Heavy spotting from front to rear

Large mouth
(extends well past eye)

Red slash under lower jaw (may be faint)

DOLLY VARDEN

No worm-like markings on dorsal fin

Oval, snake-like body

Whitish to pinkish spots, largest spots smaller than pupil

Head does not dominate body

White leading edges on lower fins

EASTERN BROOK TROUT

Red spots with blue halos

Worm-like markings on back and dorsal fin

Pinkish-orange paired fins edged in white

KOKANEE

No distinct black spots on sides

Long anal fin (13 or more rays)

Cutthroat Trout get their name from the red slash under their jaw. You will find both resident and sea run cutthroat in rivers and lakes. Cutthroat are predatory fish, feeding extensively on small fish such as sculpins and sticklebacks.

In lakes, the slow growing fish prefer colder water and spawn in the spring, which may be as late as mid June-early July in the high mountain lakes. The most productive times of the year to fish for cutthroat are during the salmon fry migration from March through May and the stickleback spawning times of July through September. In spring, try fly-fishing (a silver minnow imitation), bait fishing (small minnows) or casting a small silver lure to land one of these prized fish. Gold or silver bodied Muddler Minnow or Wool Head Sculpin are two fly patterns to try. Sinking line with short leaders is preferred to work the steep shorelines of lakes. Spincasting Kitimat lures, Panther Martin spinners or trolling Willow Leafs/Ford Fenders can also be effective. For kids a worm and bobber can often do the trick using light test and a small hook. Cast around the drop-off areas as the cutthroat tend to cruise near shore areas in search of baitfish.

As the waters warm, you will need to go deeper. In bigger lakes, trolling a 4-5 inch Cowichan spoon deep may land a trophy fish. However, casting dry flies like black gnats, Elk Hair Caddis, Tom Thumbs or ant patterns should not be ruled out. During the stickleback spawning season in late summer and early fall try working olive or grey stickleback patterns along weed beds or near the bottom. Fishing around the drop-offs or near stream mouths along the lake with fast sink line and long leaders is another possibility. During the cooler periods fly anglers will need to use searching patterns such as black broadhead leeches or Woolly Buggers.

Sea-run cutthroat run in schools, chasing spawning salmon. In the spring they feast on the salmon fry. Try using minnow patterns (Muddler Minnow), Woolly Buggers, small Krocodile lures, spinners as well as worms or powerbait. Presentation is not that important since the feed varies in size and travel in fry balls. Look for feeding activity and cast across the current slightly downstream. Fly-anglers should use a floating line with a long leader and weighted fly.

During the fall, they'll grab salmon eggs or anything close. Attractor patterns, such as Woolly Buggers and sparkle leeches are good bets in winter when food is scarce. Fishing the estuaries or beaches is an art that requires good knowledge of when the tides are moving. It is also essential to match the size and colour of the fry (in spring) or eggs (in fall) the cutthroat are chasing.

Dolly Varden are often confused with bull trout, another species of the char family. Dollies are more common in coastal areas and can reach up to 6.5 kg (14 lbs) in bigger lakes and the sea-run stream version have been known to top 9 kg (20 lbs). Dollies in the 2-5 kg (5-10 lb) range are more common. They are recognized by the pinkish spots on the body. They prefer cold, clean water, grow slowly and spawn in fall.

Their primary diet is insects, eggs and small fish. Troll a green or orange Flatfish or a Krocodile lure. Trolling plugs or larger lures on a downrigger with a flasher can produce big fish. Fishing the creek mouths with bait balls (a large cluster of worms or cured roe) suspended near the bottom can be deadly. Also, jigging with a bucktail and flasher in the winter or spring near a large creek mouth can be very successful.

On rivers and streams, they will chase down eggs, lures and minnow fly patterns that simulate distressed fish. Fishing from September through January can be quite productive as the smaller resident fish are joined by the bigger fish that leave cold, deep lakes or the ocean in fall to spawn. Both prefer deep, slower areas of the river. The aggressive fish are mainly caught on lures, but do take minnow and streamer fly patterns if you can get them deep. Fly anglers need to use high-density or fast sinking lines and big flashy olive baitfish patterns. Drifting egg patterns, such as a weighted Glo Bug, salmon flies, golden stoneflies and fall caddis flies also work. The smaller resident fish are much more aggressive and will feed throughout the year as long as the stream is flowing.

Dollies are slow growing and particularly vulnerable to over fishing. As a result, tough regulations have been imposed in an effort to maintain the resource.

Eastern Brook Trout are actually misnamed char. They are only found in a few select Island lakes and streams. They prefer cooler water and do not need as much oxygen as rainbow. They are good fighters that can grow to over 1 kg (2 lbs). They feed on insects, shrimp and the odd minnow. Fly-fishing is a popular method using chironomids in the spring and various nymph patterns in summer. During their fall spawning period, attractor type flies like a Doc Spratley or Woolly Bugger can be very effective. Spincasters should try a small Deadly Dick tipped with worm or Flatfish.

Kokanee are landlocked sockeye salmon that are easily recognizable by their slim silver bodies with a forked tail. Kokanee turn a brilliant red and create an incredible display when they spawn in the late summer. In the Island lakes, kokanee average 25-30 cm (10-12 in) in size, although can be found larger on a select few lakes. Kokanee are soft mouthed, so use lures such as the Gibbs Kokanee Katcher lake troll, which incorporate a "snubber" in the troll. There are many other lake or gang trolls to use. Adding a short leader along with a Wedding Ring and maggot, Flatfish or small pink Spin-N-Glo lure is the basic set up. Troll as slow as possible in an "S" pattern so your line will speed up, slow down and change depths. Troll with one ounce of weight or less, which takes the lure to 5–15 m (15–45 ft).

Perch are aggressive feeders and are best caught by still fishing worms with a float. Perch don't grow very big, only averaging 15–30 cm (5–12 in) in size. They are quite tasty to eat, but have developed a reputation of being a pest species in BC, since they are often illegally introduced into lakes, usually destroying, or at least seriously impacting the quality of fishing for trout.

Fish Species

Perch are active throughout the year, especially during ice fishing season. They are found in many warm water lakes across the island, especially in low level lakes to the south.

Pink salmon are the smallest of the Pacific Salmon and rarely reach over 2.5 kg (5 lbs). It is best to fish them closer to the estuary to find bright, hard fighting fish. They prefer shallow water with medium currents. They return every two years. On eastern Vancouver Island they run in the even years, while on other rivers they return on odd years. Some rivers even support two runs of pinks, usually in early September.

Fly anglers can get away with a 6 or 7-weight rod. Use a floating line or slow sink line with light flies (anything with pink in it) and drift the fly allowing it to bump along the bottom. Getting them to bite, as opposed to fowl hooking them, requires drifting your fly dead slow. For an exciting alternative, try working a pink Pollywog on the surface by skating it downstream in shallow water (less than 1m/3 ft).

Sockeye are good eating, and are generally easy to catch. They run in schools and can reach 7 kg (15 lbs) in size, but generally are half that size. Sockeye prefer current seams and riffles on downstream sides of gravel bars. During early morning and evening they can be in less than 1.5 m (4 ft) of water, but go deeper in the day. They have diamond-like scales and prominent eyes that make them one of the easiest salmon to identify. Look for them to begin entering the rivers in June, but it is not until late July that the bigger runs arrive. The sockeye fishery lasts until mid-September.

Fly-fishing for sockeye requires an 8-weight rod with short leaders (5-7 ft) and 10-12 lb tippet on high density sink tip lines. Cast the fly directly across the current allowing it to sink and skip on the bottom. Small size 8 green flies are preferred, although in murky waters you will need bigger flies with a bit of sparkle. Bottom bouncing is another popular method using light enough weight (1-3 ounce pencil lead or ball weights) to bounce every three feet or so. Fish the slots between fast and slow water in no more than a few feet of water, using either fluorescent wool or a size 12 green Spin-N-Glo. Attach this to 2–3 m (6–10 ft) of heavier leader. In addition to bottom bouncing from shore, anglers can have luck drift fishing by using a float and bait (pink krill or Ghost Shrimp).

Rainbow Trout are the most common freshwater game fish in the province. They are native to many lakes and streams and are stocked in many more. Rainbow get their name from the colourful stripe they get when spawning in the spring. The fish varies in size depending on the water body and strain you catch.

They average 20-35 cm (8-14 in) in size in many of the smaller lakes. Fly-fishing is the most exciting way to catch trout. Chironomids from March to May, followed by dragonflies, damselflies, mayflies and caddis flies are the main hatches. Attractor type patterns, such as Woolly Buggers or Doc Spratleys, are also popular. During summer, troll leeches and dragonfly nymphs deep during the day when hatch activity is limited and watch for hatches to emerge. A lake troll with a Wedding Ring and worm or bait is a popular alternative for non-fly anglers. Spincasting with spoons and small spinners cast near the drop-offs or around shoreline structure also works in small lakes. Lures such as a silver Dick Nite, Flatfish, Kamlooper, Mepps or Panther Martin can all entice the rainbow to bite.

In bigger lakes, trolling is the most popular method. Trolling a lake troll with a Wedding Ring or small lure and single egg, or a Flatfish, Kwikfish or Krocodile spoon are the preferred methods. For the bigger fish, try minnow fly patterns or trolling with big lures and flashers. If fishing from shore, spincasting small lures along the drop-offs at one of the creek estuaries or in one of the many bays can be effective.

On small rivers and streams, small green and yellow stoneflies and caddis fly nymphs work well. For top water action, watch for mayfly and caddis fly hatches. During brighter periods when trout may be hesitant to rise to the surface to take hatching insects, try small stonefly and mayfly nymphs near the bottom. Good caddis fly top water imitations are the classic dry flies Tom Thumb and Elk Hair Caddis.

Steelhead are the most prized sport fish in British Columbia. They are a sea-run version of rainbow trout known for their acrobatics and fight. Hooking them is only half the battle. Winter steelhead usually run from December through April, peaking in March. Summer steelhead runs beginning in late May and peaking anywhere between June and late July. On some of the more popular rivers, these runs are hatchery enhanced and can get as large as 9 kg (20 lbs).

Steelhead are notoriously difficult to catch. The trick is to vary the presentation depending on the season and water conditions. Steelhead like slow presentations so the quicker the water, the bigger the lure. Bait is most effective in slower, warmer water

PERCH
- Spiny anterior dorsal fin
- Six to nine dark vertical bars
- No fang-like teeth
- Paired fins amber to bright orange

PINK SALMON
- White mouth, black gums
- Large oval spots
- Tiny scales
- Dirty white belly in fresh water

RAINBOW TROUT
- Small black spots mostly restricted to above the lateral line
- Radiating rows of spots on tail
- No teeth in throat at back of tongue

SOCKEYE
- Large scales
- Small black speckles
- No spots

STEELHEAD
- Fork length 50 cm or more
- No teeth in throat at back of tongue

when suspended just off the bottom. Colorado Spinners or silver Krocodiles are good alternatives when an area has been fished or is quite crowded.

Steelhead prefer to hold in shallow water close to shore, behind boulders and logs and beside rapids (not in back eddies). It is best to fish close to the bottom and cast above holding areas. Drift fishing with a float suspending a ¼" pencil lead weight above a short leader of about 30-50 cm (12-20 in) with 1/0 to #4 hooks is the most common method. However, many anglers bottom bounce. Although wool (pink or orange) and a single egg is the most popular combination, popular lures include Corkys, Spin-N-Glos, Gooey Bobs, Colorado Spinners and even plastic worms.

Marabou patterns like the Popsicle, small Muddler Minnows or weighted leech patterns are popular. Floating lines and long leaders with a dry fly like a Grease Liner can produce the fish of a lifetime. In deeper pools, work a weighted stonefly or size 10 Glo Bug along the bottom using a sink tip line and short leader.

Steelhead are heavily regulated and regulations are subject to change on short notice. Be sure to check the fisheries website before heading out.

Message From Brian Chan

FISHING CHECKLIST

Freshwater Fisheries Society of BC

- [ ] Fishing rod and reel
- [ ] Bobbers, swivels, sinkers
- [ ] Lures
- [ ] Hooks
- [ ] Extra line
- [ ] Net
- [ ] Fishing licence
- [ ] Sunscreen
- [ ] Hat
- [ ] Bug spray
- [ ] Lunch or snack
- [ ] Life jacket
- [ ] Sunglasses
- [ ] Camera
- [ ] Extra clothing
- [ ] Nail clippers
- [ ] Pliers
- [ ] Freshwater Fishing Synopsis and Regulations

gofishbc.com

Welcome to the Vancouver Island edition of the Fishing Mapbook series. This lake and stream guide has been completely updated and expanded to provide anglers with the most accurate information on not only how to get to your favourite lake or stream but also provides details on new waters to explore. Each featured fishing location has information on access, fish species present, tips on best times of the year to fish and the best fishing techniques specific to that waterbody. Contour maps or depth charts are also provided on many of the more popular and productive lakes. Knowledgeable anglers understand the value of knowing the depth of water being fished as water temperature and food availability are key factors in determining where and at what depths different fish species are found. New anglers will also see an expanded Fish Species and Fishing Techniques section which includes information on fish identification and tricks to catching them, choosing the right rod and reel or fly gear, as well as common fishing methods and tackle. There is even proper fish handling techniques in this section.

This guide includes a number of featured rivers which adds another dimension to the fishing locations found on Vancouver Island. Anglers have the opportunity to fish for rainbow, cutthroat, brown trout, steelhead and several species of salmon. Use the information in this mapbook plus the Freshwater Fishing Regulations Synopsis to get you on the lake or river of choice.

The Freshwater Fisheries Society of BC has partnered with Backroad Mapbooks on the production of the Fishing Mapbook series, as one of our strategic objectives is to inform and educate the public about fish and recreational fishing. Guidebooks are an important tool in achieving this goal. Other Society activities include delivering Learn to Fish programs for children and families, developing community fisheries within urban areas through our Fishing in the City program, promoting the Fishing Buddies program to help attract even more new and lapsed anglers to sport fishing and improving access to fishing waters. Our major responsibility is delivery of the provincial fish stocking program and many of the lakes covered in this guide are stocked on a regular basis to ensure a sustainable recreational fishery. Up-to-date stocking records for all waterbodies stocked in the province and additional information on other society activities is available on our website www.gofishbc.com.

This guidebook covers a diverse range of fishing locations from easily accessible urban fisheries that are regularly stocked with catchable sized trout to more remote lakes and streams to waters that are only accessible by walking or by boat. The diversity of fishing opportunities described in this publication will ensure the guidebook will be an important part of your fishing trips for many years to come.

Brian Chan
Fishing Ambassador
Freshwater Fisheries Society of BC

Alice Lake

Location: 40 km (24.8 mi) south of Port Hardy
Elevation: 55 m (180 ft)
Surface Area: 1084 ha (2678 ac)
Mean Depth: 31 m (101 ft)
Max Depth: 71.3 m (233.86 ft)
Way Point: 50° 28' 00" Lat - N   127° 25' 00" Lon - W

Fishing

Alice Lake is a popular destination in the Port Alice area, and holds some of the biggest rainbow trout to be found on the island. In addition, cutthroat and Dolly Varden are lurking in the depths. Although the fish are abundant, finding them in such a large lake can be tricky. Your best bet is to troll using minnow or bait imitations to find the cutthroat or dollies, while fly patterns attract the big rainbows.

The best fishing is found between April and June and in September and October when the fish are closer to the surface. Working the drop-off around any of the river and stream mouths is a good starting point. In particular, you should try around the Marble, Link or Benson River estuaries or the mouth of Pinch Creek.

For trollers, the deep lake is best fished with a lake troll with a medium size plug like a Flatfish or Rapala or lures and flies that resemble baitfish. During cooler periods, it is recommended to set these rigs up with 30 metres (100 ft) of line and vary the weight. Work the drop-offs, particularly around the many islands, points of land, around the creek estuaries and off rock cliffs, where the bigger fish hold up on occasion As the waters warm, downrigging equipment is a real asset, as you need to get your gear deep enough into the holding zones.

To help protect the breeding stocks currently, you can't keep wild rainbow over 50 cm (20 in) and there is a single barbless hook restriction. As always, be sure to check the regulations for current fishing restrictions before heading out.

Area Indicator

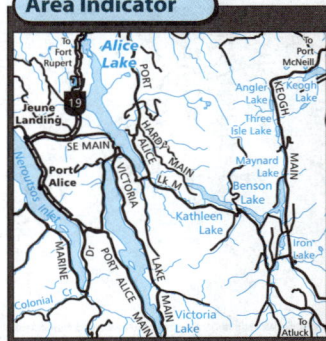

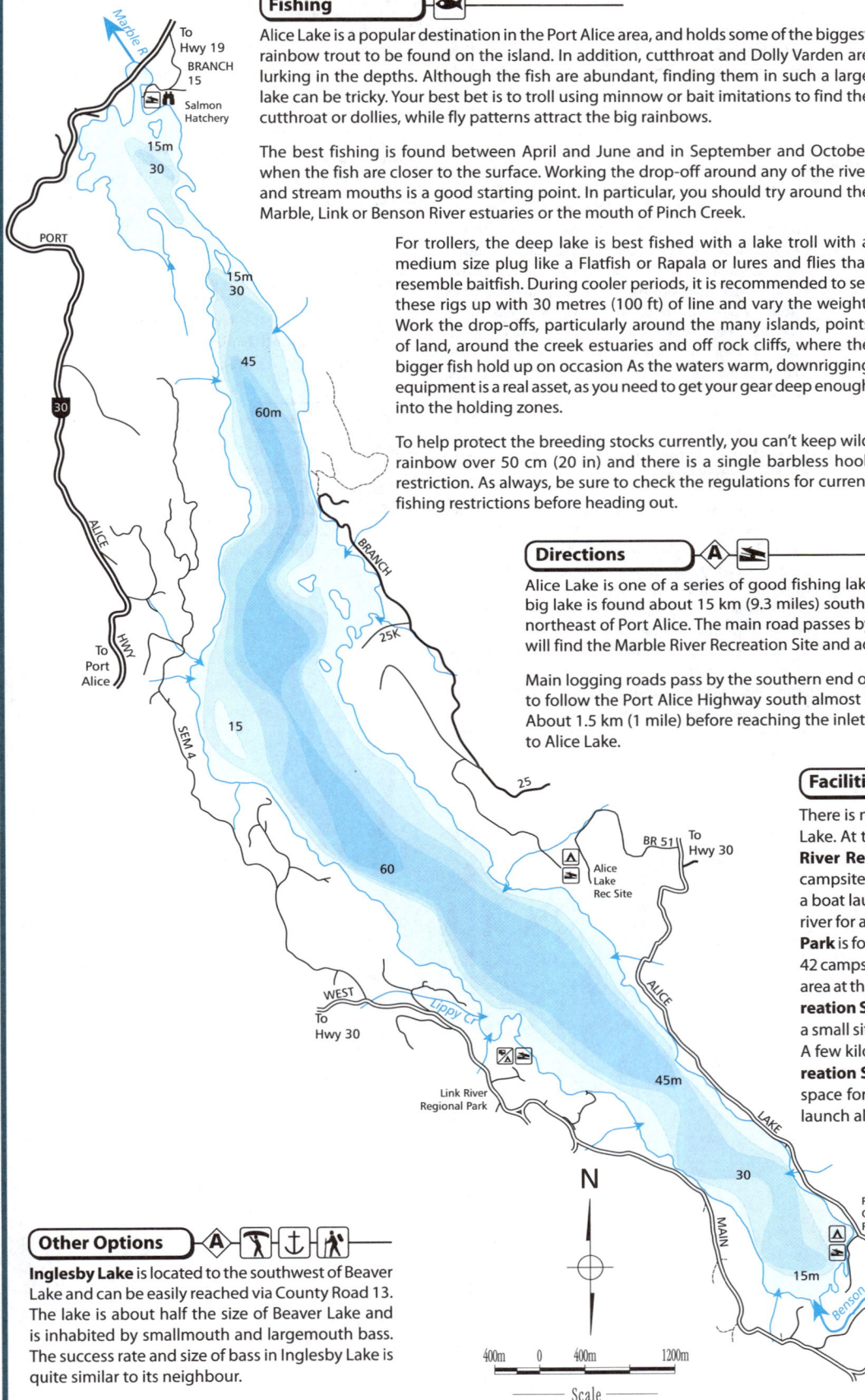

Directions

Alice Lake is one of a series of good fishing lakes found near the road to Port Alice. The big lake is found about 15 km (9.3 miles) south of the North Island Highway (Hwy 19) or northeast of Port Alice. The main road passes by the northwest tip of the lake where you will find the Marble River Recreation Site and access to the lake.

Main logging roads pass by the southern end of the lake. The quickest way to get here is to follow the Port Alice Highway south almost to Jeune Landing on the Neroutsos Inlet. About 1.5 km (1 mile) before reaching the inlet, the SE Main branches east, leading back to Alice Lake.

Facilities

There is no shortage of places to stay around Alice Lake. At the northwest tip of the lake, the **Marbel River Recreation Site** offers 33 well maintained campsites just off the Port Alice Highway. There is a boat launch, a picnic area and good access to the river for anglers and kayakers. **Link River Regional Park** is found at the south end of the lake. There are 42 campsites, a sandy beach, boat launch and picnic area at this popular regional park. **Pinch Creek Recreation Site** is found along the Alice Lake Main. It is a small site with only three campsites and a launch. A few kilometres to the north, the **Alice Lake Recreation Site** offers a slightly bigger campsite with space for ten parties. This site also features a boat launch along with a nice beach.

Other Options

Inglesby Lake is located to the southwest of Beaver Lake and can be easily reached via County Road 13. The lake is about half the size of Beaver Lake and is inhabited by smallmouth and largemouth bass. The success rate and size of bass in Inglesby Lake is quite similar to its neighbour.

N

400m 0 400m 1200m
Scale

Location: 3 km (1.8 mi) north of Gold River
Elevation: 120 m (394 ft)
Surface Area: 20 ha (49 ac)
Mean Depth: 5 m (17 ft)
Max Depth: 10 m (33 ft)
Way Point: 126° 3' 00" Lon - W 49° 48' 00" Lat - N

www.backroadmapbooks.com

Antler Lake

Area Indicator

Antler Lake
Fish Stocking Data

Year	Species	Number	Life Stage
2011	Rainbow Trout	750	Catchables
2010	Rainbow Trout	750	Catchables
2009	Rainbow Trout	500	Catchables

Fishing

Antler Lake is a small, peaceful waterbody found outside of Gold River. With such great salmon fishing in the area, it is not surprising that this little lake often goes unnoticed by area visitors. However, those in the know will find the crystal-clear waters, the beautiful scenery and steady action for trout make this a pleasant lake to visit.

The lake is home to native cutthroat trout and is stocked with 500 catchable rainbow trout each spring by the Freshwater Fisheries Society of BC. The cutthroats are abundant and usually are found in the 25-30 cm (10-12 in) range. The lake has two 9 metre (30 foot) basins and abundant growth of aquatic plants, particularly at the east end that is referred to as Yellow Pond. There is a fairly steep drop-off around the perimeter of the lake except in the Yellow Pond area where the shoals are wider. Fishing is best from April to June, and again in the fall. Trolling with flies, small spoons, Flatfish, Kwikfish or a gang troll baited with worms are common ways to fish the lake. Other anglers prefer to cast spinning gear with small lures.

For those casting or trolling flies on Antler, there are a number of reliable patterns you might want to stock in the tackle box: leeches – any time of the year; damselfly nymph – mid-June to mid-August; dragonfly nymph – early May to end of September; chironomid/ midge – early May to mid-July and the end of September; and caddisfly/sedge –mid-June to the end of August. General searching fly patterns, such as Woolley buggers, Careys, halfbacks and the Spratleys, imitate a range of food sources for rainbow and cutthroat trout, and are excellent attractors any time of the year. The flies can be trolled with a full-sink line close to the bottom.

Directions

Antler Lake is located 3 km (1.8 mi) north of Gold River off the East Road. Turn right at the 'Y' in the road before the bridge over the Gold River to find the launching site and picnic area.

Facilities

Visitors will find a cartop boat launch at the picnic site on the north side of the lake. No power boats are allowed. Full facilities are found in the town of Gold River including campgrounds and motels. There is also a campsite at Muchalet Lake, about 8 km (5 miles) north towards Woss.

Other attractions are the **Antler Lake Nature Trail**, which is a short 2 km (0.6 mi) trail that climbs up and over the hill to Scout Lake to the south.

Other Options

Star Lake, found south of Gold River, offers opportunities similar to Antler Lake and has an angling pier to make fishing from shore easier. Although a 2.5 kg (5.5 lb) rainbow was caught in Star Lake during the 2005 fall lake assessments, the lake generally produces small, stocked rainbow and cutthroat.

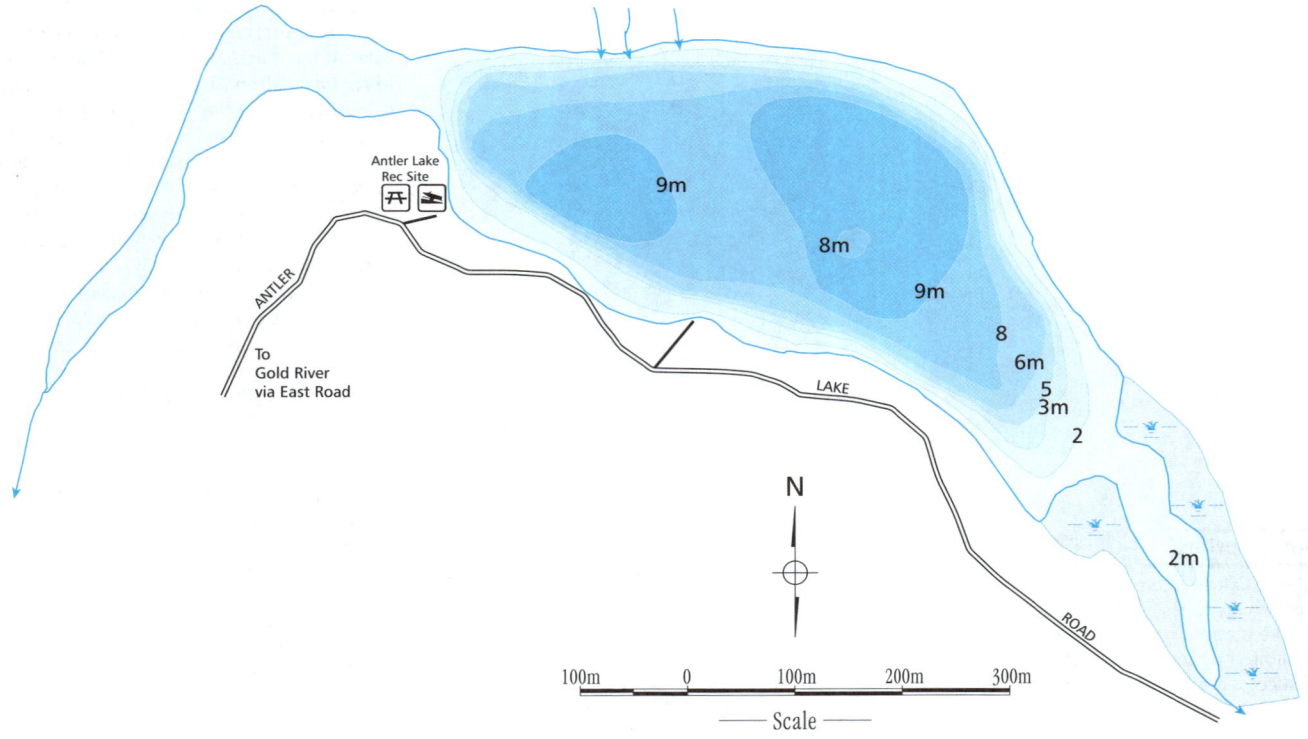

Antler Lake
Rec Site

9m

8m

9m

8

6m

5
3m

2

2m

To
Gold River
via East Road

ANTLER

LAKE

ROAD

N

100m   0   100m   200m   300m
— Scale —

Ash & McLaughlin Lakes

Fishing

Part of a popular chain of lakes north of Great Central Lake and south of Elsie Lake, Ash and McLaughlin Lakes are good fishing destinations. Both lakes provide consistent fishing for small rainbow and cutthroat trout throughout the open water season.

The cutthroat fishing in **McLaughlin** is usually a bit better due to the biannual stocking program. There are also a few Dolly Varden to 1.5 kg (4 lbs) in both lakes. However, it is the rumours of a 7.5 kg (17 lb) brown trout being landed in McLaughlin in 2003 that entices anglers to these lakes.

Fly-fishermen and spincasters are drawn to the northern tip of a small island at the southeastern end of **Ash Lake**, where the bottom drops off nicely. This area is makes for ideal fish habitat, and is one of the more productive spots on the lake. Trollers can circle the lake fairly close to shore as the lake water drops off quickly. Because the water gets so deep so close to shore, casting from shore with a bait and bobber works well too.

Fishing **McLaughlin** is quite similar in the fact that the deepest hole is towards the center of the lake and there are some nice shoals to cast a fly towards. Towards the west end of the lake, there is a neck of land sticking out into the water. Fly-fishers should try working the drop-off here, as it often proves productive.

To help locate the fish, we recommend using searching fly patterns, such as Woolley Buggers, Careys, halfbacks and Spratleys. Lures such as Flatfish, Kwikfish or a gang troll baited with worms are also common ways to fish the lake.

Area Indicator

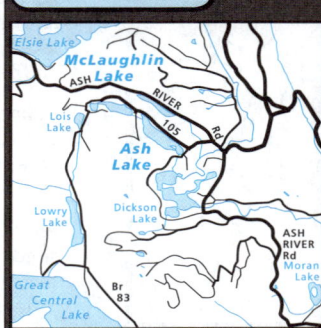

Elevation: 219 m (720 ft)
Surface Area: 41 ha (101 ac)
Mean Depth: 10 m (33 ft)
Max Depth: 28 m (91 ft)
Way Point: 125° 07′ 00″ Lon - W 49° 26′ 00″ Lat - N

McLaughlin Lake

Directions

Both lakes are reached by travelling on Highway 4 past Port Alberni to the Sproat Lake Provincial Park. At that point, head north, then west on the paved Great Central Lake Road. This road leads to the southeast tip of the big lake. From here the Ash River Road, a gravel road continues northwest. At 6.5 km and 11.7 km stay right and at 15 km stay left. After crossing Ash River, look for Branch 105 that runs past Ash Lake to McLaughlin Lake.

Access into this area may be closed or restricted. Further the roads are subject to washouts and are only maintained when active logging is in the area. Be sure to inquire locally before planning a trip into the area.

Facilities

Ash Lake does not have any developed facilities; however, it is possible to launch a cartopper at the lake in a number of locations where the road passes close. Further down the road, **McLaughlin Lake** offers a rustic launch and picnic site near the western end of the lake. Camping beside the road is also possible in the area.

McLaughlin Lake		
Fish Stocking Data		
Year	Species	Number	Life Stage
2007	Cutthroat Trout	1000	Yearling

Ash Lake
No Record of Stocking

Elevation: 206 m (675 ft)
Surface Area: 65 ha (160 ac)
Mean Depth: 14 m (46 ft)
Max Depth: 33 m (108 ft)
Way Point: 125° 05′ 00″ Lon - W 49° 25′ 00″ Lat - N

Ash Lake

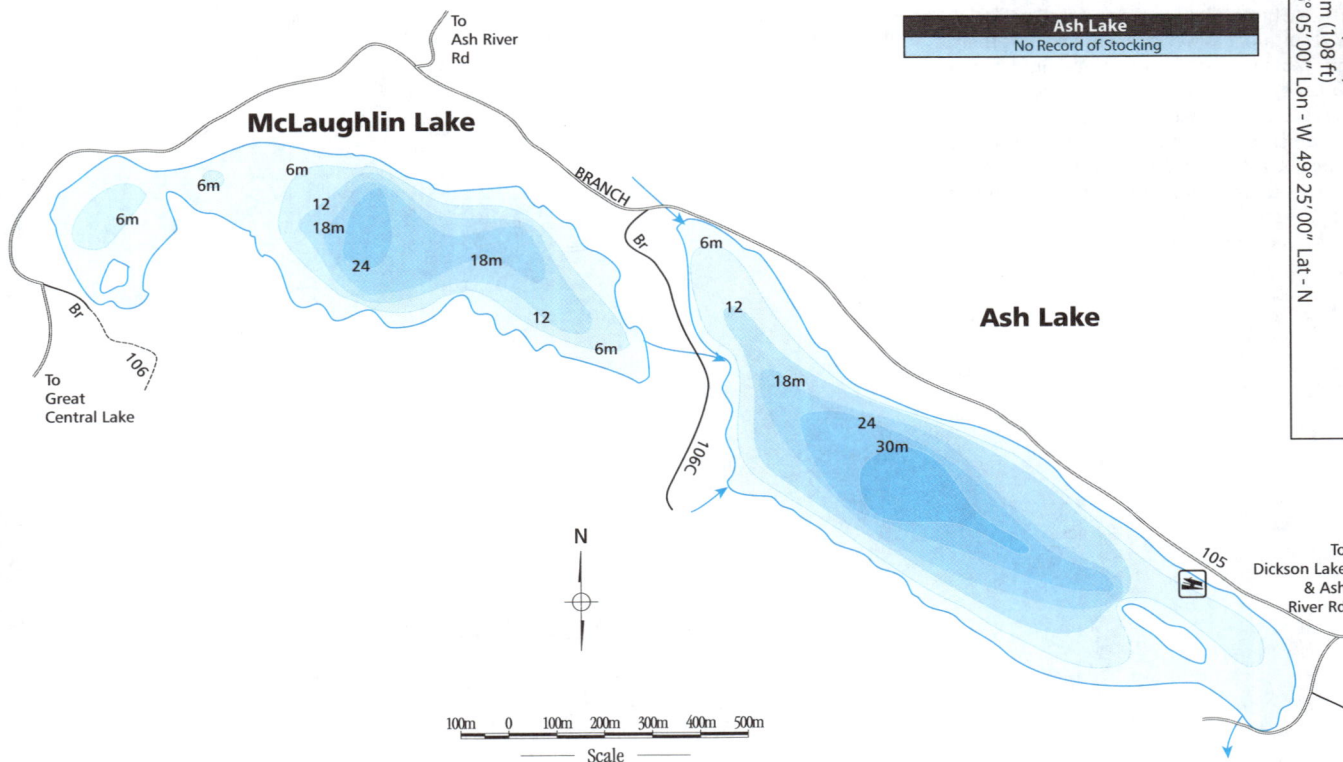

To Ash River Rd

McLaughlin Lake

6m · 6m · 6m · 6m · 12 · 18m · 24 · 18m · 12 · 6m

To Great Central Lake

BRANCH · Br · 106 · 106C · 105

6m · 12 · 18m · 24 · 30m

Ash Lake

To Dickson Lake & Ash River Rd

N

100m 0 100m 200m 300m 400m 500m
Scale

Location: 50 km (31 mi) south of Port McNeill
Elevation: 134 m (440 ft)
Surface Area: 310 ha (766 ac)
Max Depth: 77.4 m (254 ft)
Mean Depth: 31.5 m (103 ft)
Waypoint: 126° 55' 00" Lon - W 50° 13' 00" Lat - N

Area Indicator

Fishing

Situated in the spectacular Nimpkish Valley, Atluck Lake is considered one of the most scenic of the many beautiful lakes in the area. Indeed, the serene mountain setting, lack of people and good access makes this a great fishing and camping destination.

Atluck Lake is large, deep lake with good underwater structure and many inlet streams. The lake drops-off more gradually around the recreation site and the northeast end, but is much steep in the south and west end. There are also a series of islands near the middle of the lake that provide shelter from the winds and good holding areas for the fish. The lake drains into the Nimpkish River at the northeast end.

Although stocked in the past with rainbow, the lake is now a naturallyproducing waterbody home to some nice sized cutthroat, rainbow and Dolly Varden. The lake sees relatively little fishing pressure compared to those on the south Island so anglers can expect better success at times. Although the fishing holds steady during the open water season, fishing is best from May to June and again from September to October.

Being a bigger lake, trolling is the preferred method using anything that resembles the baitfish the sportfish like to chase down. Plugs, spoons or spinners in various colours and sizes are recommended. It is best to work the drop-off areas out from the boat launch, around the inlet streams and around the islands.

Fly anglers will find searching patterns, such as woolly buggers, or olive scuds (freshwater shrimp) can be effective. If using scuds, be sure to try a dead drift with a slow retrieve around creek mouths for added success.

Directions

Found about 50 km south of Port McNeill, Atluck Lake is accessed by a good 2wd gravel road. From the Island Highway (Hwy 19) between Woss and Port McNeill, look for the well signed Zeballos Main Road. Turn southwest on this road and follow it for about 9 km to the Atluck Main. This road leads west, eventually accessing the recreation site and boat launch on the northeast end of the lake.

Other Options

On the way to Atluck Lake you will pass by **Mukwilla Lake.** The 42 hectare lake has many small, wild rainbow and cutthroat as well as a few kokanee. There is a cartop boat launch available. Also in the area is **Tsiko Lake**, to the east, and **Wolfe Lake**, to the south. Tsiko or Loon Lake is a 32 hectare lake with good numbers of cutthroat trout. Fish up to 40 cm in size are not uncommon. Wolfe Lake is a 20 hectare lake with good numbers of larger cutthroat, rainbow and Dolly Varden. Like all the lakes in the area the fishing is better in the spring and fall.

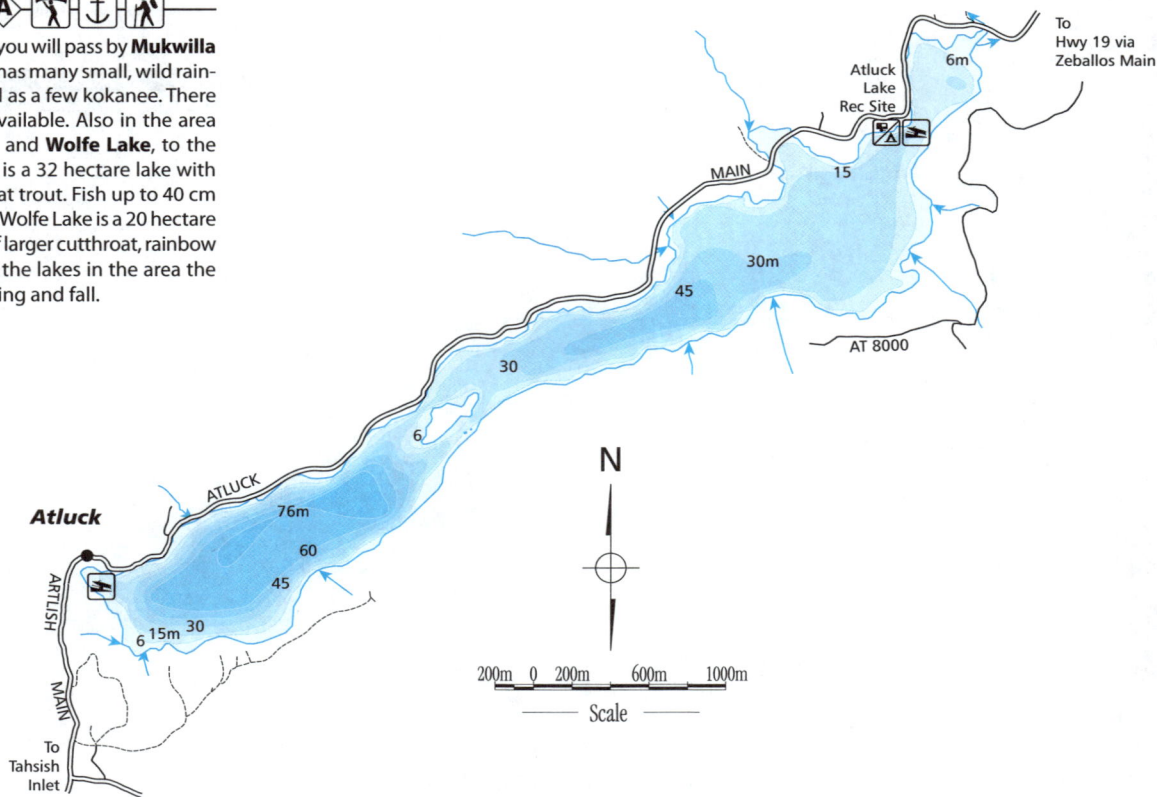

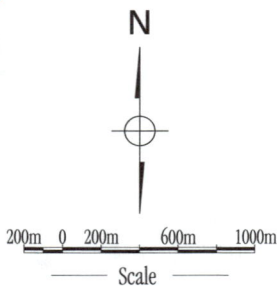

Facilities

The **Atluck Lake Recreation Site** is one of the prettier sites on the Island. The semi-open site offers great mountain views, a gravel beach and space for about five camping groups. Adding to the wilderness experience is the lack of other people. There is a boat launch onto the lake, but boaters should be wary of the winds that can pick up in the narrow valley the lake rests in. In fact, these same winds are popular with windsurfers.

Battleship Lake

Location: 23 km (14 mi) west of Courtenay
Elevation: 1,170 m (3,839 ft)
Surface area: 12.8 ha (32 ac)
Mean depth: 2.4 m (8 ft)
Max depth: 8.6 m (28 ft)
GPS Waypoint: 125° 18' 00" Lon - W 49° 43' 00" Lat - N

Fishing

The fishing season at this high elevation, hike-in lake usually starts in early July. Add the fact that the lake lies in a high snowfall area, and you have an unusually short window to fish the lake. This makes for some good fishing for plentiful, but small rainbow trout throughout the summer and into October.

Battleship Lake is an ideal fly-fishing lake. It has some inviting shoals and islands towards the north end. The drop-off is close enough to shore, particularly on the northwest shoreline, and many anglers just cast from the shore. However, packing in a float tube to reach the islands and the edge of the shoals would be a good idea.

The short season means that the fish are generally quite indiscriminate about what they'll take, and most standard mountain flies (Grizzly King, Tom's Thumb, Royal Coachman, etc) should work. Alternatively, a bait and bobber cast from shore is a good choice, as is casting a small lure tipped with a worm or small spinners. Since the fish are usually smaller than 30 cm (12 inches), it is best to use smaller flier or lures.

The lake is deep enough to avoid winterkill most years, but severe winters can have an adverse affect on the quality of fishing here. You may wish to contact the Strathcona Provincial Park staff about fishing conditions before heading out. Even so, the lake is stocked regularly to help maintain the fishery.

Area Indicator

Directions

Battleship Lake is found on Forbidden Plateau within Strathcona Provincial Park. The lake is reached by driving north of Courtenay on the Inland Highway (Hwy 19) to the turn off to the Mount Washington Ski Area. Follow the Mount Washington Strathcona Parkway Road towards the ever expanding ski village and the Paradise Meadows Trailhead. The new trailhead is located just beyond the Mount Washington Nordic ski area, about 25 km from Courtenay.

From here, it is a relatively easy walk through sub-alpine forests and meadows to the north end of Battleship Lake. The hike is just over 2 km and should take about an hour each way. Trails continue much deeper into the Forbidden Plateau and include the 8 km loop around Lake Helen McKenzie and Battleship Lake.

Facilities

There are no formal campsites on Battleship Lake, however, it is possible to continue on the Lake Helen McKenzie if you are interested in backcountry camping.

Other Options

There are several hike-in lakes in the Forbidden Plateau area that have good fishing for small rainbow. Several of the deeper, more accessible lakes are stocked, while the shallower lakes in the area do not have fish due to winterkill. One of the better options in the area is **Lake Helen McKenzie**, which is located west of Battleship Lake. It is reached by an easy 8 km (5 mile) loop trail from the Paradise Meadows Trailhead that should take about 3 hours to walk. The 55 hectare lake offers very good fishing for small, stocked rainbow (up to 35 cm/14 in) on a fly or by spincasting. Fishing is best from July until early October.

Battleship Lake Fish Stocking Data			
Year	Species	Number	Life Stage
2010	Rainbow Trout	200	Fry
2008	Rainbow Trout	200	Fry

Location: 26 km (20 mi) southwest of Campbell River
Elevation: 276 m (905 ft)
Surface area: 103 ha (255 ac)
Mean depth: 11 m (35 ft)
Max depth: 28 m (92 ft)
GPS Waypoint: 125° 30′ 00″ Lon - W 49° 59′ 00″ Lat - N

www.backroadmapbooks.com

Beavertail Lake

Area Indicator

Fishing

Stocked annually with over 7,000 rainbow trout by the Freshwater Fisheries Society of BC, Beavertail Lake is a popular fishing destination in the Campbell River area. Anglers will also find naturally reproducing cutthroat trout, Dolly Varden and kokanee to add to the fishing experience.

Beavertail is deep enough to maintain a productive fishery all summer long, but like most Island lakes the best results occur from April to June, and again through September and October. Fishing methods vary from casting flies or small lures, to trolling with flies, small spoons, spinners, plugs or lake trolls followed by a lure. For beginner anglers, or if you are new the area, trolling can be one of the most productive and easiest ways to find fish in the lake. Try a red or green wedding band, or red fire Kwikfish tipped with a piece of worm. The lure should be trolled 30–46 cm (12–18 in) behind the troll.

When fishing for kokanee, use small lures or a wedding band tipped with a worm on a gang troll. Troll slowly at mid-depth in the open water of the lake. Kokanee are soft mouthed, so it's a good idea to use a "snubber" to absorb the shock when they bite the lure.

Dolly Varden are opportunistic feeders and when they're hungry, they will hit a variety of flies or tackle. When targeting trout or kokanee, there is a good chance of hooking dollies. Small spinning lures, streamer flies and salmon eggs also work well.

Fly anglers looking for trout can enjoy success throughout the year by paying attention to current hatches. Damsel-flies emerge mid-June to mid-August; dragonfly nymphs can be effective from early May to the end of September; chironomid/midge hatches occur early March to mid-July and the end of September; and the caddisfly/sedge hatch takes flight mid-June to the end of August. Leech and halfback nymph patterns are successful all year long.

Directions

Drive west on the Gold River Highway (Hwy 28) for 16 km (10 mi) to Camp 8 (the Timberwest marshalling yard and offices). Turn right (west) onto the Elk River Mainline, an all-season, gravel logging road and proceed west for about 6 km (3.7 mi) until the lake comes into view on the north side of the road. A boat launch is found at the pullout on the mainline on the south side of the lake.

Facilities

There are two informal camping and launching sites on Beavertail Lake. The main launching site is found off the south side of the lake at the pullout off the Elk River Mainline. This site can be rather noisy with large trucks barrowing down the road. For those interested in camping, it is recommended to take the rough Beavertail Road that leads along the west side of the lake. After crossing a small stream, a small spur road branches left (west) to the lake and a rustic area to set up base camp.

Other Options

Reginald Lake is found off the rough Beavertail Road and is considered one of the more popular fisheries in the area. This is no doubt due to the annually stocking of rainbow. In recent years, the stockings have included catchable size trout to help bring the average fish size up.

Beavertail Lake			
Fish Stocking Data			
Year	Species	Number	Life Stage
2011	Rainbow Trout	2,000	Yearling
2009	Rainbow Trout	5,000	Yearling

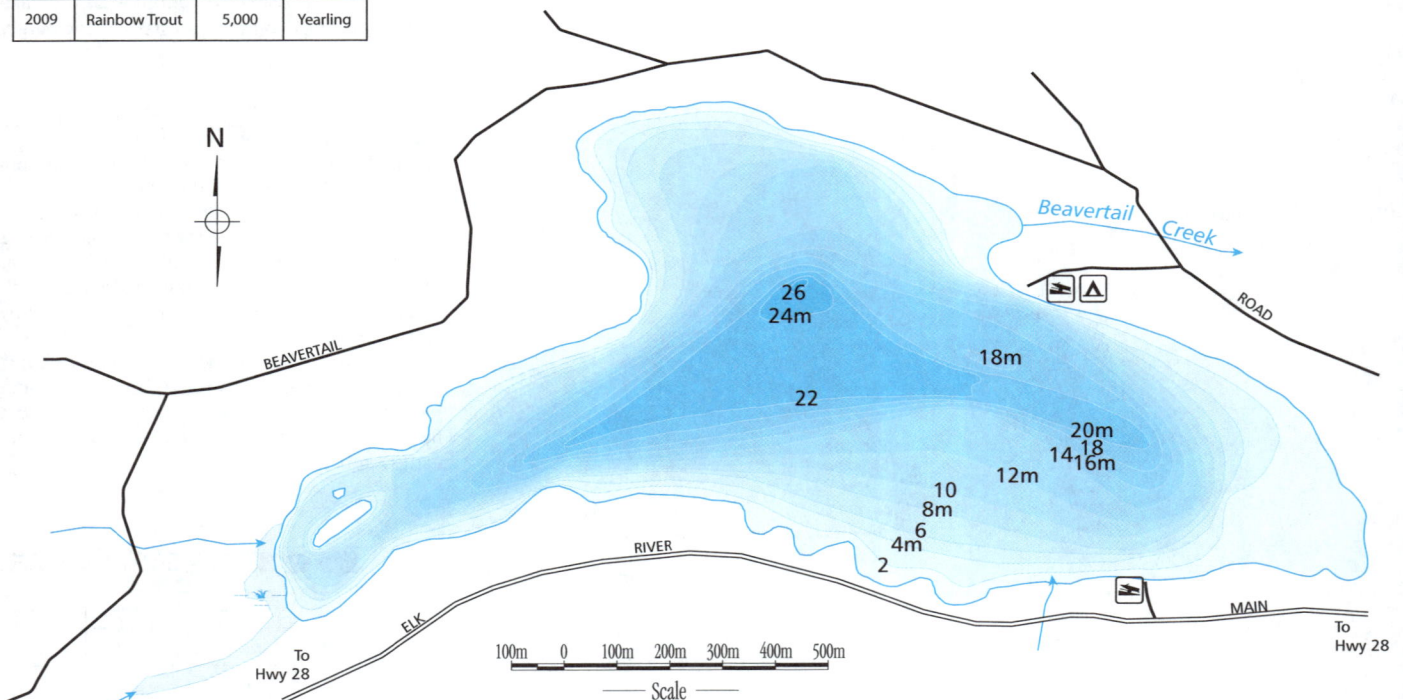

© Mussio Ventures Ltd.

Benson Lake

Location: 35 km (22 mi) southwest of Port McNeill
Elevation: 107 m (350 ft)
Surface Area: 77 ha (190 ac)
Mean Depth: 27 m (88 ft)
Max Depth: 55 m (180 ft)
Way Point: 127° 14′00″ Lon - W 50° 23′00″ Lat - N

Fishing

Boasting of large rainbow, cutthroat and Dolly Varden, Benson Lake is one of a series of good fishing lakes in the area. It is a very deep, low elevation lake meaning that trolling during the spring and fall is a good bet. Locals say that the lake is a great belly boat lake, too. You can hand-launch a boat on the west side of the lake. In addition to offering great fishing, it is a very picturesque lake, with lots of wildlife to see.

Using the depth chart provided, you should focus your efforts around the areas that the drop-off is quite pronounced, most notably the northern shore of the lake, as well as off a pair of points along the southern shore. Of course the inlet and outlet of Benson River, as well as the mouths of the other feeder streams are also prime holding areas for the trout and dollies.

If casting from shore, try to match the hatch or use bait suspended near the bottom at the edge of the drop-off. Spincasting with roostertails has proven effective. One of the better hatches is the winged carpenter ant hatch in late April or early May. During these few days, the fishing can be fast and furious, though if your timing is off and you show up too late, the fishing are usually laying low as the trout work on digesting the ant's tough exoskeleton.

If trolling, work as close to shore as possible using searching patterns or popular trout and dolly lures.

Other Options

Benson River is the small river that leads into Benson Lake. It is a catch and release stream that boasts a fair rainbow trout population that take well to the fly. Alternatively, you could try any of the other nearby lakes that include **Kathleen** and **Maynard**. Both offer similar fisheries for trout, cutthroat and Dolly Varden and are described in more detail later in the book.

Directions

Lying in a deep valley that is home to several good fishing lakes, Benson will not disappoint visitors. However, the long, bumpy ride from Highway 19 might. The most direct access is to follow the Keogh Main, which can be picked up on the south side of the highway just outside of Port McNeill at the Giant Burl. This long windy road takes you past Keogh, Angler, Three Isle, Maynard, Iron and Lac Truite before finally hitting Wady Main. Follow Wady Main north to the private launching site.

From the Port Alice Road, you can follow SE Main past Alice Lake. Before crossing the Benson River, Alice Lake Main continues east past Kathleen Lake and eventually winding down to Benson.

Either way you are looking at a rough ride, especially if you plan on bringing in a trailer.

Facilities

There is a private boat launch on the south side of the lake that visitors can use. Nearby Kathleen and Maynard Lakes offer recreation sites from which to set up base camp.

Area Indicator

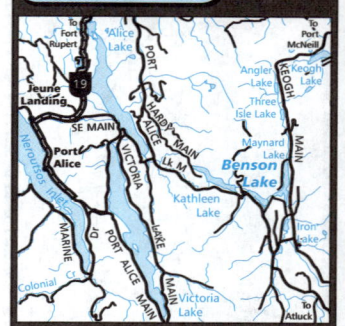

Scale

100m 0 100m 200m 300m 400m 500m

— Scale —

Benson R

6m
15
22m
30
38m
45
53m

ALICE
To
Hwy 30

LAKE

MAIN

dam

ROAD

Benson R

MERRY WIDOW

N

Location: 9 km (5.6 mi) south of Nanaimo
Elevation: 396 m (1,299 ft)
Surface Area: 3 ha (7.5 ac)
Mean Depth: 4.2 m (14 ft)
Max Depth: 8.5 m (28 ft)
Way Point: 123° 56'00"Lon - W 49° 05'00" Lat - N

Blind Lake

Area Indicator

Fishing

Blind Lake has good numbers of native cutthroat and small, stocked rainbow. And by small, we mean small. (Says one angler: "I half expected them to still have attached yolk sacs…." In truth, they can get to 24 cm/10 inches or so.) The fishing is definitely better in the spring and fall. However, the lake is at a high enough elevation to have some success during the summer months.

The magic time to fish the lake is right after ice off, when the fish stick to the top layer of water. The long winter months saps the oxygen from the lowest levels of the lake, and this, coupled with the fact that the only food available is in the shoals, means that the fish are easy to find and ravenous, willing to take most anything you offer. Because the water temperature is only around 4° C (39°F), it is still too cold for any hatches to occur, so fly fishers should stick with an attractor pattern like a Woolly Bugger or a General Practitioner.

After the spring turnover (and the inevitable few weeks of poor fishing it causes), the fish can still be found in the shallows, especially as this is the start of hatch season. As the top layer of water warms up, the fish begin to retreat down to a depth of 5–7 metres (15 or 20 feet), coming into the shoal area of the lake to feed. The biggest shoals are found at the east and west ends of the lake. A lake troll followed by a small spoon or spinner along the drop-off can produce. However, you are better off casting towards shore to work the drop-off.

If you do not have a small boat or flotation device, the water depth drops off rapidly from shore allowing for good shore casting. Try casting bait and bobber, a small spinner or a fly that matches the current hatch. When you don't see any evidence of a hatch in progress, your best bet is to use a general nymph pattern such as a Doc Spartley, Carey or half-back, or try a small leech pattern. This is particularly effective during the summer and into the fall.

Directions

Blind Lake is located within the Nanaimo River Valley. To reach the lake, head south on Highway 1 from Nanaimo and take the Nanaimo River Road exit just before crossing over the Nanaimo River Bridge. Pass by the White Rapids Road leading north and the next road heading off to the right will be a short spur road that brings you to Blind Lake. The lake is located within a kilometer of the Nanaimo River Road.

Other Options

Within a short drive of Blind Lake on the White Rapid Road, there are several small lakes. **Harewood Lake** is the largest of the lakes at 10 hectares. It has small cutthroat, which are best fished in the spring or fall. Other lakes to try are **Stark Lakes, Myles Lake** or **Overton Lakes**. Access to these lakes is limited due to private property and fishing reports are limited.

Facilities

There are no developed facilities at the lake.

Blind Lake Fish Stocking Data			
Year	Species	Number	Life Stage
2011	Rainbow Trout	500	Yearling
2010	Rainbow Trout	500	Yearling
2009	Rainbow Trout	500	Yearling

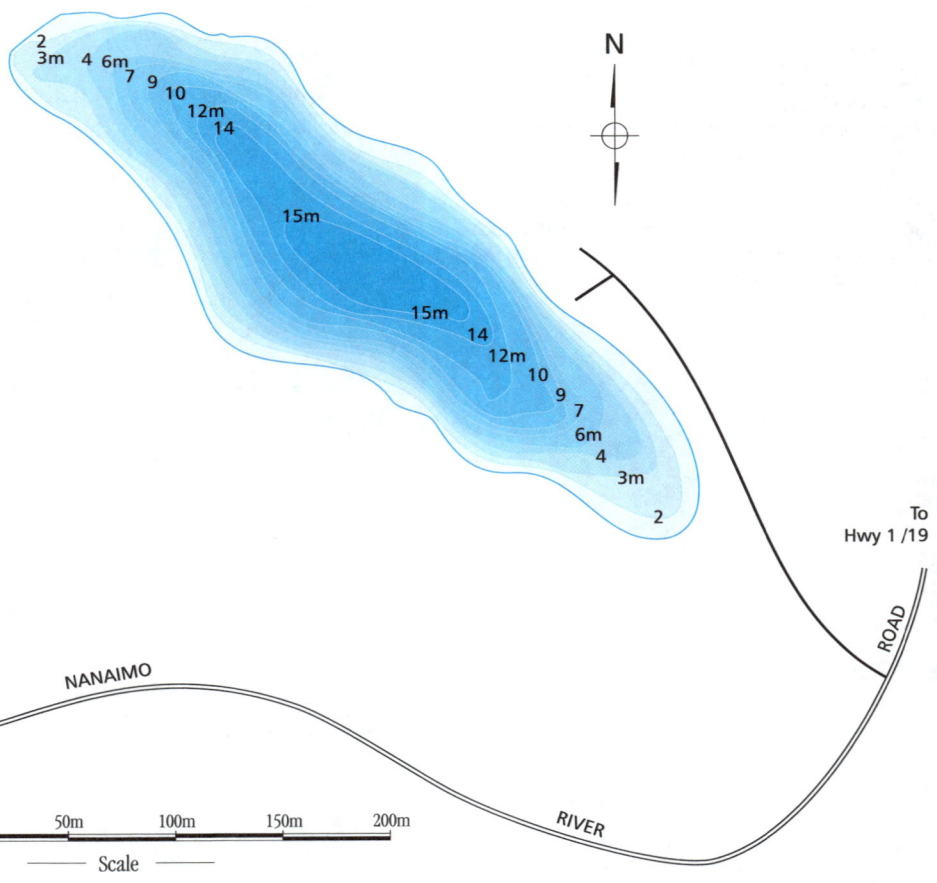

Blue Grouse Lake

Location: 18 km(11 mi) southwest of Campbell River
Elevation: 421 m (1,380 ft)
Surface Area: 6.7 ha (17 ac)
Mean Depth: 3.2 m (10.5 ft)
Max Depth: 16.5 m (54 ft)
Way Point: 125° 19' 00" Lon - W   49° 50' 00" Lat - N

Fishing

Blue Grouse Lake offers good fishing for generally small rainbow especially in the spring or fall. One source describes the lake as "overflowing" with rainbow, but we suspect that's a bit of an overstatement, considering it is only stocked with 1,000 fish annually. Then again, it is a very small lake…

Given the small size of the lake and the fact it is stocked, the trout rarely grow over 30 cm in size. However, there are reports of 35 cm (14 in) fish being caught here.

The lake has expansive shallows on both the east and west ends of the lake. Shore fishing is limited because of the shallows. If you search along the north side of the lake, you will find a couple spots where you might be able to cast a line out far enough to hit the transition area between the shoals and the deep section of the lake where the trout cruise looking for food. Otherwise, it is well advised to bring a float tube or small boat and cast a fly or a small lure along the drop offs on the east and west end of the lake.

Fly anglers can enjoy success throughout the year by paying attention to current hatches. While the shallows at the east and west ends of the lake make shore fishing difficult, it does mean the lake has fairly large hatches. Chironomids start as early as March; dragonflies emerge in early May, followed by damselflies and caddisflies in mid-June. Leeches and halfback nymph patterns can be used year round.

Facilities

At the southeast end of the lake, you will find a place to launch together with a rustic camping site.

Other Options

Regan Lake is south of Blue Grouse Lake on Rossiter Main. The 20 hectare lake has fair numbers of cutthroat and rainbow averaging 35 cm (14 in) in size. Fishing is best in the spring and fall primarily by fly-fishing or spincasting.

Directions

Blue Grouse Lake is a small lake located in the Oyster River Valley. Road access into this area is restricted so you will have to pay attention to road signs in the area to see if you can even drive in. Even if the roads are open, the lake is tricky to find and the help of a local is recommended. At the very least, make sure you have a copy of the Vancouver Island Backroad Mapbook and a GPS with the Backroad GPS Maps to help track your course.

The lake is accessed by heading north on the Inland Highway (Hwy 19) from Courtenay. You will need to cross the Oyster River and take the Cranberry Lane exit, which links up with the Duncan Bay Main. Follow this road back across the river and stay right to access Piggott Main. This logging road leads southwest. Look for Branch Road 181, which courses east.

From here on in, you'll need to pick your route carefully through the maze of backroads that may or may not be signed. You will need to find Branch 181E and then 110G, which will eventually bring you to Blue Grouse Lake. Note also that recent logging has created many new roads and temporary road names in the area.

Area Indicator

Blue Grouse Lake
Fish Stocking Data

Year	Species	Number	Life Stage
2010	Rainbow Trout	300	Yearling
2008	Rainbow Trout	900	Yearling

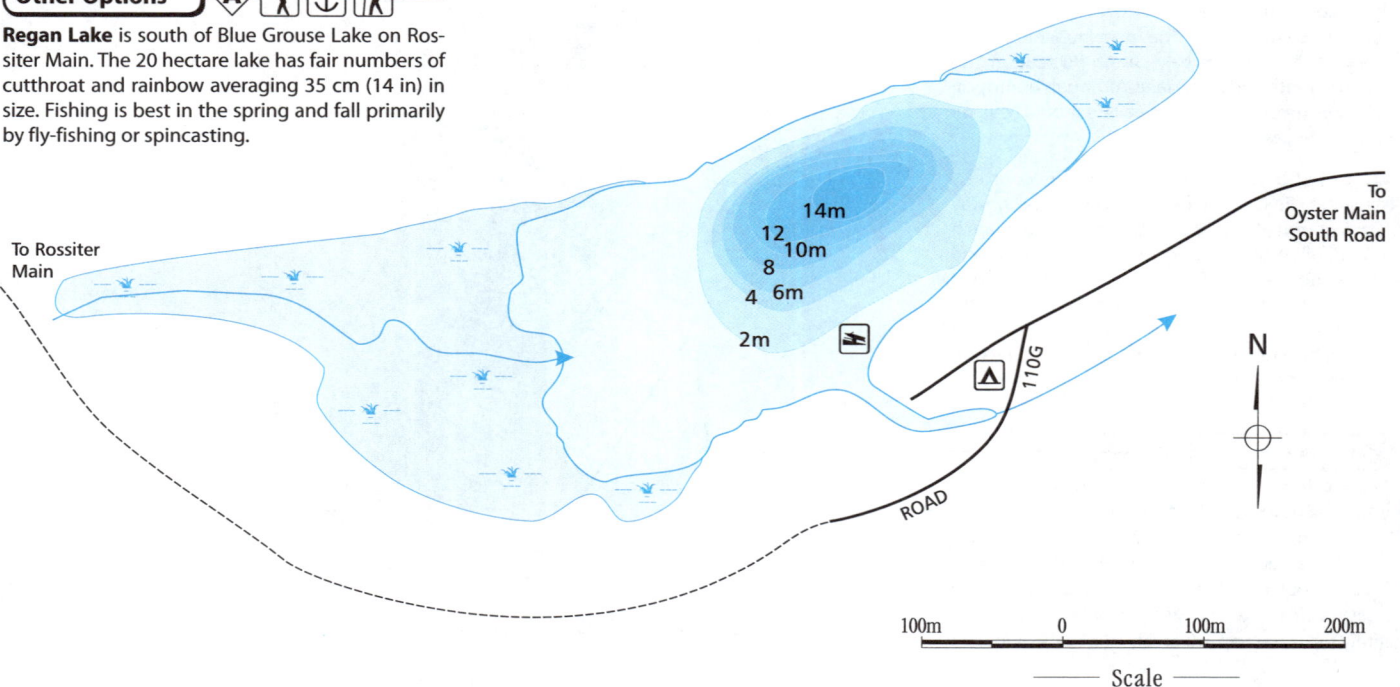

Location: 29 km (18 mi) southeast of Port McNeill
Elevation: 268 m (880 ft)
Surface Area: 901 ha (2,225 ac)
Mean Depth: 85 m (279 ft)
Max Depth: 161 m (528 ft)
Way Point: 126° 47' 00" Lon - W 50° 22' 00" Lat - N

www.backroadmapbooks.com

Bonanza Lake

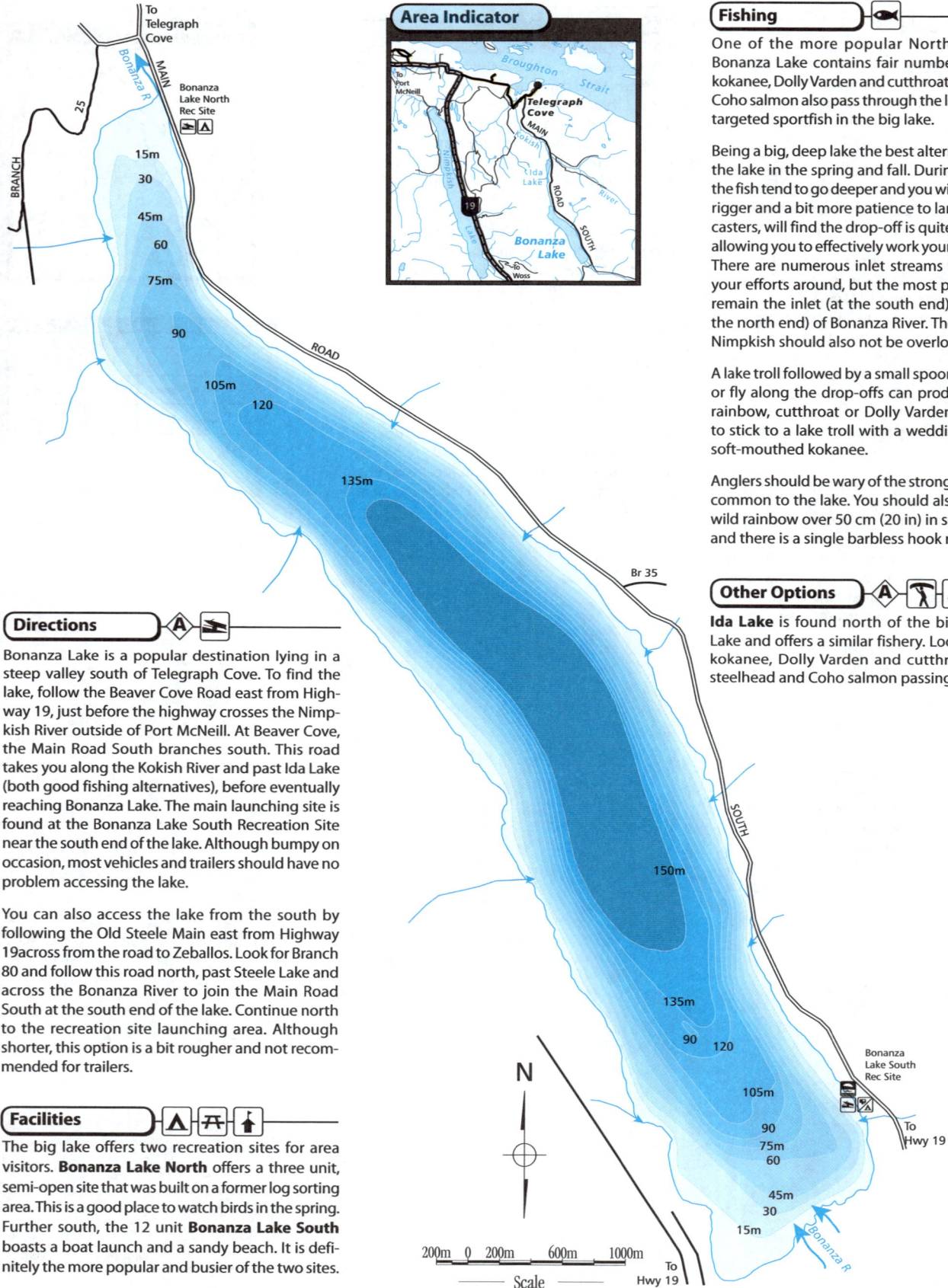

Area Indicator

Fishing

One of the more popular North Island lakes, Bonanza Lake contains fair numbers of rainbow, kokanee, Dolly Varden and cutthroat. Steelhead and Coho salmon also pass through the lake, but are not targeted sportfish in the big lake.

Being a big, deep lake the best alternative is to troll the lake in the spring and fall. During the summer, the fish tend to go deeper and you will need a down-rigger and a bit more patience to land them. Shore casters, will find the drop-off is quite close to shore allowing you to effectively work your fly, bait or lure. There are numerous inlet streams to concentrate your efforts around, but the most promising areas remain the inlet (at the south end) and outlet (at the north end) of Bonanza River. The mouth of the Nimpkish should also not be overlooked.

A lake troll followed by a small spoon, spinner, plug or fly along the drop-offs can produce catches of rainbow, cutthroat or Dolly Varden. You are best to stick to a lake troll with a wedding ring for the soft-mouthed kokanee.

Anglers should be wary of the strong winds that are common to the lake. You should also note that no wild rainbow over 50 cm (20 in) in size are allowed and there is a single barbless hook restriction.

Other Options

Ida Lake is found north of the bigger Bonanza Lake and offers a similar fishery. Look for rainbow, kokanee, Dolly Varden and cutthroat as well as steelhead and Coho salmon passing through.

Directions

Bonanza Lake is a popular destination lying in a steep valley south of Telegraph Cove. To find the lake, follow the Beaver Cove Road east from Highway 19, just before the highway crosses the Nimpkish River outside of Port McNeill. At Beaver Cove, the Main Road South branches south. This road takes you along the Kokish River and past Ida Lake (both good fishing alternatives), before eventually reaching Bonanza Lake. The main launching site is found at the Bonanza Lake South Recreation Site near the south end of the lake. Although bumpy on occasion, most vehicles and trailers should have no problem accessing the lake.

You can also access the lake from the south by following the Old Steele Main east from Highway 19 across from the road to Zeballos. Look for Branch 80 and follow this road north, past Steele Lake and across the Bonanza River to join the Main Road South at the south end of the lake. Continue north to the recreation site launching area. Although shorter, this option is a bit rougher and not recommended for trailers.

Facilities

The big lake offers two recreation sites for area visitors. **Bonanza Lake North** offers a three unit, semi-open site that was built on a former log sorting area. This is a good place to watch birds in the spring. Further south, the 12 unit **Bonanza Lake South** boasts a boat launch and a sandy beach. It is definitely the more popular and busier of the two sites.

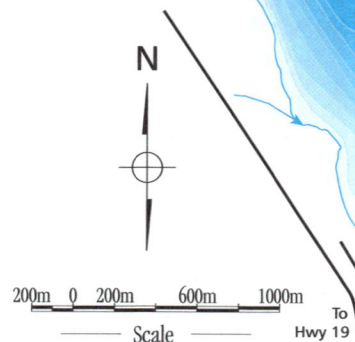

Scale: 200m 0 200m 600m 1000m

© Mussio Ventures Ltd.

Boomerang Lake

Location: 10.5 km (6.5 mi) west of Nanaimo
Surface Area: 11ha (27 ac)
Elevation: 362 m (1,188 ft)
Mean Depth: 5.2 m (17 ft)
Max Depth: 12.5 m (41 ft)
Way Point: 124° 09'00" Lon - W   49° 11'00" Lat - N

Fishing

Stocked annually with cutthroat by the Freshwater Fisheries Society of BC, Boomerang Lake is one of those hidden mountain lakes that might seem like too much effort to get to, but is well worth the effort to visit. It is high enough in elevation to offer a good fishery throughout the open water season.

Although the cutthroat tend to remain small, with a 12 in (30 cm) fish being a good-sized fish for the lake, the fishing is usually pretty steady. There are also reports of rainbow and brook trout in the lake. Outside of the arm that extends east, most of the lake provides good fishing prospects since there is a prominent drop-off that circles the lake and some nice shoals to work. Shore fishing is definitely possible with the southern most shoreline being the better area. However, like most small waterbodies, a float tube or small boat would improve success.

Trolling with flies, small spoons, Flatfish, Kwikfish or a lake troll baited with worms are common ways to fish the lake. Other anglers prefer to cast small Mepps or Panther Martin spinners.

Facilities

Boomerang Lake is a remote lake with no developed facilities. It is possible to launch small boats and picnic or even camp at the south end of the lake.

Directions

Similar to most remote south Island lakes, access into this area may be closed or restricted. It is best to inquire locally before planning a trip into the area.

Boomerang Lake is located to the west of Nanaimo along a series of backroads. From the north end of Nanaimo you will need to find Doumont or Biggs Roads, which are found on either end of Brannen Lake. These roads join and turn into Weigles Road, which eventually turns into gravel. A gate may impede travel as you climb up to eventually meet Branch Road 142, just north of Boomerang Lake. A short jaunt south on the 142 should take you to the lake.

From the north, just outside of Nanoose, look for the 155 Main Road branching south off of Highway 19. This road has restricted access and may be gated. Shortly after the pavement ends, Branch Road 142 leads southeast. This long and often bumpy road eventually leads to the north shore of Boomerang.

Regardless of the route in, it is recommended to have a high clearance vehicle and to bring along a copy of the Vancouver Island Backroad Mapbook. A GPS with the Backroad GPS Maps to help track your route in is also a helpful devise.

Area Indicator

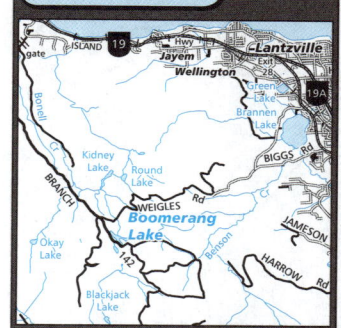

Other Options

Boomerang Lake is central to several small lakes. On the south side of the 142 Branch Road you can find **Cottle Lake**. To the north are **Round** and **Kidney Lakes** that are accessed off a rough side road from Weigles Road. These lakes are rumoured to offer fair fishing for trout in the spring and fall. Round lake is described in greater detail later in the book.

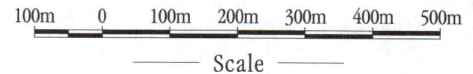

To Hwy 19 via Englishmen River Rd

BRANCH

3m

6

9m

12

142

To Nanaimo via Weigles Rd

N

Cottle Lake

100m 0 100m 200m 300m 400m 500m

Scale

Boomerang Lake			
Fish Stocking Data			
Year	Species	Number	Life Stage
2008	Cutthroat Trout	500	Yearling
2007	Cutthroat Trout	500	Yearling
2006	Cutthroat Trout	500	Yearling

Location: 10 km (6 mi) northwest of Nanaimo
Elevation: 76 m (249 ft)
Surface Area: 109 ha (269 ac)
Mean Depth: 12 m (39 ft)
Max Depth: 20 m (66 ft)
Way Point: 124° 03′00″ Lon -W 49° 13′00″ Lat - N

www.backroadmapbooks.com

Brannen Lake

Area Indicator

Fishing

Brannen Lake is a popular urban lake next to the Nanaimo Parkway (Highway 19). The lake is a productive lake and is known for its large cutthroat and rainbow, which can grow to 2.5 kg (5 lbs). While the average is only 30 cm (12 in), that size is nothing to sneeze at. There is an annual stocking program in place in the lake to ensure a healthy population of trout, while a few kokanee and even smallmouth bass are also found in the lake.

Trolling is your best bet particularly during late March to mid June and again in the fall from late September to mid November. However, shore casters will find the lake and has distinctive drop-offs around its entire shoreline allowing you to get out to where the fish like to hold. During the summer, you will need to work deep during the day or wait for early morning or late evening rises.

The most productive fishing method is to cast a fly or small lure tipped with a worm towards the shore nearby to the drop-offs. Lake trolls followed by a small spinner or lure along the drop-offs can also produce catches of rainbow, cutthroat or kokanee. Bass anglers can have a lot of fun using surface lures during overcast or low light periods, while crank baits, spinner baits or soft plastics fished close to docks, fallen trees and other protected areas never seem to disappoint.

Directions

Brannen Lake is easy to find, located next to the Nanaimo Parkway about 10 km (6 miles) northwest of downtown Nanaimo. The best access to the lake is to turn east along Metral Drive, which is accessed from Highway 19A just past Mostar Road. Once on Metral, look for Godfrey Road on the left (west) and follow this road Dunster Road. Dunster leads to the public access point and boat launch.

Signs mark the directions to the lake.

Facilities

It is possible to launch a small boat at the end of Dunster Road on the east side of the lake. Visitors will also find a private campsite located at the south end of the lake. The campsite provides a boat launch and lakeshore access for customers.

Brannen Lake			
Fish Stocking Data			
Year	Species	Number	Life Stage
2011	Rainbow Trout	5,000	Yearling
2010	Rainbow Trout	3,000	Yearling
2009	Rainbow Trout	15,280	Yearling

Other Options

Within a few kilometers of Brannen Lake are **Long and Diver Lakes**. These popular trout and smallmouth bass fisheries are highlighted later in this book. Also in the area is **Green Lake**. It is found off Aulds or Jenkins Road at the north end of Nanaimo. Stocked with trout, it also provides a good opportunity for smallmouth bass.

© Mussio Ventures Ltd.

Brewster Lake

Location: 30 km (4 mi) northwest of Campbell River
Elevation: 189 m (620 ft)
Surface Area: 413 ha (1,020 ac)
Mean Depth: 24.5 m (81 ft)
Max Depth: 56 m (185 ft)
Way Point: 125° 34' 00" Lon - W 50° 06' 00" Lat - N

Fishing

One the larger lakes on the Sayward Forest Canoe Route, Brewster Lake is home to several recreation sites including canoe access only and drive-in access sites with boat launches. Anglers will find good numbers of stocked cutthroat and rainbow trout and the odd Dolly Varden. The lake is deep enough to maintain a steady fishery throughout the year.

A canoe or boat is recommended to help you explore this large lake. There are some nice shoals around the islands at the north end to try during the spring and fall. However, if you do not have a boat, shore fishing is certainly possible since the water drops off quite rapidly, especially on the western shore.

Trolling with flies, small spoons, Flatfish, Kwikfish or a lake troll and small spinner baited with worms are common ways to fish the lake. Other anglers prefer to cast spinning gear with small lures, while fly anglers will need to match the hatch.

Facilities

Home to several different recreation sites, there is no shortage of places to stay around Brewster. **Apple Point Recreation Site** is an open, grassy site with a steep gravel boat launch on the southeast shore. This six unit site has enough room for large trailers. **Brewster Camp** is located just off the southern tip of the lake and offers a couple open grassy sites ideal for destination campers. It is managed without fees, unlike nearby **Brewster Lake Recreation Site**, which is managed with fees. It is a 19 unit semi-open site that is a prime camping spot for tenters that features a sandy beach and boat launch for small boats. **Camp 5** is set amongst an Alder stand on the site of the historic Camp 5 logging camp. Found just past Apple Point near the southwest end of Brewster Lake, there is space for five camping groups and a cartop boat launch.

In addition to the many drive-in campsites, there is also a boat access only site on the northwest shore of the lake, as it is part of the **Sayward Forest Canoe Route**. This 47 km (29 mile) circuit covers 14 different lakes and is best done in a counter clockwise direction. Allow 3 or 4 days and expect to cross 7.5 km (4.7 miles) of portages

Other Options

Picking nearby lakes to test your luck is not that difficult. In fact, virtually all the lakes on the Sayward Forest Canoe Route are known to produce trout in varying degrees. **Gray Lake** is the closest lake and is found via a 100 metre portage to the south. It is stocked regularly with rainbow to ensure a steady fishery.

Directions

Home to several recreation sites, access into Brewster Lake is fairly easy. About 15 km north of Campbell River, you can pick up the Menzies Mainline just north of the sawmill on Highway 19 at Menzies Bay. This gravel road leads past Mohun Lake to the south side of Brewster Lake and the signed turn off to Brewster Lake Recreation Site some 16 km later. The Apple Point, Brewster Camp and Camp 5 Recreation Sites are found a short distance further along.

Alternatively, head west of Campbell River on Highway 28 to the John Hart Dam turnoff. Follow this road north over the start of the infamous Campbell River to the Loveland Bay Road. Continue west along this road, which soon turns to gravel and leads to the Campbell Lake and then Gray Lake Roads. The later road branches north to the south end of Brewster Lake. Although longer (about 36 km), this is the more scenic route in.

Area Indicator

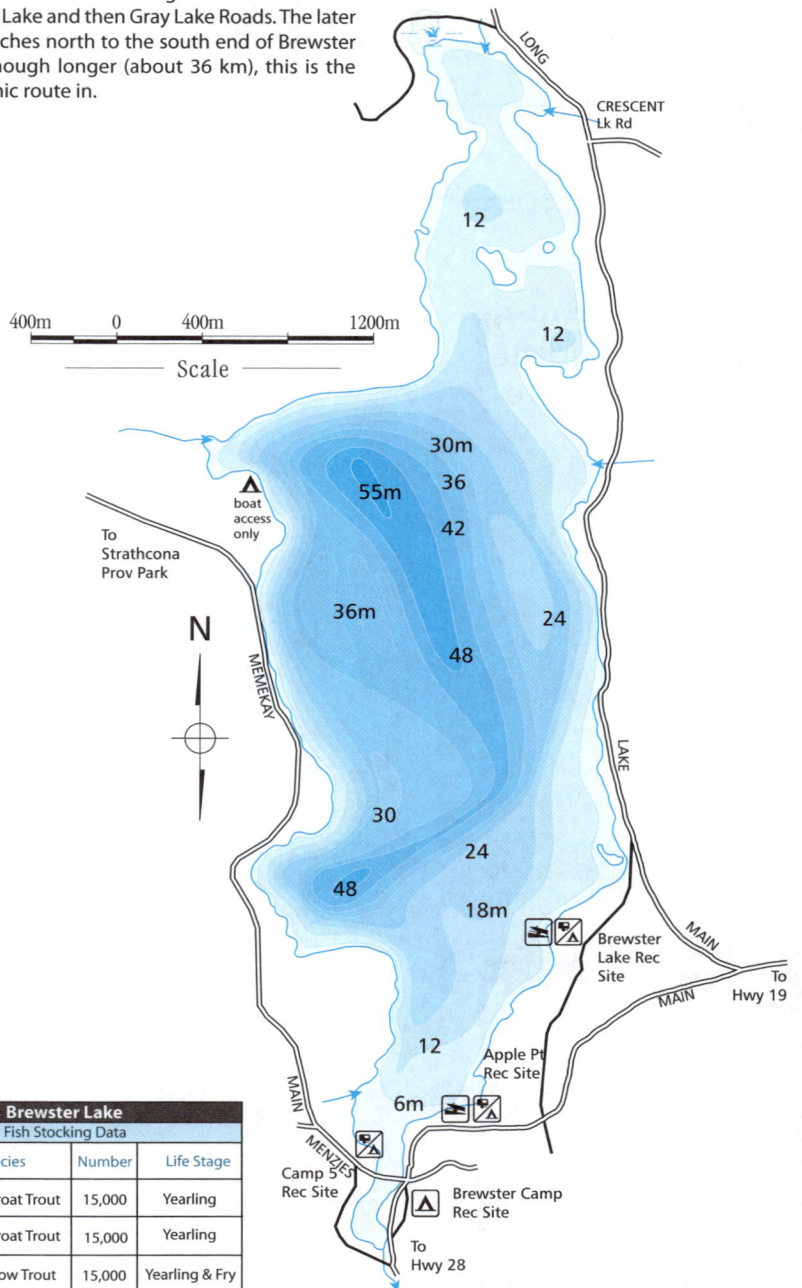

Scale

400m   0   400m   1200m

— Scale —

Brewster Lake			
Fish Stocking Data			
Year	Species	Number	Life Stage
2004	Cutthroat Trout	15,000	Yearling
2003	Cutthroat Trout	15,000	Yearling
2003	Rainbow Trout	15,000	Yearling & Fry

Location: 49 km (30 mi) west of Campbell River
Elevator: 223 m (732 ft)
Surface Area: 3,095 ha (7,645 ac)
Mean Depth: 61 m (201 ft)
Max Depth: 121 m (396 ft)
Way Point: 125° 33' 00" Lon - W 49° 43' 00" Lat - N

www.backroadmapbooks.com

Buttle Lake

Buttle Lake Narrows

Upper Campbell Lake

To Campbell River

Park Headquarters

Driftwood Bay Campsite

Buttle Lake Campsite

To Gold River

Buttle Lake

To Strathcona-Westmin Provincial Park

500m   0   500m   1000m 1500m
Scale

Ridge Route

Phillips

N

(South) Buttle Lake

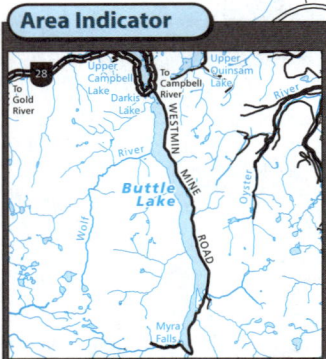

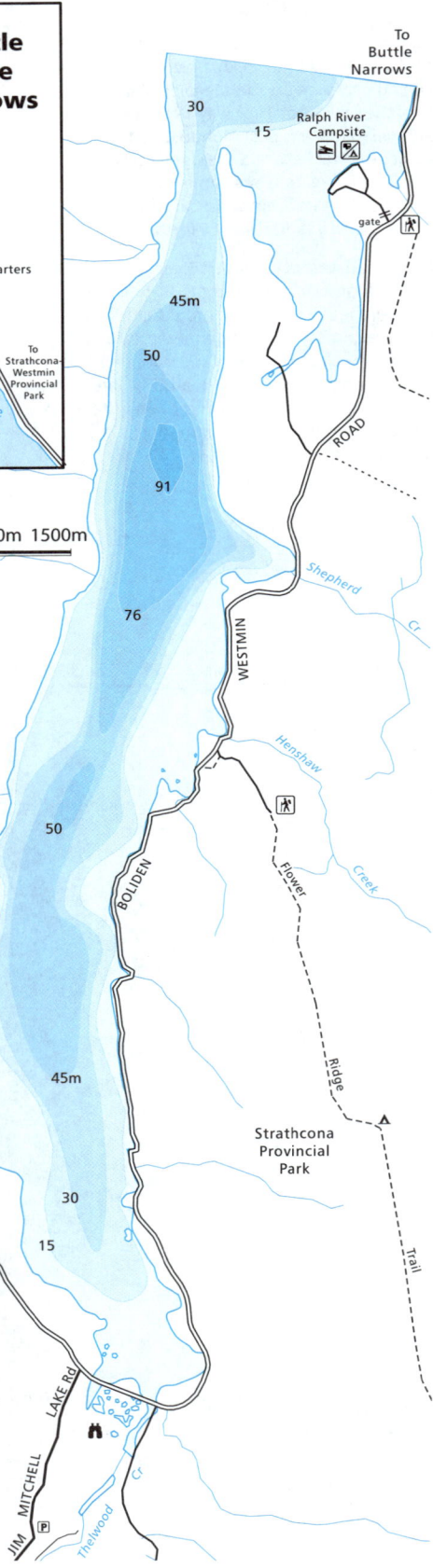

To Buttle Narrows

Ralph River Campsite

gate

30
15
45m
50
91
76
50
45m
30
15

ROAD

Shepherd Cr

WESTMIN

Henshaw

Flower

Creek

Ridge

Trail

Strathcona Provincial Park

BOLIDEN

Myra Falls ★

Strathcona-Westmin Provincial Park

Area Indicator

To Gold River

Upper Campbell Lake

To Campbell River

Upper Quinsam Lake

Darkis Lake

River

WESTMIN MINE ROAD

Buttle Lake

Wolf River

Oyster River

Myra Falls

JIM MITCHELL

LAKE Rd

Thelwood Cr

Fishing

A favourite with writer Roderick Haig-Brown, Buttle Lake is one of the most beautiful Island lakes. Nestled in the confines of Strathcona Provincial Park, some of the more prominent peaks rising above the lake include Mount McBride, Marble Peak, Mount Phillips, Mount Myra and Elkhorn Mountain. It is a man-made waterbody and the water levels fluctuate throughout the year. As a result, we have only shown pieces of the big lake with contours.

Stretching over 32 kilometres long, anglers will need to be wary of the flooded forest, with deadheads and submerged stumps being encountered, particularly close to shore. The lake is also prone to sudden, strong winds. Hazards aside, the fishing can be pretty good throughout the spring, summer and fall for small, but abundant cutthroat and rainbow. There is also the odd Dolly Varden that can reach 40 cm (16 in) in size taken.

Being such a big, deep lake, trolling is the primary fishing method. The deep lake is best fished by trolling a lake troll with a medium size plug like a Flatfish or Rapala. It is recommended to set these rigs up with 30 metres (100 ft) of line and no weight. Work the drop-offs particularly around the many islands, points of land or around the creek estuaries. If you are unable to fish from a boat, try bait fishing from shore near a creek mouth or rock ledge. In particular, the picnic sites off of the Westmin Mine Road provide access to a few creeks mouths where you should find the odd cruising trout or deep holding dolly to lure.

Please note that the tributaries feeding the large lake are closed to fishing.

Directions

Located in Strathcona Provincial Park, the northern tip of Buttle Lake is accessed from Highway 28 after passing along Upper Campbell Lake en route to Gold River. Westmin Mine Road branches south from the highway at Buttle Narrows providing good access to the eastern shore and southern tip of the big lake.

Facilities

Forming the heart of Strathcona Park, Buttle Lake offers a variety of marine and drive-in access campsites along with a few picnic areas. The most popular campsite is the **Buttle Lake Campground** at the north end. It features 85 sites, a beach, playground and boat launch. The **Ralph River Campground** is found about 35 km along the Westmin Mine Road. It hosts 75 campsites set amid the towering old-growth Douglas fir. The boat launch is found a bit further north at the **Karst Creek Picnic Site. Augerpoint and Lupin Falls** are the other picnic sites on the eastern shore.

For those looking for a bit more seclusion, there are five marine campsites offering room for about 4 campers each. From north to south they are **Rainbow Island, Mount Titus, Wolf River, Marble Rock and Phillips Creek.**

Other Options

Upper Campbell Lake is the big body of water that lines Highway 28 on the way from Campbell River to Gold River. Fishing is good for small cutthroat, rainbow and Dolly Varden. If the wind is too strong on either of the big lakes, try **Darkis Lake**, found via a short trail on the road to the Buttle Lake Campground.

Cameron Lake

Location: 22 km (13.5 mi) west of Parksville
Elevation: 193 m (633 ft)
Surface Area: 477 ha (1,179 ac)
Max Depth: 43 m (141 ft)
Perimeter: 13.6 km (8.4 mi)
Way Point: 124° 37' 00" Lon - W 49° 17' 00" Lat - N

Fishing

Cameron Lake is a pretty lake found next to Highway 4. The deep lake is unusual for Vancouver Island, as it contains some brown trout. These fish are notoriously hard to catch but do reach enormous sizes (6 kg/14 lbs). There are also rainbow, cutthroat and kokanee. Another nice thing about the lake is the fact that, despite its low elevation, the waters remain cool throughout the summer and fishing remains relatively consistent throughout the open water season.

Given the size of the lake and its depth, the best way to fish for trout is by trolling. Lake trolls are popular because they can attract both trout and kokanee and are relatively easy to use. There are many shapes, sizes and colours of lures that have proven effective trolling for trout, while kokanee prefer Wedding Rings or small lures with bait. Some of the most common trolling lures include Krocodiles, Kwikfish, Flatfish and Dick Nite spoons.

For the fly angler, most typical hatches found on the Island occur on Cameron Lake. However, due to its size it is best to troll leeches or similar searching patterns. Later in the season, the sedge hatch can create a frenzy of action if timed right. Similarly, terrestrial insect patterns such as grasshoppers can entice trout to rise for a nice meal.

If you are looking for brown trout, it is best to work near cover. They seem to prefer flies over lures and have been known to chase down baitfish or even small mice or frog imitations similar to bass.

Fishing with a small boat or a float tube is tough because the lake is known for sudden strong winds that may blow in the wrong direction. If you are restricted to shore fishing, the lake drops off quickly from the shoreline allowing you to get past the shallows. Casting in the estuary of the Cameron River or the outflow of the Little Qualicum River are two good areas to try. Use a single salmon egg, worm or powerbait fished near the bottom.

Directions

Cameron Lake is found about 22 kilometres (13.5 miles) west of Parksville or 26 kilometres (16 miles) east of Port Alberni next to Highway 4. The beautiful lake makes a dramatic backdrop as Highway 4 squeezes its way between the cliffs and the lake. The main access point is found on the east side of the lake.

Facilities

Little Qualicum Falls Provincial Park protects the south and east shore of the lake, providing both day-use facilities and camping. The picnic area and beach provide good access to the east end of the lake, while the 95 unit campsite is found next to the Little Qualicum River, near the falls. Camping is available from the end of April to the end of September. It is best to reserve a campsite through www.discovercamping.com if you plan to camp here on weekends.

MacMillan (Cathedral Grove) Provincial Park, home of the famous old-growth forest, is located to the west of Cameron Lake. It has picnic facilities as well as hiking trails, but is generally not used as an access point for the lake.

A nice resort is also found on the east end of the lake, next to the day-use area. The resort offers a lovely beach, camping, a boat launch and rentals among other amenities.

Other Options

The **Little Qualicum River** drains the big lake is one of the storied river fisheries on the east coast of the Island. Unfortunately, the popular river is also heavily regulated. There are many closures including the once popular winter steelhead run as well as catch and release restrictions on brown and cutthroat trout. Anglers will also find some Chinook that return in August, along with sea-run cutthroat. For more details and hot spots be sure to see the river description later in the book.

Area Indicator

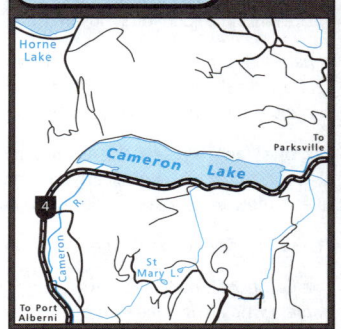

Cameron Lake			
Fish Stocking Data			
Year	Species	Number	Life Stage
2007	Rainbow Trout	2,205	Yearling

Campbell River
Stream Length: 14.5 km (9 mi)
Geographic: 125° 17'00" Lon - W   50° 2'00" Lat - N

Quinsam River
Stream Length: 42.0 km (26.1 mi)

Campbell & Quinsam Rivers

Fishing

The Campbell River attracts a lot of attention for such a short river. Yes, it is a large volume river, but it is only 5 km (3 miles) long. The Campbell River was made famous in the writing of Canada's most famous angler, Roderick Haig-Brown, and it still remains one of BC's best known rivers.

It wasn't always so short. The Campbell's headwaters are in Strathcona Provincial Park, but a trio of dams has tamed the waters of the Campbell, leaving only this short section to fish. But in that short distance lies some of the greatest river fishing on the Island. And anglers know it, too. During the opening days of steelhead season, anglers stand nigh elbow to elbow on the banks.

Part of its fame is due to the fact that it is one of the few east coast rivers that has two steelhead runs. While many rivers have winter steelhead, the Campbell is the only east coast river with both. Part of its fame comes from the fact that this is Tyee country, and while many of these are caught out in the sea, many more are taken in the river. Unfortunately, steelhead stocks have been at very low levels for the last few years.

The summer steelhead run begins in June, but really starts to cook in August and September. The winter steelhead run begins in November and continues through to April.

The Campbell's main tributary is the Quinsam River, and it shares many of the same fishing traits as the Campbell. However, it is a much smaller volume stream, and anglers who are intimidated by the Campbell's raw power might find the Quinsam easier to understand. Currently, the river has a number of closures, so check current regulations before heading out.

The most popular fishing holes are just below where the Quinsam and the Campbell meet. However, just upstream on the Quinsam is a hole that has become extremely productive. There is even a special handicapped fishing platform here. Another spot that sees a lot of attention is the Sandy Pool, just below the logging bridge.

Other popular fishing holes include the Pumphouse Pool, which is the last section of water that is open to non-fly-fishers, and is often packed with locals and visitors alike. It is common to find people from around the globe fishing here.

Above the Pumphouse Pool is the Mid-Island Pool, a fly-fishing only pool that produces well for steelhead in both seasons. Flies for steelhead are usually attractor patterns, including the Woolly Bugger, Kaufmanns Stone and the Meg-A-Egg.

Just below the dam is the Powerhouse Pool, the last fishing hole on the Campbell before it turns into a series of lakes.

In addition to its internationally famous steelhead runs, the Campbell and the Quinsam have resident and sea-run cutthroat and a few resident rainbow. The rivers also see strong returns for Coho, pink and Chinook salmon in addition to a few sockeye and chum.

Facilities

The city of Campbell River offers all services including an impressive set of retailers that can give you the lowdown on what is currently hot on the rivers. Closer to shore, **Elk Falls Provincial Park** provides a campsite, trails and a few parking/picnic areas. The Quinsam also runs through the park where trails and a fishing platform are well used. Further upstream there is a salmon hatchery.

Directions

Access to the short Campbell River is found off Highway 28 as well as from several locations in Elk Falls Provincial Park. The Quinsam can also be accessed from the park, as well as from Quinsam Road.

Campbell/Quinsam River
Fishing Pool Location Names
1. Canyon (Powerhouse) Pool
2. Mid-Island Pool
3. Pumphouse Pool
4. Sandy Pool
5. Line Fence Pool
6. Quinsam Pool

Map courtesy of Backroad Mapbooks

Chemainus Lake

Location: 3 km (1.9 mi) southwest of Chemainus
Elevation: 83 m (272 ft)
Surface Area: 4.3 ha (10.5 ac)
Mean Depth: 4 m (13 ft)
Max Depth: 7.9 m (26 ft)
Way Point: 123° 45' 00" Lon - W 48° 55' 00" Lat - N

Fishing

Chemainus Lake is a small, shallow, marshy lake that offers a good smallmouth bass fishery. There are also many small, stocked rainbows, thanks to the aggressive stocking program of the Freshwater Fisheries Society of BC and the odd brook trout in the lake. The trout might be small (a 35 cm/14 in fish is considered a trophy), but they are abundant.

Given the close proximity to town, the lake receives heavy fishing pressure, especially in the spring and fall when the fishing is better. Given the low elevation, you can fish as early as March, but the waters start to warm by the end of June. It is best to avoid this lake in the summer and return later in September and October.

The northern most part of the lake has the deepest water. Working the fringes around this area while casting from a boat is a good idea. Since the lake is lined with water lilies, casting from shore is difficult. However, working a dragonfly or damselfly nymph next to the lilies is very productive if you can get out on the water.

Chemainus Lake is also known as a good chironomid lake. The insect begins to hatch as early as March when there is a spell of warmer weather. However, the better fishing is in April any time from mid-morning onward when the insects are emerging. During the day, the best way to catch fish using a chironomid imitation is to us an intermediate sinking line or a sinking tip line. Work a black or brown-bodied fly in 6-9 metres (20-30 feet) of water such that it is within a few feet of the bottom. Slowly retrieve the fly or use a strike indicator and leave the fly just off the bottom. Later in the evening, work a size #14-16 brown or black-bodied imitation near the surface on a floating line.

The smallmouth bass tend to hang out in the deeper water found at the middle of the lake. They can be taken on the fly on standard trout patterns such as Woolley Buggers, Doc Spratleys, etc. Some people have used Bass Bugs (poppers) to good effect, but those are more commonly used for largemouth bass.

Directions

Chemainus Lake is an easily accessed as the lake is within a half kilometer of the Island Highway (Hwy 1). To reach the lake, head south of the town of Chemainus and take River Road. This paved road will take you southwest to the walk-in launching site.

Facilities

Visitors will not find much development around this small lake. It is possible to hand launch small boats and there is an old wharf people use to cast from.

Other Options

Chemainus Lake is across the highway from Fuller Lake. Fuller Lake has bigger fish, but the fishing is slower. Like Chemainus Lake, Fuller has a good chironomid hatch, particularly in April. There is a detailed write-up on **Fuller Lake** elsewhere in the book.

Chemainus Lake			
Fish Stocking Data			
Year	Species	Number	Life Stage
2011	Rainbow Trout	1,500	Catchables
2010	Rainbow Trout	4,454	Catchables
2009	Rainbow Trout	2,790	Catchables

Area Indicator

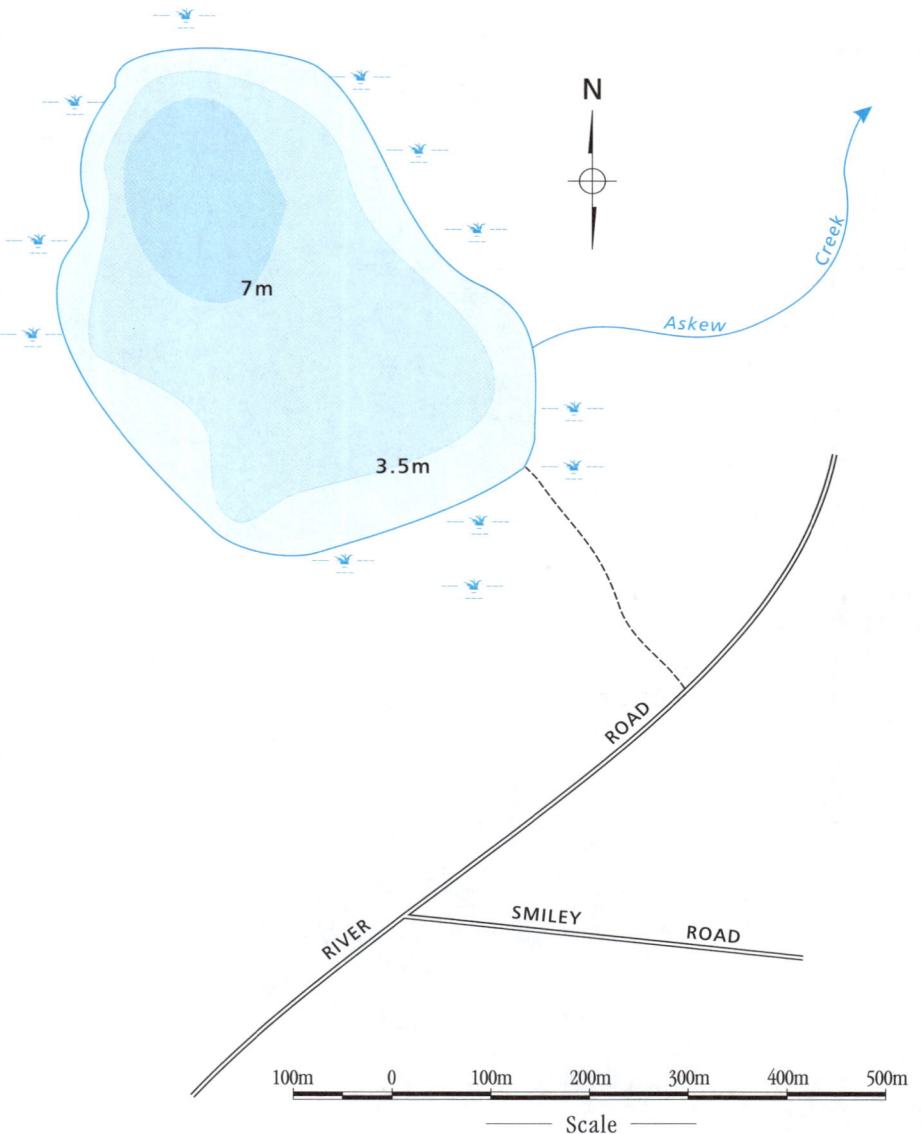

7 m

3.5 m

N

Askew Creek

ROAD

RIVER

SMILEY ROAD

Scale

100m   0   100m   200m   300m   400m   500m

Circlet & Moat Lakes

Area Indicator

Circlet Lake

Elevation: 1,182 m (3,878 ft)
Surface Area: 28.5 ha (70.5 ac)
Mean Depth: 23 m (77 ft)
Max Depth: 54 m (177 ft)
Way Point: 125° 23'00" Lon - W 49° 42'00" Lat - N

Moat Lake

Elevation: 1,175 m (3,855 ft)
Surface Area: 95 ha (234 ac)
Mean Depth: 25 m (83 ft)
Max Depth: 84 m (276 ft)
Way Point: 125° 23'00" Lon - W 49° 41'00" Lat - N

Fishing

Circlet & Moat Lakes are found in the Forbidden Plateau area of Strathcona Provincial Park. Even though the fish are stocked, the gorgeous lakes have surprising large rainbow that regularly reach 30–35cm (12–14 in) in size. Being remote, high elevation lakes with a limited fishing season, the trout are often eager to take most flies or small lures and spinners during the summer and early fall.

Circlet Lake is almost circular in nature with a deep hole right in the middle. The lake is easily fished from shore because the water level drops rapidly around its entire perimeter. However, the cliffs and steep terrain make the western side a little treacherous to tackle.

Despite being the biggest lake on the plateau, **Moat Lake** is also easily fished from shore, with the best areas being found along the southeastern side of the lake. It would also be an ideal lake to bring a float tube to. There are several enticing areas, including the fringe areas around Stuart Wood Island to work a fly, small lure or spinner in. The waters are crystal clear offering a few exciting moments when you can see the fish rising for your fly or lure.

Directions

The lakes are best accessed from the Paradise Meadows Trailhead near Mount Washington Ski Hill. The new trailhead is located just beyond the Mount Washington Nordic ski area, about 25 km from Courtenay.

The hike into these lakes is very long and difficult and is likely to discourage most fishermen. The difficult trail stretches about 9.5 km (5.9 mi) one-way as you break out of the sub-alpine forests and meadows around Lake Helen McKenzie and climb up to the rolling sub-alpine area beyond Hairtrigger Lake. Just beyond Sid's Cabin, the trail splits with the north branch leading to Circlet and the south branch to Moat. In all, you climb about 300 m (1,300 ft) in elevation and should take about 4 hours to reach either lake. Stunning views of the rugged nearby mountain peaks, great fishing and a very remote setting reward hikers for their efforts.

Facilities

There is a designated, wilderness campsite for backpackers situated at the northeast corner of the Circlet Lake. Despite signs of camping, there are no designated campsites at Moat.

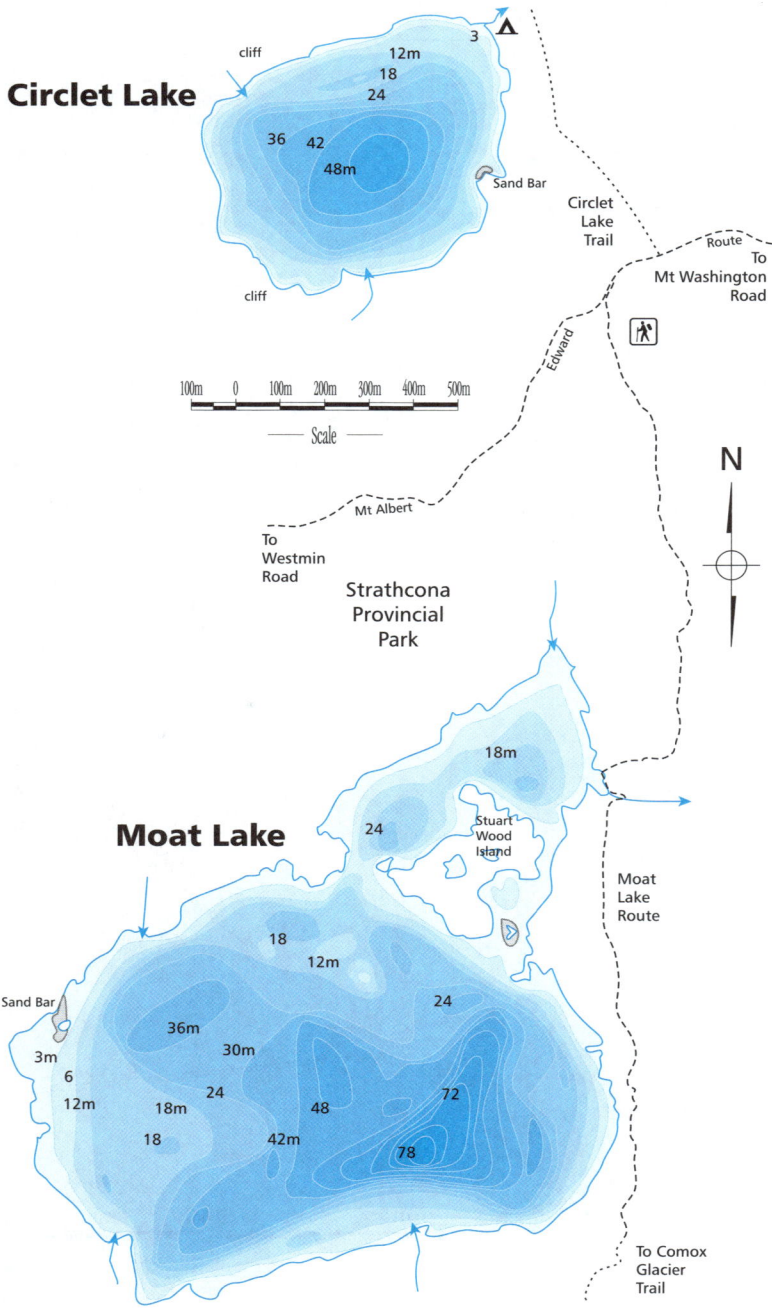

Circlet Lake			
Fish Stocking Data			
Year	Species	Number	Life Stage
2010	Rainbow Trout	580	Fry
2008	Rainbow Trout	400	Fry

Moat Lake			
Fish Stocking Data			
Year	Species	Number	Life Stage
2010	Rainbow Trout	400	Fry
2008	Rainbow Trout	400	Fry

Colliery Dam Lakes

Location: 3 km (2 mi) south of Nanaimo
Elevation: 110 m (360 ft)
Surface Area: 1.4 – 2.3 ha (3.5 ¬ 5.7 ac)
Max Depth: 6.5 m (21 ft)
Waypoint: 123° 58′ 00″ Lon - W 49° 43′ 00″ Lat - N

Fishing

Colliery Dams Park in Nanaimo is a popular local retreat for summer swimming, hiking year round and, of course, fishing. The two man-made lakes found here are stocked with catchable-sized rainbow trout several times throughout the year. The easy access and close proximity to the city makes this an ideal location for the Freshwater Fisheries Society of BC 'Fishing in the City' program.

The lakes were formed when a dam was created to provide water for the Harewood No.1 Mine. A concrete dam and spillway separate the two lakes, while the Chase River enters the park through a large culvert at the north end. An old canal at the south end of the Lower Lake allows the river to drop into a nice waterfall. Adding to the mix is a series of trails that loop around the lakes and beyond. These trails provide good shore fishing access.

Being small lakes, fishing is best in the spring and fall. The classic bait and bobber set up using small hooks with anything from worms to salmon eggs or Power Bait is a popular alternative here. The trick is to suspend the bait just off the bottom where the trout like to hide. A lightweight spinning rod-and-reel combo with 6-pound test is all you need. Spincasting with small lures like the Panther Martin, Mepps Black Fury, Gibbs Silvex, and Blue Fox spinners are also effective.

There are also several spots on the lakes where there is enough room to fly-fish. Try patterns like chironomid pupa, leeches and damselfly nymphs during the spring and fall months when water is cooler is recommended.

The Freshwater Fisheries Society of BC offers regular Learn to Fish classes at Colliery Dams. They even have a YouTube video on where to fish the lakes. Check out gofishbc.com for more details.

Area Indicator

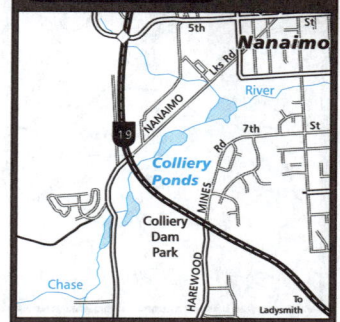

Colliery Dams			
Fish Stocking Data			
Year	Species	Number	Life Stage
2011	Rainbow Trout	5000	Catchables
2010	Rainbow Trout	9000	Catchables
2009	Rainbow Trout	6000	Catchables

Directions

Found off Nanaimo Lakes Road south of the Nanaimo Parkway (Hwy 19) signs lead the way to Colliery Dams Park. From the Parkway, go east on 5th Street near the Malaspina University-College and turn south onto Wakesiah Avenue. Turn right onto Nanaimo Lakes Road at the four way intersection and a parking spot will be found on the left, just before the Parkway underpass.

Alternatively, from Highway 19A in Nanaimo, turn west on Pine Street and then left onto 5th Street. Continue to Harewood Road and turn left again. Continue straight and the road turns into the

Nanaimo Lakes Road and the parking spot described above. A short trail leads to the lakes.

Facilities

Colliery Dams Park is a small, 28 hectare, park that is a very popular swimming location in the summer. There are three beach areas on the Upper Lake that make nice picnic spots. About 2.5 kilometres of trails loop through the forest, past waterfalls and around the two man-made lakes. Kids especially enjoy exploring the caves found off the main trail, as well as the large boulders found just south of the bridge between the two lakes. In addition to the park trail system, the **Parkways Trail**, which is part of the **Trans Canada Trail**, crosses through the park.

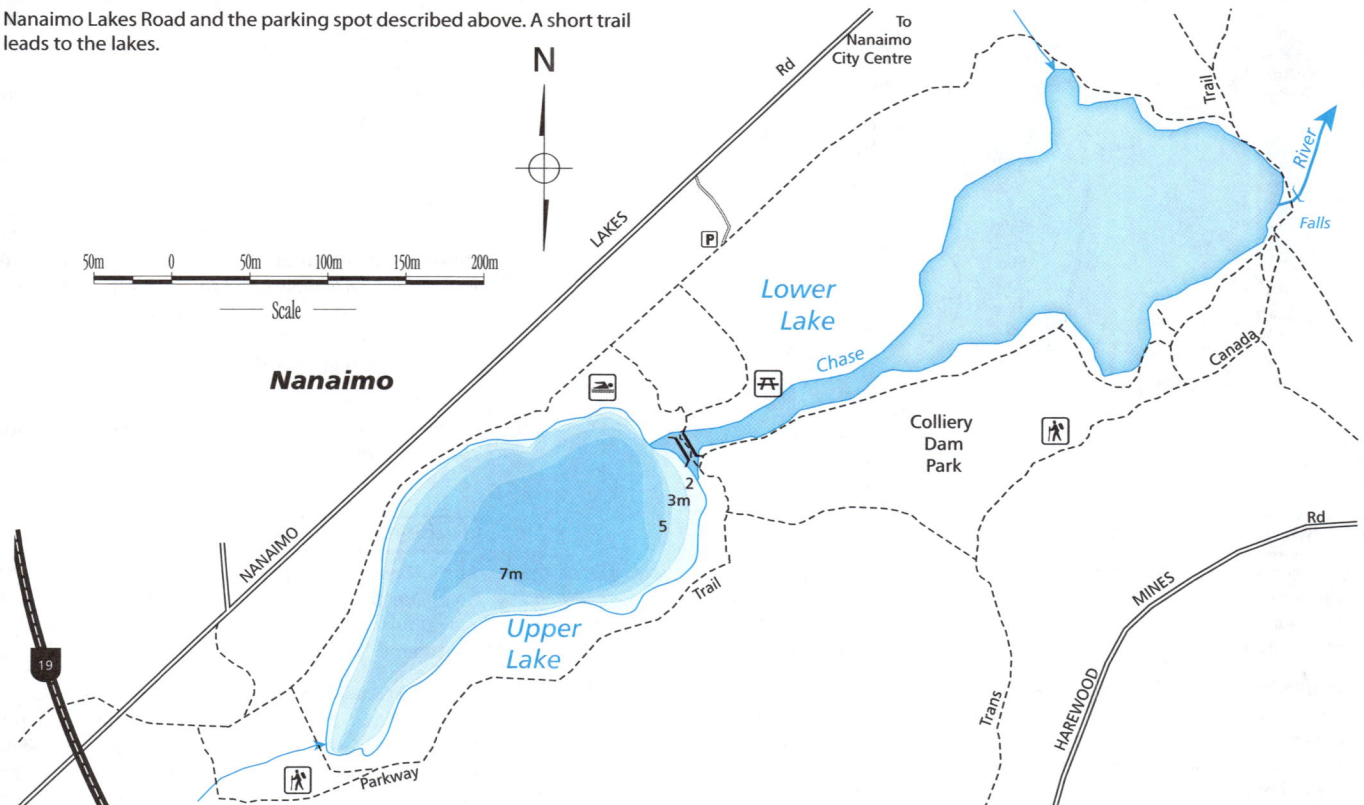

Location: 10 km (6.2 mi) southwest of Courtenay
Elevation: 134 m (440 ft)
Surface Area: 2,100 ha (5,187 ac)
Mean Depth: 61 m (200 ft)
Max Depth: 109 m (358 ft)
Way Point: 125° 10'00" Lon - W 49° 37'00" Lat - N

Comox Lake

Comox Lake

Area Indicator

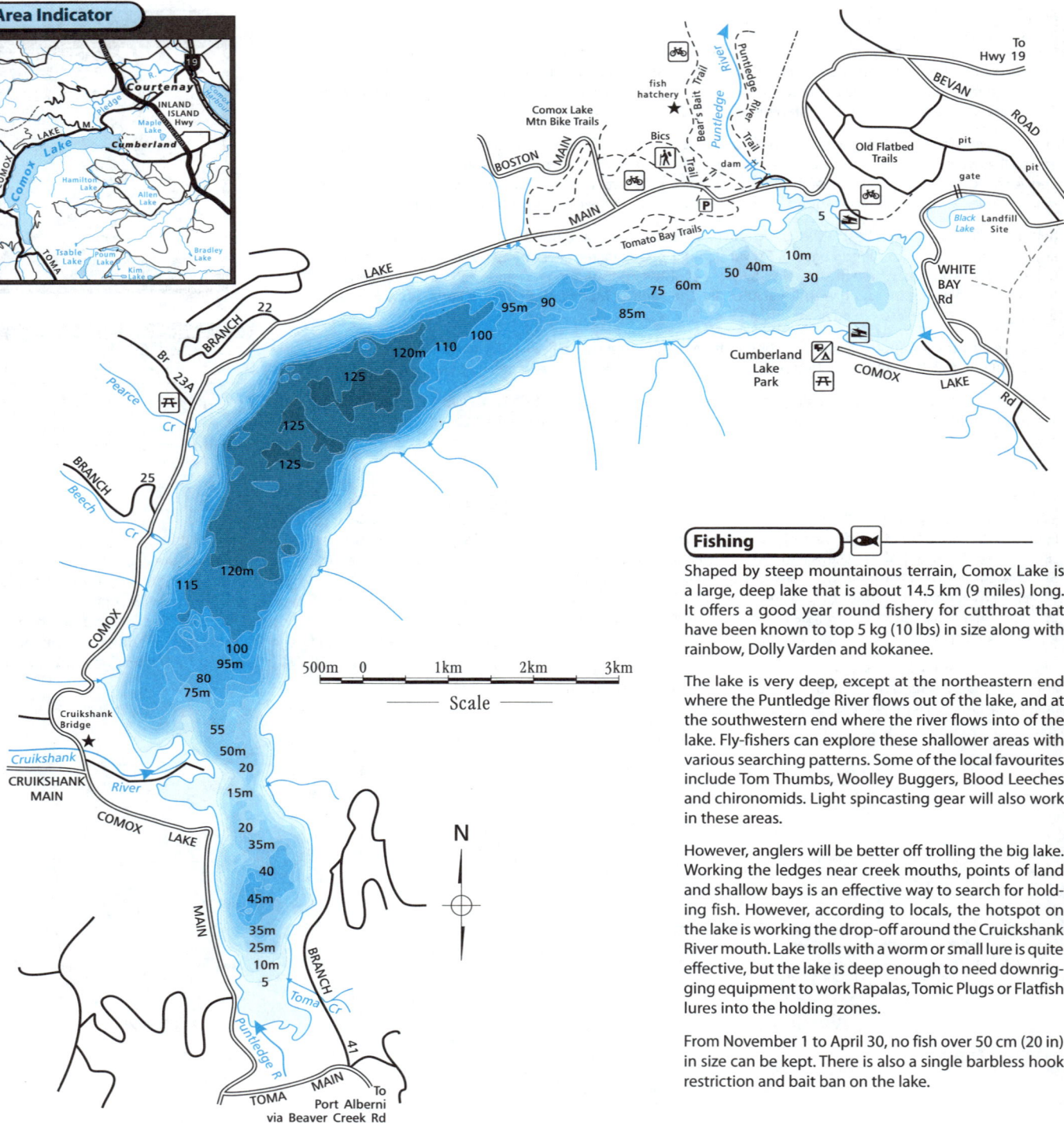

Fishing

Shaped by steep mountainous terrain, Comox Lake is a large, deep lake that is about 14.5 km (9 miles) long. It offers a good year round fishery for cutthroat that have been known to top 5 kg (10 lbs) in size along with rainbow, Dolly Varden and kokanee.

The lake is very deep, except at the northeastern end where the Puntledge River flows out of the lake, and at the southwestern end where the river flows into of the lake. Fly-fishers can explore these shallower areas with various searching patterns. Some of the local favourites include Tom Thumbs, Woolley Buggers, Blood Leeches and chironomids. Light spincasting gear will also work in these areas.

However, anglers will be better off trolling the big lake. Working the ledges near creek mouths, points of land and shallow bays is an effective way to search for holding fish. However, according to locals, the hotspot on the lake is working the drop-off around the Cruickshank River mouth. Lake trolls with a worm or small lure is quite effective, but the lake is deep enough to need downrigging equipment to work Rapalas, Tomic Plugs or Flatfish lures into the holding zones.

From November 1 to April 30, no fish over 50 cm (20 in) in size can be kept. There is also a single barbless hook restriction and bait ban on the lake.

Directions

Comox is found southwest of Courtenay and west of Cumberland. The best way to reach the lake is to travel to Cumberland from either Highway 19 or 19A along the Comox Parkway and then Dunsmuir Road. At Cumberland, follow the signs directing you to the lake via Comox Lake Road. This paved route brings you to the Cumberland Lake Park on the southeastern shore.

Another route to the lake is to follow the Lake Trail Road southwest from Courtenay. This road crosses under Highway 19 and meets the Comox Lake Main. Shortly after, this road turns to gravel and leads to the northeast end of the lake. There is a private launch site here for members of the Courtenay Fish and Game Club or you can continue along the good gravel road all the way along the western shore of the lake. Due to private property and the steep shoreline, there are few access points further along the road.

Facilities

At the **Cumberland Lake Park** you will find a paved boat launch, campground and a picnic area. The park is a popular retreat for locals and can be quite busy in the summer.

The **Courtenay Fish and Game Club** also provides a good boat launch at the northeast corner of the lake off the Comox Lake Main. If you plan to visit this lake often, we recommend you joining the club for access to this launch and some great local fishing advice.

Cowichan Lake

Location: Town of Lake Cowichan
Elevation: 158 m (518 ft)
Surface Area: 6,201 ha (15,325 ac)
Mean Depth: 50 m (164 ft)
Max Depth: 152 m (499 ft)
Way Point: 124° 16'00" Lon - W   48° 52'00" Lat - N

Directions

The town of Lake Cowichan is easily accessed from the Cowichan Valley Highway (Hwy 18) west from Duncan. From town, both paved and good forestry roads circle the lake providing access to the many parks and recreation sites that line the popular lake.

Area Indicator

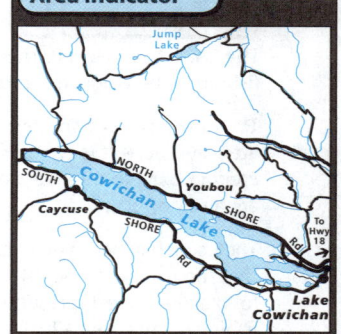

Fishing

Cowichan Lake is one of the largest and most popular lakes on the Island. However, with over 100 kilometres of shoreline to search for rainbow, cutthroat, kokanee, dollies and the odd brown trout it is not that difficult to find your own fishing area. The trout are said to grow to 3 kg (7 lbs) but you are more likely to catch one in the 1 to 1.5 kg (3 lb) range. The kokanee tend to be very small and are usually not targeted by anglers.

The best time to fish the lake is in early and late winter as well as during the spring and fall shoulder seasons. However, the lake is big enough to be produce through-out the year. The deep lake is best fished by trolling a lake troll with a small spinner tipped with worm in the 6–9 metre (20–30 ft) range. However, large tomic plugs, Flatfish or Rapala lures are other recommended lures. Work the drop-offs particularly around the many islands, points of land or around the creek estuaries.

If you are unable to fish from a boat, try bait fishing from shore near a creek mouth or rock ledge. Use a single salmon egg, worm or powerbait fished near the bottom. Salmon eggs or roe are particularly effective in the fall when the salmon migrate through the lake.

For fly-fishermen, the lake can be a challenge due to its size and the afternoon winds. But there are some spring hatches that can create some frenzied action.

Given the fishing pressure, the lake is heavily regulated. Currently, there is a 2 cutthroat trout limit per day and none can be larger than 50 cm (20 in) in size. Also, there is a single barbless hook requirement and no bait fishing is allowed between November 15 and April 15. Trollers should be wary that strong winds can pick up quickly creating big waves and unsafe conditions for smaller boats.

Facilities

Cowichan Lake has numerous facilities to help you explore the lake including resorts, campgrounds, parks and recreation sites. **Lakeview Park** is located within a few kilometers of the town of Lake Cowichan. It has both a boat launch and a campground ideal for visitors interested in exploring the eastern end of the lake. **Gordon Bay Provincial Park** is found a bit further west along the South Shore Road. Just past Honeymoon Bay look for the park turn-off on Walton Road. This popular park features a 126 site campground with a sani-dump, showers, boat launch and picnic area.

There are also six different recreation sites on the lakeshore offering various levels of service from park-like drive-in campsites with boat launches to rustic tenting only sites. Continuing past Gordon Bay on the south shore, the sites in order are **Caycuse** (27 sites), **Nixon Creek** (48 sites) and the ever-popular **Heather Campsite** (70 sites). **Maple Grove** (61 sites) is the only drive-in site on the north shore, while **Spring Beach** and **Bald Mountain** offer more rustic, boat or foot access sites on the east side of the lake.

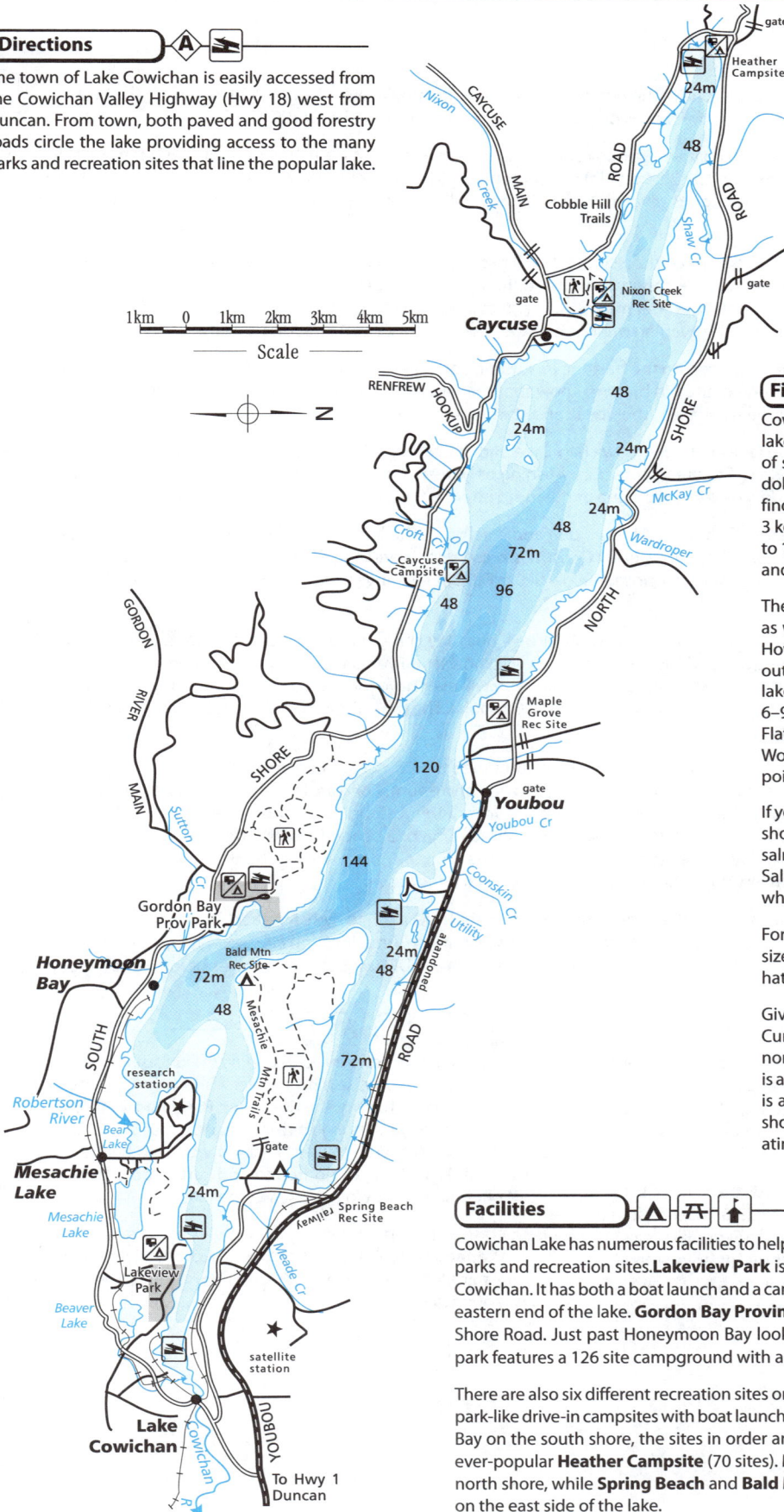

REGION 1

Cowichan River

Stream Length: 50.1 km (31.1 mi)
Geographic: 123° 57' 00"Lon - W   48° 46' 00" Lat - N

www.backroadmapbooks.com

Cowichan River

Fishing

The Cowichan River is famed in song and story as one of the best trout streams in the province. And, since BC has some of the best river fishing in the world, it stands to reason that the Cowichan is one of the great trout streams in the world.

The river has three species of trout: native cutthroat and rainbow, and stocked brown trout. It is the brown trout that get most of the attention here. It is common to catch browns in the 2.5 kg (5 lb) weight range, and stories of fish three times that size keep anglers coming back to the river again and again. Fly anglers revel at the dry fly possibilities, while minnow imitations and Woolly Buggers are also popular.

The Cowichan has its own mini-ecosystem unlike any on the Island, in that it has a strong population of insects, crustaceans and annelids that the trout eat. The fishing starts to heat up in the spring after the spring runoff has tapered off, and when the trout begin to rise for mayflies. A well-presented size 12 Adams any time after mid-April is a great imitation of the trout's primary source of food. The best fishing occurs from 12:30 to 2:30, and again in the evening during the caddis hatch. Use a size 14 caddis pupa fly.

When there are no hatches occurring, the trout feed on the bottom. In autumn and into winter for instance, the trout's main source of food is salmon roe. If you're chasing after one of the big browns, know that they prefer to feed in the evening. October to December is another prime-time on the river, when the trout are at their peak and starting to spawn.

The best fishing happens in the upper reaches between Cowichan Lake and Skutz Falls. Places like the Rock Pool, Spring Pool and Horseshoe Bend Pool are good places to start. Be sure to note the fly-fishing only restriction in this area. Egg patterns, rolled muddlers, pheasant tails, hare's ear nymphs and caddis patterns are some of the more popular fly patterns to have.

Of course, the river also hosts good returns of Chinook, Chum, Coho and steelhead. The latter enter the river in mid-December, and landing one of these silver bullets has historically made a great Christmas present for Island anglers. However, they don't get into the upper river until mid-January, and the river is currently closed below Skutz Falls. In recent years, the river has been one of the better steelhead streams on the east side of the Island.

Cowichan steelhead usually weigh between 3 and 5 kilograms (6–11 lbs), but they can get much bigger than that. Coaxing one of these beasts to chase a fly can be a challenge. One thing for certain, you will know if you've successfully gotten a steelhead's attention as, pound for pound, steelhead are about the most aggressive sportfish you will ever have the pleasure of landing. Marabou patterns like the Popsicle, small Muddler Minnows or weighted leech patterns are popular. The most important thing with winter steelhead is to drop the fly right in front of their nose.

Because the trout and the steelhead get all the attention, the salmon returning to the Cowichan seem to attract little notice. However, there are a number of anglers who come to the river in October, simply for the Coho return. Coho are a maddeningly unpredictable fish; one day they will take anything you throw at them, the next they won't go for anything. Coho usually only chase moving flies, Rolled Muddlers can work, as can a size 4 to 8 gold or silver Muddler Minnow, a Mickey Finn or a beaded Woolly Bugger. Try olive colours on bright days and brighter colours on darker days. In September and October, the Chinook return as well. The stocks were doing well for many years, but recent returns have been low due to drought and poor survival rates at sea.

Extensive restrictions are in place to ensure a productive fishery for years to come. In addition to fly-fishing sections only, bait is allowed in certain sections at certain times of the year. Anglers need to be wary of seasonal closures, location closures, and catch and release restrictions. As always, check the BC Freshwater Fishing Regulation as well as with the DFO website for closures before heading out.

Directions

The upper reaches of the river lie south of Highway 18, but the river can only be accessed by vehicle at Skutz Falls or from the town of Lake Cowichan. The old 70.2 Mile Railway Bridge is a popular access point, and the river can be accessed off Greendale Road and Hudgrover Road.

To get to Skutz Falls, take Highway 18 towards the town of Lake Cowichan. Watch for Skutz Falls Road, 7 km (3.6 miles) east of Lake Cowichan. Drift fishing the river down to Skutz Falls is also popular, although the river does pass through private land. While the river is currently closed below Skutz Falls, the famed Cowichan River Footpath is still a great way to experience the river from Duncan to Skutz Falls.

Facilities

The Cowichan River flows through the city of Duncan, which offers all amenities including fishing retailers, accommodations and restaurants. Above the city, the **Cowichan River Footpath** brings you to the **Cowichan River Provincial Park**, which stretches out along the river from the town of Lake Cowichan to below Skutz Falls. There is a 43 site campground and cartop boat launch at **Stoltz Pool** as well as a picnic area at the falls.

Beyond the falls, an old railgrade has been converted into the **Trans Canada Trail**, although it does not follow the river as closely as most anglers would like. In this section, anglers need to be aware of private property.

Cowichan River

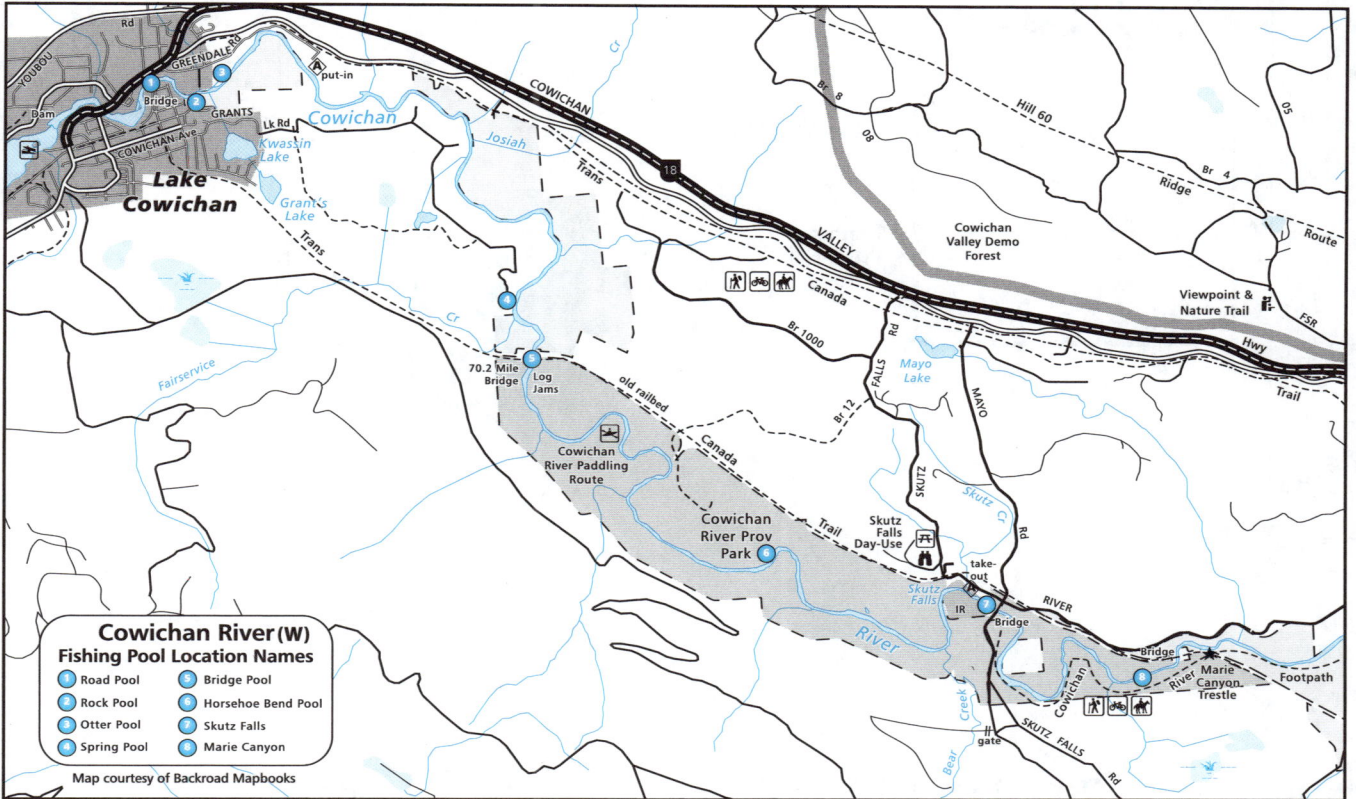

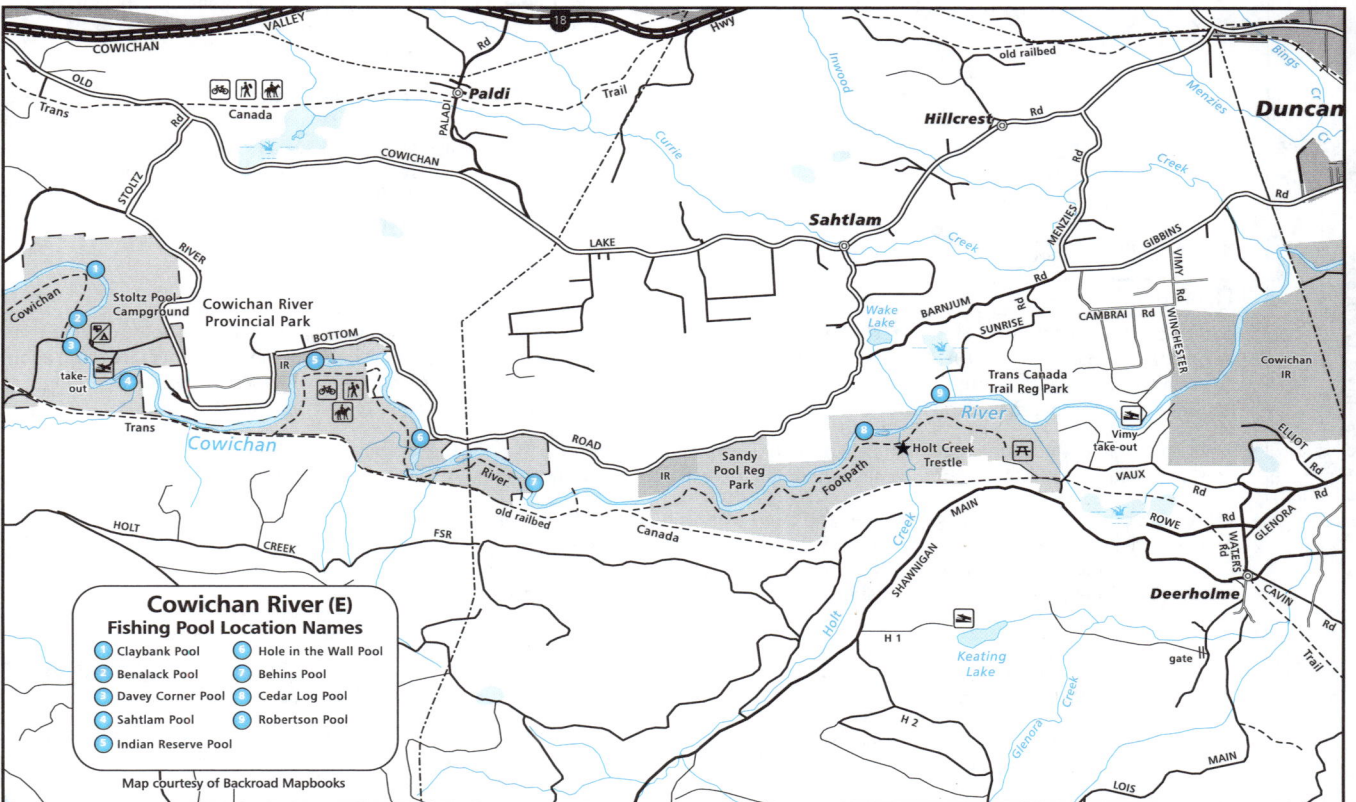

Cowichan River (W)
Fishing Pool Location Names

- Road Pool
- Rock Pool
- Otter Pool
- Spring Pool
- Bridge Pool
- Horsehoe Bend Pool
- Skutz Falls
- Marie Canyon

Map courtesy of Backroad Mapbooks

Cowichan River (E)
Fishing Pool Location Names

- Claybank Pool
- Benalack Pool
- Davey Corner Pool
- Sahtlam Pool
- Indian Reserve Pool
- Hole in the Wall Pool
- Behins Pool
- Cedar Log Pool
- Robertson Pool

Map courtesy of Backroad Mapbooks

Location: 23 km (14 mi) west of Courtenay

Croteau & Lady Lakes

Lady Lake

Elevation: 1,171 m (3,842 ft)
Surface Area: 13 ha (33 ac)
Mean Depth: 4 m (13 ft)
Max Depth: 10 m (33 ft)
Way Point: 125° 19' 00" Lon - W 49° 43' 00" Lat - N

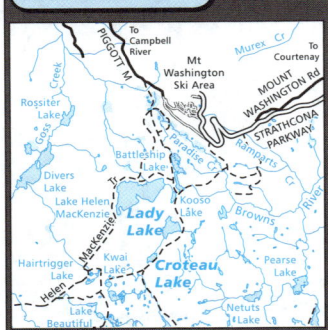

Area Indicator

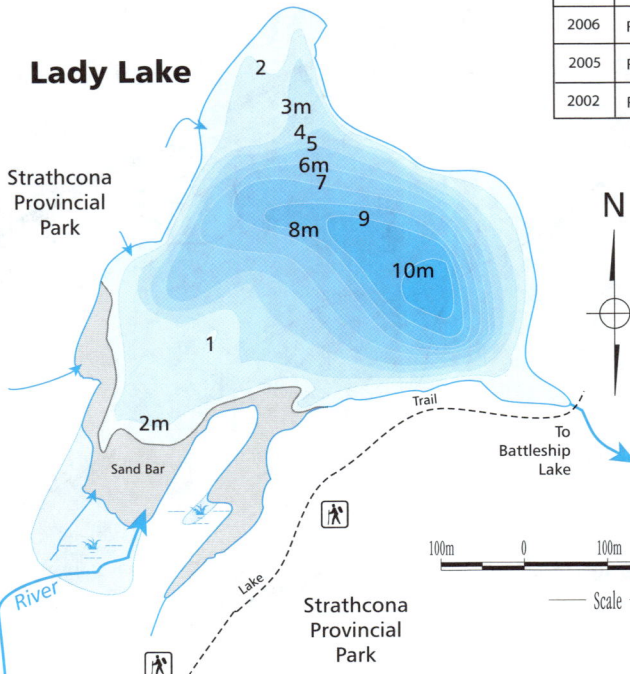

Lady Lake

Strathcona
Provincial
Park

2m
Sand Bar

Trail

To
Battleship
Lake

Lake

Strathcona
Provincial
Park

River

Lady Lake			
Fish Stocking Data			
Year	Species	Number	Life Stage
2006	Rainbow Trout	500	Fry
2005	Rainbow Trout	2,000	Fry
2002	Rainbow Trout	2,000	Fry

N

100m 0 100m 200m 300m
— Scale —

Croteau Lake

Croteau Lake

Elevation: 1,220 m (4,003 ft)
Surface Area: 3.4 ha (8.4 ac)
Mean Depth: 4 m (13 ft)
Max Depth: 10 m (33 ft)
Way Point: 125° 19' 00" Lon - W 49° 42' 00" Lat - N

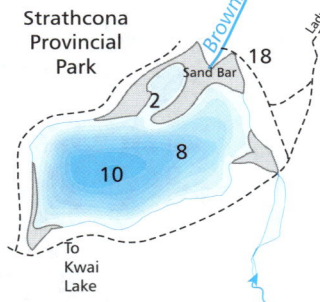

Strathcona
Provincial
Park

Browns

Sand Bar

18

Lady

2

8

10

To
Kwai
Lake

Directions A

Croteau Lake is one of the many small hike-in lakes found on the Forbidden Plateau of Strathcona Provincial Park. The lake is reached via the Paradise Meadows Trailhead, which is located just beyond the Mount Washington Nordic ski area, about 25 km from Courtenay.

From here, it is a relatively easy walk through sub-alpine forests and meadows to the north end of Battleship Lake. Once past Battleship Lake, the left fork turns into Lady Lake Trail and brings you past the eastern shores of Lady Lake to Croteau Lake. The hike beyond Battleship is a little more challenging, but should only take two to three hours to walk into Lady Lake (about 4.5 km in) or Croteau (about 6 km in).

Fishing

Stocked every few years by the Freshwater Fisheries Society of BC, Croteau and Lady Lakes host a healthy population of rainbow trout. The trout are generally small, averaging 10-12 in (25-30 cm) in size, but they are easily caught using a fly, small lure or spinner. Another nice thing about these small mountain lakes is the fact that the fishing remains active throughout the summer months with August being the best month to fish. Generally speaking the season lasts from late June until early November before the ice begins to form again.

The deepest part of the Croteau Lake is right in the middle with prominent drop-offs along the southern and western shoreline. It is at those two locations where shore fishing is best. The eastern shoreline, nearby to the informal camping sites, is shallower and not as suited to shore fishing.

Lady Lake is one of the larger lakes in the area and offers a beautiful setting for visitors to enjoy. With expansive shallows at the southwest end of the lake near the estuary of Browns River the fish tend to congregate here in the early part of the season. Fly-fishing can be a lot of using most any mountain fly (Grizzly King, Tom's Thumb, Royal Coachman, etc) or small spinner. Later in the year or during brighter periods, it is best to work the deeper parts of the lake by casting from the eastern shoreline where the water drops off quickly.

Facilities

There are no designated campsites on either lake. Camping is possible at Lake Helen McKenzie to the north or Kwai Lake to the south.

Croteau Lake			
Fish Stocking Data			
Year	Species	Number	Life Stage
2005	Rainbow Trout	2,000	Fry
2002	Rainbow Trout	2,000	Fry

Darkis Lake

Location: 35 km (22 mi) southwest of Campbell River
Elevation: 224 m (735 ft)
Surface Area: 11 ha (27 ac)
Mean Depth: 3 m (10 ft)
Max Depth: 5 m (16 ft)
Way Point: 125° 37' 00" Lon - W   49° 50' 00" Lat - N

Fishing

Darkis Lake is a small, walk-in fishing lake located to just outside Strathcona Provincial Park. It is only a shot walk from the Buttle Narrows Campground and has become increasingly popular since it is such a great trout fishing lake. Fully half of the lakeshore, if not more, is easily accessible by trail and is open enough to offer shore casting. Some areas are even clear enough to accommodate the backcast of a fly angler.

Spincasters will find that a good old bobber and worm cast from shore will produce as well as anything you can throw out there. The only drawback is that the lake shore is quite shallow and lined with logjams making shore casting a bit of a challenge. If you really want to catch fish, a float tube or even a canoe will go a long ways. Trolling the lake with a leech, nymph or small spoon will usually produce well, as will setting up off the drop-off and casting towards shore, retrieving along the bottom.

The best fishing comes right after the lake is stocked with catchables by the Freshwater Fisheries Society of BC in mid-May. As the summer wears on the fishing gets worse, not just because the water warms up so much (which it does), but because the lake is quickly fished out. The triploid rainbow that are added each year do not spawn, meaning there is no reproducing population here. While they theoretically get bigger than other species of fish, there is lots of fishing pressure here, and most of the fish are gone by June. There are also native cutthroat in the lake, but most of the big fish are caught and kept, too.

Fly anglers will find there are a number of hatches that occur concurrently at the lake in May when the lake is stocked. There are chironomid hatches that occur on the lake, but by the time the fish are stocked, there are usually bigger and better hatches happening around the same time. Don't discount a nice, slow chironomid or blood worm pattern, but if you aren't having much luck, check if there is another food source that is drawing the fish's attention. Of course, a dragonfly nymph will often work well when there is no active hatch.

Other Options

Buttle Lake is a huge lake, a short walk away from Darkis. The lake holds rainbow, cutthroat and Dolly Varden. There are two boat launches on the lake including one at the Buttle Narrows Campground.

Directions

Darkis Lake is a small, hike-in lake found just outside of Strathcona Provincial Park. To get to the lake, take Highway 28 west from Campbell River to the Buttle Narrows Campground, a distance of about 40 km (25 miles).

From the campground, follow the signed Partius Lake Trail for about 300 m (1,000 ft) to the lake. The trail is easy, and carrying a canoe to the lake is not a problem.

Facilities

There are no facilities at the lake itself, but the lake lies 300 metres from the **Buttle Lake Campground** in Strathcona Provincial Park. This is one of the largest campgrounds in the park, with 85 vehicle accessible campsites, some right along the lakeshore. Reservations are accepted through www.discovercamping.ca, or by calling 1-800-689-9025.

Area Indicator

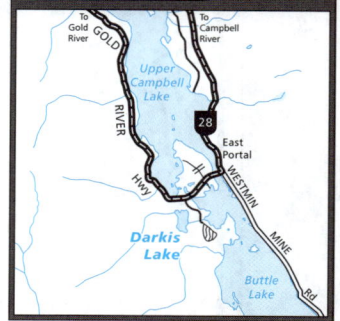

Darkis Lake			
Fish Stocking Data			
Year	Species	Number	Life Stage
2011	Rainbow Trout	500	Catchables
2010	Rainbow Trout	500	Catchables
2009	Rainbow Trout	500	Catchables

To Hwy 28

1 m

2

3 m

4

5 m

N

Partius Lake Trail

Darlington & Francis Lakes

Darlington Lake

Elevation: 240 m (787 ft)
Surface Area: 13 ha (33 ac)
Mean Depth: 17.5 m (58 ft)
Max Depth: 28 m (92 ft)
Way Point: 124° 43' 00" Lon - W 48° 57' 00" Lat - N

Francis Lake

Elevation: 230 m (755 ft)
Surface Area: 42 ha (105 ac)
Mean Depth: 24 m (78 ft)
Max Depth: 41 m (135 ft)
Way Point: 124° 42' 00" Lon - W 48° 57' 00" Lat - N

Area Indicator

To Port Alberni

FRANKLIN

Franklin Camp

Darlington Lake

BAMFIELD (SARITA) Rd

Francis Lake

SOUTH

MAIN

To Nitinat Lake

Directions A

These two lakes are found close to Franklin Camp on the way to Bamfield. To find the lakes from Port Alberni, head south through town, following the signs pointing to Bamfield. You will soon be travelling south on the often bumpy, gravel Bamfield (Sarita Main) Road. Continue past the China Creek Campsite and Museum Creek Main. The next major intersection (about 35 km south of Port Alberni) is the site of Franklin Camp and the turnoff to the lakes.

At Franklin Camp, head southeast on South Main or the Carmanah Mainfor about 2 kilometres and you will pass by Darlington Lake. About 500 metres east of Darlington Lake, you will come to Francis Lake.

Fishing

Known to provide good fishing for small rainbow and Dolly Varden, these two lakes make a fine destination for those looking to get away from it all.

Both lakes are deep enough to maintain a steady fishery throughout the ice-free season, making them appealing destinations when other lakes have slowed down. However, the lakes are not exactly high elevation, and the best fishing still happens in the spring (May to June) and fall (September to October).

Anglers will find that both lakes fish quite similar. Both lakes have small shoal areas, with the bottom quickly dropping off, nearly right from the shoreline. This means that the lakes are easy to fish from the shore. On Francis Lake, most people just cast from the shore right beside the launch area. Of course, if you can bring a boat or canoe you should be able to work the drop-off, shoals and deeper holding areas depending on the time of day and season.

Trolling a lake troll or a lure tipped with a worm around the perimeter of the lakes is perhaps the most productive fishing method, but do not rule out fly-fishing or casting small lures closer to shore. As always, fly anglers are best to match the hatch, while small spinners like Mepps or Panther Martin rarely disappoint.

Darlington Lake

To Port Alberni via Hwy 4

6m 12 24

27m

FIRE ACCESS ROAD

BRANCH 32

Kenney Cr

FRANKLIN

N

Francis Lake

6m 12 24

36m

SOUTH

30

18

MAIN

To Port Renfrew via Hwy 14

100m 0 100m 200m 300m 400m 500m
Scale

Facilities

Darlington Lake offers no developed facilities, but visitors will find a rustic, cartop launching area on the western shoreline of the lake. This launch site is found off a short access road from South Main.

Francis Lake, on the other hand, offers a camping area complete with a dock on the western shore. It is possible to launch small boats here. This access point is also found off South Main.

Other Options A

Chemainus Lake is across the highway from Fuller Lake. Fuller Lake has bigger fish, but the fishing is slower. Like Chemainus Lake, Fuller has a good chironomid hatch, particularly in April. There is a detailed write-up on Fuller Lake elsewhere in the book.

Dickson Lake

Location: 28 km (17 mi) northwest of Port Alberni
Elevation: 200 m (656 ft)
Surface Area: 119 ha (295 ac)
Mean Depth: 4 m (13 ft)
Max Depth: 16 m (53 ft)
Way Point: 125° 05′ 00″ Lon - W 49° 24′ 00″ Lat - N

Fishing

Dickson Lake is one of several lakes north of Great Central Lake and south of Elsie Lake. Anglers will find good numbers of small cutthroat and rainbow in Dickson. As an added bonus, some of the summer-run steelhead are able to navigate over Dickson Falls and enter the lake. Occasionally, a trout fisherman receives a big surprise when he hooks one of those fish.

It is a perfect fly-fishing lake given its many bays and shallows. The Ash River flows into a northeastern bay of the lake and flows out of the lake at the southeastern corner. One bay is only 2 metres deep so in all; the lake has a good flow of nutrients into the lake and some expansive shallows for rearing insects. Fly-fishing the edge of the shoals is a good bet. If you want to troll, focus your efforts around the two deeper holes towards the northern most part of the lake. Otherwise, you will be catching a lot of "weed trout".

Fly anglers looking for trout can enjoy success throughout the year by paying attention to current hatches. Damselflies emerge mid-June to mid-August; dragonfly nymphs can be effective from early May to the end of September; chironomid/midge hatches occur early March to mid-July and the end of September; and the caddisfly/sedge hatch takes flight mid-June to the end of August. Leech and halfback nymph patterns are successful all year long.

Please note that no fish over 50 cm (20 in) in size can be kept and there is a bait ban and single barbless hook restriction on the lake.

Directions

Dickson Lake is reached by traveling on Highway 4 past Port Alberni to the Sproat Lake Provincial Park. At that point head north, then west on the paved Great Central Lake Road. This road leads to the southeast tip of the big lake. From here the Ash River Main, a good gravel road continues northwest. Continue on the main road avoiding the notable turn offs at 6.5 km and about 10.5 km and look for Branch 102 leading west. This gated road provides access to the south side of the lake. Alternatively, many simply launch at the mouth of the Ash River off the main road and work their way into the lake.

Facilities

The lake lacks any developed facilities. It is still possible to camp at roadside or launch a small boat.

Area Indicator

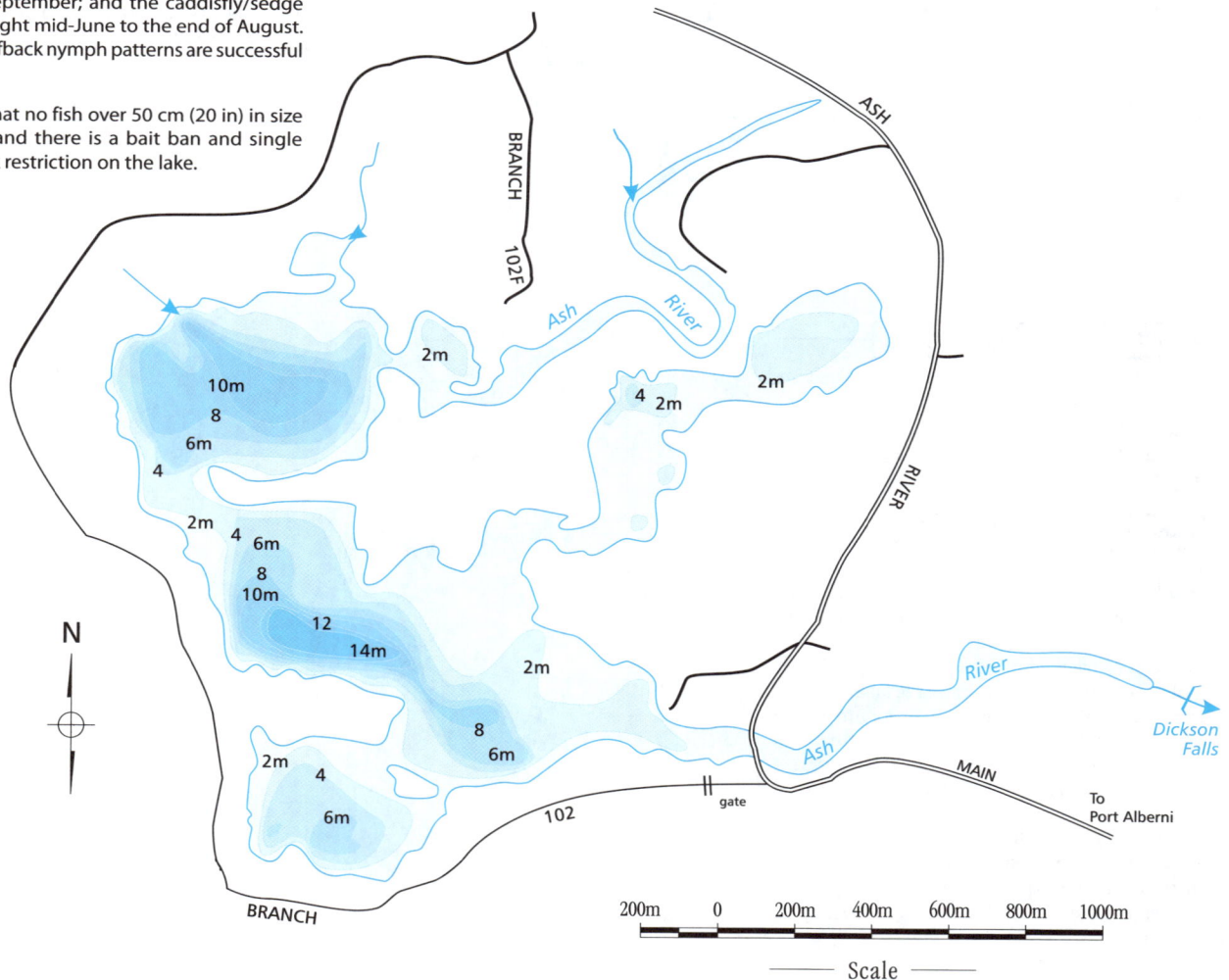

Other Options

The Ash River Road crosses the Stamp and Ash Rivers, while providing access to several good fishing lakes. **Ash, McLaughlin and Turnbull Lakes** all offer reasonable fishing for trout and dollies. The **Stamp River** is part of one of the better river fishing systems on the Island for steelhead and salmon. Look for more details on all of these waterbodies in other sections of the book.

Location: 40 km (25 miles) west of Port Alberni
Elevation: 670 m (2,198 ft)
Surface Area: 59 ha (145 ac)
Mean Depth: 13 m (42 ft)
Max Depth: 32 m (105 ft)
Way Point: 125° 17' 00" Lon - W 49° 19' 00" Lat - N

Doran Lake

Area Indicator

Directions

Doran Lake lies in the hills at the west end of Sproat Lake, about 40 km (25 miles) west of Port Alberni. About 2 km (1.2 miles) west of Sproat, take the Branch 500 logging road north from Highway 4. Keep on the main road by staying left at the first two junctions and then right for the remaining junctions to find the lake.

Branch 500 is rough in places and seems to get rougher the further you travel up the hill. A 4wd vehicle is a definite advantage to make it all the way in.

Fishing

Doran is a small mountain lake in the Sproat Lake area that offers good fishing for steelhead and rainbow from late spring (late May) through the fall. However, the best time to fish the lake is in September and October. The lake is generally iced over from November to April.

Doran is one of those lakes where fish stocking had an adverse affect. They now rely on natural reproduction to maintain the fish stocks. In the past, the trout were known to reach some nice sizes with 1 kg (2 lb) fish being relatively common. Although the steelhead stocking in the mid nineties resulted in some big fish, the food sources declined rapidly, and the program was abandoned. However the lake has been slow to recover. Today, catching a larger trout is a rarity. The fish average 25-30 cm (10-12 inches) in size.

The lake has several deep holes where you can work the fringes and drop-off areas. In particular, the northwest and northeast corners of the lake have nice holes surrounded by prominent shoals to provide the ideal trout habitat. Another nice area is to the north of the small island situated towards the south end of the lake. There is an inviting ledge in that area.

Trolling with flies, small spoons, Flatfish, Kwikfish or a gang troll baited with worms are common ways to fish the lake. Other anglers prefer to cast spinning gear with small lures.

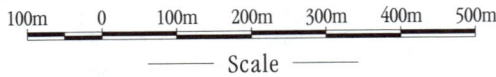

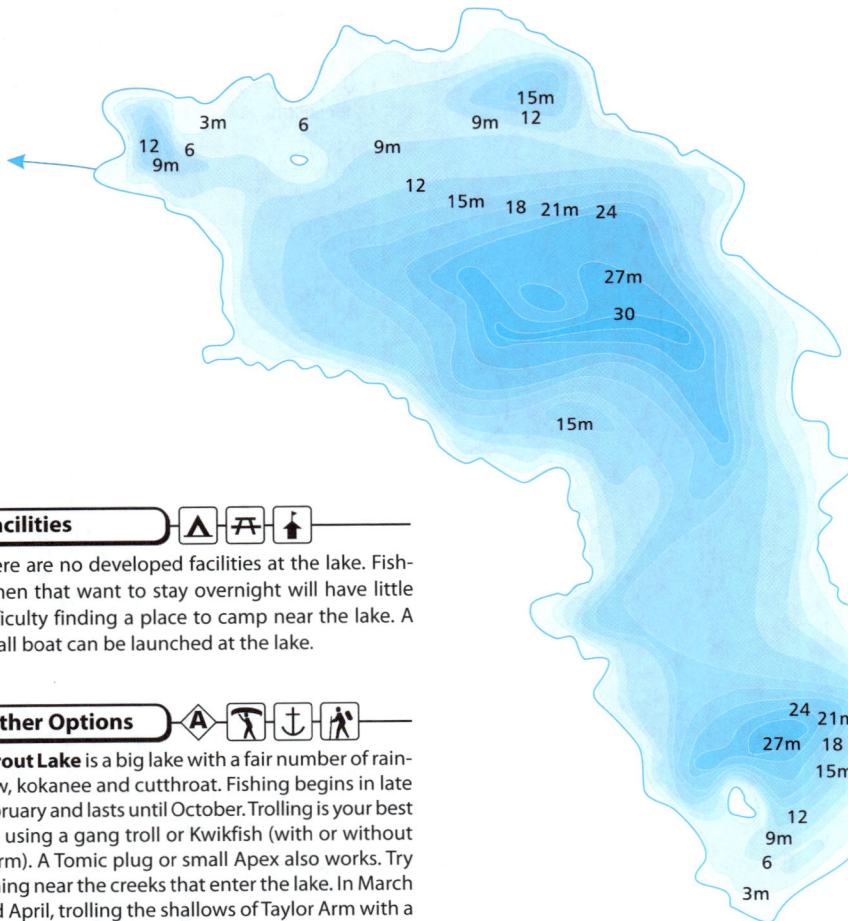

Facilities

There are no developed facilities at the lake. Fishermen that want to stay overnight will have little difficulty finding a place to camp near the lake. A small boat can be launched at the lake.

Other Options

Sprout Lake is a big lake with a fair number of rainbow, kokanee and cutthroat. Fishing begins in late February and lasts until October. Trolling is your best bet using a gang troll or Kwikfish (with or without worm). A Tomic plug or small Apex also works. Try fishing near the creeks that enter the lake. In March and April, trolling the shallows of Taylor Arm with a minnow imitation can produce some cutthroat in the 10 lb (4.5 kg) category. The 3,800 hectare lake has private resorts, a provincial campsite and good boat launching facilities. Access is via Highway 4. Watch for fishing restrictions. Other nearby Lakes include **Kennedy Lake**, which holds some large cutthroat, and **Muriel Lake**, where you will find smaller fish, but more of them.

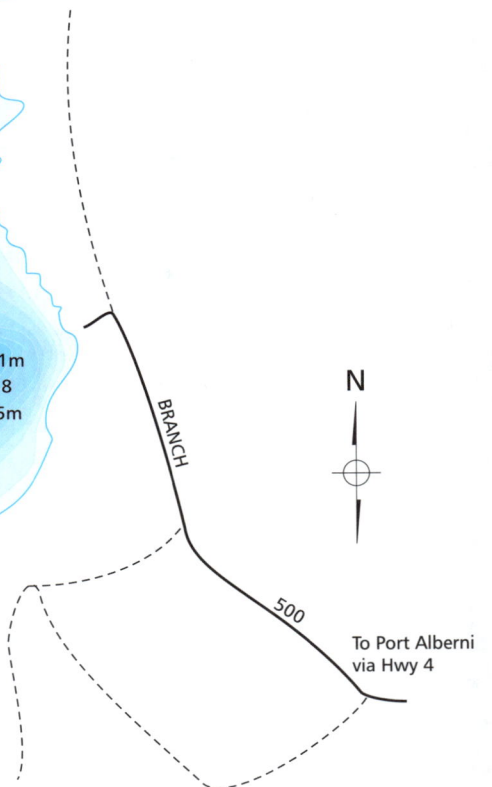

Dougan (Rogers) Lake

Location: 11 km (7 mi) southeast of Duncan
Elevation: 45 m (150 ft)
Surface Area: 10 ha (25 ac)
Mean Depth: 8.5 m (28 ft)
Max Depth: 22 m (72 ft)
Way Point: 123° 37' 00" Lon - W 48° 43' 00" Lat - N

Fishing

Aided by an aggressive stocking program by the Freshwater Fisheries Society of BC, Dougan Lake is fairly productive for small rainbow and the odd cutthroat. Rumours are the odd trout reaches 1.5 kg (4 lbs) in size, but most are less than 30 cm (12 in) in size.

Fly-fishing and bait fishing in spring (March to May) and in fall (September to October) is your best bet as there is an algae bloom in the summer months that pretty well puts a halt to the fishing.

The lake is quite deep towards the middle of the lake. The south and north ends drop off rapidly to allow for shore fishing, if you can find a spot to cast beyond the lilies and avoid the trees that overhang the lake. The island on the west side of the lake is a good area to focus around if you are casting a fly or lure from a boat. There are some nice fringe areas around the island where some big trout cruise. Anglers are also well advised to fish near the three natural springs that feed Dougan Lake in the south or where Patrolas Creek in the northwest drains the lake.

Dougan Lake is known as a good chironomid lake. The hatch usually peaks in April. In the morning or during the day, try using a chironomid imitation on an intermediate sinking line or a sinking tip line. Work a black bodied fly in 6-9 metres (20-30 feet) of water such that it is within a few feet of the bottom. Slowly retrieve the fly or use a strike indicator and leave the fly just off the bottom. In the evening, use a floating line and keep the fly just below the surface.

If you have access to a boat, the lake is deep enough to troll with a gang troll or small lure. Circle the perimeter of the lake close to the drop-off area. However, note the electric motor only restriction in place at the lake.

Directions

Dougan Lake is located next to the Island Highway (Hwy 1) north of Mill Bay and south of Duncan. The lake is just north of the traffic light at the Cobble Hill Road junction.

Other Options

Part of the reason Dougan Lake is only moderately used is the fact two of the Islands premier fishing destinations lie in close proximity. **Shawnigan Lake** is a beautiful recreational lake home to cutthroat, rainbow, kokanee and smallmouth bass. However, it is lure of the famed **Cowichan River** to the north that often distracts area visitors. With great trout, salmon and steelhead fishing there are few better destinations in the province. Look for more details on both later in this book.

Facilities

Visitors will find a full service campground in the area along with a place to launch smaller boats on the east side of the lake.

Area Indicator

Dougan Lake			
Fish Stocking Data			
Year	Species	Number	Life Stage
2011	Rainbow Trout	1,500	Catchables
2010	Rainbow Trout	2,683	Catchables
2010	Steelhead	2,500	Catchables
2009	Rainbow Trout	3,294	Catchables
2009	Stealhead	4,000	Catchables

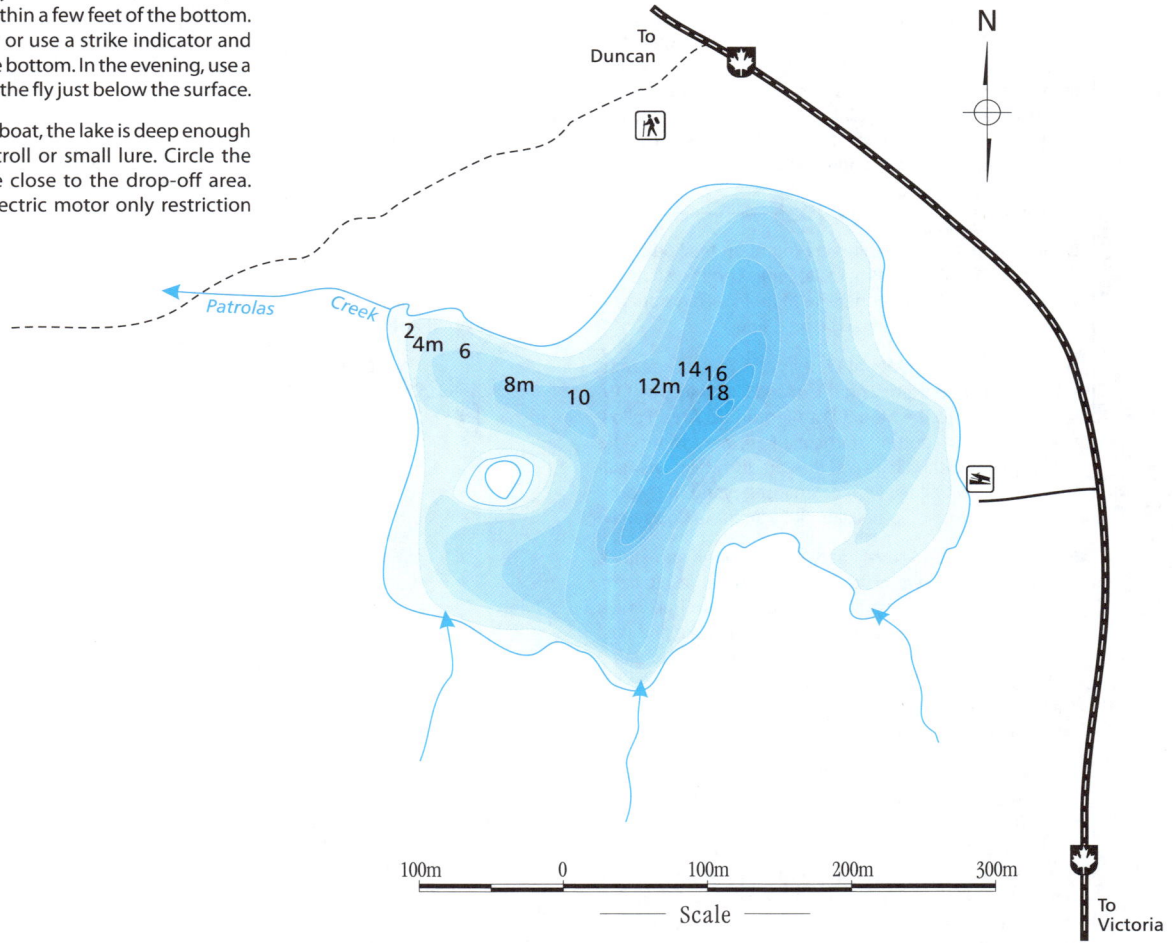

To Duncan

N

Patrolas Creek

2 4m 6
8m 10 12m 14 16 18

100m 0 100m 200m 300m

Scale

To Victoria

Location: 19.5 km (12 mi) west of Courtenay

Douglas & McKenzie Lakes

Area Indicator

Douglas Lake Fish Stocking Data			
Year	Species	Number	Life Stage
2005	Rainbow Trout	2,000	Fry
2002	Rainbow Trout	2,000	Fry

McKenzie Lake Fish Stocking Data			
Year	Species	Number	Life Stage
2005	Rainbow Trout	2,000	Fry

Elevation: 935 m (3,068 ft)
Surface Area: 7 ha (18 ac)
Mean Depth: 4 m (13 ft)
Max Depth: 12 m (40 ft)
Way Point: 125° 16'00" Lon - W 49° 41'00" Lat - N

Fishing

Found a long distance from the nearest road, Douglas and McKenzie Lakes do not see a lot of visitors. But those that venture in will be rewarded with beautiful scenery and some good fishing for descent size rainbow trout. There are also reports of cutthroat trout in McKenzie Lake.

Although these lakes are found on the famed Forbidden Plateau area of Strathcona Provincial Park, they lie a little lower than most of the other lakes. As a result, the season starts a little earlier (late June to early July) and extends into late October. However, snow on the trails might limit anglers from benefiting from these extra couple weeks.

Douglas Lake is the smaller of the two, but it is also the deeper lake allowing for much easier shore fishing. One of the better areas is at the outflow creek just south of the memorial cairn. Those attempting to fish **McKenzie Lake** without getting out on the water should try the northern half of the lake. Regardless, as long as you can get out beyond the weeds of either lake, most any fly or small lure should produce trout that average 30–35 cm (10–12 in) in size. The stocked trout generally come fairly easily to most presentations due to the limited fishing season.

Directions

Douglas and McKenzie Lakes are found on the Forbidden Plateau of Strathcona Provincial Park. The lakes can be accessed by trail from either the Mount Washington side or the old Forbidden Plateau ski area side.

To access lakes from Mount Washington, you will need to drive north of Courtenay on the Inland Highway (Hwy 19) to the turn off to the Mount Washington Ski Area. Follow the Mount Washington Strathcona Parkway towards the ever expanding ski village and the Paradise Meadows Trailhead. The new trailhead is located just beyond the Mount Washington Nordic ski area, about 25 km from Courtenay.

From here, it is a relatively easy walk through sub-alpine forests and meadows to the north end of Battleship Lake. Continue past Battleship along the Lady Lake Trail which brings you past the eastern shores of Lady Lake and past Croteau Lake. Shortly after Croteau Lake, there is a junction in the trail. Take the left trail, which is the Forbidden Plateau Trail. That trail leads past Panther Lake and Johnston Lake before reaching Douglas Lake some 13 km (5.5 hours) later.

To reach the lakes from Forbidden Plateau Ski Hill, begin your ascent along the Becher Trail from the old ski area. It is a fairly difficult hike that passes through a variety of landscapes en route to Murray Meadows, which is beyond the lakes. Due to the elevation gain and rustic nature of the trail, it should take 5 to 6 hours to hike the 12 or kilometres into McKenzie Lake. On either trail, the hike is very long and strenuous discouraging most fishermen.

Elevation: 935 m (3,068 ft)
Surface Area: 10 ha (25 ac)
Mean Depth: 2.4 m (8 ft)
Max Depth: 5.1 m (17 ft)
Way Point: 125° 15'00" Lon - W 49° 41'00" Lat - N

Douglas Lake

Strathcona Provincial Park

Forbidden Plateau

memorial cairn

McKenzie Lake

To Johnston Lake & Mt Washington Ski Area

Forbidden Plateau Trail

McKenzie Meadows

forest

forest

Forbidden Plateau

forest

To Forbidden Plateau Ski Area

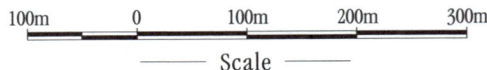

100m 0 100m 200m 300m

Scale

Facilities

Douglas Lake has a designated camping area located on the east end of the lake. **McKenzie Lake** also offers a designated campsite. It is found on the southern end of the lake.

Drum Lake

Location: 19 km (12 mi) northeast of Gold River
Elevation: 317 m (1040 ft)
Surface Area: 22.5 ha (56 ac))
Mean Depth: 12.7 m (42 ft)
Max Depth: 24 m (79 ft)
Way Point: 125° 52′ 00″ Lon - W   49° 50′ 00″ Lat - N

Fishing

Drum Lakes are located on the western boundary of Strathcona Provincial Park between Campbell River and Gold River. Although often referred to as one lake, it is actually two separate basins, which are separated by a shallow neck. Boats can pass through the narrows; however, you may have to duck as a trail bridge over the channel doesn't provide a great deal of headroom.

Angling access to the shoreline is good with both the east and west basins being accessible from the southern shoreline of the narrows. Many anglers cast spinning gear or fly-fish for the rainbow trout, cutthroat trout and Dolly Varden that await the avid angler. The lakes are stocked with 1,000 cutthroat every second year by the Freshwater Fisheries Society of BC.

Due to the sharp drop-offs into the lake's two basins, you will find most anglers trolling close to shore along the shallow shoals, or casting into the bays and vegetation along the shoreline. The peak times for anglers to target trout in the shallower areas are May, June, September and October; however, fishing is considered good through most of the year.

Anglers will have success with both spinning or fly gear. A lake troll followed by a small spoon, spinner, plug or fly along the drop offs can produce catches of rainbow, cutthroat or Dolly Varden. The rainbow and cutthroat generally feed on the 'hatch of the day,' so with the right fly imitation at the right time, the likelihood of action on the line increases dramatically. During the spring and fall hatches, the best fly-fishing areas are the shoals where the fish move in to feed. Chironomids can hatch any time from mid-morning onward, so almost any time of the day can be good for this type of angling. When you don't see any evidence of a hatch in progress, your best bet is to use a general nymph pattern such as a Doc Spartley, Carey or halfback, or try a small leech pattern. In the summer, when the majority of the hatches have tapered off, Drum Lake's trout will once again turn their full attention to such staple food source as leeches and dragonfly/ damselfly nymphs. Fishing imitations of these menu items will very likely net results.

Area Indicator

Directions

Found off Highway 28 about 73 km (45 miles) west of Campbell River on the way to Gold River, Drum Lake makes a fine rest area. There are two parking areas. One is located at Crest Creek onthe lower basin, while the better access point is located across the highway from the Elk River Trailhead. It is a short 150 metre (490 ft) walk from the trailhead to the cartop boat launch here.

Facilities

Found in **Strathcona Provincial Park**, an informal launch site as well as picnic and swimming area are found at the pebble beach located across the highway from the signed Elk River Trailhead. The challenging **Crest Mountain Trail** is also found between the two lake basins for those looking for a stiff climb up to the scenic alpine. There are no resorts or campsites in the immediate vicinity.

Other Options

Crest Lake is found further west on the south side of Highway 28, just past the tiny Mud Lake. Crest Lake is noted to be a stocked cutthroat lake, although we have no recent reports to confirm if a fishery exists or not.

Drum Lake			
Fish Stocking Data			
Year	Species	Number	Life Stage
2008	Cutthroat Trout	1,000	Yearling
2006	Cutthroat Trout	1,000	Yearling

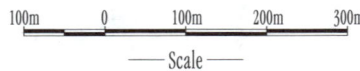

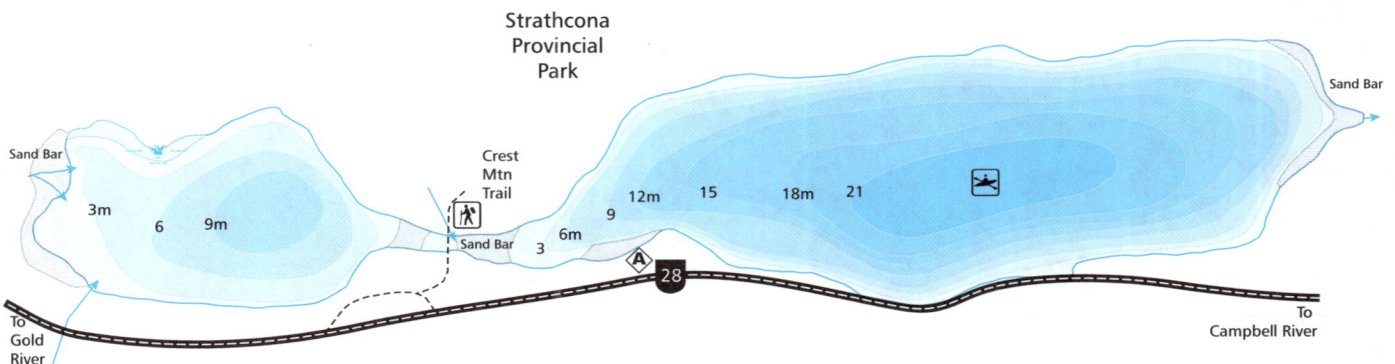

N

100m   0   100m   200m   300m

— Scale —

Strathcona
Provincial
Park

Sand Bar

Sand Bar

Crest Mtn Trail

Sand Bar

3m   6   9m

12m   15   18m   21

9

3   6m

28

To Gold River

To Campbell River

Location: 20 km (12.5 mi) northwest of Victoria
Elevation: 134 m (440 ft)
Surface Area: 8.4 ha (21 ac)
Mean Depth: 6.3 m (21 ft)
Max Depth: 17 m (53 ft)
Way Point: 123° 28'00" Lon - W 48° 33'00" Lat - N

Durrance Lake

Durrance Lake

Durrance Lake Fish Stocking Data			
Year	Species	Number	Life Stage
2011	Rainbow Trout	2,000	Catchables
2010	Rainbow Trout	4,000	Catchables
2009	Rainbow Trout	4,000	Catchables

Fishing

Durrance Lake is a popular retreat for Victoria anglers. The shorelines are protected by parkland and the fishing is fairly consistent with cutthroat, stocked rainbow, smallmouth bass and even pumpkinseed sunfish. To help offset the heavy fishing pressure, the Freshwater Fisheries Society of BC stocks the lake several times a year with rainbow.

Given the low elevation, trout fishing suffers from the summer doldrums due to warming water. Trout anglers will find the best times to fish the lake between April and June, and then again in September to October, especially if fly-fishing. However, bass prefer warmer water and anglers pursuing smallmouth can enjoy success during the early summer. For bass, there are some inviting lily pads and fallen logs along the shoreline where you should throw your bass plug. The southeast tip is also a good area to sample around spawning season. Early in the morning during overcast periods or at dusk is the best time to fish for bass. Smallmouth will take to the fly, and tend to go after patterns similar to what trout like: Doc Spratleys, Woolley Buggers and leech patterns especially. Smallmouth are not consistent surface feeders, so a sinking line usually works best.

The east and south ends of the lake are quite shallow and have limited fishing opportunities from shore. However, these areas are effectively worked with a fly or light gear from a float tube. Trolling with flies, small spoons, Flatfish or Kwikfish are common ways to fish the lake. Other anglers prefer to cast spinning gear with small lures. If trolling the lake, be careful of snags in the water and the fact that the treeline is right up to the water.

There is an electric motors only restriction on the lake.

Area Indicator

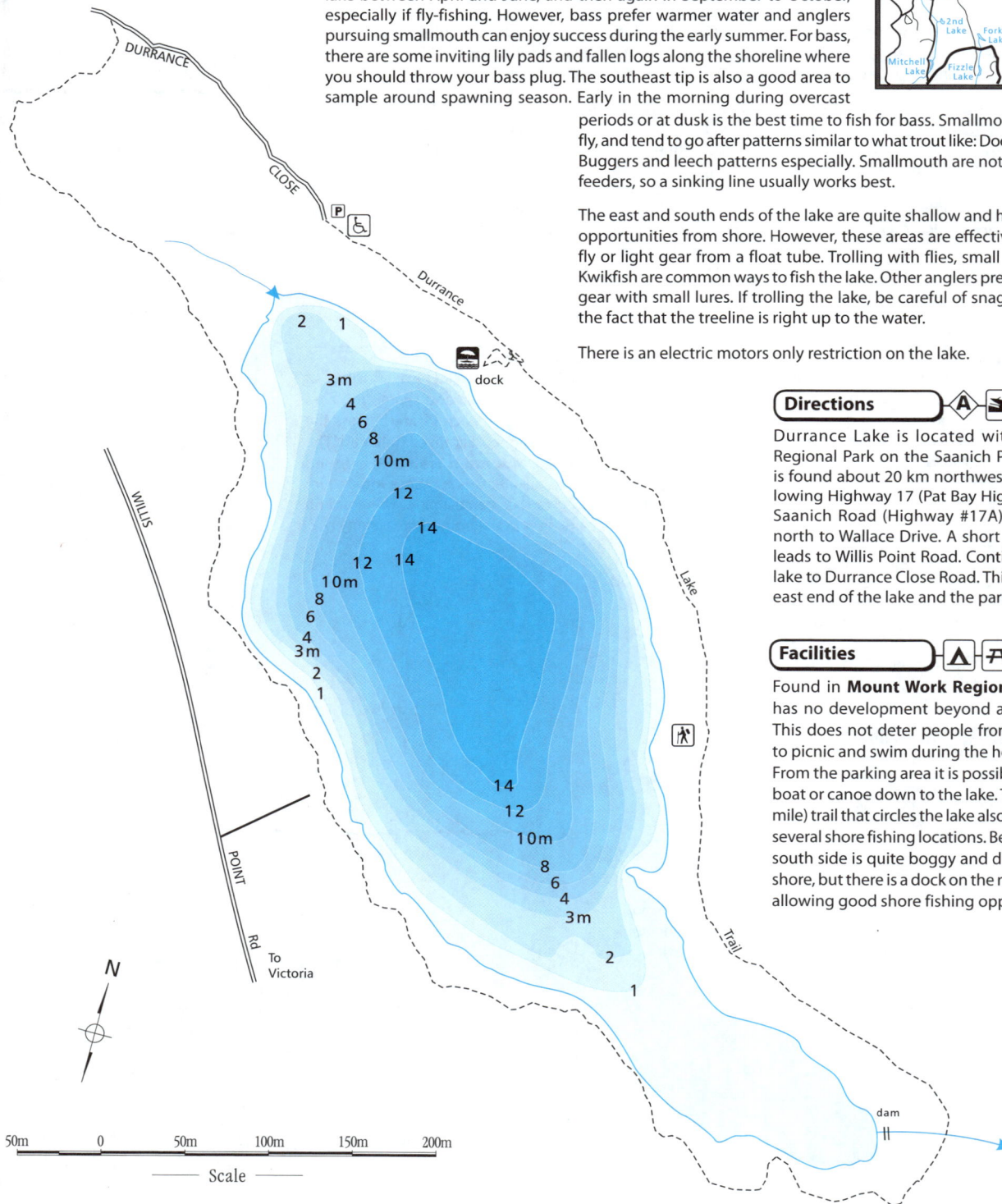

Directions

Durrance Lake is located within Mount Work Regional Park on the Saanich Peninsula. The lake is found about 20 km northwest of Victoria by following Highway 17 (Pat Bay Highway) to the West Saanich Road (Highway #17A). Follow this road north to Wallace Drive. A short jaunt on this road leads to Willis Point Road. Continue west past the lake to Durrance Close Road. This road leads to the east end of the lake and the parking area.

Facilities

Found in **Mount Work Regional Park**, the lake has no development beyond a nice trail system. This does not deter people from visiting the area to picnic and swim during the heat of the summer. From the parking area it is possible to bring a small boat or canoe down to the lake. The short 1.7 km (1 mile) trail that circles the lake also provides access to several shore fishing locations. Bear in mind that the south side is quite boggy and difficult to fish from shore, but there is a dock on the northeast shoreline allowing good shore fishing opportunities.

N

50m 0 50m 100m 150m 200m
— Scale —

Echo Lake

Location: 20 km (12.5 mi) southwest of Campbell River
Elevation: 220 m (720 ft)
Surface Area: 24 ha (59 ac)
Mean Depth: 6 m (20 ft)
Max Depth: 14 m (46 ft)
Way Point: 125° 24'00" Lon - W 49° 59'00" Lat - N

Fishing

Just a short drive from Campbell River, Echo Lake has been developed as a put-and-take fishery to encourage visitors and residents to partake in the joys of reeling in a fighting rainbow at the end of the line. Each year, Echo is generously stocked with a thousand catchable rainbow in the spring and again in the fall by the Freshwater Fisheries Society of BC. The lake is also home to good-sized populations of resident cutthroat trout and Dolly Varden, which are also popular for anglers.

You don't need to be an expert on the science of the sport to catch fish here. With a basic fly or spinner rod, a net and a few tried-and-true standbys in your tackle box, your chances are good any time of the year. True, the fishing slows down in summer, but not as much as you would expect from a smaller, low elevation lake.

Following the shore west from the boat launch will bring you to an extensive shoal area, while heading west from the picnic area will take you to an area where there is a pronounced drop-off just off shore. It will be the anglers that find the perfect location between shoal (where the fish like to feed) and deeper water (where fish like to hang out, especially in summer) who will have the best success.

Lake trolls are popular because of their effectiveness and ease of use. There are many shapes, sizes and colours of lures that have proven effective trolling for trout and dollies. Some of the most common trolling lures include chrome/orange and chrome/blue Krocodiles, silver or black/silver speckled Kwikfish, Flatfish and Dick Nite spoons in nickel or nickel/red. Local tackle shops in Campbell River will be able to provide advice on the best sizes and colours of lures for targeting trout and dollies in Echo Lake.

In the spring when the water is cool, the aquatic insects are hatching and the fish are feasting, your odds at luring fish with fly gear are excellent. As always, casting flies that match the hatch will be highly productive.

In the fall, or in the spring when there is no active hatch, try a fly like the Carey Special or the Doc Spratley. These flies imitate a range of food sources for rainbow and cutthroat trout, are excellent attractor patterns any time of the year. Other common patterns that produce good results are the pheasant-tail nymph, 52 Buick, halfback and baggie shrimp. This small selection of fly pattern in various sizes and colours will imitate most aquatic insects targeted by trout. Flies can be trolled with a full sink line in 20–38 cm (8–15 ft) of water, close to the bottom, or cast and retrieved. Varying your speed while trolling or retrieving the fly can be effective at enticing fish to bite.

Area Indicator

Echo Lake
Fish Stocking Data

Year	Species	Number	Life Stage
2011	Rainbow Trout	1,250	Catchables
2010	Rainbow Trout	2,000	Catchables
2009	Rainbow Trout	2,000	Catchables

Directions

Echo Lake is located 20 km (12.5 mi) southwest of Campbell River next to Highway 28 en route to Gold River. The lake is easily accessed at two locations directly off the highway.

Facilities

A good boat launch for non-motorized boats is found just off the highway. There is also a place to picnic, while camping is found nearby at the **Miller Creek Recreation Site** to the west.

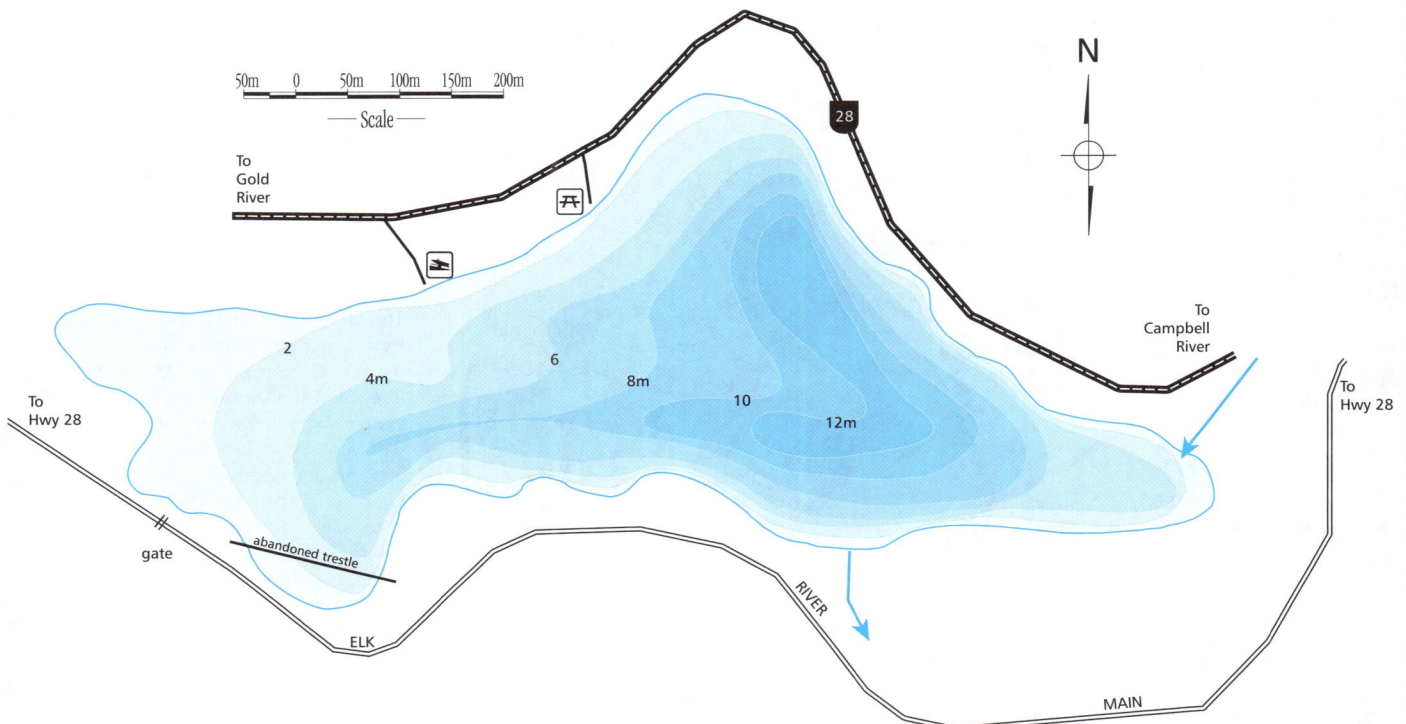

Elk & Beaver Lakes

Elk Lake

Elevation: 220 m (720 ft)
Surface Area: 247 ha (610 ac)
Mean Depth: 8 m (25 ft)
Max Depth: 19 m (63 ft)
Way Point: 123° 24'00" Lon - W 48° 32'00" Lat - N

Beaver Lake

Elevation: 220 m (720 ft)
Mean Depth: 3 m (11 ft)
Max Depth: 8 m (26 ft)
Way Point: 123° 22'00" Lon - W 48° 31'00" Lat - N

Area Indicator

Fishing

Known as Victoria's freshwater playground, Elk and Beaver lakes offer a great diversity of year-round activities. Swimmers, sailors, water-skiers, rowers and paddlers share the well-stocked waters of these two adjoining lakes with anglers. This multi-use recreation area is situated in Elk Beaver Lake Regional Park.

The wide range of recreational pastimes found on the surface of the lakes is matched by the wide variety of fish species below. Elk Lake is stocked each year with generous quantities of rainbow trout by the Freshwater Fisheries Society of B.C. Largemouth and smallmouth bass are also sought with great success by anglers, while coastal cutthroat, brown bullheads (also known as catfish), pumpkinseed sunfish, common carp and, more recently, thriving numbers of yellow perch also roam the lakes.

The best trout fishing occurs in the spring and fall when other recreational use is less prevalent and when insect hatches generate peak feeding periods. The season can start as early as late March when chironomids start to hatch. They are at their peak in April and are best caught with black or brown-bodied flies. Although the most common method of trout fishing on these lakes is a slow troll, some anglers idle their boats around the perimeter, or anchor in the small bays to cast towards rising rainbows during an insect hatch. Years ago, debris was sunk about 20 m (50 ft) from shore around the main body of Elk Lake to create artificial reef cover for the fish. Anglers should try trolling spinners, spoons and plugs with or without a lake troll. Flatfish, Gibbs Croc (or Krocodile) in nickel or chrome with a blue or fire-orange stripe, or Mepps and Panther Martin spinners are common lures for trout. Cast or trolled, olive coloured leech patterns usually perform well.

In the mornings and evenings, surface lures can provide explosive action for largemouth and smallmouth bass, especially in summer. In shallow waters, try crank baits, spinner baits or soft plastics fished close to docks, fallen trees and other protected areas. In deeper water, try deep-running crank baits or soft plastics. From the fishing pier on Elk Lake, bass anglers report success with orange or chartreuse powerbait.

There are motorboat power restrictions on both lakes.

Directions

Elks and Beaver Lakes are located next to the Pat Bay Highway (Highway 17), about 13 km north of Victoria on the drive to the ferry terminal at Swartz Bay. Several exits lead from the highway to the eastern shores of the lakes. These include Haliburton, Claremont, Piedmont, Cordova Bay or Sayward Roads.

Facilities

The lakes are in **Elk Beaver Lake Regional Park**, a popular daytime retreat for the residents of Greater Victoria. Around the circumference of the lakes is a well-developed trail system and numerous foreshore access points with a range of facilities. Four of the picnic areas are equipped with wheelchair-accessible washrooms. There are two boat launches on Elk Lake, one at the northern tip, the other at the rowing club on the east. A fishing pier is located on Elk's northwestern shore.

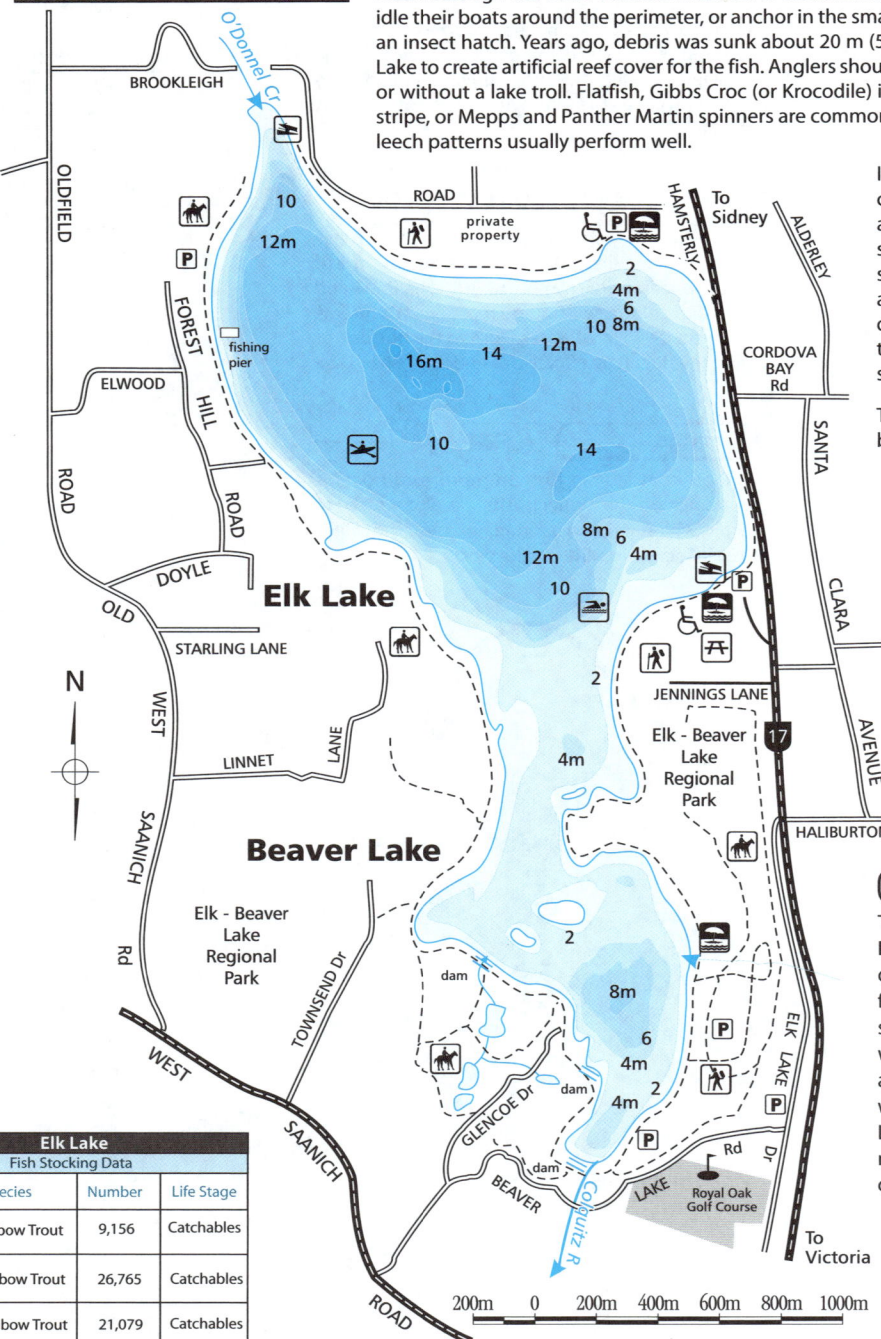

Elk Lake Fish Stocking Data			
Year	Species	Number	Life Stage
2011	Rainbow Trout	9,156	Catchables
2010	Rainbow Trout	26,765	Catchables
2009	Rainbow Trout	21,079	Catchables

Beaver Lake Fish Stocking Data			
Year	Species	Number	Life Stage
2007	Rainbow Trout	21,000	Catchables/ Yearling

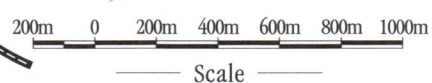

Elsie Lake

Location: 33 km (20.5 mi) northwest of Port Alberni
Elevation: 195 m (640 ft)
Surface Area: 1,107 ha (2,735 ac)
Mean Depth: 8 m (25 ft)
Max Depth: 21 m (68 ft)
Way Point: 125° 09' 00" Lon - W 49° 27' 00" Lat - N

Fishing

Elsie Lake is the largest of the series of lakes found in the Ash Valley north of Great Central Lake. The lake is a very popular weekend destination due in part to its reputation as being one of the better fishing lakes in the area. Visitors will find naturally reproducing cutthroat, rainbow and steelhead that average 25–35 cm (10–14 in) in size. However, trout over 1.5 kg (3 lbs) are regularly taken.

During the spring and fall the lake is quite large and trolling is the preferred method of fishing so that you can cover more area. Try using a lake troll (Willow Leaf, small spinner or wedding ring and worm) or searching fly pattern (Doc Spratley, Carey Special or leech) along the shoreline east of the island. However, do not be surprised if you show up during the summer and find the lake has all but disappeared due to summer draw down. At this time, the island becomes part of the shoreline and there is a big drop from the treeline to the water. It is quite an ugly site since the bottom of the lake is filled with stumps; a scar from the logging practices decades ago.

For a large lake, Elsie Lake is relatively shallow. The deepest area is in the eastern most half of the lake where you will find three distinct holes. The area around the island at the west end drops off rapidly so fly-fishing or spincasting that area is a good bet. Also, the mouth of the Ash River at the eastern end of the lake is a good place to cast a bobber and bait or a fly.

Directions

The lake is reached by traveling on Highway 4 past Port Alberni to the Sproat Lake Provincial Park. At that point, head north then west on the paved Great Central Lake Road, which leads to the southeast tip of the big lake. From here the Ash River Road, a gravel road continues northwest. At 6.5 km and 11.7 km stay right and at 15 km stay left. The Ash River Road will soon bring you along the northern shores of Turnbull Lake then along the southwestern shores of Elsie Lake.

Accessing the northern side of the lake can be a challenge due to washouts on the former Long Lake or Branch 110 Road. If you can get to the north end, there is a rustic camping area and launching site.

Facilities

Elsie Lake is a relatively remote lake with no developed facilities. Visitors will find rustic boat launching areas at the northeast end of the lake as well as along the Ash River Road at the south end of the lake. Camping is certainly possible in the area and there are some established sites to use. The mouth of the Ash River is a nice place to camp.

Area Indicator

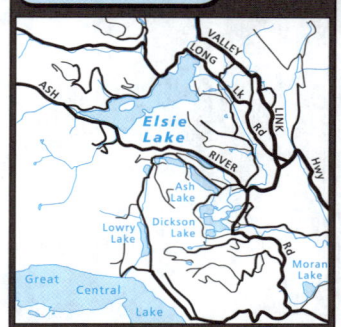

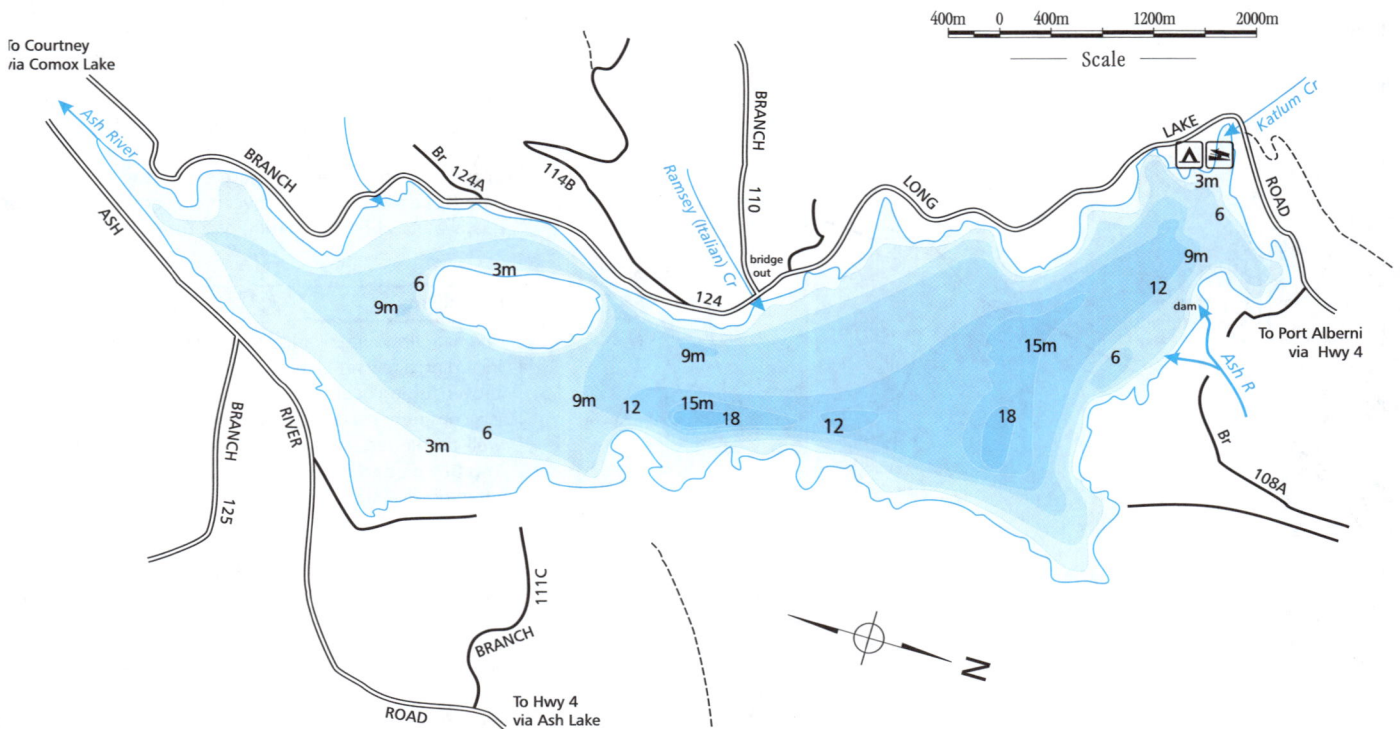

Other Options

Within the Elsie Lake area there are numerous small lakes to choice from. Full write-ups and depth charts of **Turnbull, McLaughlin, Dickson and Ash Lakes** are found elsewhere in this book. All these lakes have rewarding fishing for rainbow, cutthroat and even Dolly Varden in the spring and fall.

Stream Length: 39.2 km (24.4 mi)
Geographic: 124° 16'00"Lon - W   49° 18'00" Lat - N

Englishman River

Fishing

The Englishman River is a small volume, pretty river that flows northeast from Arrowsmith Lake to the ocean just south of Parksville. The river has been sorely abused in the past, and has been one of the most endangered streams on Vancouver Island. But the river is doing all right now, thanks to a variety of groups including the Nature Trust who have fought long and hard to see the river recover.

The river is best known for its steelhead, and although returns are low (target numbers are around 500), they are a lot better than they were a few years ago. In 2007, parts of the river closed to steelhead fishing were opened again. Fishing is enhanced by hatchery stocking programs.

The river also has some great fishing for native rainbow and cutthroat, both resident and sea-run, which can be taken on the fly or with small lure (say a fluorescent Panther Martin). The trick is getting your gear right to the bottom, where the trout hold and feed. Probably the easiest thing to do is to is to attach sinkers about two feet from the leader, so that the sinkers bounce on the bottom while your lure dances merrily about a foot or two off the bottom. Too much weight is better than too little (its okay if your sinkers just sit on the bottom), but you probably aren't going to have much success if you gear drifts overtop the fish.

In addition to steelhead, all five species of salmon are present. However, outside of a few jack Coho caught in the fall, salmon numbers tend to be low for most species. On the other hand, fishing the Englishman River estuary can be good for the small run of sea-run cutthroat trout that is also present.

Directions

The Englishman River can be accessed at many points along its 30 km (18.5 mile) length, especially in the Parksville area. Both Highway 19 and 19A cross the river just east of the city, providing angler access to some productive waters. Further upstream, the river is paralleled on the northwest side by the Englishman River Road to a point near Englishman River Falls Provincial Park. The park itself is accessed by Errington Road, off Highway 4. Upstream of the park, the river is accessed from the 155 Main, a gated road that follows the river most of the way up to its headwaters, although getting past the gates is doubtful.

Facilities

The river flows near Parksville, which offers all amenities including a few retailers to pick up local knowledge and proven fishing gear. Closer to the mouth of the river, there is a comprehensive regional park system that includes a well-developed trail system for anglers to use. Both the **Top Bridge and Englishman River Regional Parks** are often used as staging area by local anglers.

If you are interested in camping in the area there are two nearby provincial parks. **Rathtrevor Beach** is found near the estuary and provides 150 drive-in along with 25 walk-in sites. Further upstream, **Englishman River Falls** is another popular destination that includes 103 riverside campsites as well as a nice trail system along the river. There is no fishing allowed within the boundaries of this park.

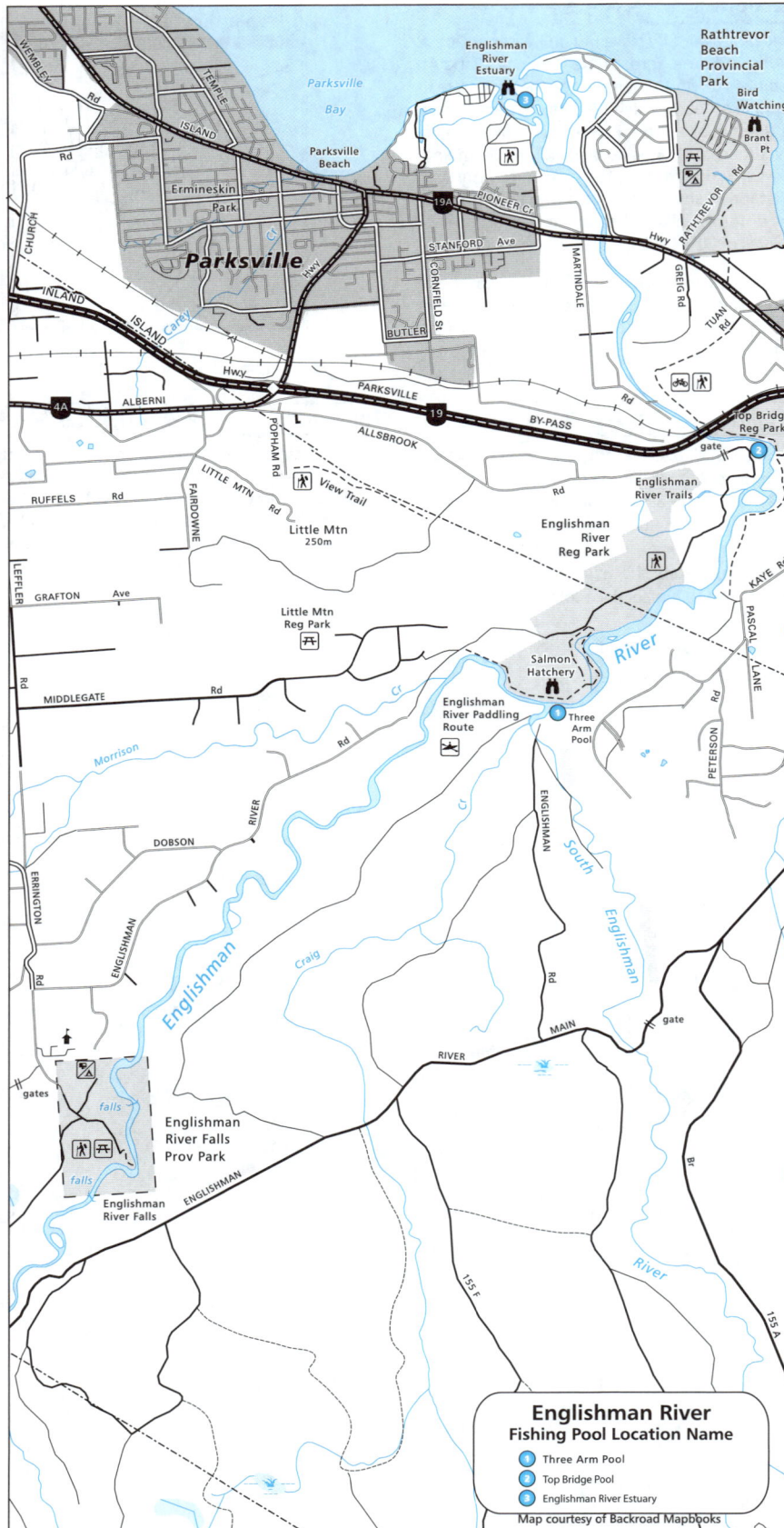

Englishman River
Fishing Pool Location Name

1. Three Arm Pool
2. Top Bridge Pool
3. Englishman River Estuary

Map courtesy of Backroad Mapbooks

Esary Lake

Location: 9 km (5.5 mi) north of Port Alberni
Elevation: 252 m (827 ft)
Surface Area: 13 ha (32 ac)
Mean Depth: 3 m (10 ft)
Max Depth: 7 m (23 ft)
Way Point: 124° 46' 00" Lon - W 49° 20' 00" Lat - N

Fishing

Esary Lake is a catch and release only lake located east of Horne Lake. Known to produce bigger than average cutthroat, this shallow lake is best fished early spring or later in the fall. During the summer, the lake becomes rather warm and stagnant and it is not worth fishing at that time.

In addition to being quite shallow, shore fishing is restricted because of the marshy nature and debris around shoreline. Anglers are well advised to bring a pontoon boat or float tube or something, to get out on the water and cast towards shore. The northern most part of the lake narrows into a small bay. There is a deeper pocket of water here with a drop-off. Fish like to hold in the deeper water, coming into the shallow waters to feed, so this is a good place to work a nymph fly pattern or small lure.

In the spring, when the water is cool, the aquatic insects are hatching and the fish are feasting, your odds at luring fish with fly gear are excellent. The Carey Special and the Doc Spratley, which imitate a range of food sources for cutthroat, are excellent attractor patterns any time of the year. Other common patterns that produce good results are the pheasant-tail nymph, 52 Buick, halfback and baggie shrimp. This small selection of fly pattern in various sizes and colours will imitate most aquatic insects targeted by trout. Flies can be trolled with a full sink line in 20–38 cm (8–15 inches) of water, close to the bottom, or cast and retrieved. Varying your speed while trolling or retrieving the fly can be effective at enticing fish to bite.

Area Indicator

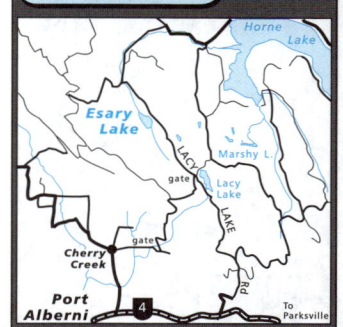

Directions

Esary Lake is located east of Horne Lake and north of Port Alberni. The best way to access the lake is to drive east on Highway 4 (Port Alberni Highway) past Loon Lake to the Lacy Lake Road turn-off. This road, if the gate is open, leads north past Lacy Lake to Esary Lake. If you are able to drive in, a short hike from the old road brings you to the lake.

An alternative route from the north is to drive the Horne Lake Road west of Qualicum Beach. Drive to the end of Horne Lake and through the Horne Lakes Cave Provincial Park. About a kilometre past the caves on the Horne Lake Forest Road, a spur road branches south leading past Esary Lake to link with the Lacy Lake Road.

In addition to a high clearance truck, it is recommended to bring along a copy of the Backroad Mapbook for Vancouver Island and a GPS with the Backroad GPS Maps to help navigate into this remote lake.

Other Options

Lacy Lake is found south of Esary Lake. The lake has fair numbers of cutthroat and rainbow. Spincasting and fly-fishing in the spring and summer is your best bet. The lake does not have any developed facilities but it is possible to launch a small boat at the lake.

Facilities

There are no facilities at the lake. You can pack in a small boat or canoe to the lake and launch it from shore.

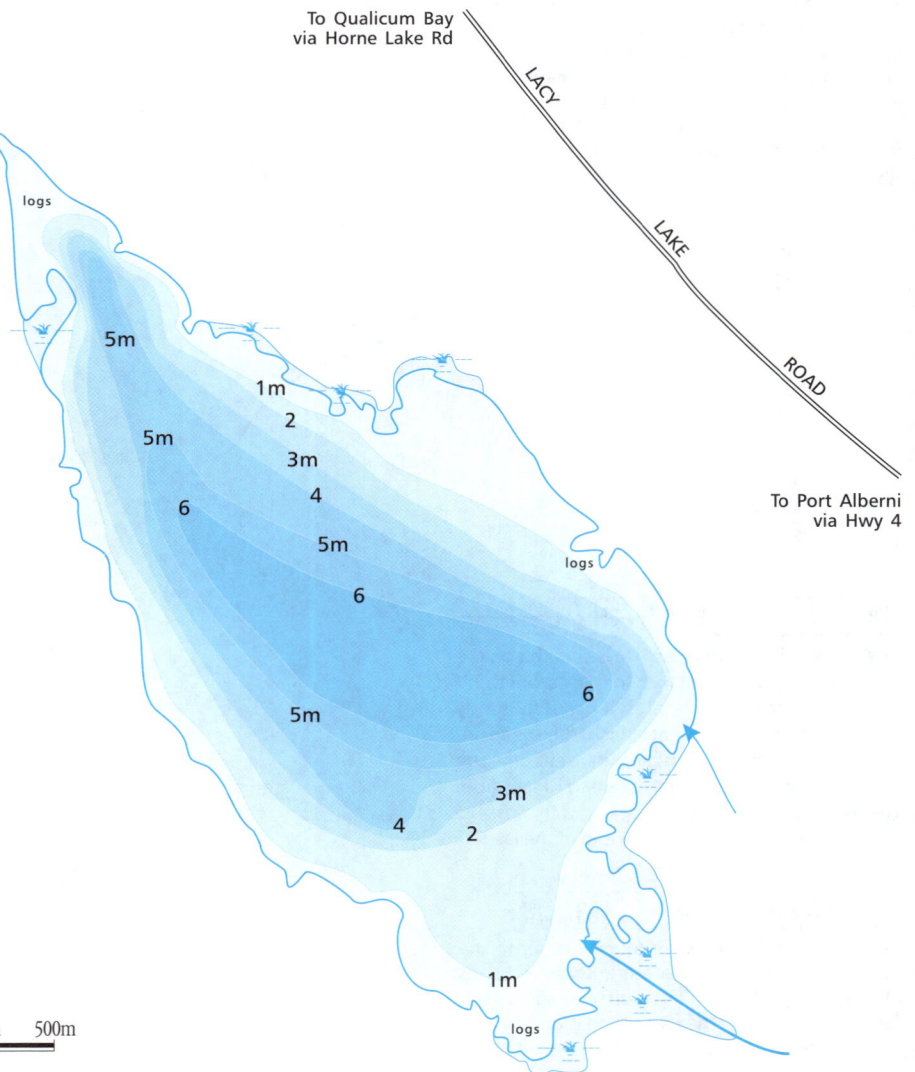

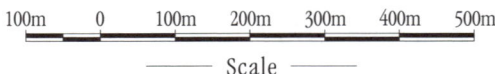

Location: 6.5 km (4 mi) northeast of Port Renfrew
Elevation: 3 m (10 ft)
Surface Area: 33 ha (82 ac)
Mean Depth: 2.3 m (7.5 ft)
Max Depth: 5 m (16 ft)
Way Point: 124° 21′ 00″ Lon - W 48° 35′ 00″ Lat - N

www.backroadmapbooks.com

Fairy Lake

Area Indicator

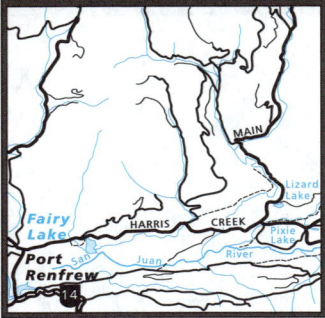

Fishing

Fairy Lake is located on the West Coast of the Island nearby to Port Renfrew. Locals and visitors alike ply the waters of this small, low elevation lake looking for cutthroat and Dolly Varden, which both average 30 cm (12 in) in size. The cutthroat are both resident and sea run.

Since the lake is almost at sea level, the lake offers an early season fishery. In fact, you can start fishing the lake by mid-March. By late spring, fishing has usually slowed right down as the shallow lake waters warm rather quickly. The fishing picks up again in the fall. Between October and April, there are a number of restrictions, including: artificialfly only, bait ban, and catch and release restrictions.

At other times of the year, bait fishing and casting a small lure tipped with a worm works well. If you don't have a boat or a float tube, try fishing the southeast corner of the lake. Even if you are on the water, this corner of the lake will produce the best.

The deepest part of the lake is at the south end of the lake where Fairy Creek drains into the lake. This is another good place to concentrate your efforts, whether you are casting from a boat or from shore. The rest of the lake is very shallow and fishing is marginal except during the early part of the year when trout may cruise the shoals in search of food.

For clues to what the cutthroat may prefer, look for what is hatching or even under rocks to see what type of nymphs are attached to the underwater rock structure. If fishing is slow or there is no hatch evident, try a leech pattern or small streamer to find cruising cutts. If these aren't working, try a standard attractor pattern like a Woolly Bugger or Doc Spratly.

There is an engine power restriction (10 hp) on the lake.

Directions

To find the lake, head west to Port Renfrew from Victoria via the West Coast Highway (Hwy 14). Once at Port Renfrew, head north crossing the San Juan River on the newly established Pacific Marine Road linking Port Renfrew with Lake Cowichan. Fairy Lake is found on the right, about 6.5 km down this road. The good access allows RVs or cars to access the lake.

Facilities

The **Fairy Lake Recreation Site** is situated on the western shores of the lake. The large open, RV friendly site has 36 campsites, a beautiful sandy beach, dock and cartop boat launch. There is an on-site supervisor and a fee to camp here after the site dries out in early summer. A nature trail leads from the shoreline east along the creek. It is also possible to launch a boat from the north end of the lake.

Other Options

Lizard and **Pixie Lakes** are found further to the east off the new Pacific Marine Road and Lens Main respectively. Both lakes offer steady fishing for rainbow trout. Of the two, Lizard is usually a bit better since it is stocked. Look for more details on these lakes later in the book.

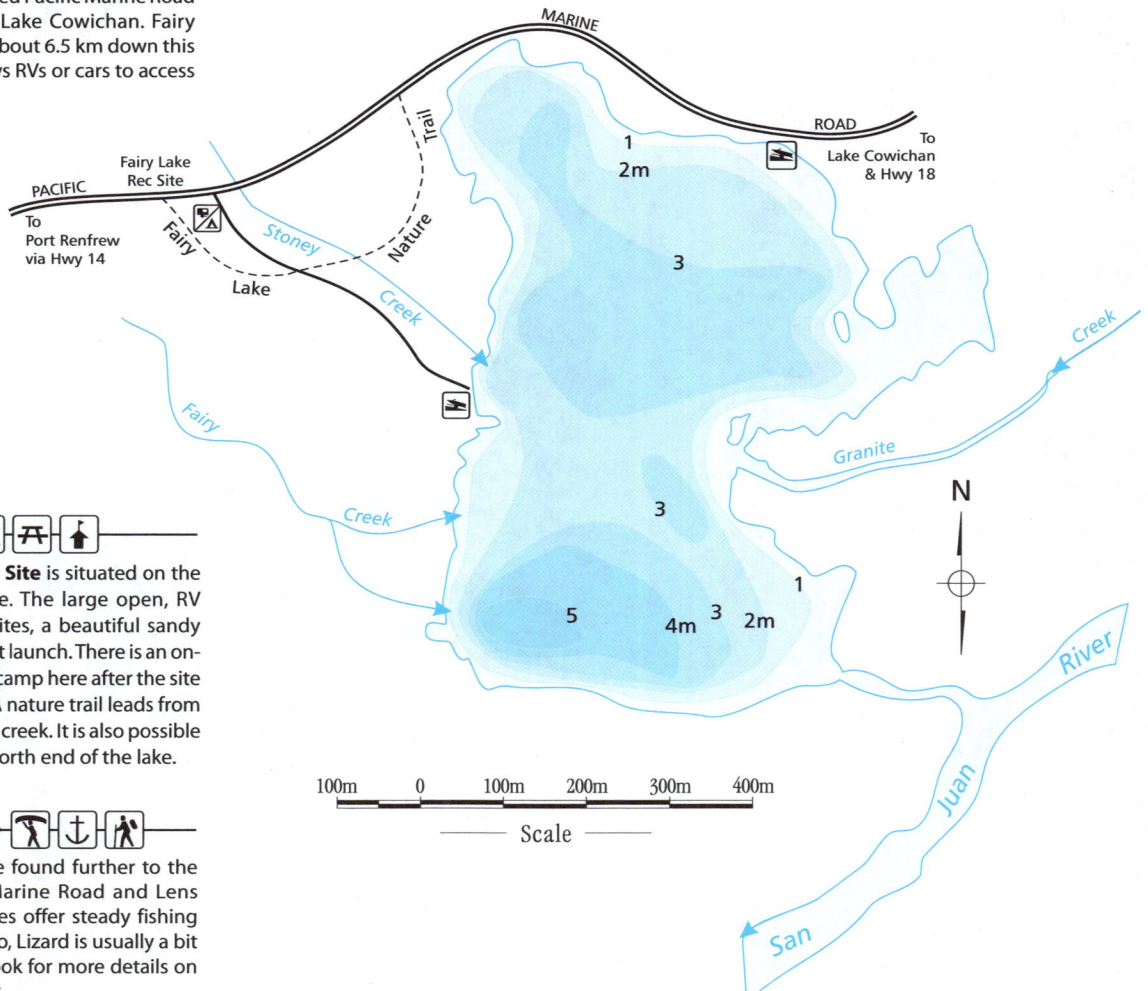

Flora Lake

Location: 55 km (34 mi) south of Port Alberni
Elevation: 198 m (650 ft)
Surface Area: 15 ha (37 ac)
Mean Depth: 7.5 m (25 ft)
Max Depth: 15 m (50 ft)
Way Point: 124° 43'00" Lon - W 48° 52'00" Lat - N

Fishing

Flora Lake is found north of Nitinat Lake and south of Franklin Camp. While it is still road accessible, it is quite a ways from the nearest pavement, and as a result, sees less use than lakes farther east.

The lake holds good numbers of small stocked rainbow and wild cutthroat. Fishing can be particularly good in the spring and fall with May and June as well as September to October being the prime months to visit the lake.

For the most part, the water level drops off rather quickly allowing for some decent shore fishing. The deepest hole is at the west end near the inflow creek. This area provides ideal fish habitat and the fish hang around near the drop-off collecting insects that flow into the lake from the creek. This is a good spot to fly-fish or spincast. There is also a large shoal area at the east end of the lake; while shoals generally don't provide the best fishing, this is a good place to try during a hatch.

Fly anglers looking for trout can enjoy success throughout the year by paying attention to current hatches. Damselflies emerge mid-June to mid-August; dragonfly nymphs can be effective from early May to the end of September; chironomid/midge hatches occur early March to mid-July and the end of September; and the caddisfly/sedge hatch takes flight mid-June to the end of August. Leech and halfback nymph patterns are successful all year long.

The lake is deep enough to troll. Try a small lure tipped with a worm, the trusty old lake troll (Willow Leaf and worm) or searching fly patterns.

Area Indicator

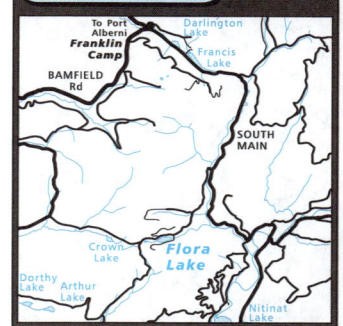

Directions

To reach the lake from the north, travel to Port Alberni on Highway 4. At Port Alberni, head south through town following the signs pointing to Bamfield. Continue south on the Bamfield Road for about 35 km to the old Franklin Camp. At this point look for the Carmanah Main heading east and follow this road southeast passing Darlington and Francis Lakes to the 8.5 km mark where the Flora Lake Main branches west or right. It is about 5 or so kilometers to the lake.

To reach the lake from the south, travel to the town of Lake Cowichan on the Cowichan Valley Highway (Hwy 18). Continue to the west end of the lake via North Shore Road. Once at the west end of Cowichan Lake, head west along the Nitinat Main all the way to the Nitinat Junction at 18.5 km. Head north over the bridge and proceed along the Little Nitinat River via Carmanah Main. You will come to the Flora Lake Road turnoff at the 8.5 km mark. Cross the Little Nitinat River on that road and drive to the lake.

Both routes require a long trip along bumpy logging roads. A truck, GPS with the Backroad GPS Maps and a copy of the Backroad Mapbook for Vancouver Island are recommended.

Facilities

The **Flora Lake Recreation Site** is found at the north end of the lake. It offers six rustic lakeshore campsites as well as a cartop boat launch.

Other Options

Crown Lake is located a few kilometers west of Flora Lake on the Flora Lake Main. The lake offers fair fishing for generally small trout.

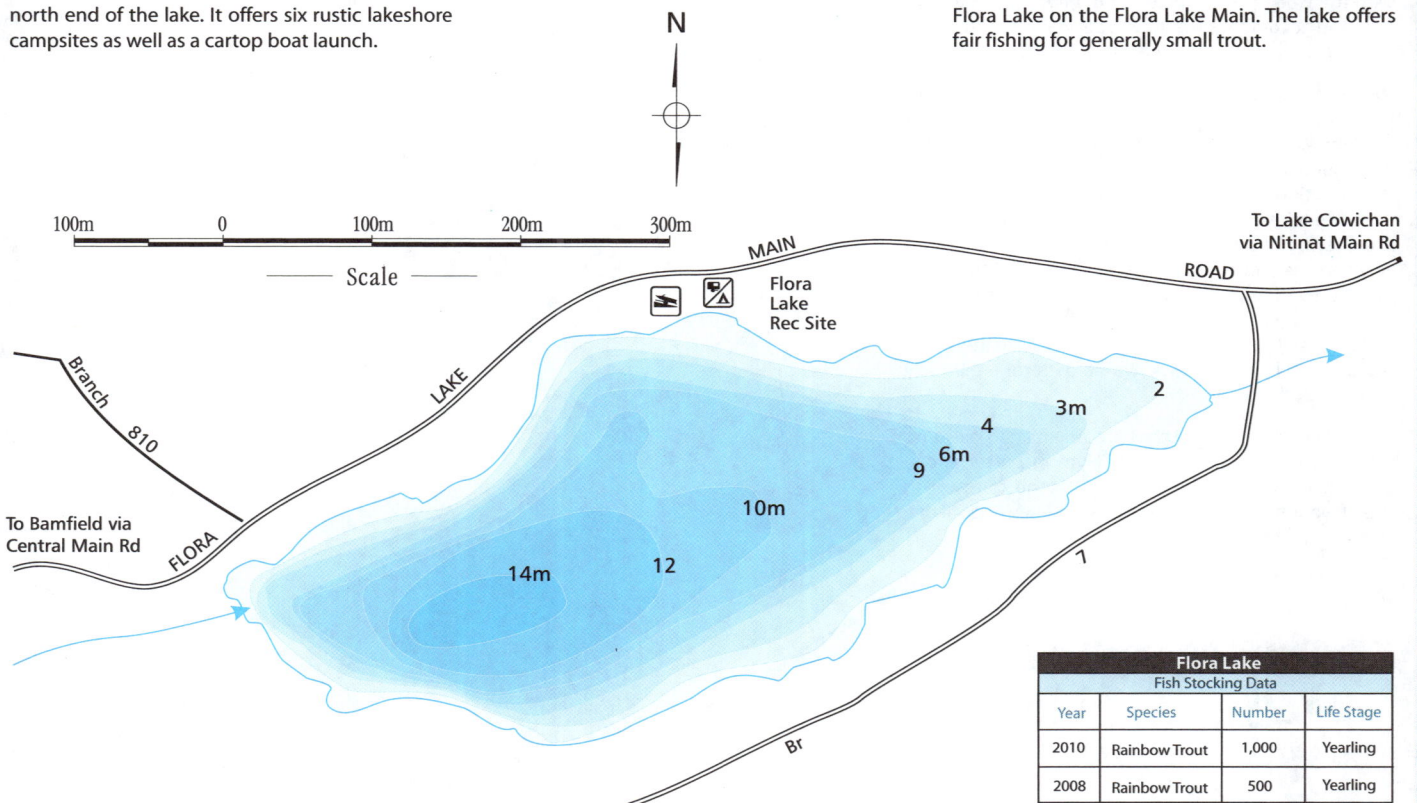

N

100m	0	100m	200m	300m

— Scale —

Flora Lake Rec Site

To Lake Cowichan via Nitinat Main Rd

MAIN

ROAD

Branch 810

To Bamfield via Central Main Rd

FLORA

LAKE

2
3m
4
6m
9
10m
14m
12
7
Br

Flora Lake			
Fish Stocking Data			
Year	Species	Number	Life Stage
2010	Rainbow Trout	1,000	Yearling
2008	Rainbow Trout	500	Yearling

Location: 15 km (9.3 mi) west of Victoria
Elevation: 81 m (266 ft)
Surface Area: 12 ha (30 ac)
Mean Depth: 3 m (10 ft)
Max Depth: 5.5 m (18 ft)
Way Point: 123° 31′ 00″ Lon - W 48° 28′ 00″ Lat - N

www.backroadmapbooks.com

Florence Lake

Area Indicator

Directions

Florence Lake is found east of Victoria off the Trans-Canada Highway (Highway 1). To access the east end of the lake, head north on the Florence Lake Road from the highway at a point just west of the Millstream Road junction. To reach the west side, take an immediate left on Brock Avenue off the Florence lake Road once you leave the highway.

Facilities

Florence Lake is an urban lake with no public facilities. However, hand launching small boats is certainly possible. But please be courteous to the local property owners that bound on the lake and be sure to avoid trespassing on private lands.

Other Options

Langford and Glen Lake are located to the south of Florence Lake and offer rainbow, cutthroat and even smallmouth bass fishing. These urban lakes receive more than their fair share of fishing attention but operate on a put and take fish stocking program to ensure the trout fishery maintains. More details on the lakes are found later in this book.

Florence Lake Fish Stocking Data			
Year	Species	Number	Life Stage
2007	Rainbow Trout	2,000	Catchables
2006	Rainbow Trout	2,000	Catchables
2005	Rainbow Trout	2,000	Catchables
2005	Cutthroat Trout	2,000	Catchables

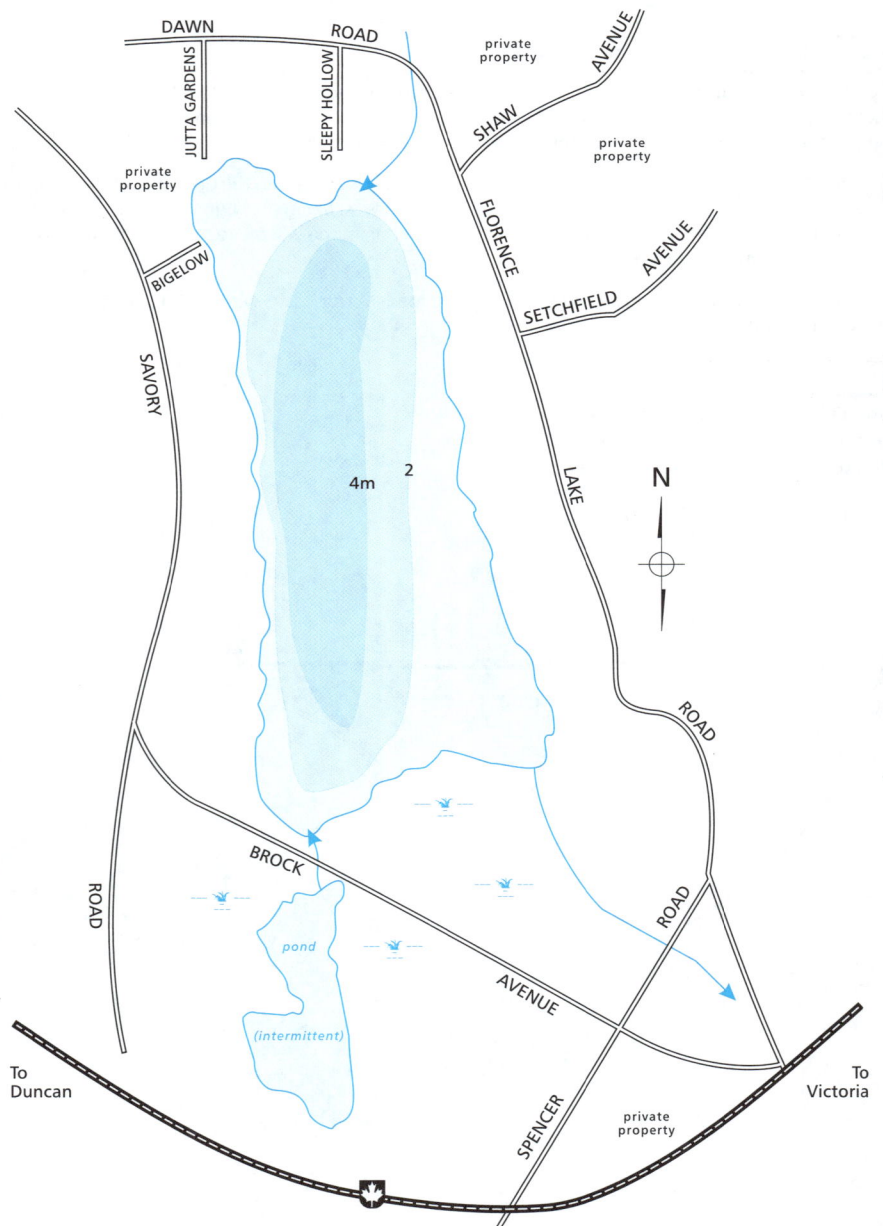

Fishing

Located in the city of Langford, Florence Lake is an urban lake that sees a lot of fishing pressure from locals. To help offset the pressure, the Freshwater Fisheries Society of BC maintains an annual rainbow trout stocking program. There are also a few cutthroat in the lake.

The lake is managed as a put and take fishery, and is stocked with a couple thousand catchable rainbows every year. As a result of the fishing pressure, the trout have little chance to grow to decent sizes and a 30 cm (12 in) fish is considered a trophy here.

Because the lake is so shallow (the deepest spot in the lake is only 5.5 m/18 ft deep), it heats up rather quickly. It is not surprising then that the lake is best fished in the early spring (March to May) and later in fall (October). Visitors will also find the lake has a marshy shoreline that is not well suited for shore casting. Rather than fighting with the weeds, you should bring a float tube or small boat and get out towards the deeper water. Cast towards shore is also a much more effective fishing technique.

If you are using spinning gear, it is recommended to use light gear and small spinners such as a Mepps or Panther Martin. However, fly anglers are likely to have more success on the lake due to the prominent shoals. Pay attention to the current hatches remembering that Island hatches generally maintain the same pattern. Chironomid/midge hatches occur early March to mid-July and the end of September; dragonfly nymphs can be effective from early May to the end of September; damselflies emerge mid-June to mid-August; and the caddisfly/sedge hatch takes flight mid-June to the end of August. Leech and halfback nymph patterns are usually successful all year long.

In the fall, when the hatches are few or non-existent, leech patterns still work well. Nymph patterns can produce as well, but most fly fishers tend to resort to their favourite attractor pattern, like a Carey Special or a General Practitioner.

50mm 0 50m 100m 150m 200m
Scale

© Mussio Ventures Ltd.

Frederick & Pachena Lake

Elevation: 83 m (272 ft)
Surface Area: 40.9 ha (101 ac)
Mean Depth: 13 m (43 ft)
Max Depth: 23 m (75 ft)
Way Point: 125° 02' 00" Lon - W 48° 51' 00" Lat - N

Fishing

Found just east of Bamfield on the West Coast of Vancouver Island, these lakes do not see a lot of fishing pressure. Like many Island lakes, they are often passed over for more popular salmon fishing out of Bamfield.

Frederick Lake is known for its early season fishery for fair numbers of small rainbow and cutthroat as well as Dolly Varden. However, it is rumoured that September is the best time to fish **Pachina Lake**. The fish are generally small, as the lakes are poor in nutrients.

Visitors will find that **Frederick Lake** drops off rapidly from shore, at least in places, allowing for decent shore fishing. However, the more effective method of fishing is to troll. There is a boat launch at the north end of the lake, just off the Bamfield Road.

Pachena has a few nice shoals to work that allows for some decent fly-fishing in the early spring. Later in the year try trolling using searching patterns or small lures. The lake has two inviting islands, one at the northeast end of the lake and one in the middle. Try fishing a general searching pattern like a Doc Spratly or Wooly Bugger.

Area Indicator

Frederick Lake

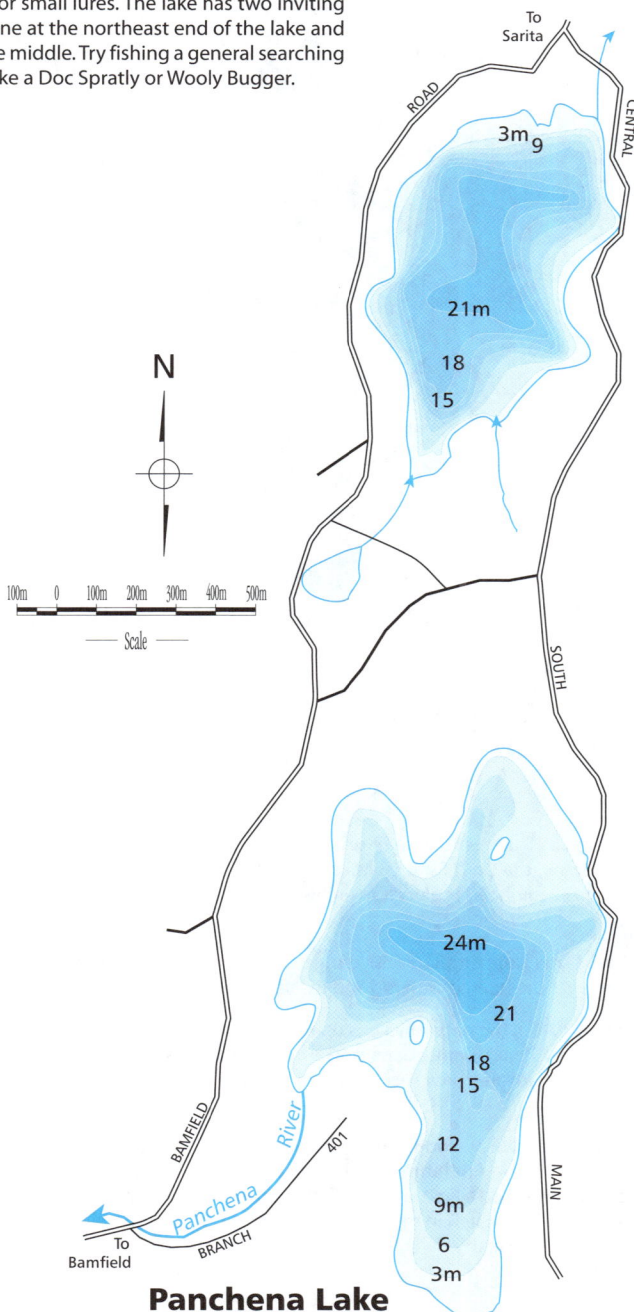

To Sarita

3m 9

21m

18

15

N

100m 0 100m 200m 300m 400m 500m
— Scale —

Directions A

Frederick Lake is easily found since it lies next to the Bamfield Road about 12 km before entering Bamfield. **Pachena** lies directly to the south, but is often missed by visitors since it is a bit off of the road. Although cars can make the journey, visitors coming in from Port Alberni should be wary of the long and bumpy logging road. It is over 65 km of logging road travel.

Facilities ▲ 🏕 🛶

There is an informal boat launch and picnic site located at the north end of **Frederick Lake**. **Pachena** doesn't offer much in the way a facilities, although hand launching small boats is certainly possible. Camping is found further south at Pachena Beach. It is certainly not recommended to camp along the Bamfield Road as there is a lot of road traffic noise and plenty of dust. Of course, there is camping around Bamfield, too, as well as at Sarita, just north of Fredericks Lake. Visitors may choose to stay at the Pachena Bay Campground, which is a spectacular location just off the beach.

Other Options A 🚶 ⚓ 🚶

Rosseau Lake is located off the Central South Main (good 2wd access) near Frederick and Pachena Lakes. The lake has good fishing for small rainbow and cutthroat that average 20–25 cm (8–10 in) in size as well as some small kokanee and smallmouth bass. Look for more details on this lake later in the book.

Elevation: 88 m (289 ft)
Surface Area: 59 ha (145 ac)
Mean Depth: 11 m (35 ft)
Max Depth: 26 m (86 ft)
Way Point: 48° 50' 00" Lat - N 125° 02' 00" Lon - W

24m

21

18

15

12

9m

6

3m

Bamfield

Panchena River

401

BRANCH

To Bamfield

Panchena Lake

Location: 15 km (9.3 mi) north of Duncan
Elevation: 55 m (180 ft)
Surface Area: 24 ha (59 ac)
Mean Depth: 8.5 m (28 ft)
Max Depth: 17 m (56 ft)
Way Point: 123° 43' 00" Lon - W 48° 54' 00" Lat - N

www.backroadmapbooks.com

Fuller Lake

Area Indicator

To Ladysmith
Chemainus
1A
Chemainus Bay
RIVER Rd
Chemainus Lake
HENRY
Chemainus River
Fuller Lake
River
To Duncan

Fuller Lake
Fish Stocking Data

Year	Species	Number	Life Stage
2011	Rainbow Trout	7,806	Catchables/Fry
2010	Rainbow Trout	7,556	Catchables
2010	Steelhead	4,024	Catchables
2009	Rainbow Trout	7,351	Catchables
2009	Steelhead	7,119	Catchables

Directions

The lake is nestled between the Island Highway and Highway 1A (Chemainus Road) to the south of Chemainus. Signs mark the turn-off to the park at the south end of the lake.

Facilities

Fuller Lake is an urban lake surrounded by private residents, a golf course and a park. At the south end of the lake you will find **Fuller Lake Park**. At the park, there is a picnic site and a cartop boat launch.

Scale

100m   0   100m   200m   300m   400m

Fishing

Fuller lake provides the rare opportunity to pursue larger trout in a picturesque, easily accessible, semi-urban environment. For these reasons, the lake is a popular destination anglers and the Freshwater Fisheries Society of BC helps maintain the trout fishery with several stockings of catchable size rainbow every year. Some of these trout are rumoured to reach up to 2.5 kg (6 lbs) in size. Aside from rainbow, anglers also enjoy an active smallmouth bass fishery along with the odd cutthroat trout and brown bullhead.

Fuller's trout anglers use a variety of methods: casting or trolling flies, spinning with small lures, trolling with gang trolls and worms, and still-fishing with artificial baits or worms. Small spoons, flatfish and Kwikfish in a frog pattern, or one that is yellow-bodied with red and black dots, are other good choices for trolling.

In warm summer weather, when the trout become less active and move to deeper water, the pace quickens on the lake's lively smallmouth bass fishery. In the mornings and evenings, surface lures perform well. In shallow, protected waters, crank baits, spinner baits, powerbaits or soft plastics produce excellent results. Bass prefer rocky areas, or sheltered spots under docks, stumps and fallen trees, and there are many such places to fish along the shore at Fuller Lake. In deeper water, try deeprunning crank baits or soft plastics.

If your preference is fly-fishing, Fuller Lake is one of the more active lakes to test. It is known as a good chironomid lake with the tiny insect beginning to hatch as early as March when there is a spell of warmer weather. However, the better fishing is in April through May, especially in the evening when the insects are emerging. At that time, work a size 14-16 brown or black bodied imitation near the surface on a floating line. Bloodworm patterns worked near the bottom also work well early in the season. April brings mayfly hatches followed by the caddisfly/sedge hatch in mid-May. April through to early June produces a wealth of opportunities for nymph and dry-fly-fishing on Fuller. The Tom Thumb is often a productive dry-fly choice, while the all-purpose Doc Spratley, one of the best searching patterns, can be used to represent most major insects, as well as leeches.

An electric motor only restriction applies at the lake.

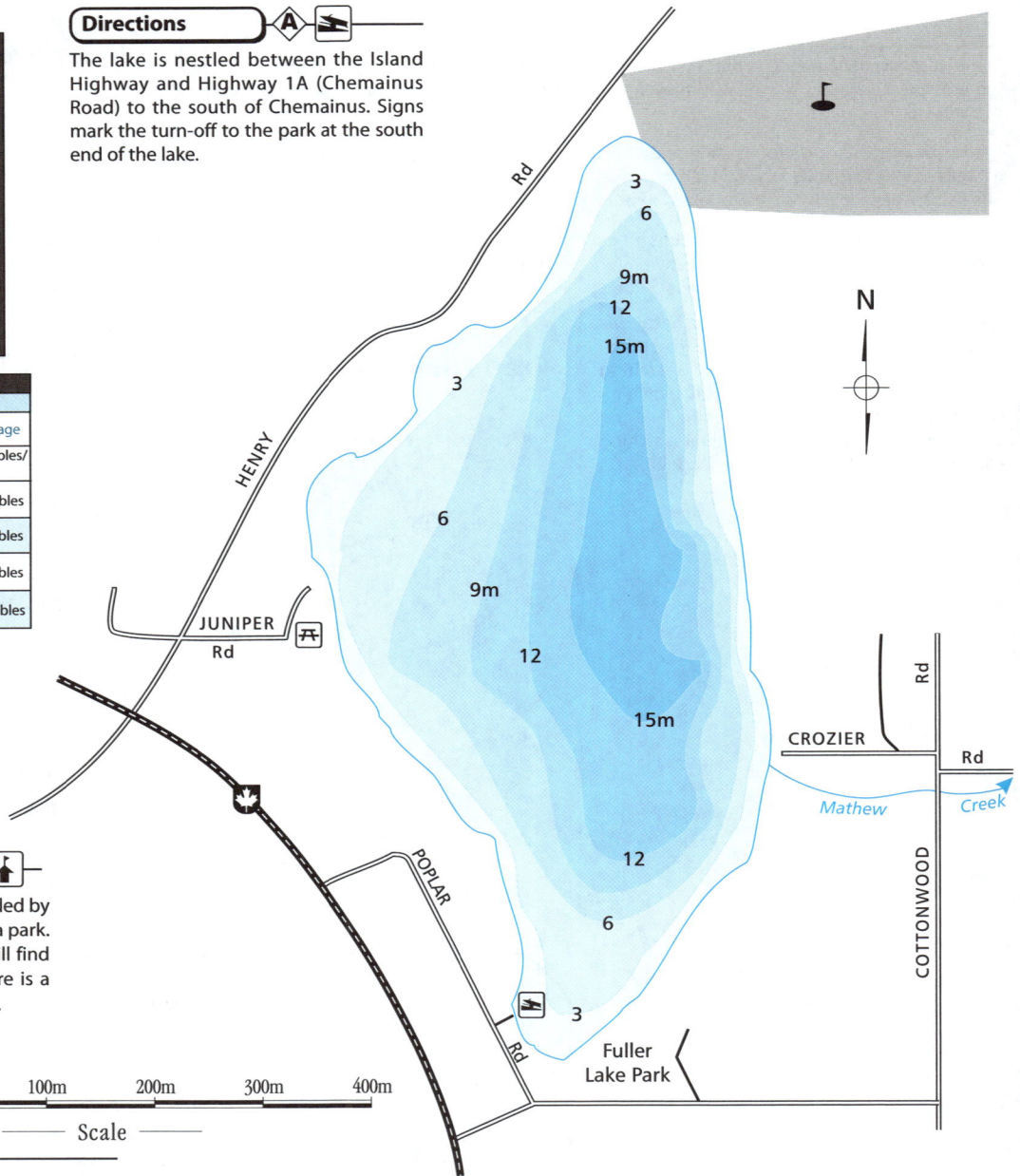

HENRY Rd
JUNIPER Rd
POPLAR Rd
CROZIER
COTTONWOOD Rd
Rd
Mathew   *Creek*
Fuller Lake Park

3
6
9m
12
15m
3
6
9m
12
15m
12
6
3

N

Georgie Lake

Location: 16 km (10 mi) west of Port Hardy
Elevation: 224 m (735 ft)
Surface Area: 472 ha (1166 ac)
Mean Depth: 16.3 m (53 ft)
Max Depth: 42.4 m (139 ft)
Way Point: 127° 40'00" Lon - W 50° 44'00" Lat - N

Fishing

Found west of Port Hardy this lake is far enough north to deter most from visiting it. As a result, the lake is rumoured to be one of the better north Island lakes for cutthroat fishing. There are also a few wild rainbow and Dolly Varden to tease anglers, but most of the fishing attention is focused on the cutthroat.

The fish are generally small since the water in the lake is acidic and not rich in nutrients, but the odd dolly can reach 1.5 kg (3 lbs) in size. Another nice thing about this lake is the fact fishing remains fairly consistent through out the open water season that generally lasts from May through October.

Being a fairly big and deep lake, most anglers prefer to troll. However, it is possible to cast from the southern shore since there are prominent drop-offs in certain areas. One thing anglers should note is the fact that the lake is acidic and nutrient poor meaning there is not a lot of insect activity here. Fly anglers should stick to minnow type fly patterns. However, it has been said that working a mosquito pattern can actually get a fair number of strikes, especially in the early evening. Try working a number 12 or 14 in the area right around the campsite.

Using a small lake troll or a black Flatfish as you work your way around the lake usually works well. However, locals know that the best place to troll is about halfway down the lake. While there is no real structure here to attract the fish, there is a fist farm holding tank. While the farm itself is private property, the area around the farm is not, and the overburden from the farm tends to attract lots of other fish to the area. You can troll through here, or you can just cast from your boat, using a Flatfish or even a simple worm.

Directions

As far as Island lakes go, they do not get much more north than this. In fact, you will need to travel to the end of the Island Highway near Port Hardy to find this one. Just before entering town, the Holberg Road branches west. Follow this paved road to the Georgie Lake Forest Service Road, which is found at about the 7 km mark on the Holberg Road. Turn north on the Georgie Lake Road and continue to the east end of the lake where you will find a recreation site from which to access the lake.

Facilities

The **Georgie Lake Recreation Site** is found on the east end of the lake offering a nine unit campsite, a nice sandy beach and a boat launch. At the north end of the beach, a moderately difficult 7 km (4.3 mile) return trail cuts though the old growth forest along the lakeshore to Songhees Lake.

Area Indicator

Other Options

On the road to Holberg, anglers can also sample a couple of nearby waterbodies. **Kains Lake** is found about 14 km (8.5 miles) west of Port Hardy and holds fair numbers of slow growing cutthroat. A little further west, **Nahwitti Lake** also reports good fishing for small cutthroat along with a few dollies and kokanee. There is recreation site and cartop boat launch on Nahwitti.

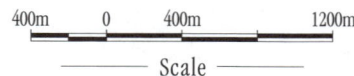

400m 0 400m 1200m

Scale

To Port Hardy via Holberg Rd

Georgie Lake Rec Site

Location: 21 km (13 mi) west of Victoria
Elevation: 67 m (220 ft)
Surface Area: 17 ha (42 ac)
Mean Depth: 6 m (21 ft)
Max Depth: 14 m (46 ft)
Way Point: 123° 31'00" Lon - W 48° 26'00" Lat - N

www.backroadmapbooks.com

Glen Lake

Glen Lake

Area Indicator

To Duncan
Florence Lake
GOLDSTREAM Rd
Langford
1A
Langford Lake
Glen Lake
Colwood Lake
JACKLIN
GLEN Lk Rd
To Sooke
14
To Victoria

Fishing

Being an urban lake, it is not too surprising to see that Glen Lake receives more than its fair share of angling attention. On top of being stocked annually with catchable sized rainbow by the Freshwater Fisheries Society of BC, the lake also holds a few cutthroat and is becoming known a decent smallmouth bass fishery. The low elevation lake also opens up quite early with the fish becoming active as early as March.

Trout anglers will find the lake is best fished for trout in March to June and again in September to October. Despite the number of private residences lining the lake, shore fishing is possible. In particular, the southwest shore off of the Galloping Goose Trail is a good place to try. However for best results, try getting out on the lake with a pontoon boat or canoe and casting toward the lily pads with a worm tipped lure or a damselfly or dragonfly nymph. Another alternative is to spincast or fly-fish near the outflow creek at the south end of the lake.

In the summer months when the trout fishing is at a stand still, the bass fishery is often good. Use a plug or attractor type fly and cast it into the weedy areas of the lake. If you're finding you are catching more reeds than fish, try using a Texas or Carolina Rig to keep your hook from getting snagged. Or try using a worm on a hook and just bob for bass. Look for places with lots of structure where the bass like to hide, such as a sunken log or rock overhang.

Anglers often like to us bass bugs or poppers, but you might be better off using a smaller fly, especially in the dog days of summer. Of course, it can be difficult to keep a clean line when casting dry flies into weeds, but a heavier line along with some creative twitching when retrieving should help you avoid most snags. Although the heavier line and larger lure is not as elegant as other forms of fly casting, it can prove just as satisfying when you put the popper exactly where it was supposed to go.

There is an electric motor only restriction at the lake. Also, an irrigation system was installed in recent years to help water quality and the fishery.

Directions

Glen Lake is located southwest of Langford, about 21 km west of Victoria. Take Highway 14 (the Sooke Highway) to Glen Lake Road and then head north. Take a right on Glenview Drive and you will reach a small park to access the northwest end of the lake. Continue onto Glennan Road to find another small park and the main launch area.

Facilities

Glen Cove Park, off Glennan Drive, is the main access point for visitors wishing to launch small, non-motorized boats. On the opposite side of the lake, **Glen Lake Park** also offers day-use facilities. Most of the area in between is housed by private residences that line the lake. However, the **Galloping Goose Trail** does skirt the south shore providing for some shore access.

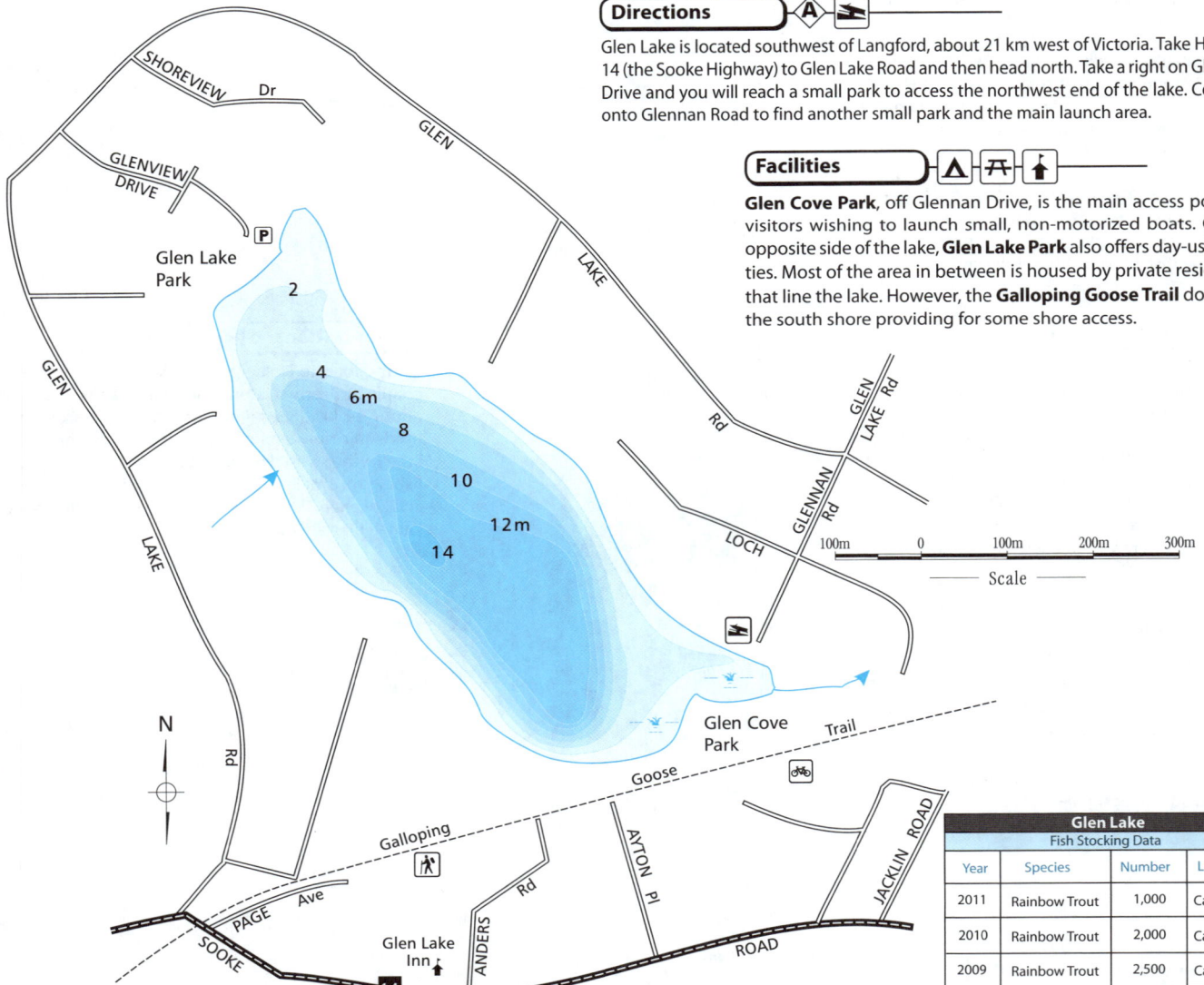

SHOREVIEW Dr
GLEN
GLENVIEW DRIVE
P
Glen Lake Park
2
4
6m
8
10
12m
14
GLEN LAKE Rd
Rd
GLENNAN Rd
LOCH
100m   0   100m   200m   300m
Scale

N

Glen Cove Park
Trail
Goose
Galloping
PAGE Ave
ANDERS Rd
AYTON Pl
JACKLIN ROAD
SOOKE
ROAD
Glen Lake Inn
14

Glen Lake			
Fish Stocking Data			
Year	Species	Number	Life Stage
2011	Rainbow Trout	1,000	Catchables
2010	Rainbow Trout	2,000	Catchables
2009	Rainbow Trout	2,500	Catchables

Gold River

Stream Length: 54.8 km (34.1 mi)
Geographic: 126°4'00" Lon - W   49°44'00" Lat - N

Fishing

Gold River gets its name from the sediments that turn the river's water into a golden yellow-green colour. The west coast river is one of the top five steelhead streams in the province, featuring big runs of both summer and winter steelhead. While other rivers are hatchery enhanced, the Gold River is not.

Chasing summer run steelhead is arguably some of the most fun you can have with a rod in your hand. While the winter steelhead run here is one of the biggest of any river, the fish tend to find a holding pool and stay there, ignoring your lure unless you drop it on their nose. On the other hand, summer steelhead will chase a fly or lure around the river, and once you've snagged one, will explode out of the river into the air like it is jet propelled.

This is not to say that you should not come here in winter. There is great satisfaction in convincing a winter steelhead to take a bite. Depending on your personal style and preference, you may favour one over the other. Or you may just be addicted to steelhead. And if you are, this is the river for you.

Flowing out of Gold Lake, the river gains stream as it makes its way south to its confluence with the Muchalat River north of town. It is here that anglers gain an interest in the river, as upstream of the confluence it is closed to fishing. Places to fish include the Muchalat Pools, the Helicopter Run and Rileys Riffle. The later is a pool downstream from the confluence of the Gold and the Ucona Rivers. Sometime referred to as the Garbage Hole, it is not impossible to hook a dozen, sometimes two, steelhead on the right day.

Fly-fishers will find the Gold fast and unrelenting in winter. While it is certainly possible to fish a fly here in winter, it takes a good touch and a heavy line. Much easier to use a heavier lure that you can bounce along the bottom. Winter steelhead rarely expend any excess energy, and unless the lure is within inches, they'll most likely just ignore it. Do what you can to attract the fish's attention. This includes fishing garish lures like a neon orange Spin and Glow or a pink Gooey Bob.

There are small returns of all five species of salmon, as well as sea-run cutthroat trout and Dolly Varden. However, numbers are quite low, and few people ever fish the Gold for anything other than steelhead.

Directions

The Gold River flows through the town of Gold River, which is found at the end of Highway 28 from Campbell River. From the townsite, you can choose to head upstream by simply keeping right at the first intersection. Follow East Road keeping left to access the Gold River Main on the western banks or turning right to keep on East Road. Side roads lead to the river, but most start from the Muchalat Pools.

However, the fish in the Gold tend to hang out in the lower river, which is accessed by following Muchalat Drive south out of town. There are a number of places along the road where the river can be accessed.

Facilities

Gold River the town provides most amenities including restaurants, accommodation and even fishing retailers. Those interested in camping can look for the **Gold River Lions Campground** south of town. There are also a few picnic sites along the river.

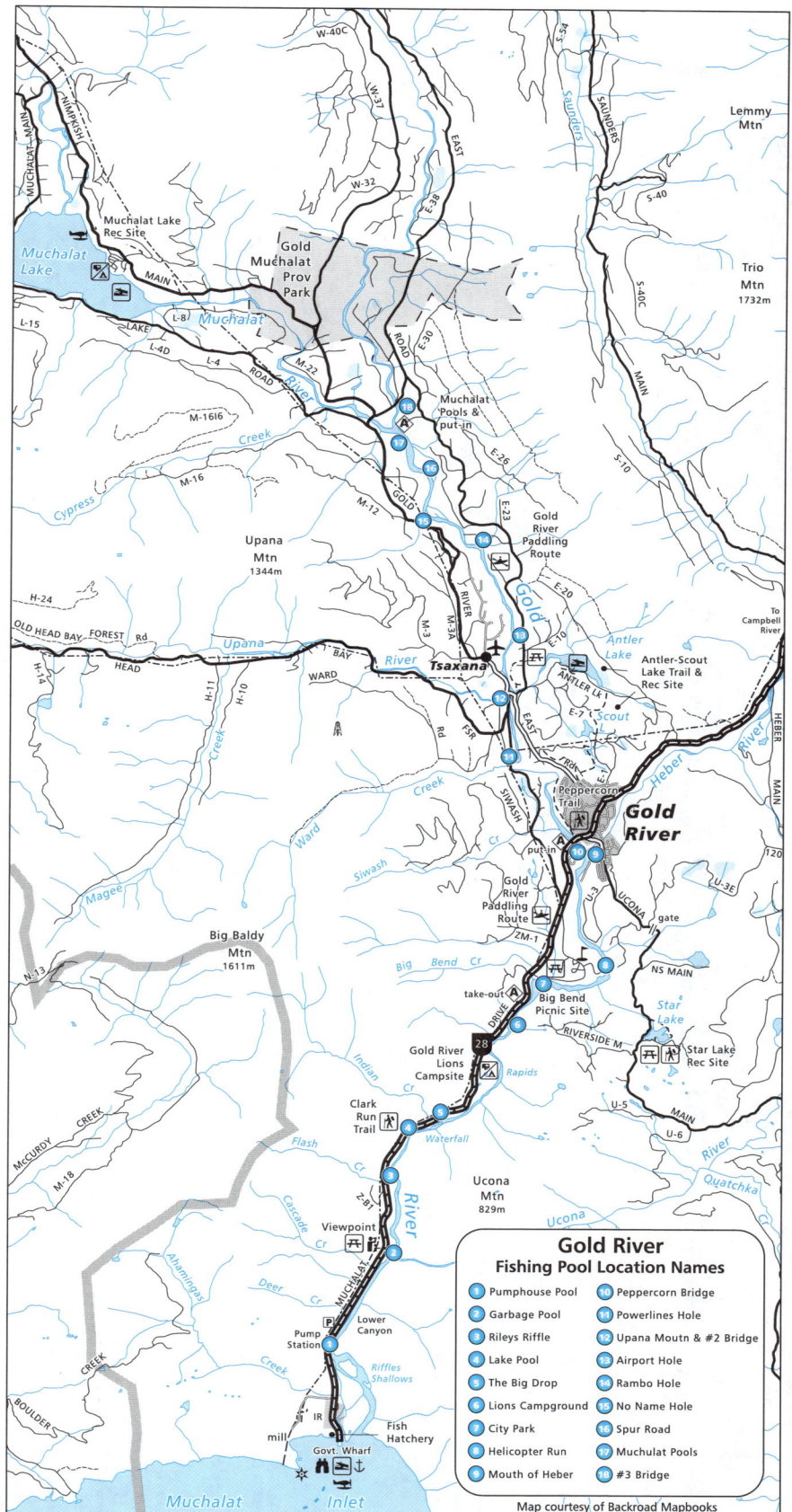

Gold River
Fishing Pool Location Names

1. Pumphouse Pool
2. Garbage Pool
3. Rileys Riffle
4. Lake Pool
5. The Big Drop
6. Lions Campground
7. City Park
8. Helicopter Run
9. Mouth of Heber
10. Peppercorn Bridge
11. Powerlines Hole
12. Upana Mountn & #2 Bridge
13. Airport Hole
14. Rambo Hole
15. No Name Hole
16. Spur Road
17. Muchalat Pools
18. #3 Bridge

Map courtesy of Backroad Mapbooks

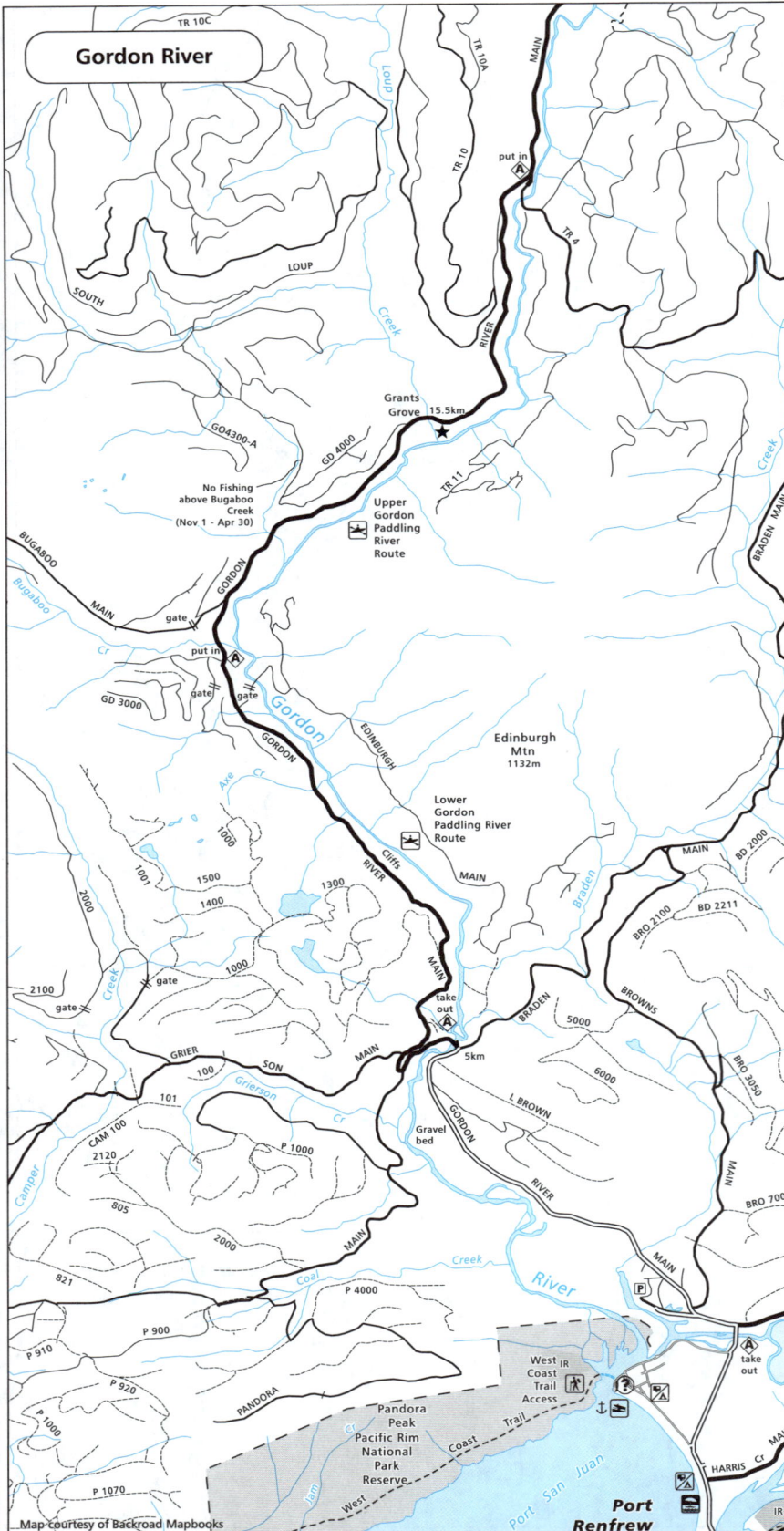

Stream Length: 49.6 km (30.8 mi)
Geographic: 124° 26′ 00″Lon - W   48° 36′ 00″ Lat - N

Gordon River

Gordon River

TR 10C

Loup Creek

TR 10A

MAIN

put in

TR 10

TR 4

LOUP

SOUTH

RIVER

Grants Grove   15.5km

GO4300-A

GD 4000

TR 11

No Fishing above Bugaboo Creek (Nov 1 - Apr 30)

Upper Gordon Paddling River Route

BRADEN MAIN

BUGABOO MAIN

Bugaboo Cr

GORDON

gate

put in

gate   gate

Gordon

GD 3000

EDINBURGH

Edinburgh Mtn 1132m

Axe Cr

Lower Gordon Paddling River Route

1000

1001   1500

1400   1300

Cliffs

RIVER

MAIN

Braden Cr

MAIN

BD 2000

2000

1000

BRO 2100   BD 2211

2100

gate

gate

MAIN

take out

BROWNS

BRO 350D

BRO 700

GRIER   SON

100   101

Grierson Cr

CAM 100   2120

805

2000

821

P 1000   P 900

P 910

P 920

PANDORA

P 1000

P 1070

Coal Creek

P 4000

5km

Gravel bed

GORDON

L BROWN

5000

6000

RIVER

Creek

River

MAIN

P

West Coast Trail Access

Pandora Peak Pacific Rim National Park Reserve

West Coast Trail

West

IR

Port San Juan

Port Renfrew

take out

HARRIS Cr   MAIN

IR

Map courtesy of Backroad Mapbooks

Fishing

The Gordon River is a small, fast flowing stream that drains into Port San Juan, north of Port Renfrew. Like most of the rivers in the area, the river holds small populations of native cutthroat and rainbow. The river also has tiny returns of Chinook, chum and Coho but is best known for its steelhead fishing.

There are two runs of steelhead on the Gordon, a summer run in June and early July and a winter run in February and March. In summer, the Steelhead return to the river well before it is time to spawn. As a result, they are not as single-minded as winter steelhead, and are willing to chase a lure around the river. Fly anglers can even convince them to rise to a dry fly, like a Steelhead bee, a Steelhead caddis or a pink pollywog.

The best time to fish the Gordon is after it has rained. Even then, the river is very shallow, with the fish splashing through the shallowest sections as they make their way from pool to pool. One of the most common and most adaptable rigs for steelhead fishing is fast water bobber fishing. The basics of the rig include a weight for getting the lure to the bottom, a lure, and a bobber. The weight should be enough to keep the gear bouncing along the bottom, but not so much that it stays in one place.

The trick is to get the lure down to eye level with the fish. This is important, especially in winter when the steelhead will move maybe six inches to chase after food. The Gordon is a clear river, except when winter storms kick up a lot of dirt. When the river is dirty, try using a flashy lure, like a spinner or neon-coloured spoon will work. When it is running clear, try a Gooey Bob.

Use weights or a weighted line to get the gear down to where the fish are and a strike indicator to let you know when you've got a fish on. Bunny Leeches, Marabou Flies, Egg patterns and bright coloured flies with lots of reds and oranges work well in winter, but if they aren't producing, don't be afraid to fall back to a simple Woolly Bugger.

While the Gordon is generally a shallow, clear river, that does not mean that you will be able to see what is happening at all times. In some of the deeper holding pools it is difficult to see what's happening, and the use of a float or bobber will help reveal what is happening beneath the surface.

Directions

The Gordon River flows into Port San Juan, north of Port Renfrew, which is located at the end of Highway 14, west of Victoria. The river is accessed along the Gordon River Main which follows the river all the way to its headwaters.

The best access to the river is at a bridge over the river at kilometre 5 along the road. Below here there are many gravel beds to work, while north of here the canyons restrict access but create deeper holes to sample. Finding your own hole will take a bit of exploring off of the main road.

Facilities

The Gordon River is found just north of Port Renfrew, where you will find camping and beach access along with a few stores. Nearby Fairy Lake has a recreation site that is a popular place to stay for anglers when they are in the area.

Gracie Lake

Location: 20 km (12.5 mi) west of Port Alberni
Elevation: 391 m (1,283 ft)
Surface Area: 38 ha (94 ac)
Mean Depth: 19 m (63 ft)
Max Depth: 43 m (141 ft)
Way Point: 125° 05′ 00″ Lon - W   49° 13′ 00″ Lat - N

Fishing

Gracie Lake is considered one of the better rainbow fisheries in the southern part of Vancouver Island. To help maintain the fishery, the Freshwater Fisheries Society of BC stocks the lake every other year with rainbow trout.

Given the depth of the lake, the water does not warm significantly in the summer months allowing for decent fishing throughout the ice-free season. However, the better fishing is in April to June and September to October.

If casting from shore, visitors will find the northwest shore has a fairly descent drop off that allows for a few good casting areas. During cooler periods and earlier in the season there are also some nice shoal areas to cast a fly or small lure into. One favourite area is found around the outflow creek in the bay at the southeast end of the lake. Try using a small spoon or wet fly like a Doc Spratley during these times.

Given the size and depth the lake, Gracie is also good trolling lake. A lake troll with your lure tipped with a worm or powerbait or searching type fly patterns are good options to start with. However, there's nothing that says you can't just find a nice spot and spincast from a small boat or tube. There is a knob on the southern shore of the lake, and fishing either side of this can be productive.

Please note that there is an electric motor only restriction at the lake.

Directions

Gracie Lake is located south of Sproat Lake on the way to Nahmint Lake. To find the smaller lake, continue past Port Alberni on Highway 4 and look for McCoy Lake Road just after crossing the Somass River. Follow this road west to the Stirling Arm Main Road. Continue on this logging road past the notable road junction at about the 21 km mark. The Stirling Arm Main continues southwest climbing the pass and skirting the eastern shore of Gracie Lake. It is a short walk from the road down to the lake.

Despite the fair distance of logging road travel, most vehicles should have no trouble getting to the lake.

Facilities

Resting in the mountains between Sproat and Nahmint Lakes, there are no developed facilities on Gracie. It is possible to camp near roadside and hand launch small boats on the northwestern side of the lake. For a somewhat more formal camping area, continue southeast to Nahmint Lake where you will find a small recreation site near the northern end of the scenic lake.

Area Indicator

Other Options

Nearby Sproat and Nahmint Lakes are two larger lakes worth trying if the fishing is slow at Gracie Lake. **Sproat Lake** is easily accessed off Highway 4 and offers fair numbers of rainbow, kokanee and cutthroat to 4.5 lbs (2 kg). It is best to troll the lake from late February until October or try casting near the creek mouths. **Nahmint Lake** is located off the Nahmint Mainline and is rumoured to hold some nice sized rainbow as well as a few smaller cutthroat. Try fly-fishing or spincasting where the river enters and leaves the lake. Watch for fishing restrictions.

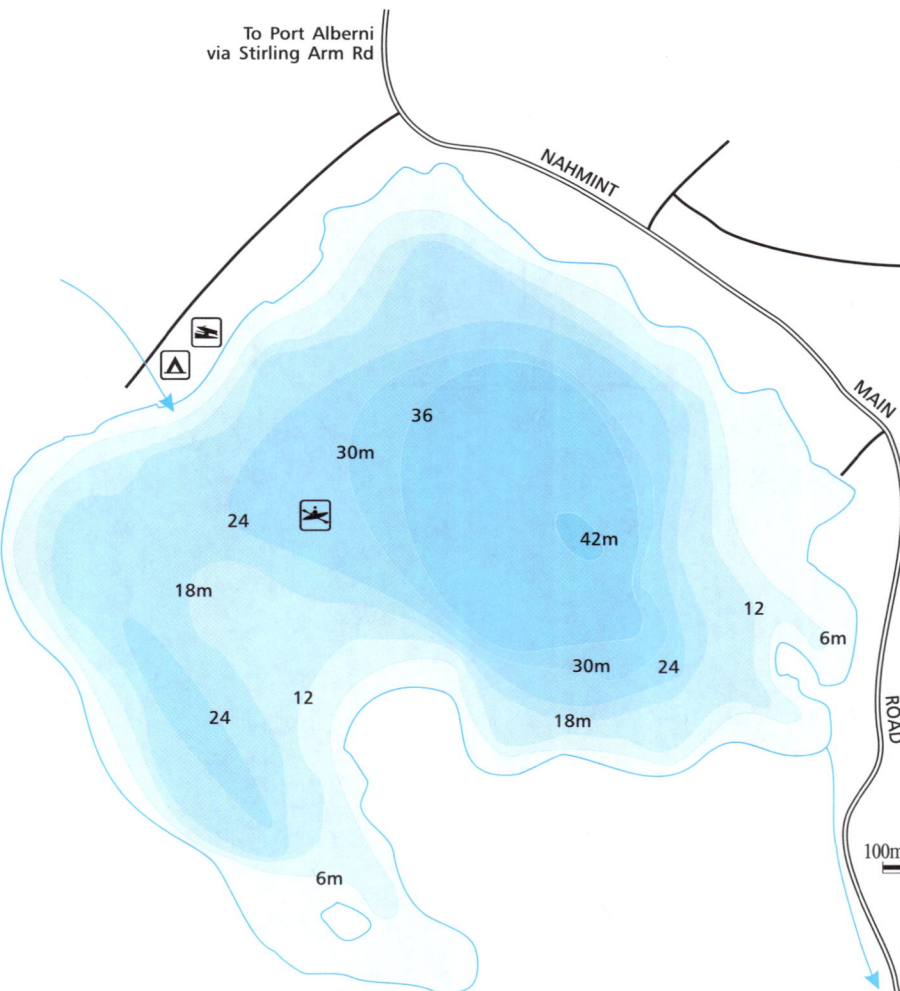

To Port Alberni
via Stirling Arm Rd

NAHMINT

MAIN

ROAD

36

30m

24

42m

18m

12

6m

30m   24

12

18m

24

6m

To Nahmint Lake

N

Gracie Lake			
Fish Stocking Data			
Year	Species	Number	Life Stage
2010	Rainbow Trout	600	Yearling
2008	Rainbow Trout	750	Yearling

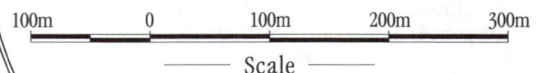

100m   0   100m   200m   300m

Scale

Location: 16 km (10 mi) west of Port Alberni
Elevation: 82 m (269 ft)
Surface Area: 51 km² (31.7 mi²)
Max Depth: 294 m (965 ft)
Waypoint: 125° 15' 00" Lon - W 49° 15' 00" Lat - N

Great Central Lake

Area Indicator

Fishing

Stretching 45 km (28 miles) long, Great Central Lake is one of the biggest of a series of big lakes along the spine of Vancouver Island. At 294 metres (965 feet), it is also the second deepest lake on the Island. Thanks in no small part to the hatchery at Robertson Creek there is healthy fish returns in the creeks and rivers around the lake. There is also good fishing for some of the Islands biggest rainbow and cutthroat trout as well as the odd Dolly Varden in the big lake. Rainbow and cutthroat have been reported over 3.5 kg (8 lbs) here.

It is a beautiful, crystal clear lake that has little development and thus few people fishing the big lake. Carved by the last ice age, the lake level is regulated by dams located on either end of the lake built in the 1920's. Prior to the lake being raised it was the site of a large logging and saw milling operation which ran several railroad logging camps as well as a floating "A" Frame camp. In fact, the steep unfriendly shoreline of the lake made it necessary to build housing on floats and since the late 1800's there have been floating homes on Great Central Lake.

Today, the Department of Fisheries fertilize the lake every summer to help the sockeye spawn and grow quicker. This results in a thick algae bloom that definitely hinders the fishery when the waters warm. As a result it is best to fish the lake between April and June or September and October. However, the lake does not freeze so year round fishing is possible.

Your standard big lake trolling gear (bucktails, Rapalas, or anything that resembles small baitfish) for rainbow and cutthroat is recommended. There is plenty of shoreline to explore so patience is a key here. But don't be surprised if you hook into a sockeye. These big, acrobatic fish have caught more than the odd trout angler off guard. For something different, try black ant fly patterns in summer. Working the inflow streams either on the fly or suspended with a bobber can be a lot of fun.

Unfortunately, the condition of the dams, especially the small wooden dam at Boot Lagoon at the east end, is deteriorating rapidly due to lack of maintenance. The lake is reported to be drawn down to 50-year lows.

Directions

Found about 16 west of Port Alberni, the big lake is accessed at the end of Great Central Lake Road to the north of Highway 4. If you have a smaller boat or want a more rustic camping adventure, continue along the Ash River Main to Branch 83. Follow this road west to the rough side road leading to Scout Beach Recreation Site.

Facilities

Formerly Ark Resort, the **Great Central Lake RV Resort & Marina** is the main facility to the lake. Newly renovated, they provide camping, canoe and boat rentals and a launch onto the lake. Those with smaller boats or canoes can launch and camp at **Scout Beach Recreation Site** along the north shore, while another boat access only campsite is found at the start of the popular **Della Falls** trailhead. If you have an extra day or two, be sure not to miss these spectacular falls that are one of the biggest in Canada falling over 440 metres (1,443 feet). But the 15 km trek up to the falls is not to be taken lightly.

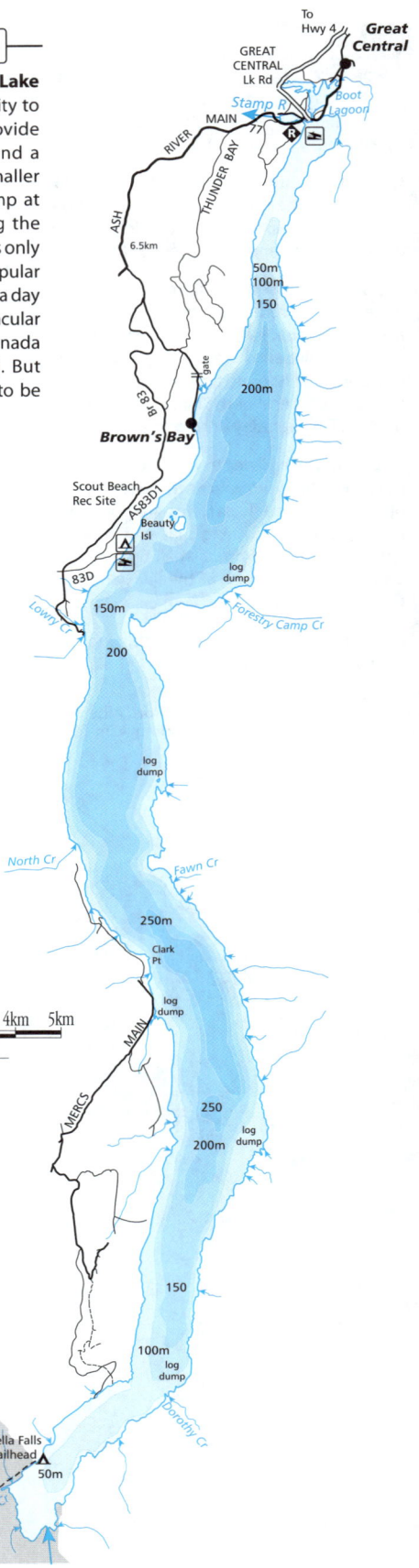

Green Lake

Location: 13 km (8 mi) northwest of Nanaimo
Elevation: 93 m (305 ft)
Surface Area: 13.4 ha (33 ac)
Mean Depth: 6 m (20 ft)
Max Depth: 9 m (29.5 ft)
Way Point: 124° 04' 00" Lon - W 49° 14' 00" Lat - N

Fishing

Green Lake is a rural lake that is found in the northwest end of Nanaimo. The Freshwater Fisheries Society of BC stocks the lake on occasion with rainbow trout to help maintain the trout fishery, while bass anglers revel in the fact the lake holds smallmouth. There are also a few cutthroat in the lake. Due to the heavy fishing pressure, the fish tend to be small with a 35 cm (14 in) fish being considered big.

The lake is not very deep, and trolling is not the best option here. Still, people do troll the lake. Using light gear on a shallow troll will work early in the season before the fish start to head too deep.

Still, it is much better to spincast or fly-fish. For trout, the lake is best suited for an early season fishing or late fall fishery. Spincasters can try a standard assortment of light gear. In the spring, fly anglers will do best by matching the hatches. During the fall, or when there is no active hatch, resort to the typical arsenal of leeches, nymphs, or attractor patterns like a Doc Spartley.

When the water warms (during the early summer), so does the bass fishing. There is a small but growing community of anglers in BC who are passionate bass fishers. Bass are not as big as salmon, or as pretty as trout, but they are canny, cautious fish that stick to areas where it is difficult to lure them from their lairs. Successfully dropping a line alongside the fallen tree and convincing the fish to bite is a thrill known to a select few. Tube baits are good for fishing a little deeper, while fishing a Texas, Carolina or Florida rig will help keep your hook weed free when casting into reedy waters where smallmouth like to hang out.

In summer, bass like to move out into deeper water early in the day, and move into the shallows during the day. Often a simple presentation like a worm or jig can prove quite effective. Jigging is a great way to fish for bass as the fish like to hang out around structure like stumps and weeds and overhangs. Rather than try and cast into these areas, you can simply drop a line down and begin jigging.

Given the rural nature of Green Lake, there are a number of residences that line the lake and shore fishing is limited. A small boat (there is an electric motor only restriction at the lake) or float tube is your best bet. However, some enterprising anglers use the active E & N Railroad to access the northeastern shore. Beware of trains!

Area Indicator

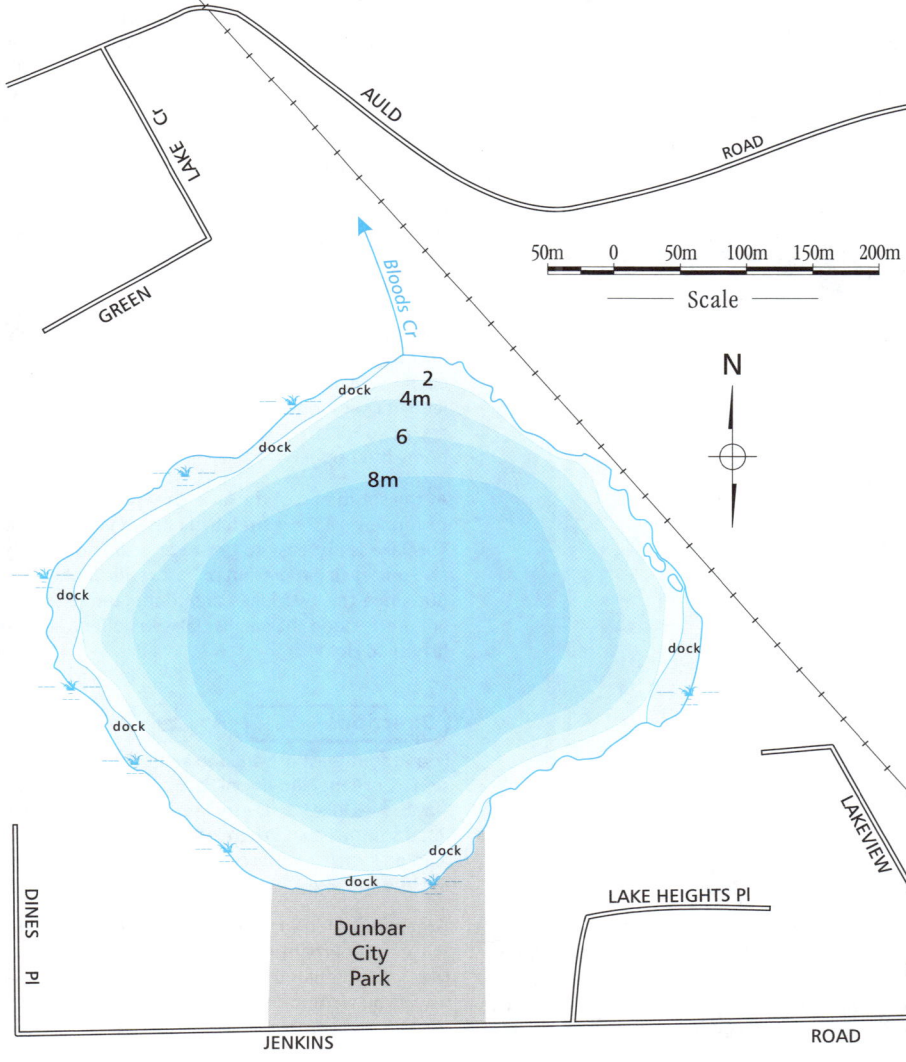

Directions

Green Lake is found northwest of the Nanaimo city centre off the Inland Island Highway. You will need to take the Dumont Road exit to link up with Jenkins Road. Follow Jenkins west to Dunbar City Park, which is the main access point to the lake.

Other Options

Brennen Lake is another popular lake located just south of Green Lake. Cutthroat and rainbow are reported to reach 2.5 kg (5 lbs) in size here. **Long** and **Diver Lakes** are also found nearby and offer good fishing for rainbow and cutthroat trout as well as smallmouth bass.

Facilities

Dunbar City Park provides day use facilities and a place to launch small, non-motorized boats.

Green Lake			
Fish Stocking Data			
Year	Species	Number	Life Stage
2011	Rainbow Trout	2,000	Catchables
2010	Rainbow Trout	2,250	Catchables
2009	Rainbow Trout	3,000	Catchables

Scale: 50m 0 50m 100m 150m 200m

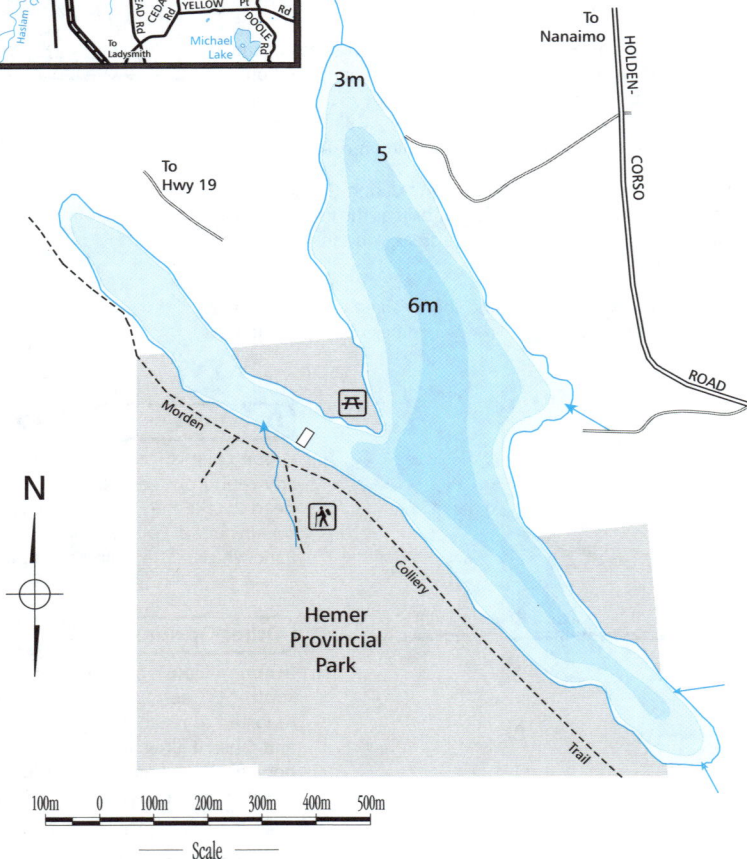

Holden & Greenway Lake

Holden Lake

Area Indicator

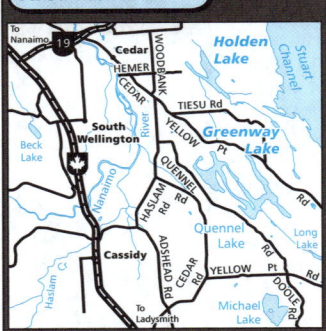

Elevation: 8 m (26 ft)
Surface Area: 38 ha (94 ac)
Mean Depth: 4.4 m (63.5 ft)
Max Depth: 6.5 m (22 ft)
Way Point: 123° 49'00" Lon - W 49° 6'00" Lat - N

Holden Lake Fish Stocking Data			
Year	Species	Number	Life Stage
2009	Cutthroat Trout	1,000	Yearling
2008	Cutthroat Trout	1,000	Yearling
2007	Cutthroat Trout	1,000	Yearling

Holden Lake

To Hwy 19

To Nanaimo

3m

5

6m

Morden

Hemer Provincial Park

Colliery

Trail

N

| 100m | 0 | 100m | 200m | 300m | 400m | 500m |

— Scale —

Greenway Lake

Elevation: 19 m (62 ft)
Surface Area: 2.2 ha (5.5 ac)
Mean Depth: 3.3 m (11 ft)
Max Depth: 4.6 m (15 ft)
Perimeter: 0.75 km (0.5 mi)

Greenway Lake

To Holden Lake

To Nanaimo via Tiesu Road

INGRAM Rd

5m

Greenway Lake
No Record of Stocking

Facilities

Hemer Provincial Park is a day-use only park with an extensive trail system including pit toilets and park benches. Bird watching is a popular pastime in the area or you can explore the trail system that connects with Boat Harbour to the east.

Fishing

At the heart of Hemer Provincial Park, Holden Lake is a small, peaceful lake that provides a nice fishing experience for stocked cutthroat trout, small rainbow and a thriving smallmouth bass population. The close proximity to Nanaimo makes this a fairly busy fishery throughout the year. To help maintain a trout fishery, the Freshwater Fisheries Society of BC stocks the lake annually with about a thousand cutthroat.

Anglers will find plenty of shoreline structure that makes ideal cover for both trout and bass. Fly fishers looking for trout might want to try a leech or a nymph, while a small spoon will work for spincasters. Cast close to the logs and bush or near the lily pads.

The marshy waterway that feeds and drains the lake is also a good area to try for bass. In the summer, when the water warms up, the trout retreat to the cool, deep waters, while the bass come out to play. Despite the marshy shoreline in areas, the lake does provide some good shore angling potential, especially since bass like to hang out in protected areas like weeds. Try rigging your hook so that it doesn't snag using a Texas rig. Bass anglers may want to try jigging, too, using a bobber and a worm. Jigging is a great way to fish for bass, as it allows you to get the lure in closer to the cover the bass love so much, without worrying about snagging it as you would when casting and retrieving. Also, bass tend to be wary of things that move to fast, and a lure that sits in the water, twitching occasionally will often prove to be just the thing to get their attention. It isn't the most exciting form of angling (at least to some), but it can be productive. If you have a belly boat, you can slowly move position in an attempt to draw out the fish.

If you are looking for the big bass, you will usually find them deeper in the water, under the most cover available. As a general rule, they will only feed at twilight, so don't be disappointed with the size of your catch if you take off in time to make it home by supper.

At the south end of the lake, **Greenway Lake** can be found via a short stretch of rather marshy water. This lake is not easy to get to or well known. It is also unclear if either trout or bass reside in the lake. But since the two lakes are connected, chances are pretty good the smaller lake will offer a similar fishery to Holden.

Directions

Found southeast of Nanaimo in the Cedar area, the signs for Hemer Provincial Park can be seen on the way to the Duke Point Ferry Terminal. Take the Cedar Road southeast and then look for the Hemer Road leading east. It is a short walk from the parking area to **Holden Lake**.

Greenway is found further south off Ingram Road. Private property may impede direct access to the lake, so be prepared to navigate the marshy waterway if you want to try your luck here.

Hoomak Lake

Location: 10 km (6 mi) east of Woss
Elevation: 240 m (787 ft)
Surface Area: 94 ha (232 ac)
Mean Depth: 12 m (39 ft)
Max Depth: 37 m (121 ft)
Way Point: 126° 31' 00" Lon - W 50° 12' 00" Lat - N

Fishing

Found east of Woss, alongside Highway 19, Hoomak Lake is a fair sized roadside lake that is accessed from a rest stop on the south side of the highway. The lake produces decent catches stocked cutthroat that come readily to a fly or lure early in the year. There is also a native population of Dolly Varden which can get to 2 kg (4 lbs).

The lake is mostly hidden from the highway behind a screen of trees, but a short trail leads to the lake. You will need a canoe or a float tube to fish the lake since shore fishing is next to impossible, as the lake is pressed in on all sides by thick brush.

Locals advocate getting to this lake as early in the year as possible, which is usually April. By the end of May, the fishing begins to tail off, and even in fall it doesn't match the quality of fishing as there is early in the year.

The lake is a popular lake with fly fishers, as the shoreline has plenty of weeds, which in turn mean that there are a lot of insect hatches here, from chironomids to dragonflies, to mayflies and caddisflies. It is the latter that attract the most attention from top water fly anglers. They usually hatch a little later in the year, starting in May. In a good hatch, almost anything you throw out onto the water will result in a strike. However, when the hatch is light, the fish don't get into a feeding frenzy, and are much more particular about what they will go for. It's times like these where the experienced fly angler rises to the surface (so to speak), as it is important to match the size, shape, colour and motion of the caddisfly, to entice the fish to bite. An assortment of colours and sizes is a good thing to have, too.

When there is no active hatch, trolling is your best option. Using a leech or a nymph pattern trolled slowly around the lake, or an attractor pattern like a Woolly Bugger will usually produce well. Try using a Gold Ribbed Hare's Ear as a mayfly nymph imitator.

Spincasters can try an assortment of spoons and spinners. Cutthroat are often easily attracted to flashy, showy lures, so if you're finding a chrome spoon isn't working, try something a little showier. The fish are fairly voracious predators and if you can make them think they're chasing a minnow, so much the better. Pure gold F4 or F5 Flatfish seem to work really well.

The stocking program for cutthroat will be ending in 2009, as the population is self-sustaining.

Area Indicator

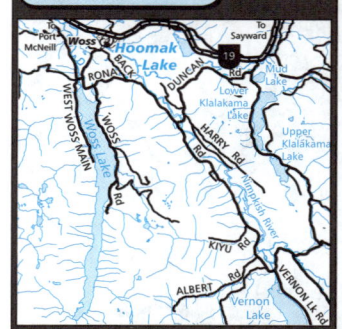

Hoomak Lake Fish Stocking Data			
Year	Species	Number	Life Stage
2007	Cutthroat Trout	2,000	Yearling

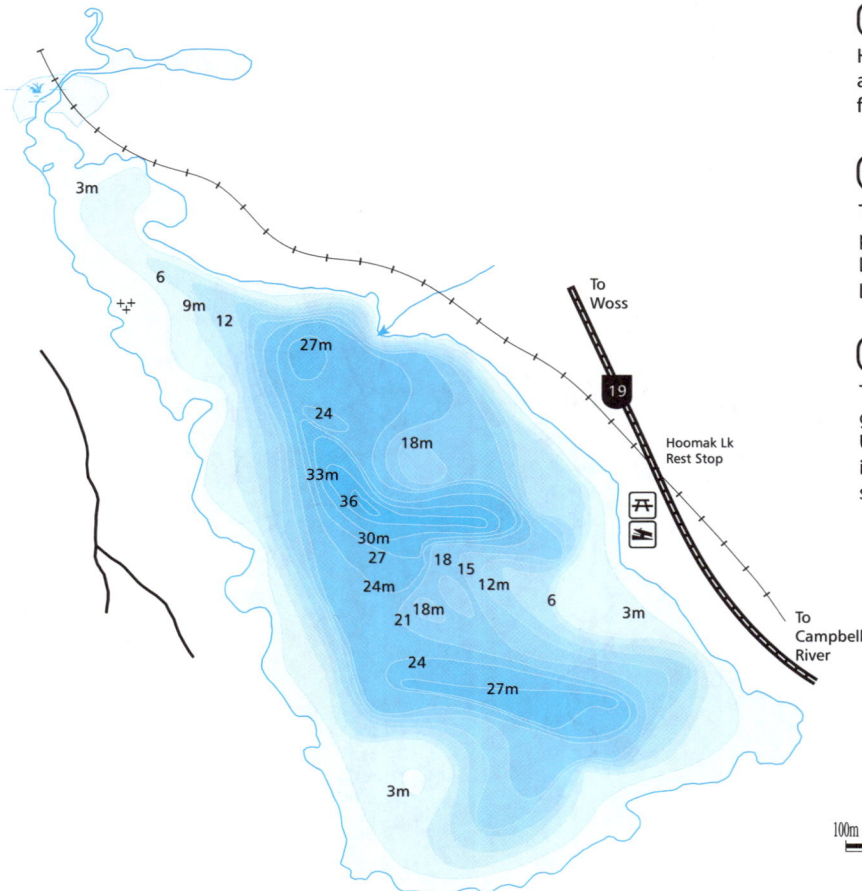

Directions

Hoomak Lake lies 10 km (6 miles) east of Woss alongside the Island Highway (Highway 33). Watch for a pull-out on the south side of the highway.

Facilities

There is a rest area off the highway, complete with picnic tables. For those looking to overnight, nearby Lower Klalakama Lake to the southeast or Woss Lake to the southwest both provide recreation sites.

Other Options

There are a number of great fishing lakes in the general Woss area. The closest to Hoomak Lakes are **Upper** and **Lower Klalakama**, written up elsewhere in this book. These popular fishing lakes also hold stocked cutthroat and native Dolly Varden.

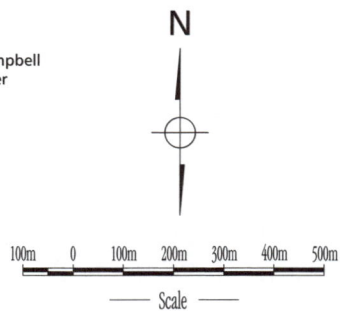

100m 0 100m 200m 300m 400m 500m
— Scale —

www.backroadmapbooks.com

Horne Lake

Location: 18 km (11 mi) west of Qualicum Beach
Elevation: 123 m (404 ft)
Surface Area: 960 ha (2,371ac)
Mean Depth: 20 m (66 ft)
Max Depth: 61 m (200 ft)
Way Point: 124° 42' 00" Lon - W   49° 20' 00" Lat - N

Area Indicator

Horne Lake			
Fish Stocking Data			
Year	Species	Number	Life Stage
2007	Cutthroat Trout	15,000	Yearling
2006	Cutthroat Trout	15,000	Yearling
2005	Cutthroat Trout	15,000	Yearling

Fishing

Horne Lake is best known for its unique cave system at the west end of the lake. However, anglers in the know relish in the fact the crystal clear waters provide good fishing for cutthroat along with rainbow and kokanee. There are also unconfirmed rumours of brook trout in the lake.

For most of the eighties and early nineties, the lake was being stocked with steelhead, and some still survive here. However, over the last few years the lake has been aggressively stocked with cutthroat trout by the Freshwater Fisheries Society of BC. Considering that 15,000 fish are dumped in annually, there is no doubt cutthroat fishing should be good here.

The low elevation lake is big and deep enough to maintain a year round fishery. Generally speaking though, the fishing is better between April and June and again in September and October.

It is possible to shore fish, or even just cast from the dock, but most anglers prefer to troll the big lake using a lake troll, light gear like a Flatfish, or even a wet fly like a Woolly Bugger. There is good fishing just off the boat launch at the west end of the lake. Try trolling along the drop-off along the northern shore, or near the mouth of the Qualicum River, south of the launch. Another area to try is towards the east end of the lake, where you'll find a pair of islands that offer good structure for the fish.

The lake is fairly big, and can get windy. Boaters should remain mindful of the weather.

Directions

Horne Lake is a well-developed lake that is lined with private residents northwest of Parksville. Although the lake is only found about 5 kilometres down the Horne Lake Road from Highway 19, the main public access point is found at the west end of the lake about 13 km from the highway.

The road is mainly gravel and is actively used by logging trucks seven days a week. Caution is advised.

Facilities

Horne Lake Regional Park lies on the west end of the lake and provides a nice boat launch as well as camping and a separate day-use area complete with beach. The large 105 hectare (260 acre) park boasts both lake and river frontage and a series of trails. Campsite reservations are available through the Regional District of Nanaimo at 250-248-7829 or http://www.hornelake.com/reservations.htm.

Adjacent to the regional park is the ever popular **Horne Lake Cave Provincial Park**. It is certainly worth the effort to take a tour of these unique caves.

Other Options

The **Qualicum River** flows into and out of Horne Lake and is a popular fishery itself. The river holds cutthroat, best caught in fall, Chinook and Coho also found in fall and a highly regulated steelhead fishery. Anglers can easily access the river from the parks on the west side of the lake.

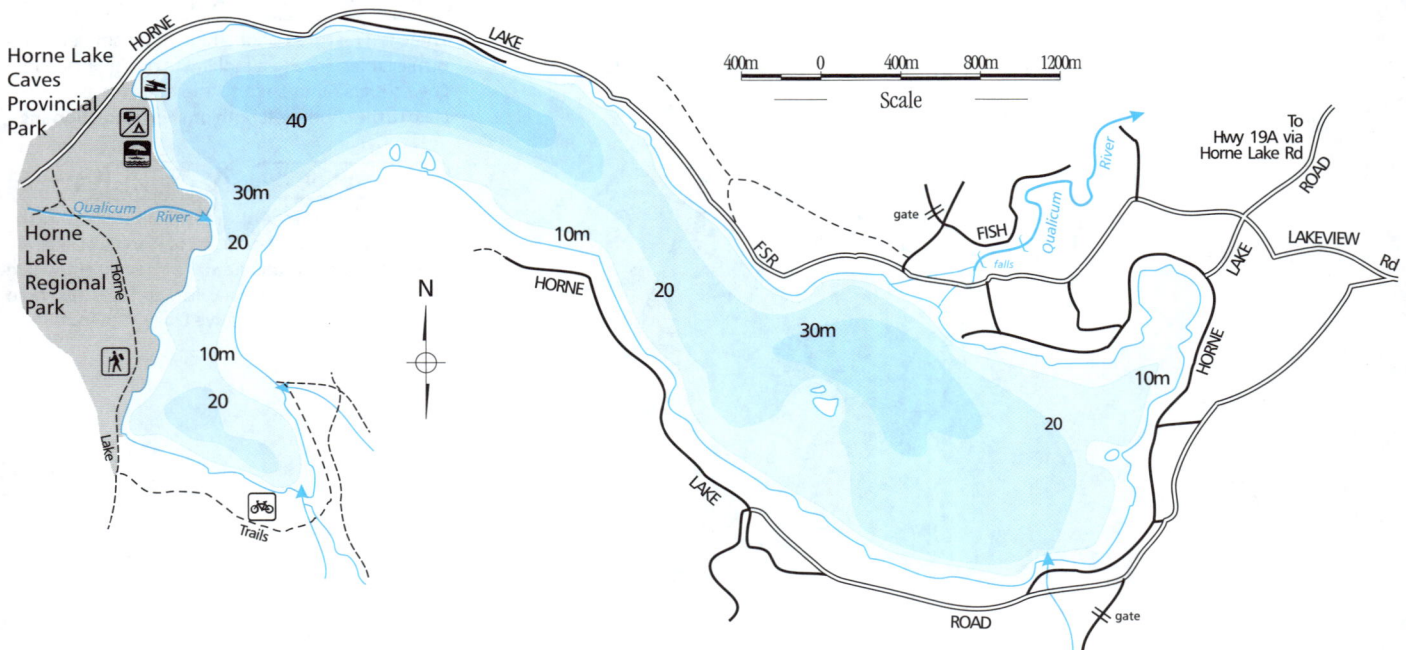

Iron Lake

Elevation: 175 m (574 ft)
Surface Area: 19.56 ha
Perimeter: 2.6 km (1.6 mi)
Mean Depth: 7.5 m (25 ft)
Max Depth: 21 m (69 ft)
Way Point: 127° 13' 00" Lon - W 50° 22' 00" Lat - N

Directions

Iron Lake is located south of Maynard Lake on the Keogh Main. The Keogh Main is found off the Island Highway (Highway 19), less than 2.5 miles (about 5 km) past the Campbell Way turnoff into Port McNeil.

The mainline is a busy logging road, and is closed from time to time during active hauling periods. Depending on where they are logging, it may be possible to access the lake from the Alice Lake Main, but check ahead before heading out.

Facilities

There is a recreation site at the south end of Iron Lake, but it offers little more than a boat launch and a place to park. Better camping is found at Maynard and Kathleen Lakes.

Area Indicator

Fishing

Iron Lake is one of the smallest lakes in the mess of lakes found south of Port McNeil. While the other lakes in the area (including Kathleen, Benson and Keogh) are better known, Iron Lake sees its fair share of anglers, too. They come here for the cutthroat trout fishing, although the lake holds good numbers of Dolly Varden, too. The cutts can get up to 45 cm (18 inches), but average 30 cm (12 inches).

The lake is hemmed in by a pair of logging roads that split, go past the lake on either side, then rejoin on the other side of the lake, so access to the lake is fairly good. Unfortunately, the lake is not a good shore fishing lake, for a variety of reasons; extensive shoals, brush and some marshy areas all combine to make it a poor shore fishing lake. Better to bring a belly boat or even a small cartopper.

Right after ice up is one of the best times to fish here, as the fish are basically all found in a narrow band of water right near the surface, usually cruising the shoals. During the winter, the lower levels of the lake are mostly depleted of oxygen, and this doesn't change until the lake warms up to about 4°C (39°F). Coupled with the fact that the fish are ravenous, these first few weeks can be a magical time for fishing this small lake.

As spring progresses, the water begins to warm, and the fish settle into a band of water about 5 metres (15 feet) down known as the thermocline. At this time they also come up into the shoals to feed. The preferred method of fishing here is using a simple worm and bobber set up. Drop a worm so it hangs just at the edge of the transition between the shoals and deeper water.

Spincasting also works well, using a spoon or spinner. Again, work the transition between the shoals and the deeper water, positioning your boat or belly boat in the deeper water. Let your lure sink down to the bottom, and then retrieve slowly towards the deeper water; fish are more likely to strike at food heading towards them than food heading away.

Even if you are having little or no luck, Iron Lake is a pretty lake, with plenty of wildlife. It is a great place to be, although, the main haul logging road is next to the lake, so you'll have to deal with the noise and dust from the occasional truck passing by. Speaking of logging, note that the road is an active haul road, and may be closed for periods of time when they are hauling. Check with a local tackle shop, or cross your fingers and hope for the best.

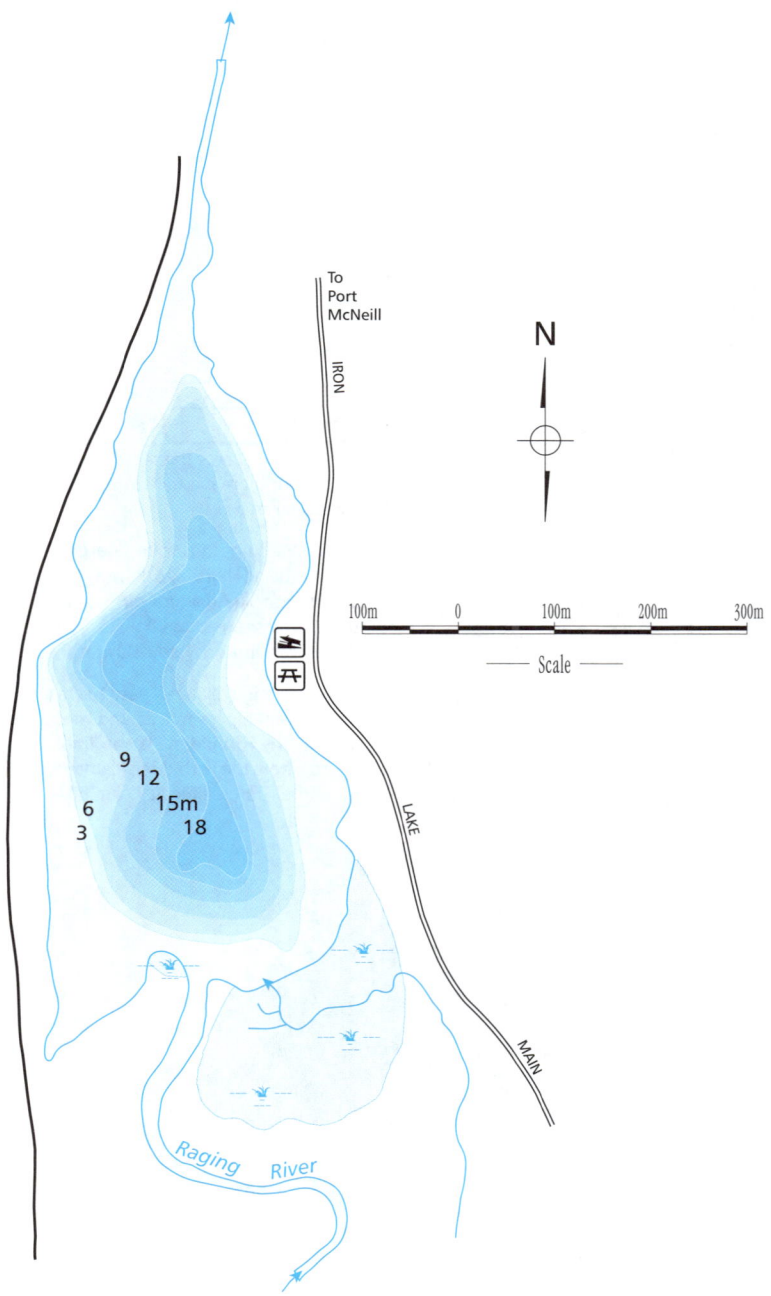

To Port McNeill

IRON

N

100m 0 100m 200m 300m

— Scale —

LAKE

9
12
6   15m
3   18

MAIN

Raging River

Location: 23 km (14 mi) west of Courtenay

Johnston & Panther Lakes

Area Indicator

Johnston Lake

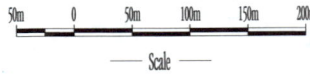

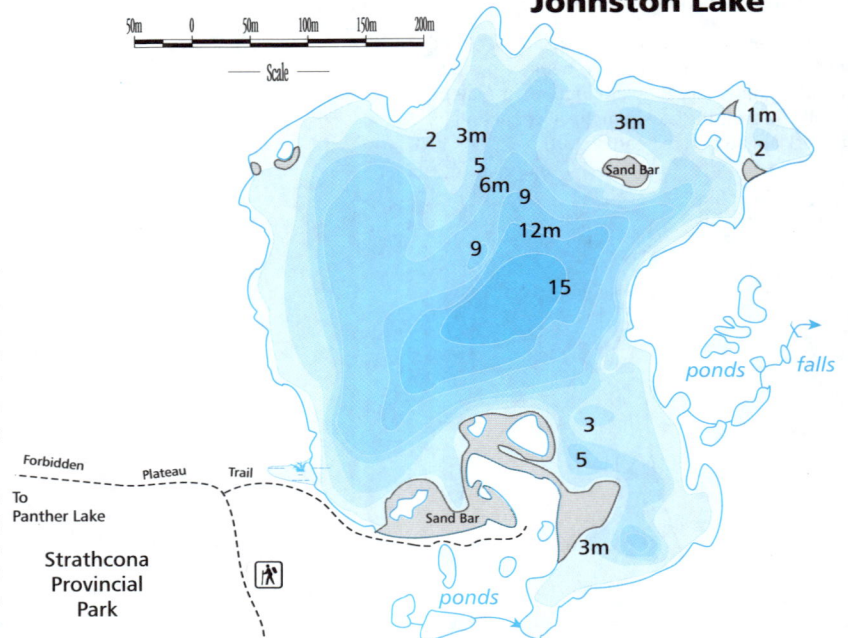

Elevation: 1,113 m (3,650 ft)
Surface Area: 14 ha (35 ac)
Mean Depth: 5.3 m (17 ft)
Max Depth: 18 m (59 ft)
Way Point: 125° 18'00"Lon - W 49° 41'00" Lat - N

Panther Lake Fish Stocking Data			
Year	Species	Number	Life Stage
2005	Rainbow Trout	2,000	Fry

Johnston Lake Fish Stocking Data			
Year	Species	Number	Life Stage
2002	Rainbow Trout	2,000	Fry

Fishing

Located far from the nearest trailhead, these two lakes do not see a lot of anglers. Although the lakes are stocked on occasion, the rainbow seem to be quite big when compared to other high elevation fisheries. The trout average 25-30 cm (10-12 in) in size and can put up a good fight with light gear.

The fishing season is weather driven. In low snow years, you can get on the lakes by the early part of July, while in big snow years you might have to wait until August. As a general rule, the fishing can be slow at first, but when the waters begin to warm, fishing really heats up. By late October-early November, the ice begins to form again.

Johnston Lake is bigger and deeper. The bay at the south end of the lake is extremely inviting as it has several deeper pockets with a lot of fringe area to cast towards. If you are keen enough to pack in a floatation device, try at the northeast end where there is a submerged island and a deeper hole. For shore fishermen, it is better to work your way around to the west side of the lake where there is a prominent drop-off.

Panther Lake is managed as a trophy lake with fly only restrictions and a one fish limit. With expansive shallows around the inflow and outflow creeks, shore fishing can be difficult outside a few select areas. A float tube will improve success. Try casting small flies towards the reed covered shallows as the fish tend to cruise those areas in search of food.

Panther Lake

Elevation: 1,081 m (3,545 ft)
Surface Area: 11 ha (27 ac)
Mean Depth: 7.5 m (25 ft)
Max Depth: 21 m (69 ft)
Way Point: 125° 19'00"Lon - W 49° 41'00" Lat - N

Directions

Most people access the lakes from Mount Washington, but there is a trail from the old Forbidden Plateau ski area as well.

Mount Washington is found north of Courtenay. Take the Inland Highway (Highway 19) to the Mount Washington Ski Area turn-off. Follow the parkway to the Paradise Meadows Trailhead, just beyond the Mount Washington Nordic ski area.

From here, it is a relatively easy 10 km (6 mile) walk through sub-alpine forests and meadows to the lakes via the Forbidden Plateau Trail. You can also get here from the Forbidden Plateau Ski Hill, along the Becher Trail, a difficult 17 km hike.

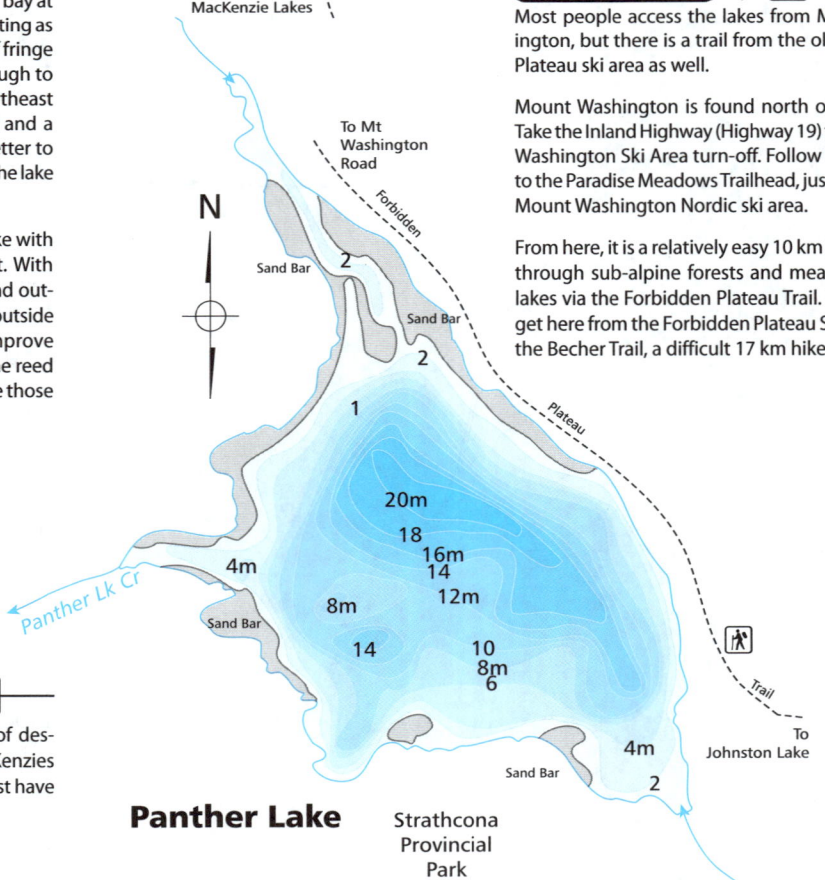

Facilities

BC Parks discourages camping outside of designated areas. Nearby Douglas and McKenzies Lakes to the west and Kwai Lake to the east have designated campsites.

Johnston Lake

Panther Lake
Strathcona Provincial Park

Kains Lake

Location: 19 km (11.8 mi) west of Port Hardy
Elevation: 307 m (1,007 ft)
Perimeter: 10.5 km (6.5 miles)
Max Depth: 11 m (36 ft)
Way Point: 127° 41′ 00″ Lon - W 50° 42′ 00″ Lat - N

Fishing

Kains Lake is a good sized lake that is found in the northwest part of the Island. It is considered one of the best cutthroat lakes on the north Island and the fishing can be fast and furious at times.

Lying near the coast creates a fairly wet environment, especially in winter. Because of all the rain, the lake's nutrients tend to get washed out quickly. This means that there is not as much food for the lake's resident cutthroat to eat, which means that, although there are plenty of them, they don't grow very fast. Finding a fish above 30 cm (12 inches) can be a bit of a challenge.

Although small, the cutthroat are fairly indiscriminate about what they will chase. Part of that has to do with the fact that there just is not a lot of food for them to eat, so they will chase after anything that looks like food. Part of it, too, is the fact that cutthroat are like water-bound magpies, in that they tend to be attracted to things that glitter. Yes, presenting a perfectly tied nymph will often entice them to bite, but so will throwing something with lots of flashy, pretty silver bits.

The lake drops off quickly, with sharp transitions between the shoals and the deeper water, so it is possible to fish the lake from the shore. However, most anglers prefer to bring along a belly boat or small craft to work the edges. Trolling a black Flatfish with silver or gold sparkles in the transition zone can be very productive.

There are also a number of streams that flow into the lake, which wash food and oxygen down into the lake. Fly anglers can try working these areas with a terrestrial pattern such as a flying ant, or with an attractor pattern like a General Practitioner or a Taylor's Golden Spey. During the early spring, spincasters can try working the mouths of these streams with minnow imitations. Even if there aren't any minnows coming down, the cutthroat will be attracted to the silver and gold patterns (they love shiny!).

Area Indicator

Directions

Kains Lake is located along the Holberg Road, 9 miles (15 km) west of Port Hardy. Take the Island Highway (Highway 19) out of town to the Holberg Road/Grandville Street turn-off. Follow this road west until you see the lake on your right.

Facilities

There are no officially developed facilities at the lake, but it is possible to hand launch a boat, and there is space to set up a tent or camper beside the lake. There are recreation sites with campgrounds at nearby Georgie and Nahwitti Lakes. Visitors should come prepared for wet conditions, even in summer.

Other Options

North of Kains Lake is **Georgie Lake**, which has lots of small cutthroat. The lake sees little use, and the fishing is good, even if the fish are small. There is a recreation site with camping and a boat launch. Further to the west along Holberg Road is **Nahwitti Lake**. Like the other lakes in the area, it has plenty of small growing cutthroat. Unlike the other lakes, it also holds Dolly Varden and kokanee.

Location: 36 km (22 mi) southwest of Port McNeill
Elevation: 100 m (328 ft)
Surface Area: 127 ha (314 ac)
Mean Depth: 28 m (92 ft)
Max Depth: 60 m (197 ft)
Way Point: 127° 17'00" Lon - W   50° 24'00" Lat - N

www.backroadmapbooks.com

Kathleen Lake

Area Indicator

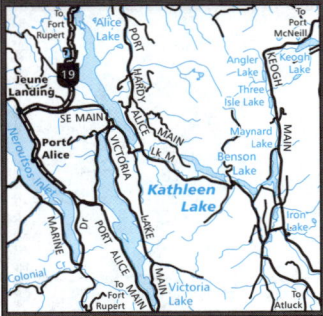

Fishing

Lying in a deep valley that is home to several good fishing lakes, Kathleen Lake will not disappoint visitors. Most anglers come to find some nice sized wild rainbow and cutthroat. There are also a few larger Dolly Varden in the lake, which maintains a relatively consistent fishery throughout the open water season from April through October.

Given the size and depth of the lake, trolling is the name of the game here. The lake is quite deep and offers a lot of nice areas to work. If trolling, work as close to the shore as possible early in the season, backing off to the edge of the drop-off once the water begins to warm up. A lake troll can work very well, as can a silver or gold Flatfish. The latter work particularly well around the inflow or outflow of Benson River or at the mouth of Wady Creek.

During the early morning or after the sun has gone down in late fall and into summer, the fish come up from the thermocline, and begin cruising the shoals in search of food. These are the magic hours for fishing. Fly fishers break out their favourite dry flies and begin to work the surface. Trollers come in closer to shore and begin working shallow diving plugs.

However, you don't have to get fancy to have good success here. You don't even need a boat, despite the fact that nearly everyone who comes here has one. The Benson River flows into the lake right near the Kathleen Lake Recreation Site, and it is possible to fish from shore here. During spring, fry and minnows come down the stream and into the big lake. Waiting for them at the mouth of the river are opportunistic, and often quite large, fish. Spoons and lures that imitate these minnows can work well, as can a simple worm and bobber set up. The trick here is to get these down almost to the bottom near the drop-off.

Directions

Found a long ways from the nearest paved road, Kathleen Lake is relatively easy to find if you have the Backroad Mapbook or the Backroad GPS Maps for Vancouver Island. The main access is from the Port Alice Road, which can be found between Port Hardy and Port McNeill on Highway 19. Follow the road to Port Alice for about 10 km where the Alice Lake Main branches south or left. Continue past the south end of Alice Lake and look for the Wady Main junction about the 23 km from the highway. Turn north or left and follow this road over the Benson River for about 3 km to the Kathleen Lake Recreation Site.

Be careful if trailering in boats as the road is often rough and bumpy. Industrial traffic is also a concern at certain times.

Facilities

The small recreation site at the southeast end of the lake offers room for about four campers in a semi-open area. Visitors will also find a decent gravel boat launch that is popular with both anglers and canoeists along with a gravel beach.

Other Options

En route to Kathleen, Benson and Maynard Lakes are both described in better detail in the book. **Benson Lake** has relatively large rainbow, cutthroat and Dolly Varden by Island standards. **Maynard Lake** has good numbers of smaller cutthroat and is best fished in the spring and fall.

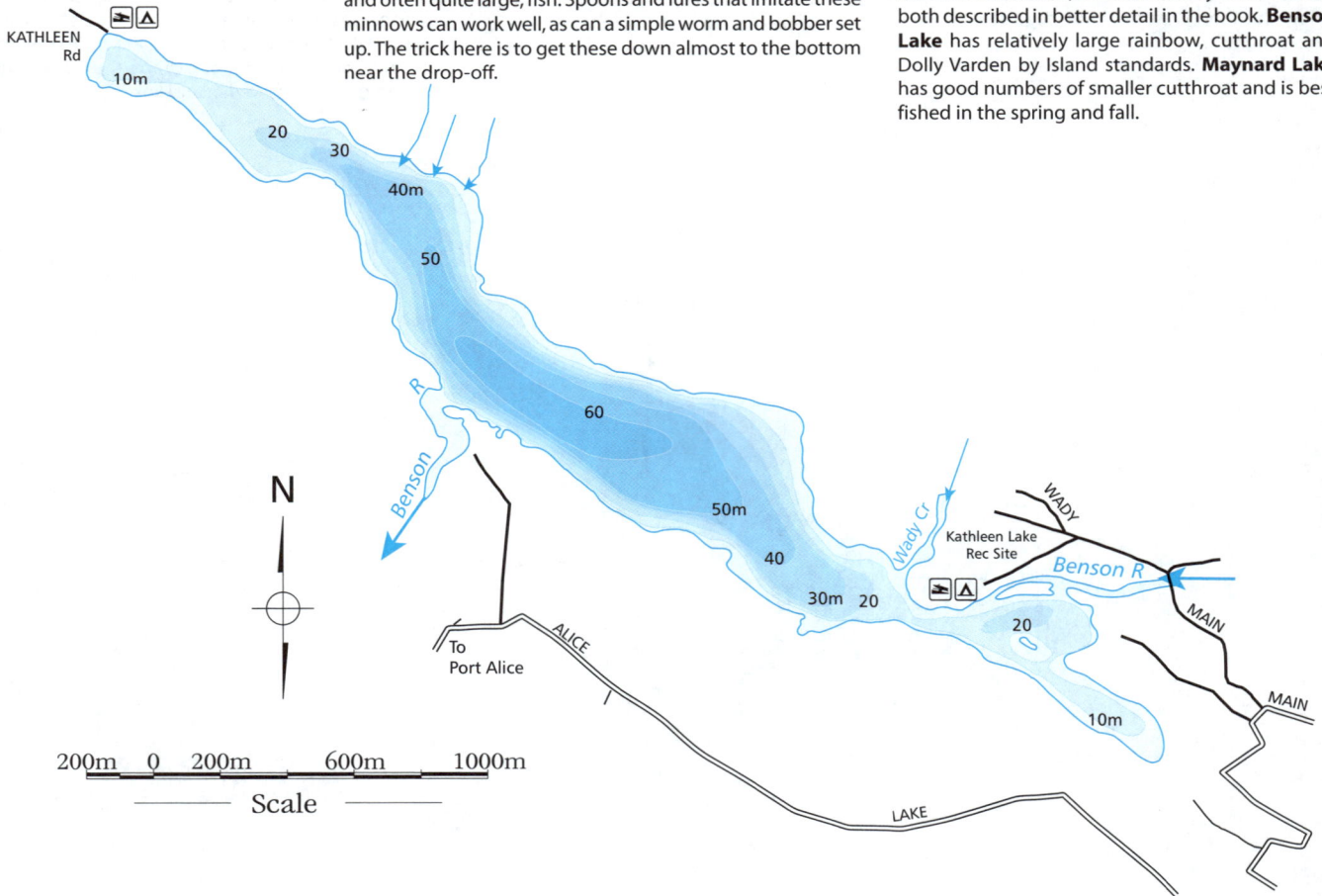

KATHLEEN Rd

10m
20
30
40m
50
Benson R
60
50m
40
30m   20
20
10m
Wady Cr
Kathleen Lake Rec Site
WADY
Benson R
MAIN
MAIN
To Port Alice
ALICE
LAKE

N

200m   0   200m   600m   1000m
Scale

Kemp Lake

www.backroadmapbooks.com

Location: 6.5 km (4 mi) west of Sooke
Elevation: 33 m (108 ft)
Surface Area: 25 ha (62 ac)
Mean Depth: 4.7 m (15.4 ft)
Max Depth: 11.5 m (38 ft)
Way Point: 123° 47' 00" Lon - W 48° 23' 00" Lat - N

Fishing

Stocked annually with cutthroat, Kemp Lake offers an early season fishery beginning in late March. It is considered one of the better south Island trout lakes due to the steady fishing and the fact that the odd trout is reported to reach 40 cm (16 in) in size on occasion. There are also a few wild rainbow as well as smallmouth bass to chase down.

Fly anglers have reported good success here as early as March, with pretty decent results continuing to June. The fishing drops off in the summertime and picks up somewhat in September and October. It is preferable to fish the lake from a boat as the lake is lined with weed beds and private residents making shore fishing a challenge.

Early in the season, the fish tend to stay in the shallow water, chasing down any bits of food they can find. They also stay in the shallow waters because the deeper waters tend to have low oxygen levels. For fly casters, this is a great time to be at the lake, as the fish tend to be fairly indiscriminate. Work the shoal areas with an attractor pattern or a leech during this early season fishing.

When the water temperature reaches about 4° C (39° F), the lake enters a time of turnover, when the water starts to circulate through the entire lake. This stirs up nutrients from the bottom, but the oxygen levels drop, which can be hard on the fish. This usually lasts a couple weeks, and fishing during this time is usually futile. After the turnover, though, the insects start to hatch, and the lake moves into its most productive time. Chironomids are the first insect to emerge, followed by mayflies, then damselflies, caddisflies, and dragonflies.

The lake has extensive weedbeds, which can be difficult to fish, but offer good cover for the fish. This means that anglers looking for success later in spring or in fall could do worse than casting towards the weeds with a wet fly such as a dragonfly or damselfly nymph.

In the summer, the trout fishing slows down to a standstill as the water gets too warm for these cold water fish. Fortunately, the lake is home to an active population of smallmouth bass. At this time, the smallmouth come into the shallows to play. They are a suspicious fish who rarely venture far from cover. Again, fishing near the weedbeds or other obvious hiding place will do well. There are special bass lures that are designed not to snag (much) in the weeds, or you can rig a hook with a worm set to protect the hook from snagging.

No powerboats are allowed on the lake.

Area Indicator

Directions

Kemp Lake is located near Sooke, just of the West Coast Highway (Highway 14). Look for the Kemp Lake Road turnoff, just west of town. Turn north and look for Chubb Road leading west to the lake, about two kilometres from the highway. This should lead to a public access point.

Although the last stretch of road is unpaved, access to the lake is relatively easy and can be done in a car.

Facilities

There are a number of private residents with docks on the north and south shore of the lake. For the general public, it is possible to launch a cartop boat or canoe on the western shores of the lake.

Kemp Lake			
Fish Stocking Data			
Year	Species	Number	Life Stage
2011	Rainbow Trout	1,000	Catchable
2010	Rainbow Trout	2,000	Catchable
2009	Rainbow Trout	2,000	Catchable

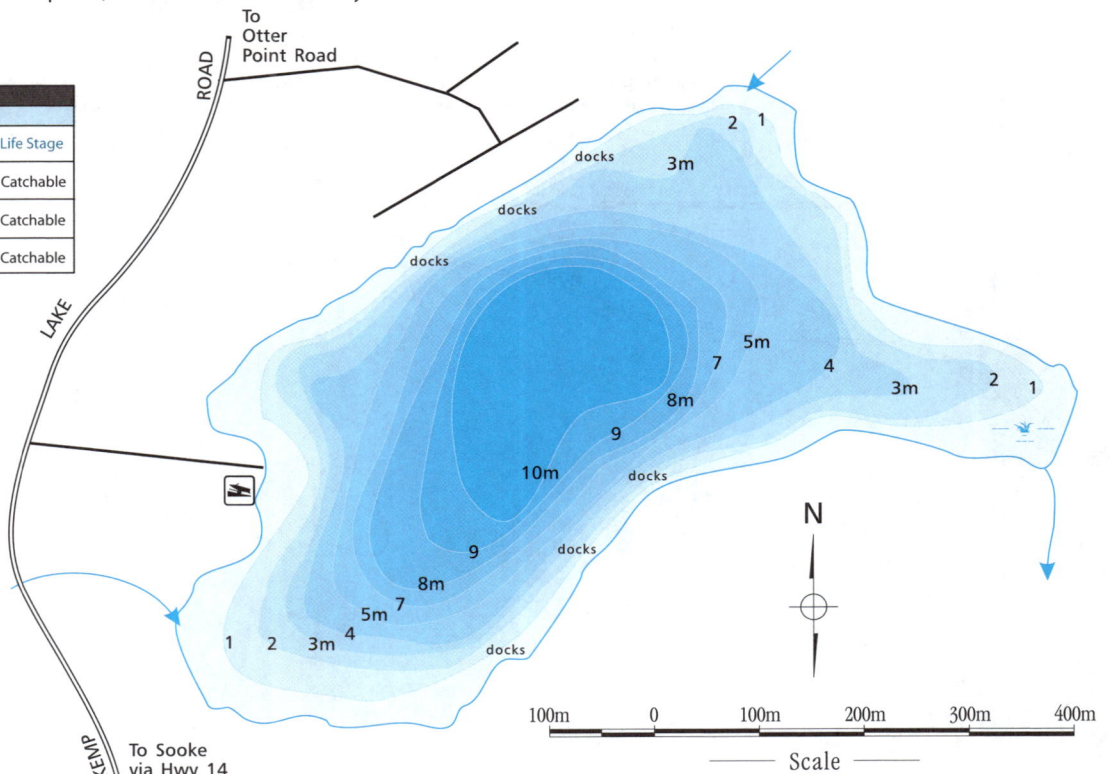

Location: 11 km (7 mi) southwest of Port McNeill
Elevation: 226 m (741 ft)
Surface Area: 80 ha (197 ac)
Mean Depth: 20 m (66 ft)
Max Depth: 45 m (148 ft)
Way Point: 127° 10' 00" Lon - W 50° 29' 00" Lat - N

Keogh Lake

Area Indicator

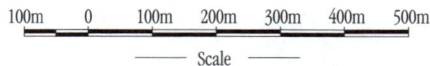

Fishing

With so many great fishing alternatives in the area, Keogh Lake is often overlooked. However, a new recreation site, good road access and fairly decent trout fishing helps bring back area residents year after year. Visitors will find both rainbow and cutthroat trout that occasionally reach 40 cm (16 in) in size. There are also rumours of the odd Dolly Varden and kokanee being landed.

Keogh is a moody lake. The fish are either biting, or they are not. This can be rather frustrating because even if you are doing everything right, if the lake is not feeling like giving up its fish, you're not going to get any.

The lake gets pretty deep, pretty quick and has several small feeder streams. This means that shore fishing is certainly possible, and access to the north shore of the lake is quite easy from Keogh Main. Basically, anywhere you can stand, you can fish, and anywhere you can fish there are fish. Unless they are not biting…

Of course, if it was just a moody lake, most people would go elsewhere. But it is the fact that the fish that are caught here are often in the 2.5 kg (5 lb) range that keeps them coming back for more. It is an abusive relationship, but many north Island anglers love the lake despite its fickle nature.

To effectively work the lake it is best to bring a boat and work the drop-off areas around any of the small streams or the mouth of the Keogh River. Although the lake is deep enough to fish throughout the summer, the best times to fish here are in May to June and again from September to October. Troll deep, around 12 m (40 ft), using slightly heavier gear than you might at some other lakes. A lake troll can be effective, as can a variety of spinners, spoons and plugs. The cutthroat seem to love shiny things, so if a realistic presentation isn't working, don't be afraid to toss out your gaudiest lure and see what bites.

Directions

Found about 11 kilometres southwest of Port McNeill, Keogh Lake is easily found off the Keogh Main. This main logging can be picked up on the south side of the highway just outside of Port McNeill at the Giant Burl. The road winds its way past Cluxewe River and up to Keogh where the roadside recreation site provides access. Most 2wd vehicles should have no trouble accessing the lake.

Facilities

On the northeast shores of Keogh, visitors will find the RV friendly **Clint Beek Recreation Site**. The treed site features room for about 14 camping groups and a man-made sandy beach. Launching a small boat is certainly possible here.

Other Options

The north Island is home to endless fishing alternatives. Small lake lovers can check out **Angler Lake**, which is found just south of Keogh Lake on the Keogh Main. It holds wild cutthroat and a few Dolly Varden. Alternatively, stream anglers can visit **Cluxewe River**, which is found just west of Port McNeill on the Keogh Main. This small river offers a good year round fishery. This is one of the few rivers (currently) with an allowable catch of hatchery steelhead.

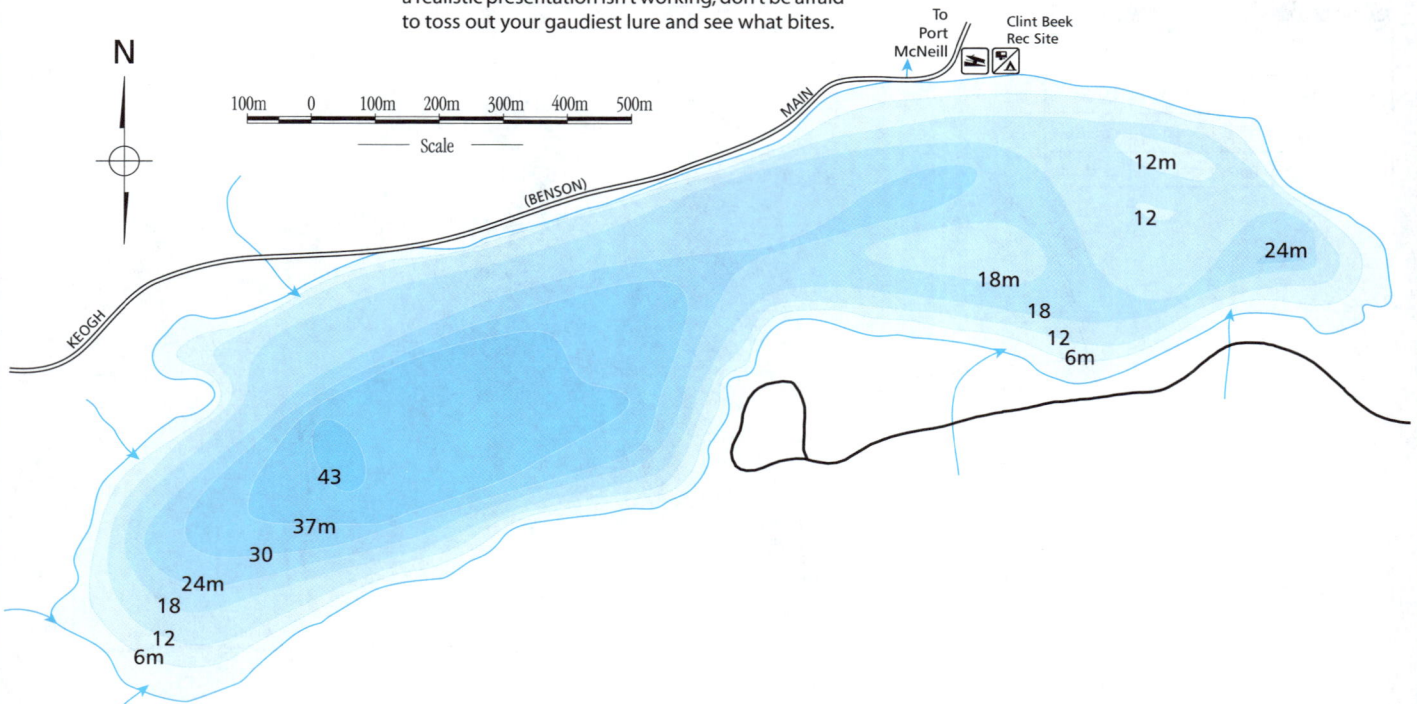

Kissinger Lake

Location: 60 km (37 mi) west of Duncan
Elevation: 191 m (627 ft)
Surface Area: 12.5 ha (31 ac)
Mean Depth: 9.5 m (31 ft)
Max Depth: 30 m (98 ft)
Way Point: 124° 28' 00" Lon - W   48° 55' 00" Lat - N

Fishing

The Cowichan Valley is an extremely popular getaway destination, with sun-drenched beaches and crystal clear waters. Kissinger Lake is found at the west end of Cowichan Lake, and has become a victim of the Cowichan's success. The word is out that Kissinger is a great place to go swimming in the summer and fishing earlier and later in the year.

In spring and fall, the lake is becoming more popular with anglers. As a result, the lake is now stocked annually with catchable rainbow trout to maintain a put and take fishery. The triploid, or sterile, fish that are stocked are supposed to grow larger and faster than the previous strain to hopefully increase the average catch size. As of 2008, the Freshwater Fisheries Society of BC will be stocking the lake twice a year with 1,000 catchable fish in spring and again in fall.

The lake is easily accessible by car and features a nice place to hand launch a boat. There is a small dock sticking out into the lake, which can be used to moor small boats, or even to fish off of. The water is quite clear, and people can often sight fish off the dock.

There is a prominent island just out from the recreation site, and fishing around the island, as well as along the drop-off around the shores, will be the most effective method. The lake is quite deep and lends itself to trolling with spoons or on the fly. The trout will usually chase after anything that looks like a minnow. Use small spoons with chrome or silver or minnow patterns like a Muddler Minnow. Fly anglers will find that trolling leeches and general attractor patterns like a Woolly Bugger is also quite effective.

The lake is noted for its warm waters in the summer, and is a popular swimming destination. Warm waters, however, are not conducive to fishing, and the fishing slows right down in summer. The lake does remain cool in its depths, but the trout tend to get lethargic at that time. Even if you do manage to catch a fish, they do not provide the same feisty fight that they do in cooler weather. If you are here in summer, troll deep, or try fishing in the evening, after the sun is no longer beating down on the lake.

There is an electric motor only restriction on the lake.

Directions

Found at the west end of Cowichan Lake, the quickest access is from the North Shore. Continue past Youbou to the Heather Campsite and follow the new road to Nitinat Lake. Once on the Nitinat Main, watch for the sign marking Kissinger Lake.

Facilities

The **Kissinger Lake Recreation Site** offers 26 campsites among trees, eight with a lake view, plus five group sites. The former logging camp is managed by Timber West as a family destination complete with a nice beach and swimming area along with a place to hand launch boats and a small dock. The lake is completely surrounded by logging roads, and active logging has left a large scar to the west of the lake. Fortunately, none of this can be seen from the water.

Other Options

Just to the east of Kissinger, **Cowichan Lake** is one of the most popular recreational fishing destinations on the Island. The big, sprawling lake has over 100 km of shoreline to search for rainbow, cutthroat, kokanee, dollies and a few brown trout. For more details on the various fishing techniques, numerous recreation sites and parks as well as a helpful depth chart, look for our page on Cowichan Lake earlier in the book.

Area Indicator

Kissinger Lake Fish Stocking Data			
Year	Species	Number	Life Stage
2011	Rainbow Trout	1,000	Catchable
2010	Rainbow Trout	2,000	Catchable
2009	Rainbow Trout	1,500	Catchable

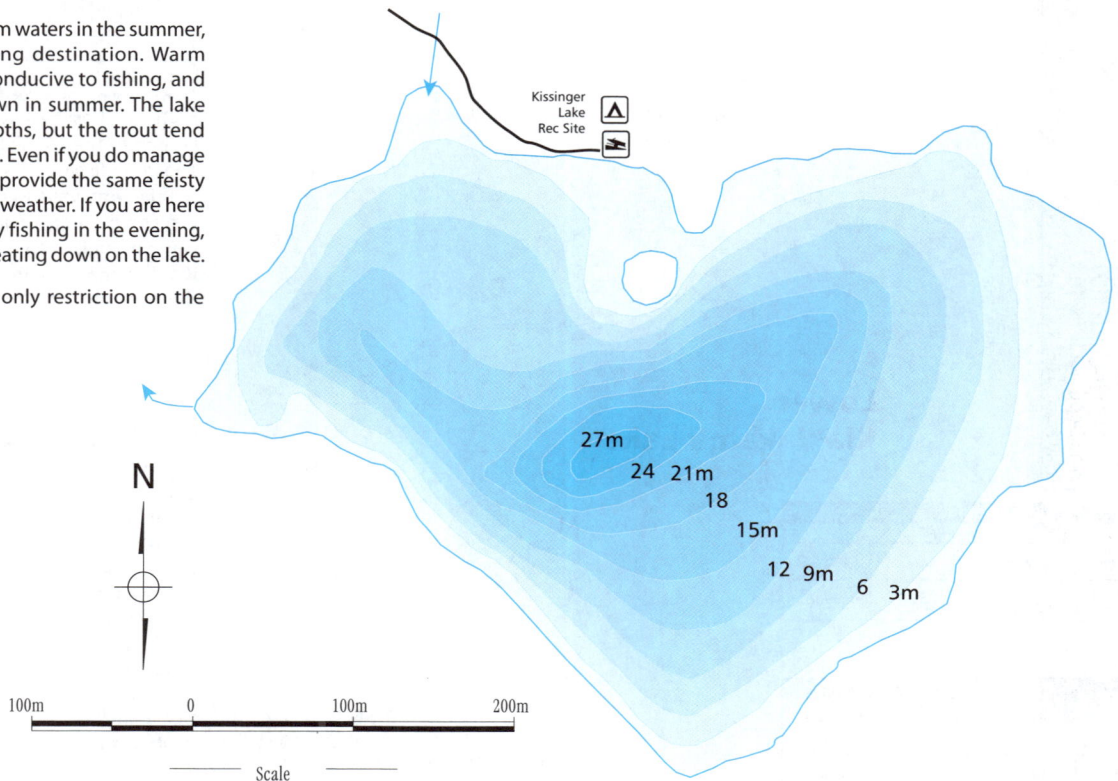

Kissinger Lake Rec Site

27m
24 21m
18
15m
12 9m 6 3m

N

100m   0   100m   200m

Scale

Upper Klaklakama Lake

Elevation: 302 m (991 ft)
Surface Area: 252 ha (622 ac)
Mean Depth: 7 m (23 ft)
Max Depth: 25 m (82 ft)
Way Point: 126° 27'00" Lon – W 50° 09'00" Lat – N

Lower Klaklakama Lake

Elevation: 306 m (991 ft)
Surface Area: 100 ha (247 ac)
Mean Depth: 7 m (23 ft)
Max Depth: 22 m (82 ft)
Way Point: 126° 26'00" Lon – W 50° 07'00" Lat – N

Area Indicator

Lower Klaklakama Lake			
Fish Stocking Data			
Year	Species	Number	Life Stage
2008	Cutthroat Trout	500	Yearling

Upper Klaklakama Lake			
Fish Stocking Data			
Year	Species	Number	Life Stage
2008	Cutthroat Trout	1,000	Yearling

Directions

Found 15 km east of Woss on Highway 19, access into these lakes is found off the signed road to the Mount Cain Ski Hill. Turn onto Mount Davie Road and then south or right again on Duncan Road. Follow this road for 2km where a left on Nimpkish Main South leads to the recreation site about a kilometre down this road. Most vehicles should be able to access the lakes.

Fishing

Some call these shimmering lakes the highlight of the Nimpkish Valley. Others are not that impressed by all the logging in the surrounding hills. No matter, those that come here come for the impressive fishing. In addition to stocked cutthroat trout, anglers will also find wild Dolly Varden. Some of these char are known to get as large a 2 kg (4.5 lbs) in size.

Similar to most lakes in the area, these lakes offer a good open water fishery with the spring and fall being the better time to visit. In fact, these lakes can open up as early as April at which time the cutthroat will take readily to most well presented offerings. Make sure you time it right, as the first couple weeks after ice off is a magic time for fishing, but when the water hits 4°C (39°F), it starts to turnover, clouding the water and dropping the oxygen levels. At this time the fish are lethargic and unwilling to chase anything. Once the turnover is finished, though, look out! The fishing becomes red hot for a few months.

Fishing is not just limited to those with boats. There are decent shoal areas around both lakes and spincasters and fly anglers will find some decent casting areas at either end of the lake. Of course, trolling is the most popular way of fishing here. Try some small spinners, lake trolls, or Flatfish. Pure gold size F4 or F5 Flatfish seem to work really well.

While the lakes can be fished into the summer, the locals advise against it. When the water warms up, the fish begin to take on a weedy taste, especially in the big lake. Unless you are practicing catch and release only, there's not much point in fishing here after about May.

Facilities

Both lakes host recreation sites that are quite popular due to the scenic destination, the easy access and good fishing. The first site found is the **Lower Klaklakama Lake Recreation Site**, which offers a fairly open camping area with room for about five camping units and a launching area. The **Upper Klaklakama Lake Recreation Site** is the nicer of the two with a sandy beach, a boat launch and a few ancient trees still standing near the site. There is room for about 4 campers at this small site.

Other Options

Just off the highway, **Hoomak Lake** offers fairly good fishing for small, stocked cutthroat and wild Dolly Varden throughout the spring and fall. Fly-fishing and spincasting from a float tube are the best methods of fishing the lake. A rest area with a cartop boat launch and forestry trail is found next to the lake. Also in the area, anglers can test their luck on the Davie River. The **Davie River** links Schoen Lake with the larger Nimpkish River. The Davie offers winter and summer steelhead runs (February to March and June to July respectively), as well as rainbow trout in summer.

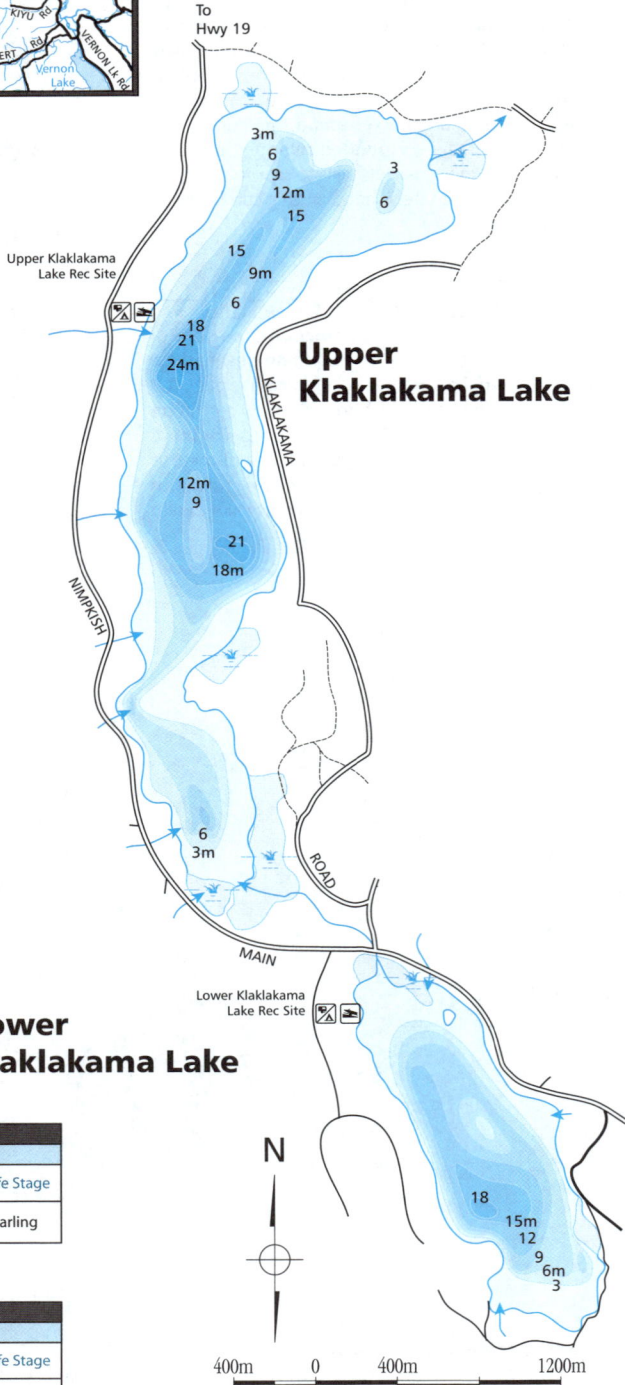

Upper Klaklakama Lake

Lower Klaklakama Lake

Langford Lake

Location: 15 km (9.3 mi) west of Victoria
Elevation: 67 m (220 ft)
Surface Area: 61 ha (151 ac)
Mean Depth: 6.5 m (21 ft)
Max Depth: 17 m (56 ft)
Way Point: 123° 23'00" Lon - W 48° 27'00" Lat - N

Fishing

Most anglers that come to Langford Lake come for the good-sized rainbow and smallmouth bass. Reports of bass being caught in the 3 kg (7 lb) class are quite common, but certainly not the norm. There are also some cutthroat in the lake since both trout species are stocked regularly. For something different, perch have been illegally introduced and provide a fun fishery for the kids.

The first thing anglers will notice when they visit this urban lake north of Victoria is the metal, pyramid shaped aerator that rises out of the lake. This is noteworthy not just because they are pointy metal objects sticking out of the water, but also because for some reason, the fish are attracted to them, too.

As a result, finding success here can be dead simple. Troll around this aerator with a lake troll and small lure tipped with bait. Once your figure out the right lure and depth to troll, catching small trout should be no problem.

If you are looking for bigger trout or bass, you will need to work the small bays, weeds, small islands and various other shore structure. The lake has had a number of bass spawning reefs added, and, once you've gotten over working around the pointy metal thingies, these should draw your attention next.

During cooler periods, the trout prefer these shallow areas and the bass prefer the deeper holes, and the fishing is better for trout. When the waters warm, the opposite is true.

Fly anglers will find a good chironomid hatch on the lake. The insect begins to hatch as early as March when there is a spell of warmer weather. The hatches continue through the spring with April being the height of the hatch. Try leeches or other searching patterns if there is no hatch on.

The bass tend to feed on chironomids, small baitfish, leeches and even tadpoles. Try attractor type fly patterns such as a Woolly Bugger or Werner shrimp. If spincasting, there are many different plugs such as a Rapala to use. Regardless, you will need to get your hook very close to cover, especially for lunker bass.

Development is encroaching on the lake, but considering its close proximity to the city, the heavy stocking program and the good trout and bass fishing, the lake is not that busy with anglers. There is an electric motor only restriction at the lake.

Area Indicator

Directions

Langford Lake is easily reached off Goldstream Avenue (Hwy 1A) to the west of Victoria. There is a place to access the off the main road or you can follow Leigh Road to the boat launch on the southwest shoreline. Goldstream Avenue is the main road through the city of Langford that connects Highway 1 with Highway 14.

Facilities

There is a boat launch off Leigh Road as well as a small area to launch canoes off Goldstream Avenue to the north. The community has established a nice trail system around the lake that includes access to some shore fishing points. There is even a wooden walkway that provides access to a fishing pier on the western side of the lake. If that is not enough, there is also an aeration system that was installed in order to improve the quality of the water for the fish.

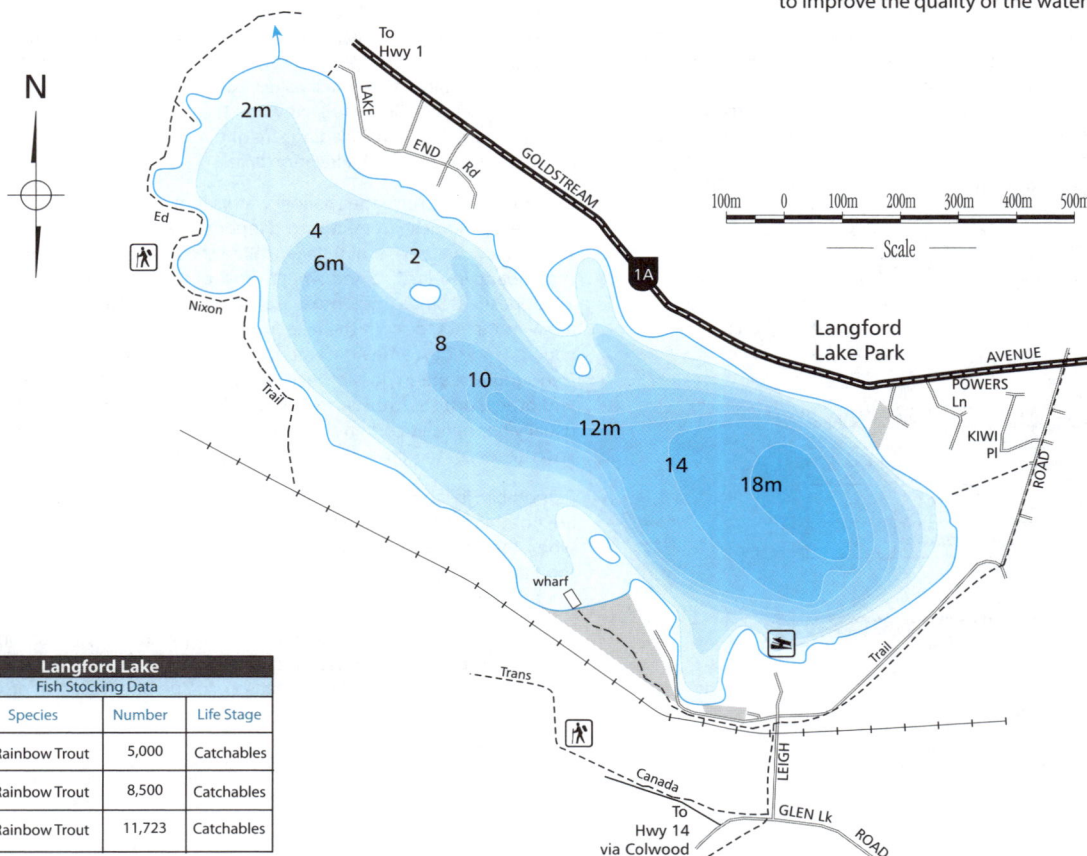

Langford Lake Fish Stocking Data			
Year	Species	Number	Life Stage
2011	Rainbow Trout	5,000	Catchables
2010	Rainbow Trout	8,500	Catchables
2009	Rainbow Trout	11,723	Catchables

Lake Beautiful & Mariwood Lake

Mariwood Lake

Elevation: 1,159 m (3,800 ft)
Surface Area: 7.4 ha (18 ac)
Mean Depth: 3.6 m (12 ft)
Max Depth:14 m (47 ft)
Way Point: 125° 20'00" Lon - W 49° 42'00" Lat - N

Area Indicator

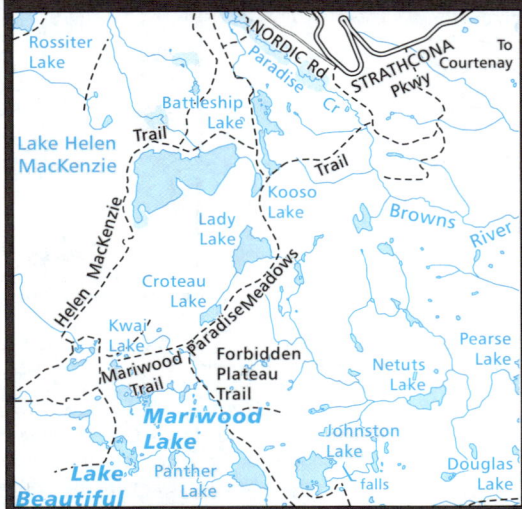

Directions

Found on Forbidden Plateau within Strathcona Provincial Park, these lakes are reached by driving north of Courtenay on the Inland Highway (Hwy 19) to the turn off to the Mount Washington Ski Area. Follow the Mount Washington Strathcona Parkway Road towards the ever expanding ski village and the Paradise Meadows Trailhead. The new trailhead is located just beyond the Mount Washington Nordic ski area, about 25 km from Courtenay.

From the trailhead, you will need to course south past several lakes including Battleship, Lady, Croteau and Kwai en route to Mount Albert Edward or Circlet Lake. Near the Kwai Lake Campsite, an easy to miss trail leads south to Mariwood Lake. Lake Beautiful is found south of Mariwood. Mariwood is found over 8 km (3 hours) from the trailhead, making both lakes far enough away from a road to discourage most fishermen.

Facilities

There are no designated campsites at either lake. Those looking to overnight in the area can stay at nearby Kwai Lake.

Lake Beautiful

Elevation: 1,130 m (3,705 ft)
Surface Area: 6 ha (15 ac)
Mean Depth: 2.6 m (8.5 ft)
Max Depth: 14 m (45 ft)
Way Point: 125° 20'00" Lon - W 49° 41'00" Lat - N

Mariwood Lake
Fish Stocking Data

Year	Species	Number	Life Stage
2005	Rainbow Trout	2,000	Fry
2002	Rainbow Trout	2,000	Fry

Lake Beautiful
Fish Stocking Data

Year	Species	Number	Life Stage
2005	Rainbow Trout	5,000	Fry
2002	Rainbow Trout	5,000	Fry

Fishing

There are a number of good fishing lakes found in the Forbidden Plateau area of Strathcona Provincial Park, and while they may not be the best known lakes in the area, Lake Beautiful and Mariwood Lake are certainly worth the effort to visit. In addition to gorgeous scenery, the limited fishing season and fish stocking program helps keep the rainbow trout fairly aggressive. These trout are reported to average 30–35 cm (12–14 in) in size and readily take most well presented flies or small lures.

However, these lakes are not vehicle-accessible. This means that the fishing pressure is lower, and the experience of fishing the lakes is all the sweeter for the hike in. Or at least, that's what some anglers would tell you. Others just find the hike-in an unnecessary evil, and many won't even bother making the effort. This is fine for the few anglers that enjoy the solitude of fishing remote, hike-in lakes.

Like other lakes on the plateau, the fishing season does not start until July, after the ice melts off the lake. Fishing remains active throughout the summer months with August being the best month. By late October to early November, the ice begins to form again.

Lake Beautiful is a shallow lake with a half dozen small islands as well as many small bays and shoals that would excite even the most casual fly angler. However, the shallow nature of the lake makes it tough to fish from shore with lures and spinners. A floatation device a real advantage here. If you are fishing from shore stay at the north end and cast towards the drop-off near the deep hole shown on the chart.

Mariwood Lake is a fly-fisher's dream lake. It has numerous islands and bays making some great casting terrain. The deepest part of the lake is off the western shore of the lake and there are several shallower holes in amongst the islands on the east side of the lake. Casting from shore is possible around most of the lake as there are prominent drop-offs throughout.

While these lakes are not above treeline, the forests surrounding the lakes are thin, and the shoreline is fairly open. This, coupled with the shallow waters, means that the fish can be easily spooked on a calm day. Approach the shoreline slowly, keeping an eye out for fish laying in wait in the shallow water. While chances are you'll have to get out on the water with a float tube (especially on Lake Beautiful), why ruin the opportunity to snag a nice sized rainbow from the shore? Wading straight into the lake is the biggest mistake made by anglers on high elevation lakes.

Rainbow like to cruise the shallow waters looking for food when they know it's safe, and quickly retreat into deeper waters when they sense a threat. The shallow water of a high lake (called the littoral zone) is where most of the aquatic insects live and where most of the windblown terrestrial bugs are deposited. Since this is most likely the place for fish to be feeding so take a few moments to scout the lake from well back from the shoreline. This, of course, works best when the water is still, and when you have a pair of polarized sunglasses (and possibly even a pair of binoculars). Watch for rises, boils, and other surface disturbances that will betray the location of the fish. This usually happens at certain times of the day (early morning or late evening), and the rest of the time, you'll have to keep an eagle eye out.

Remember, just because you don't see a fish at first glance doesn't mean they are not there. Rainbow are designed to blend with the scenery, and it's only when they move that they'll reveal their position. Take some time to scout the lake, and then start working the shallows. You'll have time to move to deeper water soon enough.

Fish found in high elevation lakes are also opportunistic, and as long as nothing seems out of place, will usually chase anything that looks like food. So small spoons and wet flies like a Doc Spratley or a Zug Bug will often produce well.

Lake Beautiful & Mariwood Lake

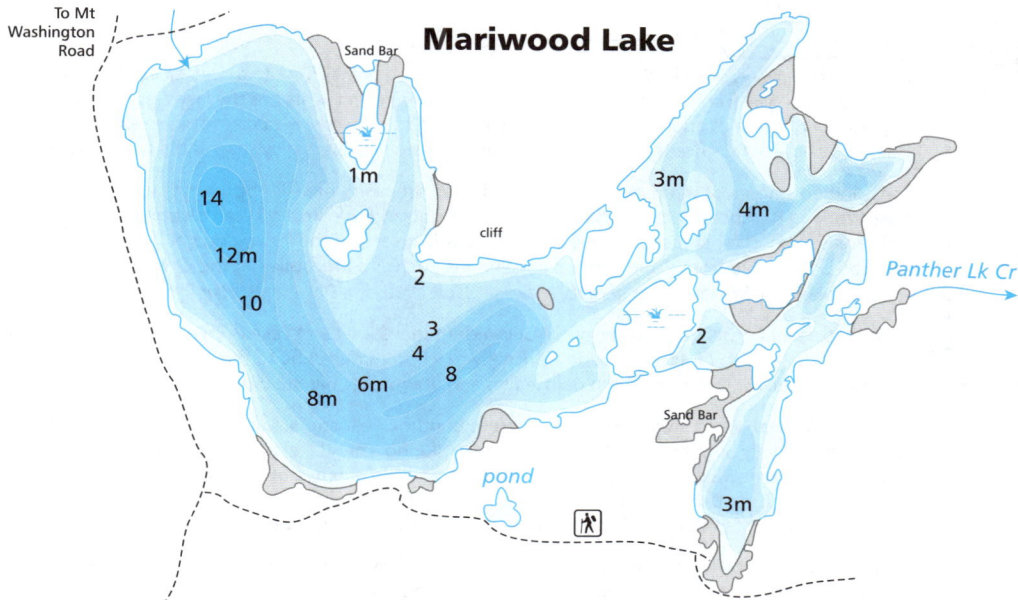

Mariwood Lake

Elevation: 1,159 m (3,800 ft)
Surface Area: 7.4 ha (18 ac)
Mean Depth: 3.6 m (12 ft)
Max Depth:14 m (47 ft)
Way Point: 125° 20' 00" Lon - W 49° 42' 00" Lat - N

Mariwood Lake

To Mt Washington Road

Sand Bar

1m

14

12m

10

cliff

2

3
4
8

8m   6m   8

3m

4m

Panther Lk Cr

2

Sand Bar

pond

3m

Strathcona Provincial Park

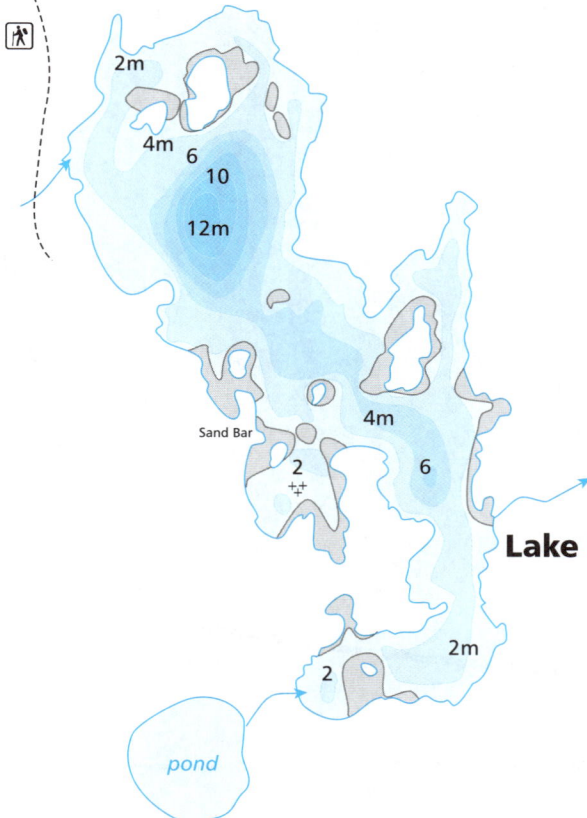

Lake Beautiful

Elevation: 1,130 m (3,705 ft)
Surface Area: 6 ha (15 ac)
Mean Depth: 2.6 m (8.5 ft)
Max Depth: 14 m (45 ft)
Way Point: 125° 20' 00" Lon - W 49° 41' 00" Lat - N

N

2m

4m   6

10

12m

50m   0   50m   100m   150m   200m

Scale

4m

Sand Bar

2

6

Lake Beautiful

2m

2

pond

Location: 83 km (52 mi) southwest of Port Alberni
Elevation: 96 m (315 ft)
Surface Area: 7.5 ha (18.5 ac)
Max Depth: 10 m (34 ft)
Perimeter: 1.5 km (.9 mi)
Way Point: 125° 26' 00" Lon - W   49° 07' 00" Lat - N

www.backroadmapbooks.com

Larry Lake

Area Indicator

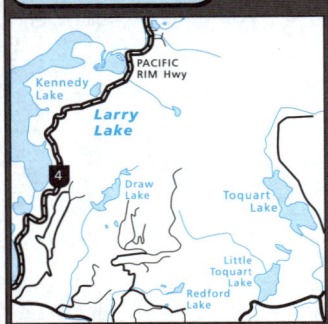

Fishing

Larry Lake has always been known as a picturesque stopping point en-route to the Pacific Rim. Tucked in between the Pacific Rim Highway (Highway 4) and Kennedy Lake, only in recent years has the lakes reputation as a fishing hot spot caught the attention of anglers. The lake has been stocked regularly with catchable size rainbow by the Freshwater Fisheries Society of BC since the mid-1990s. Today, these small trout readily snap at the hook and take to the fly.

With a limited amount of shoreline vegetation and steep drop-offs, there is opportunity to cast spinning lures along the shore. Working the shoals (the area between the shoreline and the drop-off) can be quite effective as the trout forage these areas looking for leeches and a variety of aquatic insects in the larva, pupa or nymph stage of their life cycle. Trout can be tempted from shore with casting spoons, such as a Krocodile or Croc, or by simply still-fishing bait under a bobber or off the bottom. If trolling, try a lake troll followed by a silver Flatfish or Kwikfish.

Fly anglers should watch for hatches of chironomids (midges) on Larry Lake from early April to mid-July, and again at the end of September. Caddisflies (sedges) usually hatch from mid-June to the end of August. Mayflies emerge from late spring to early summer, and both damselflies and dragonflies hatch during the summer months.

Leeches are available as a trout food source throughout the year and are always a good searching pattern. Most any variation of a Woolly Bugger is a good choice when exploring a new lake or fishing during non-hatch periods. Work the fly slow and deep on a sinking line along the shoal. Try an olive green mini leech with some sparkle tied in. Other good leech colours for Larry Lake are black, brown and maroon, tied as solid or mixed with one of the other colours. When the fishing is slow, other faithful standbys you can knot on your line are a 52 Buick, half back or a dragonfly/damselfly nymph.

Like many lakes on the west coast of the island, it tends to remain cooler in summer. At this time, many fish the deeper water out from the boat launch. Working around the islands on either side of the lake is popular during the spring and fall periods.

Directions

Larry Lake is located between the Pacific Rim Highway (Highway 4) and the east end of Kennedy Lake. It is found on the west side of the highway about 83 kilometres (52 miles) from Port Alberni on the way to Tofino.

Facilities

Although many highway travellers stop here, there are no developed facilities at the lake. Anglers will find a small area that is suitable to launch cartop boats or canoes.

Other Options

Larry Lake is tucked away in a crook between Highway 4 and **Kennedy Lake**. This large lake has a launching area a bit further along the highway as well as a few campsites around the lake. The lake is considered one of the Island's best cutthroat lakes. Try fly-fishing or spincasting a stickleback imitation to replicate the cutthroat's main diet in this lake. Watch for strong winds.

Larry Lake Fish Stocking Data			
Year	Species	Number	Life Stage
2011	Rainbow Trout	750	Yearling
2010	Rainbow Trout	750	Yearling
2009	Rainbow Trout	750	Yearling

N

To Port Alberni

To Tofino

Scale

100m   0   100m   200m

Lizard Lake

Location: 18 km (11.2 miles) northeast of Port Renfrew
Elevation: 65 m (213 ft)
Surface Area: 8.7 ha (21.5 ac)
Mean Depth: 7.5 m (25 ft)
Max Depth: 15.5 m (51 ft)
Way Point: 124° 13'00" Lon - W   48° 36'00" Lat - N

Fishing

Lizard Lake, a popular lake in the San Juan River Valley east of Port Renfrew, gets its name because it is overrun with newts. To help maintain a decent fishery, the Freshwater Fisheries Society of BC stocks the lake annually with rainbow trout. With abundant feed, these fish grow quickly and can reach 35 cm (14 in) in size. The fisheries website also says there are cutthroat in the lake, but we have no confirmed reports of these fish being caught here.

The small, low elevation lake is best fished earlier in the year. It opens up as early as April, with fishing being pretty steady through June. After the summer slow down, the fishing heats up again in late September and October.

The lake offers both prominent shoals and a deep centre to allow both shore casters and trollers to effectively work the lake. If casting from a small boat or float tube, it is best to cast towards the shoals during cooler periods when the trout like to cruise these areas looking for food. If trolling, a lake troll worked near the drop-off area is an effective method.

Trout will take readily to a variety of small lures or spinners. Local tackle shops will help you select the best sizes or colours, but you should always carry a selection of Mepps or Panther Martin spinners along with a small Krocodile or similar lure. Still fishing with a bait and bobber is always effective, while trollers will find success with a lake troll followed by a silver Flatfish or Kwikfish.

Fly fishers will find a variety of attractor patterns work well here. Leeches, Doc Spratleys and the ever-popular Wooly Bugger can all work well. At certain times of the year, in the early morning, or later in the evening, when the fish begin to rise to chase surface insects, dry flies can work well, too.

There is an electric motors only restriction at the lake.

Directions

Lizard Lake is located northeast of Port Renfrew and Highway 14. To find the lake, travel north from Port Renfrew on the new Pacific Marine Road towards Lake Cowichan. Continue past Fairy Lake and the intersection with the Lens Main at about the 16.5 km mark, stay left. Within 500 metres the lake and recreation site will be on the right. The good road access will allow cars and RV's to access the lake.

Facilities

The **Lizard Lake Recreation Site** is a newly enhanced site with space for 28 camping groups, a separate day-use area and beach and even walk-in tenting sites. There is a good gravel boat launch and two docks for smaller boats or canoeists to use. There is on-site supervision and a fee to camp here.

While in the area, be sure to explore the nearby trails and look for the big trees found in the area. These sites are noted in the Backroad Mapbook for Vancouver Island.

Other Options

Up the San Juan River Valley, you will find **Fairy Lake** and **Pixie Lake**. Fairy Lake is on the new Pacific Marine Road whereas Pixie Lake is on the Lens Main. Both offer fishing for small rainbow and cutthroat. Please refer to the sections in this book specific for those lakes. You will find a depth chart and a detailed write-up on the fishing in both those lakes.

Area Indicator

Lizard Lake Fish Stocking Data			
Year	Species	Number	Life Stage
2011	Rainbow Trout	1,000	Catchables
2010	Rainbow Trout	1,000	Catchables
2009	Rainbow Trout	1,000	Catchables

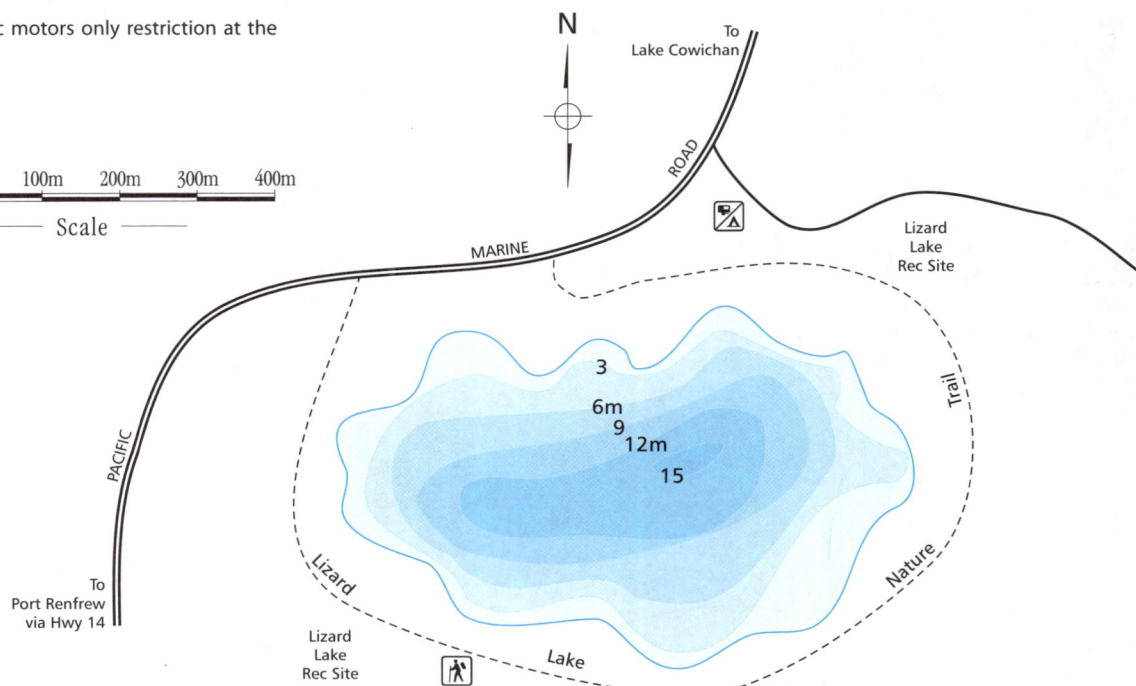

Location: 10.5 km (6.5 mi) southwest of Duncan
Elevation: 670 m (2,198 ft)
Surface Area: 15.5 ha (38 ac)
Mean Depth: 1.5 m (5 ft)
Max Depth: 5.5 m (18 ft)
Way Point: 123° 47' 00" Lon - W 48° 42' 00" Lat - N

www.backroadmapbooks.com

Lois Lake

Area Indicator

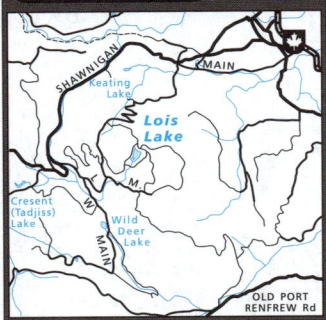

Fishing

Lois Lake is being managed as a trophy fishery. This means there are special fly-fishing only and a one trout limit restrictions to help keep the fish bigger. As a result, it is known for its good-sized rainbow and elusive brown trout that have been known to reach 3 kg (7 lbs).

The lake is high enough in elevation to provide a good late spring or early summer trout fishery. Visitors will find some very enticing shoals around the lake as well as a series of small islands around the lake to work. The best way to fish Lois Lake is to cast towards the shallows into the weed beds.

Fly anglers should try to match the hatch. Chironomids begin to emerge in April and last through to July before resurfacing again at the end of September. Caddisflies (sedges) usually hatch from mid-May to the end of August. Mayflies emerge from late spring to early summer, and both damselflies and dragonflies hatch during the summer months. Lois is considered a good lake to fish with dragonfly or damselfly nymphs. If you are open for some top water action, the Tom Thumb is often a productive dry fly choice. Those using searching patterns will not go wrong with the all-purpose Doc Spratley or leech patterns.

The Freshwater Fisheries Society of BC currently stocks the lake with rainbow trout bi-annually to help maintain a good fishery. The lake was stocked in the past with brown trout, and although they are no longer stocked here, they still remain. Brown trout are a suspicious fish, and can prove difficult to catch.

Directions A

Found to the northwest of Shawnigan Lake and southwest of Duncan, access into this lake can be a bit tricky and a 4wd vehicle is definitely an asset. Adding to the confusion is the recent proliferation of gates on the south Island. We recommend finding a local or using a detailed logging road map, such as those in the Backroad Mapbook for Vancouver Island, along with a GPS and the Backroad GPS Maps to help track the lake.

The easier access route is from the north near the hamlet of Glenora southwest of Duncan. To find Glenora Road, turn west off Highway 1 at Allenby Road and then south on Miller. This road leads to Glenora Road, which continues west to Waters Road. Turn left or south and if the gates are open, this road should join Lois Main. Continue south as the road winds its way along the east side of Glenora Creek to Branch road L 11. Take this road east and then branch south almost immediately on L 10. If all things go well, this road should help you reach the north end of Lois Lake.

Access into this area may be closed or restricted. It is best to inquire locally before planning a trip into the area.

Other Options A

Wild Deer Lake is located south of Lois Lake on W Main. This is a popular fishing lake, which is certainly worth a try for small trout. For full details on the fishing at the lake and for a depth chart, please refer to the write-up in this book specific to Wild Deer Lake.

Facilities

This remote lake offers no facilities. Visitors will find a rustic launching area and signs of camping at the north end of the lake.

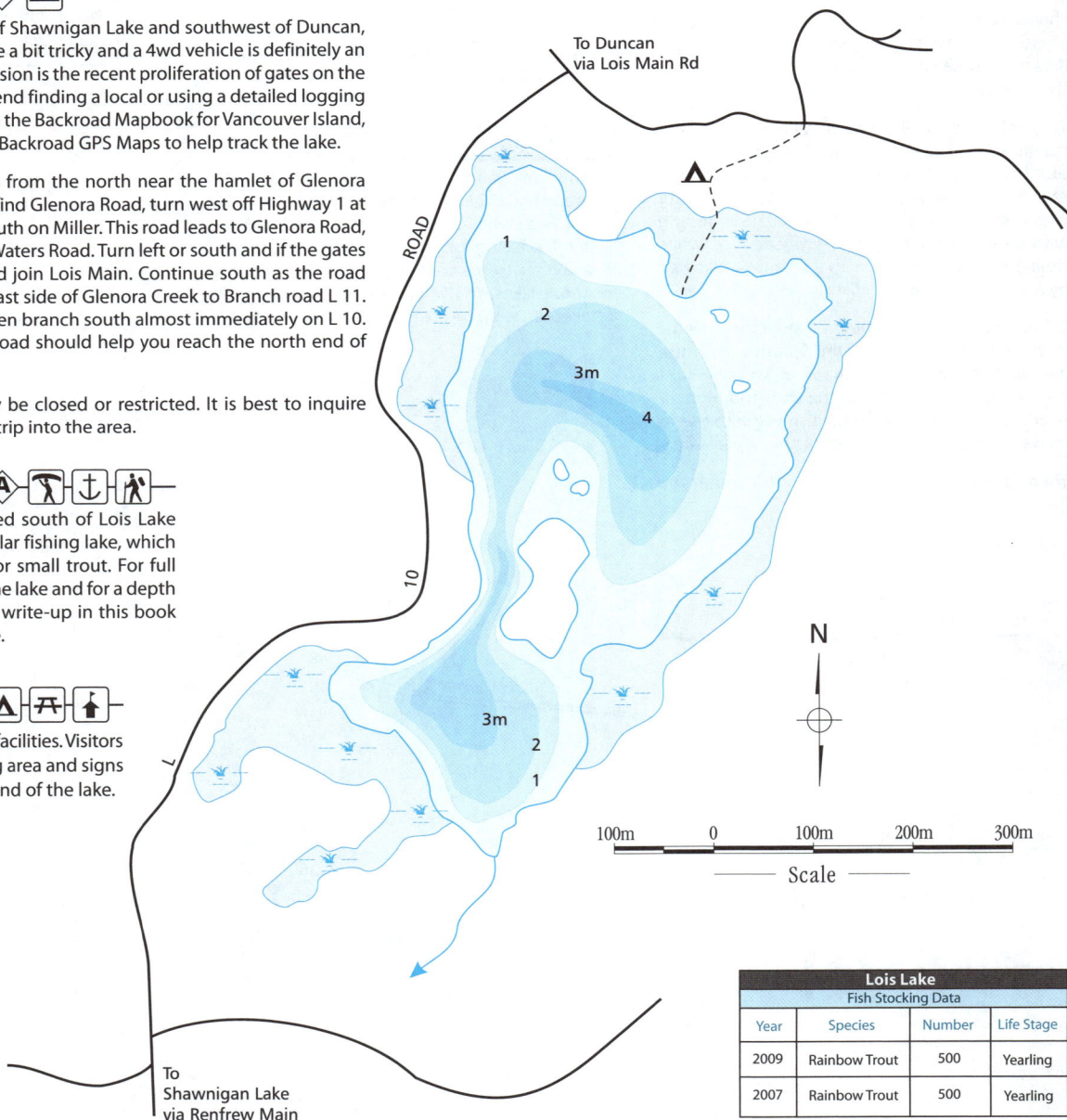

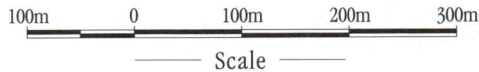

To Duncan
via Lois Main Rd

ROAD

10

L

To
Shawnigan Lake
via Renfrew Main

N

100m   0   100m   200m   300m
— Scale —

Lois Lake			
Fish Stocking Data			
Year	Species	Number	Life Stage
2009	Rainbow Trout	500	Yearling
2007	Rainbow Trout	500	Yearling

Long & Diver Lake

Elevation: 111 m (364 ft)
Surface Area: 34 ha (83 ac)
Mean Depth: 6 m (20 ft)
Max Depth: 14 m (46 ft)
Way Point: 124° 01'00"W 49° 12'50"N

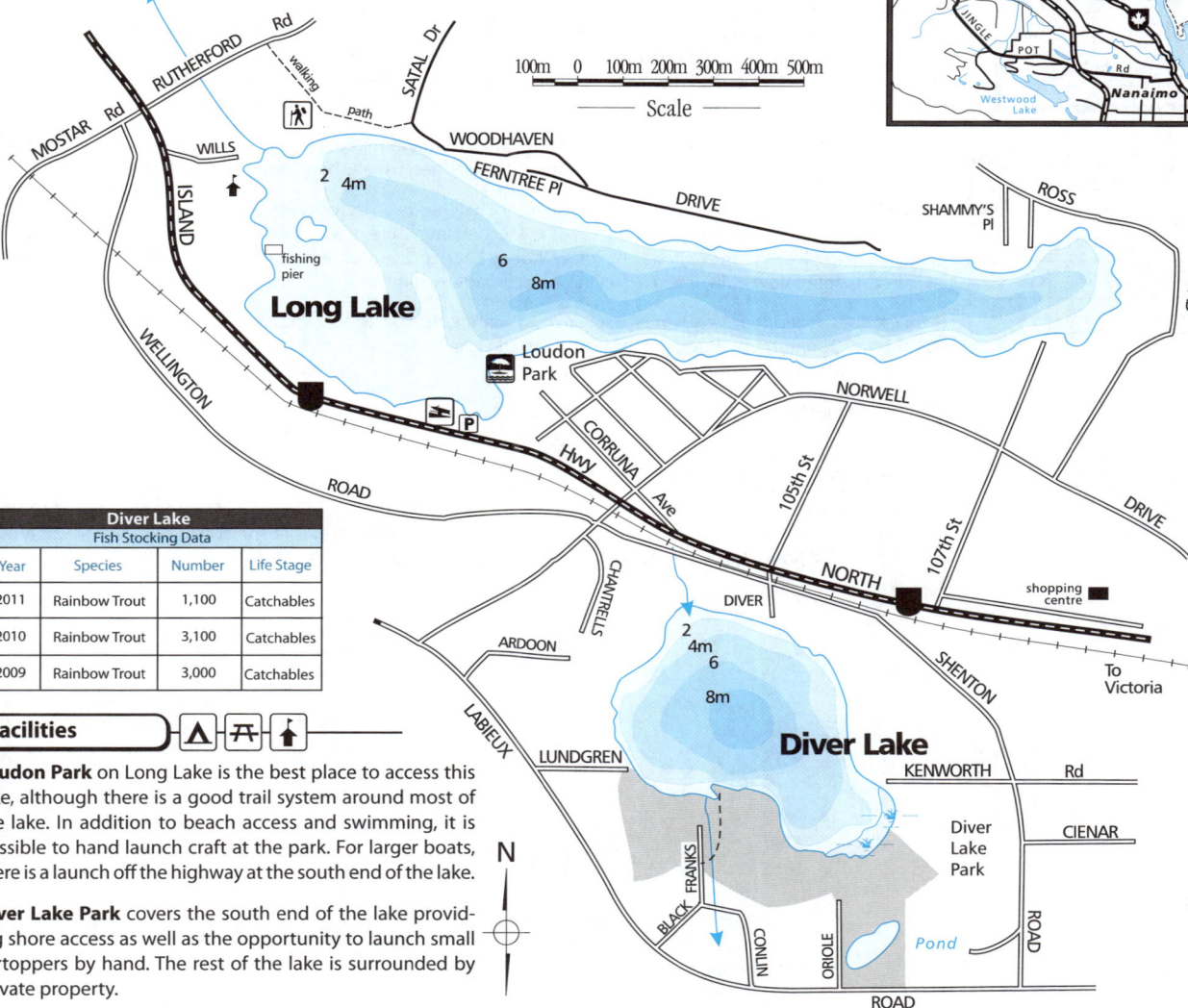

Directions

The Old Island Highway cuts between the lakes allowing for easy access. Long Lake is accessed at the south end of the lake at Loudon Park. Take Norwell Drive north from the highway and follow signs to the park. Driver Lake is also found off Norwell Drive. Follow this road west off the highway and then take the next left on Labieux Road. Signs point the way to Diver Lake Park at the south end.

Long Lake Fish Stocking Data			
Year	Species	Number	Life Stage
2011	Rainbow Trout	2,500	Catchables
2010	Rainbow Trout	9,678	Catchables
2009	Rainbow Trout	15,847	Catchables

Area Indicator

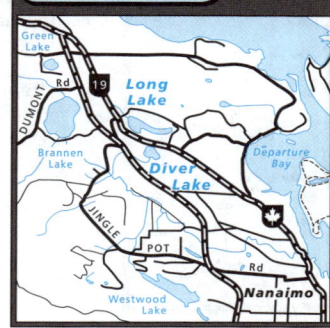

100m 0 100m 200m 300m 400m 500m

Scale

Diver Lake Fish Stocking Data			
Year	Species	Number	Life Stage
2011	Rainbow Trout	1,100	Catchables
2010	Rainbow Trout	3,100	Catchables
2009	Rainbow Trout	3,000	Catchables

Facilities

Loudon Park on Long Lake is the best place to access this lake, although there is a good trail system around most of the lake. In addition to beach access and swimming, it is possible to hand launch craft at the park. For larger boats, there is a launch off the highway at the south end of the lake.

Diver Lake Park covers the south end of the lake providing shore access as well as the opportunity to launch small cartoppers by hand. The rest of the lake is surrounded by private property.

Elevation: 108 m (354 ft)
Surface Area: 15.5 ha (38 ac)
Mean Depth: 3.4 m (11 ft)
Max Depth: 7 m (23 ft)
Way Point: 124° 01'00"W 49° 13'00"N

Fishing

Resting in the north end of Nanaimo, these lakes provide a surprisingly good fishery for both trout and bass. Of the two, Long Lake is the more popular and most developed.

Long Lake has large smallmouth bass to 2 kg (4-5 lbs) as well as stocked rainbow. Most anglers prefer casting flies and small lures through the prominent shoals. One popular casting area is from the dock on the western shore, but this location is only effective in the early spring and fall when the waters are cooler. The northern and southern shorelines have prominent drop-offs and fish like to hold here throughout the year.

Bass like attractor type flies, rubber worms or bass plugs. You need to cast them nearby to some cover such as a sunken log or lily pads where the bass tend to hide. For larger fish, try fishing the deeper areas with plugs or lake trolls and worm rigs during the winter or shoulder seasons.

When you arrive at **Diver Lake**, you should expect slower fishing for rainbow, cutthroat and smallmouth bass. The trout are stocked regularly and those fish can reach 2 kg (4.5 lbs) but average 30 cm (12 in) in size. The lake offers an early season fishery beginning in March, but fishing slows by June when the waters warm. It is not until late September, when the trout become more active.

The shoreline is marshy providing great cover for the bass and trout. Try casting a bass plug towards the lily pads. Casting a dragonfly or damselfly nymph towards the weeds is a good idea for catching the trout.

There is an electric motor only restriction on the lake.

Location: 11 km (7 mi) east of Port Alberni
Elevation: 366 m (1,200 ft)
Surface Area: 7 ha (17 ac)
Mean Depth: 6 m (20 ft)
Max Depth: 14 m (46 ft)
Way Point: 124° 42' 00" Lon - W   49° 15' 00" Lat - N

www.backroadmapbooks.com

Loon Lake

Area Indicator

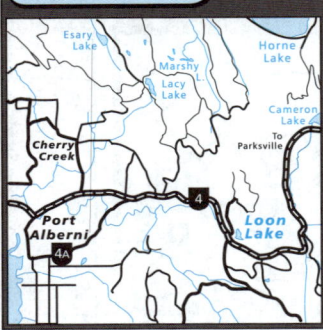

Loon Lake			
Fish Stocking Data			
Year	Species	Number	Life Stage
2011	Rainbow Trout	1,250	Catchables
2010	Rainbow Trout	2,000	Catchables
2009	Rainbow Trout	2,000	Catchables

Fishing

While it may be small in size, Loon Lake holds surprisingly large rainbow and cutthroat trout. The average catch is about 40 cm (16 in) in size, although larger fish are not uncommon. Adding to its appeal, Loon Lake is also stocked annually by the Freshwater Fisheries Society of BC with catchable size rainbow and fast growing cutthroat.

Extremely popular lake with the locals, Loon Lake is situated in mountainous terrain in the midst of a Douglas-fir forest. It is best fished by small boat or canoe as the dense growth of alder and fir around the perimeter makes access to the shoreline difficult. The best fishing takes place in the months of May, June, September and October; however, good fishing can be had throughout the summer.

The most common ways to fish Loon Lake are casting or trolling flies, small spoons, spinner and plugs. A lake troll with a wedding band and small piece of bait will produce good results almost anytime of year. Spinners, such as a Mepps or Gibbs black/orange dot, tipped with a piece of worm are good casting options. If you are able to access the lake with small boat or canoe, try trolling black/silver speckled Flatfish or Kwikfish, a Dick Nite spoon, or a Luhr Jensen brass needlefish. These lures can be accompanied by a lake troll if desired.

Fly anglers should watch for hatches of chironomids (also know as midges or gnats) from early May to mid-July, and sometimes again at the end of September. Caddisflies (sedges) usually hatch from mid-June to the end of August.

In the summer and late fall, when most of the insect hatches have tapered off, Loon Lake's trout once again turn their full attention to such staple food sources as leeches, immature dragonflies and damselflies and bloodworms. When fishing a leech pattern such as the black Woolly Bugger, or any other imitation, use a sinking line and pull the line in with long, slow pulls. If you're trolling a leech pattern, remember the slower the better.

While it doesn't happen every winter, or even most winters, the lake will occasionally freeze thick enough to support ice fishing. During these times, the locals flock to the lake to partake in this unique experience. Worms or salmon roe work especially well through the ice.

There is an electric motor only restriction on the lake.

Directions

Loon Lake is also known as Summit Lake because of its location on Highway 4 just east of Port Alberni. Look for Summit Road branching north, about 11 km (7 miles) east of town, opposite the access road to the old Mount Arrowsmith Ski Area. The lake is found a short distance later on a side road. A car should be adequate.

Facilities

Visitors will find an informal parking/picnic area at the southwest end of the lake. It is possible to hand launch small boats and canoes here. There is also a fisherman's trail around the lake.

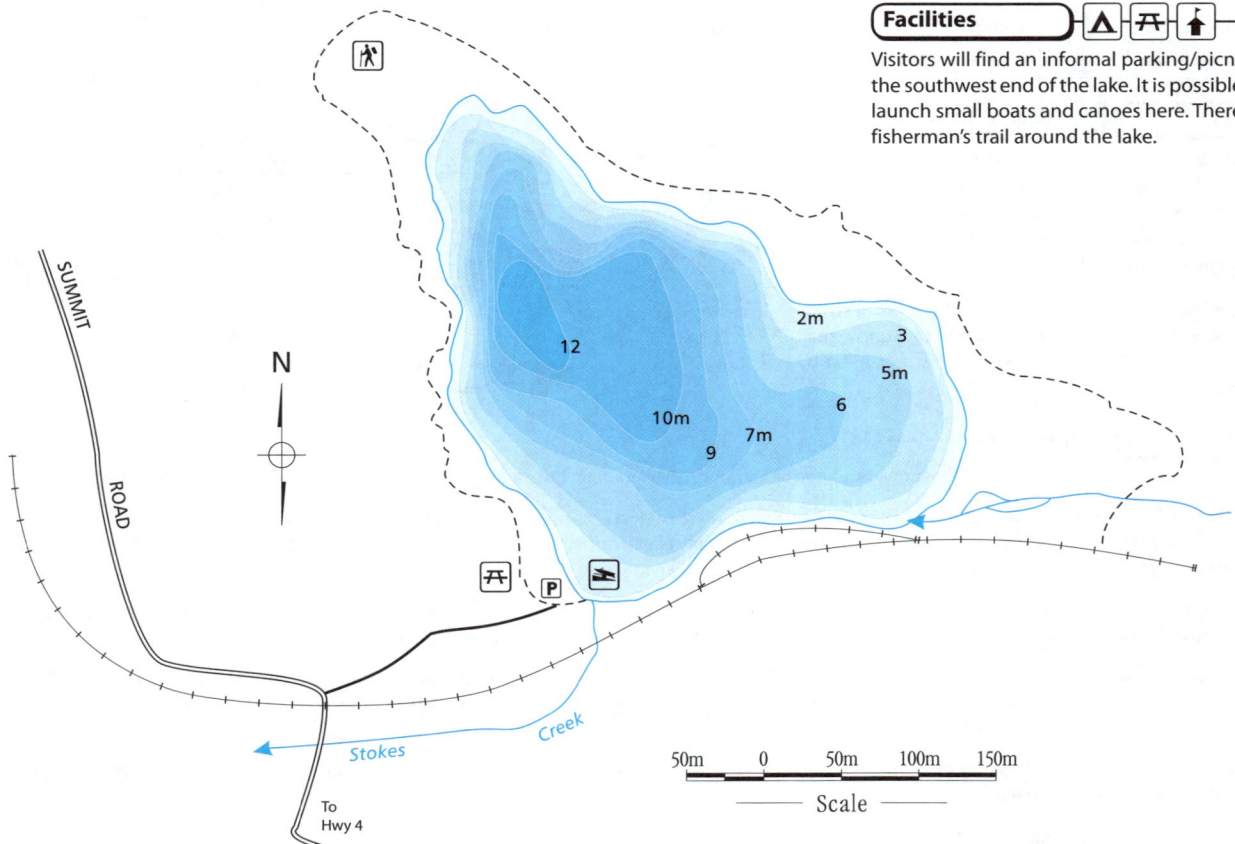

SUMMIT ROAD

N

12
2m
3
5m
6
10m
7m
9

Stokes Creek

To Hwy 4

50m   0   50m   100m   150m
Scale

Lost Lake

Location: 18 km (11 mi) south of Campbell River
Elevation: 260 m (853 ft)
Surface Area: 3.4 ha (8.5 ac)
Mean Depth: 4.2 m (14 ft)
Max Depth: 11 m (36 ft)
Way Point: 125° 15' 00" Lon - W   49° 49' 00" Lat - N

Fishing

Stocked biannually by the Freshwater Fisheries Society of BC, Lost Lake offers a decent fishery for generally small cutthroat. There are also unconfirmed rumours of kokanee here.

Fly anglers will delight at the expansive shallow around the lake, particularly near the inflow and outflow areas. The water drops off sufficiently enough to allow shore fishing, but a floatation devise will go a long ways in helping you work these shoals. Dry flies will work better at certain times of the year and at certain times of the day. Otherwise, the standard wisdom holds: figure out what the fish are eating, and offer them something that looks like food. In spring, this means matching the hatch, while in fall, or during times with no hatches, leech, nymph and attractor patterns like a Carey Special are all things to try.

However, if these aren't working, you can try mixing it up. Flies that imitate wind-blown terrestrials, like winged black ants, can often prove to be successful at certain times of the year. Alternatively, troll searching fly patterns or work small spinners at variable depths to find where the trout are holding.

Similar to many other shallow, low elevation lakes on the Island, the fishery is much better in the spring (April to June) and fall (September and October). This is because trout prefer cooler water and are much more active at these times.

Directions

Lost Lake is located in the mountains above the Inland Island Highway between Campbell River and Courtenay. Road access into this area is restricted so you will have to pay attention to road signs in the area to see if you can even drive in. Even if the roads are open, the lake is tricky to find and the help of a local is recommended.

The lake is accessed by heading north on the Inland Highway (Highway 19) from Courtenay. You will need to cross the Oyster River and take the Cranberry Lane exit, which links up with the Duncan Bay Main. Follow this road back across the river and stay right to access Piggott Main. This logging road leads southwest. Look for Branch Road 181, which courses east, past Little Lost Lake to the southwest shore Lost Lake.

Careful recent logging has created many new roads and road names in the area. A good map like those found in the Backroad Mapbook for Vancouver Island and a GPS with the Backroad GPS Maps will go a long way to helping you find this and other fine fishing lakes in the area.

Facilities

There are no developed facilities at the lake. It is easy enough to camp at roadside and launch a small cartop boat. There are rough campgrounds at a few nearby lakes (Blue Grouse, Began, Wowo), but the nearest actual official campground are back in the Campbell River/Courteney area.

Other Options

Little Lost and **Hell Diver Lakes** are found in the immediate area and are likely to hold the odd trout. However, they are not stocked and we have no recent reports on fishing these lakes so you might be better off searching for **Blue Grouse Lake**, which is found a little higher and to the east. This lake is stocked on opposite years with rainbow and fishing can be quite good for rainbow trout. It is described in more detail earlier in this book.

Area Indicator

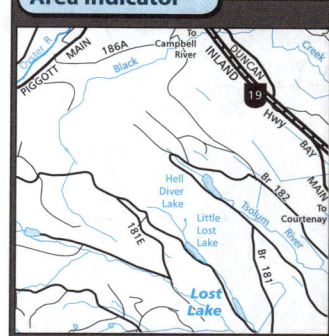

Lost Lake			
Fish Stocking Data			
Year	Species	Number	Life Stage
2007	Cutthroat Trout	500	Yearling

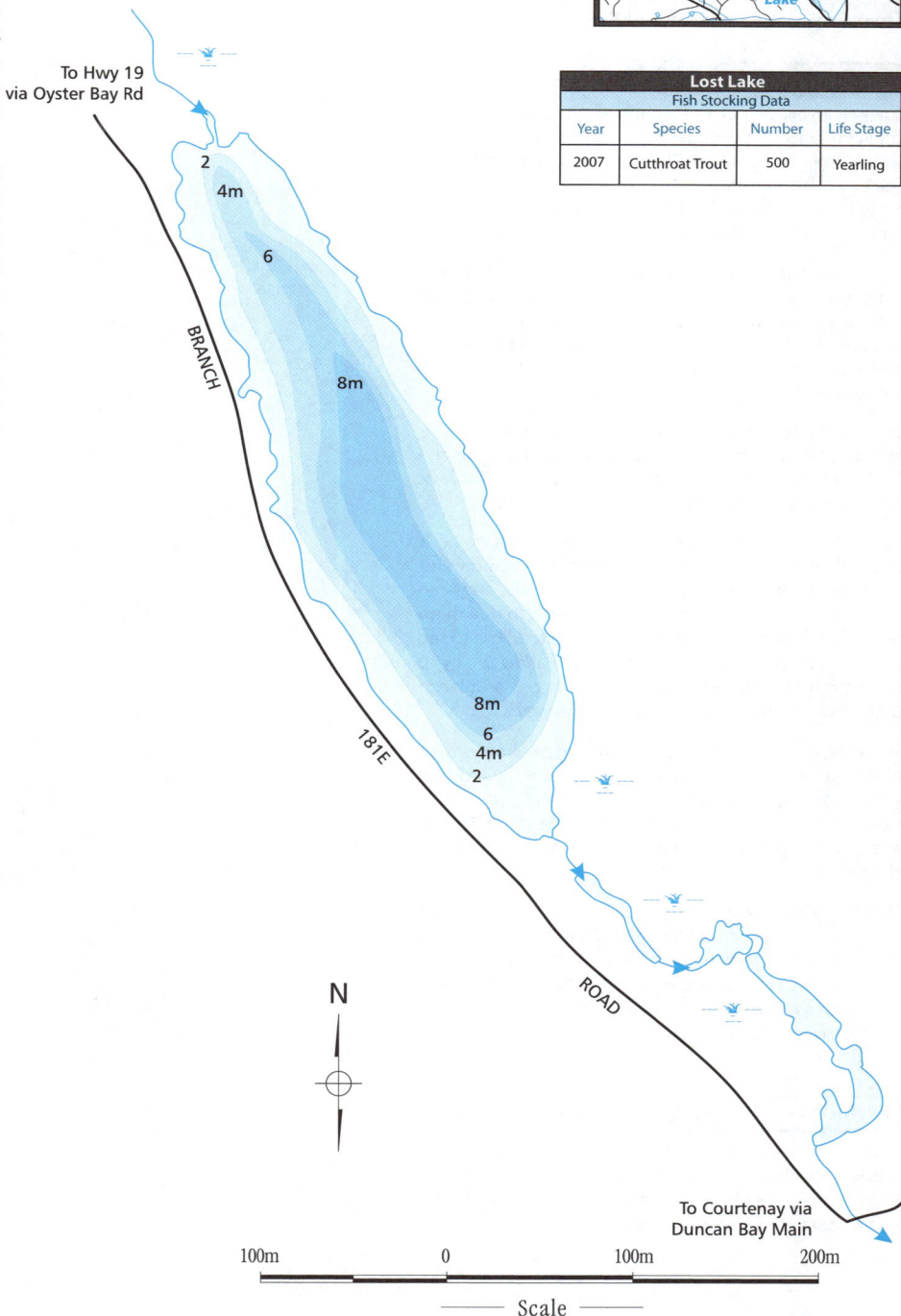

To Hwy 19 via Oyster Bay Rd

2
4m
6
8m
8m
6
4m
2

BRANCH

181E

ROAD

N

To Courtenay via Duncan Bay Main

100m   0   100m   200m

— Scale —

Location: 30 km (18.6 mi) northwest of Port Alberni
Elevation: 136 m (446 ft)
Surface Area: 46 ha (114 ac)
Mean Depth: 5 m (16 ft)
Max Depth: 11 m (36 ft)
Way Point: 125° 08' 00" Lon - W   48° 24' 00" Lat - N

www.backroadmapbooks.com

Lowry Lake

Area Indicator

Directions

Also referred to as Tuck Lake, Lowry Lake is found north of Great Central Lake off the road to Brown's Bay. With wash outs prevalent in the area and the distance of logging road travel required, we recommend bringing a higher clearance vehicle to access the lake.

The lake is reached by travelling on Highway 4 past Port Alberni to the Great Central Lake Road. Continue along the Great Central Lake Road to the community of Great Central. Continue on the graveled Ash River Road to the 6.5 mark. From that location, take Branch 83 (or 8) west. Stay right at the first fork and right again at about 7 km where there is a three way junction. The north branch here leads to the south end of Lowry Lake and the recreation site a short distance later. This road is becoming overgrown and it is no longer possible to drive to the recreation site near the north end of the lake.

Fishing

Lowry is an excellent lake for rainbow and cutthroat trout, yet experiences only moderate use by anglers. The Freshwater Fisheries Society of BC augments the lake's natural spawning with cutthroat each year. Some of these trout grow to about 35 cm (14 in) in size, but the average fish tend to be a lot smaller. Kokanee are also resident.

A good portion of Lowry Lake is fringed with overhanging alder and willow, along with beds of rushes and aquatic weeds – prime habitat for feeding trout and inviting locations for the fly angler. Unfortunately, the brushy and steep shoreline does not lend itself particularly well to shore fishing.

The best times to fish the lake are in April or May and also in the fall from September to October. At that time, fly-fishing can be quite productive. Try anchoring off one of the weedbeds and casting towards the weed beds.

For trollers, the Carey Special and the Doc Spratley, both of which imitate a range of food sources for rainbow and cutthroat trout, are excellent attractor patterns any time of the year. The best way to fish these flies is to troll them with a full sink line in 2–5 m (8–15 ft) of water, close to the bottom. Vary your speed while trolling to allow the fly to hit bottom occasionally. Also, most variations of a leech pattern will perform well throughout the year.

Trout anglers can also find success trolling small spoons, or plugs. Casting spinning gear with small lures towards the weedbeds is another reliable method. Of the hundreds of reliable spinners that can be found in tackle stores, Mepps and Bluefox spinners remain some of the most common choices and are good options.

Those looking for kokanee should remember they are soft mouthed fish. Lures such as the Gibbs Kokanee Katcher lake troll, which incorporate a "snubber" in the troll, will increase the chance of landing one. Most conventional lake trolls with a wedding band and small piece of bait will also produce good results.

Facilities

Found on the east side of the lake, the **Lowry Lake Recreation Site** is a nicely treed site on a fairly remote lake. There is space for about six camping groups along with a rustic boat launch for smaller or cartop boats.

Lowry Lake Fish Stocking Data			
Year	Species	Number	Life Stage
2008	Cutthroat Trout	500	Yearling
2007	Cutthroat Trout	500	Yearling
2006	Cutthroat Trout	500	Yearling

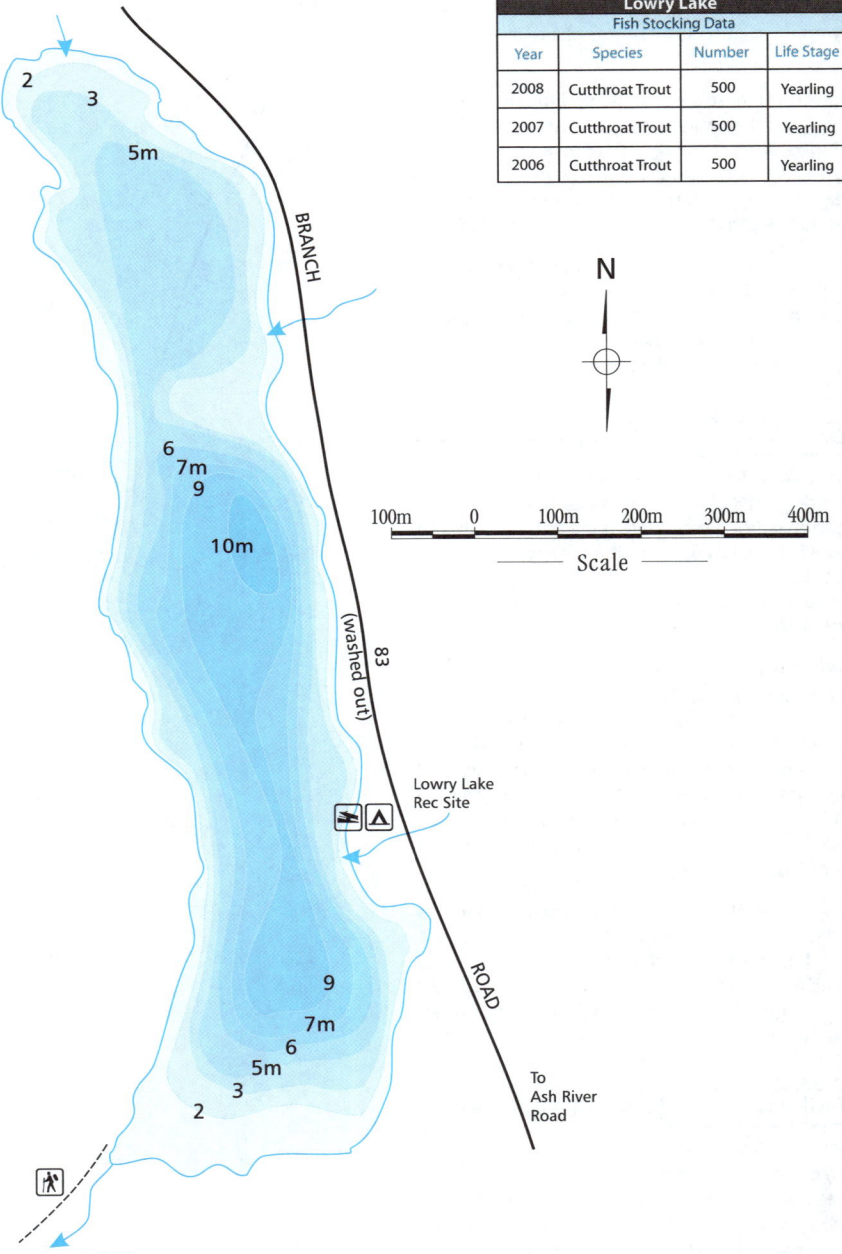

N

100m   0   100m   200m   300m   400m
Scale

BRANCH

83 (washed out)

Lowry Lake Rec Site

ROAD

To Ash River Road

2
3
5m
6
7m
9
10m
9
7m
6
5m
3
2

www.backroadmapbooks.com

Maple Lake

Location: 5 km (3 mi) south of Courtenay
Elevation: 136 m (446 ft)
Surface Area: 28 ha (69 ac)
Mean Depth: 6 m (20 ft)
Max Depth: 13 m (43 ft)
Way Point: 125° 01' 00" Lon - W 49° 38' 00" Lat - N

Fishing

Its close proximity to the town of Courtenay and the good-sized trout it produces makes Maple Lake a favourite location for local residents. To help offset the busy fishery, the Freshwater Fisheries Society of BC stocks the lake annually with thousands of catchable size rainbow trout.

Another nice aspect of the lake is the fact that it can be productive year round. However, seasoned anglers report the best fishing occurs between October and April. The lake is quite small and shallow, so the water tends to warm up by late spring.

For those fishing with a spinning or spincasting rod and reel, there are a few spots to fish along the shore, although most anglers ply the waters using cartop boats, pontoons or float tubes. Some of the frequently used lures on Maple Lake include Panther Martins (Regular Gold), Mepps (Black Fury), Gibbs Hockey Sticks or Flatfish (frog colour). Probably the simplest way to catch fish and introduce young people or novice anglers to sport fishing is by a technique known as still fishing. When still fishing from the shore or a boat, the angler casts out and waits for a bite. Floats (bobbers) can be attached to the line so the baited hook stays suspended in the water. The depth can be adjusted by simply sliding the float up or down the line.

If you're a fly angler, there are expansive shallows at the south end of the lake as well as two small islands around which to work when the waters are cooler. This area also produces in late summer when there is usually a short but productive evening bite. Others prefer working the deeper water at the north end of the lake during summer. The Carey Special and the Doc Spratley, both of which imitate a range of food sources for rainbow and cutthroat trout, are excellent attractor patterns at Maple Lake any time of the year. The best way to fish these flies is to troll them with a full sink line in 2–4 m (8–15 ft) of water, close to the bottom. Your fly should hit bottom occasionally when fishing these flies properly. Vary your speed while trolling the fly.

Leeches, damselfly nymphs and dragonfly nymphs are important food sources for Maple's trout, and these patterns remain reliable most of the year. Black, brown, olive green or maroon leech patterns, tied in many of the common commercial patterns found in tackle shops, are good choices when the fish don't seem to be biting on anything else. One successful leech imitation on Maple Lake is a No. 10 olive leech tied with Angora goat dubbing and green crystal flash in the tail.

There is an electric motor only restriction on the lake.

Directions

Maple Lake is found south of Courtenay next to the Inland Island Highway. You will need to follow the Comox Valley Parkway to Minto Road. Turn left and drive past the cemetery and under the highway to access the parking area. There is a rough boat launch available for non-motorized boats beyond the parking area. Anglers should also note the gate is closed nightly at 8 pm.

Facilities

If the gate is open, there is a cartop boat launch that is found about 200 metres from the parking lot. There is a rough road down to the launch that high clearance vehicles can negotiate; otherwise it is easy enough to carry small craft down.

Area Indicator

Maple Lake			
Fish Stocking Data			
Year	Species	Number	Life Stage
2011	Rainbow Trout	2,500	Catchables
2010	Rainbow Trout	5,981	Catchables
2009	Rainbow Trout	6,000	Catchables

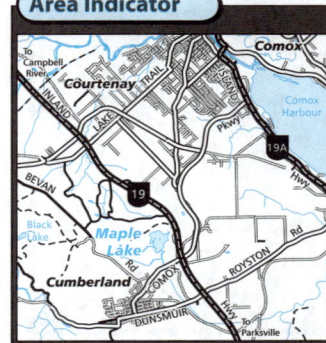

Location: 27 km (17 mi) southwest of Victoria
Elevation: 21 m (69 ft)
Surface Area: 25 ha (62 ac)
Mean Depth: 3 m (10 ft)
Max Depth: 5 m (16 ft)
Way Point: 123° 36′00″ Lon - W 48° 22′00″ Lat - N

www.backroadmapbooks.com

Matheson Lake

Area Indicator

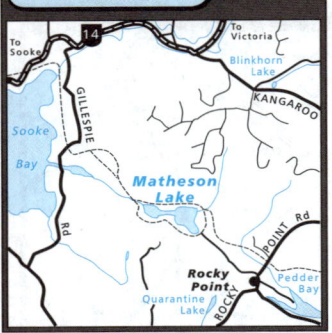

Matheson Lake Fish Stocking Data			
Year	Species	Number	Life Stage
2011	Rainbow Trout	1,000	Catchables
2010	Rainbow Trout	2,000	Catchables
2009	Rainbow Trout	2,000	Catchables

Fishing

Matheson Lake is a popular fishing lake found southwest of Victoria. The lake offers an early season fishery that begins as early as April for small cutthroat and rainbow trout. There are also a few larger Dolly Varden (to 1.5 kg/3 lbs) and smallmouth bass.

If you have a boat or float tube, try casting towards the weedbeds with a dragonfly or damselfly nymph. Alternatively, cast a small lure with a worm or use bait and a bobber. However, many people work the lake from the open shore.

As is typical of these shallow, low elevation lakes that hold both trout and bass, there are three distinct seasons. Spring is a great time for fly-fishing, as insects begin to hatch. Imitating these hatching insects is at the heart of what fly-fishing is all about. The chironomid hatch begins in April and runs to mid-July. Another early hatch is the dragonfly nymph which starts at the end of April.

In the summer months when the trout fishing is at a stand still, the bass fishery is at its best. The bass are caught on attractor type fly patterns such as a Woolly Bugger or Leech patterns. If spincasting, there are many different plugs such as Rapalas to use. The bass hang around the lily pads so cast as close to the vegetation as possible. The bigger fish tend to hold deeper, and further under cover, and snagging one of these wiley fish can be a very satisfying experience. Of course, because bass like cover, it is easy to get your gear snagged. There are specific lures that are less likely to snag the weeds, or you can use a simple hook baited with a worm in such a way as to keep the hook from snagging. There are a variety of methods, but the most popular are the Texas Rig and the Carolina Rig.

As the water begins to cool down again in fall, the bass start to retreat to the deeper areas of the lake, while the trout shake off their summer doldrums and begin feeding again in earnest. While there are occasional fall hatches, the fish are bulking up for the winter and tend to prefer larger food sources. Nymphs and leeches work well, as do attractor patterns like the Carey Special or the Woolly Bugger.

There is an electric motors only restriction at the lake and the bass must be released.

Directions

Matheson Lake is easily accessed by taking Highway 14 to the Happy Valley Highway turnoff. Head south to the Rocky Point Road turnoff and continue on the Rocky Point Road to the tiny community of Rocky Point. The access road to the park heads northwest from Rocky Point to the Matheson Lake Regional Park parking lot at the east end of the lake.

Alternatively, continue on Highway 14 past the Happy Valley Highway to Gillespie Road. Head south and you will find the trailhead into the park that leads to the west end of the lake.

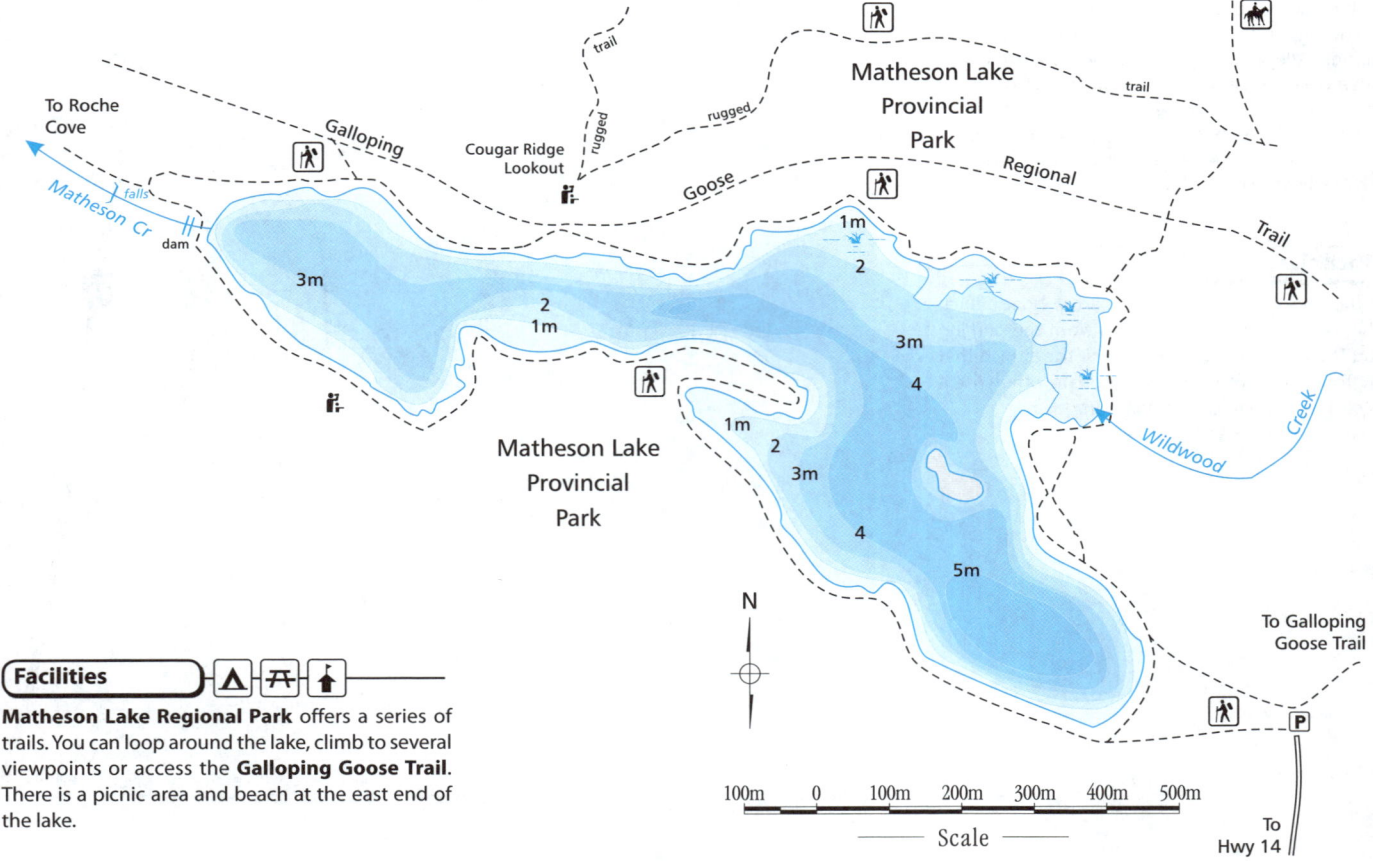

Facilities

Matheson Lake Regional Park offers a series of trails. You can loop around the lake, climb to several viewpoints or access the **Galloping Goose Trail**. There is a picnic area and beach at the east end of the lake.

Maynard Lake

Location: 25 km (15.5 mi) southwest of Port McNeill
Elevation: 175 m (574 ft)
Surface Area: 84 ha (208 ac)
Mean Depth: 13m (43 ft)
Max Depth: 39 m (128 ft)
Way Point: 127° 12′00″ Lon - W 50° 24′00″ Lat - N

Fishing

Maynard Lake is a small man-made lake found southwest of Port McNeill. The lake is known for producing well for small cutthroat to 30 cm (12 in). It is also known for producing much bigger fish on occasion, but only rarely. The lake also holds Dolly Varden and some steelhead. It is one of a group of great fishing lakes found just east of the larger Alice and Victoria Lakes.

Maynard Lake rests at a low elevation, but is fairly deep, which means that fishing slows down in summer, but doesn't stop. The trick with fishing deeper in summer is to not snag any of the submerged trees that are still at the bottom of the lake. Actually, these trees prove to be a bit of a challenge at any time of the year, creating both a snag hazard for your line and a navigation hazard for your boat.

Because of the drowned trees, trolling the lake can be a little difficult. It's not impossible, and there is a boat launch to get you out onto the lake, but losing a lure or three is a definite possibility. You might find it easier to find a nice spot and cast from the boat using a small spoon or a lure tipped with a worm. The lake is quite deep in the middle, so snagging isn't an issue here. However, the fish prefer the transition zones that unfortunately also host many of the old trees and snags.

There are large log jams at the north and south end of the lake, and a log boom down towards the dam. The jams should be approached with caution, but should be viewed with interest, especially early in the year. They not only provide cover for the fish, but there are inflow streams from both locations, which wash down all manner of food for the hungry fish.

There is a beach at the northeast corner of the lake, close enough to the inflow of Three Lakes Creek to be an attractive spot to fish. Casting from the beach with a simple worm and bobber can prove to be extremely effective. Of course, you can cast whatever you like here – spoons, flies, plugs if you really want to. The point is, you don't have to be fancy to have good success, and indeed, it is easier and often more effective to keep things simple.

Other Options

There are a number of great fishing lakes in the same area as Maynard Lake. **Benson Lake** is the closest, and is found just a short way below the dam at the southwest end of the lake. Past Benson is **Kathleen Lake**, while north of Maynard is **Keogh Lake**. All these lakes are written up elsewhere in the book.

Facilities

There is a boat launch and an informal campground at the south end of the lake. Unfortunately, it rests a little too close to Keogh Main, a busy logging road, to make it a perfect getaway spot.

Directions

Maynard Lake is found alongside the Keogh Main Road, 25 km (15.5 miles) southwest of Port McNeil. To get here, take Keogh Lake Main from the Island Highway (Highway 19) south past Keogh Lake. You will pass are a couple small lakes along the route before hit-ting Maynard.

Note that access into the area is restricted during periods of active hauling. Check with the locals before heading out.

Area Indicator

Location: 47 km (29 miles) northwest of Campbell River
Elevation: 60 m (197 ft)
Surface Area: 272 ha (672 ac)
Mean Depth: 31 m (102 ft)
Max Depth: 55 m (180 ft)
Way Point: 125° 38' 00" Lon - W 50° 18' 00" Lat - N

www.backroadmapbooks.com

McCreight Lake

Area Indicator

Fishing

Named after BC's first premier, John Foster McCreight, this lake is also known as Bear Lake. It is a very scenic lake found along the Rock Bay Forest Road that makes a popular fishing and camping destination.

Part of that popularity can be ascribed to the long fishing season. The lake is found at a fairly low elevation, but is fairly deep. The season can get underway as early as April, and continues throughout the year. While the fishing does slow down in summer, the lake still produces well for rainbow and stocked cutthroat, even on the hottest days. The lake also holds Dolly Varden and kokanee.

Because the lake is so deep, trolling is the most popular way to fish the lake. In the spring, work the drop-off with spoons, wet flies or a lake troll. In the summer, the fish head into a narrow band of water between the warm surface (littoral) water and the cold, oxygen-less depths. This area is called the thermocline, and once you have found the right depth, you can basically work the entire lake at this depth. However, there are some areas that are better than others, and the fish will still usually be found hanging around places where they can mount furtive expeditions into the shoals, which is where they find the majority of their food. Working these transition areas will produce the best results.

Another popular strategy is to try is the inlet or outlet of Amor de Cosmos Creek. Inflowing creeks wash down all manner of food and contain cool, oxygenated water. Fish tend to hang around these areas because rather than having to go find food, the food comes to them.

The water drops off quickly and the shore is open in places, making it a good lake to fish from shore. Many groups cross to the west side of the lake, to Bear Beach, and fish from the beach using a simple worm and bobber or a spoon.

McCreight Lake
Fish Stocking Data

Year	Species	Number	Life Stage
2007	Cutthroat Trout	5,000	Yearling
2006	Cutthroat Trout	5,000	Yearling
2005	Cutthroat Trout	5,000	Yearling

Directions

McCreight Lake is located about 47 km (29 miles) northwest of Campbell River. To get there, take the Island Highway (Highway 19) north for about 40 km (25 miles). Watch for the Rock Bay Road. If you cross Amor de Cosmos Creek, you've gone too far.

Turn north onto Rock Bay Road, and follow it to the lake. You can stop at Alder Grove Recreation Site, but if you bring a boat, it is much easier to launch at the McCreight Lake Recreation Site. This site is found about 6.5 km from the highway along a good gravel road.

Facilities

McCreight has not one, but four (count 'em) recreation sites on its shores. **Bear Beach** is a user maintained tenting site on the west side of the lake that is water accessed only. **Sitka Spruce** is a walk in site on the east side of the lake. **Alder Grove** is just north of Sitka Spruce, but only has space for two groups. It is best known for its beach. The biggest site on the lake is the **McCreight Lake Recreation Site**, which has four units, and a steep gravel boat launch. It is a popular site with anglers and wind surfers.

Other Options

Nearby **Stella Lake** is a popular lake with similar fishing as McCreight. Between the two is **Pye Lake**, which has cutthroat and Dolly Varden. Both are written up elsewhere in the book.

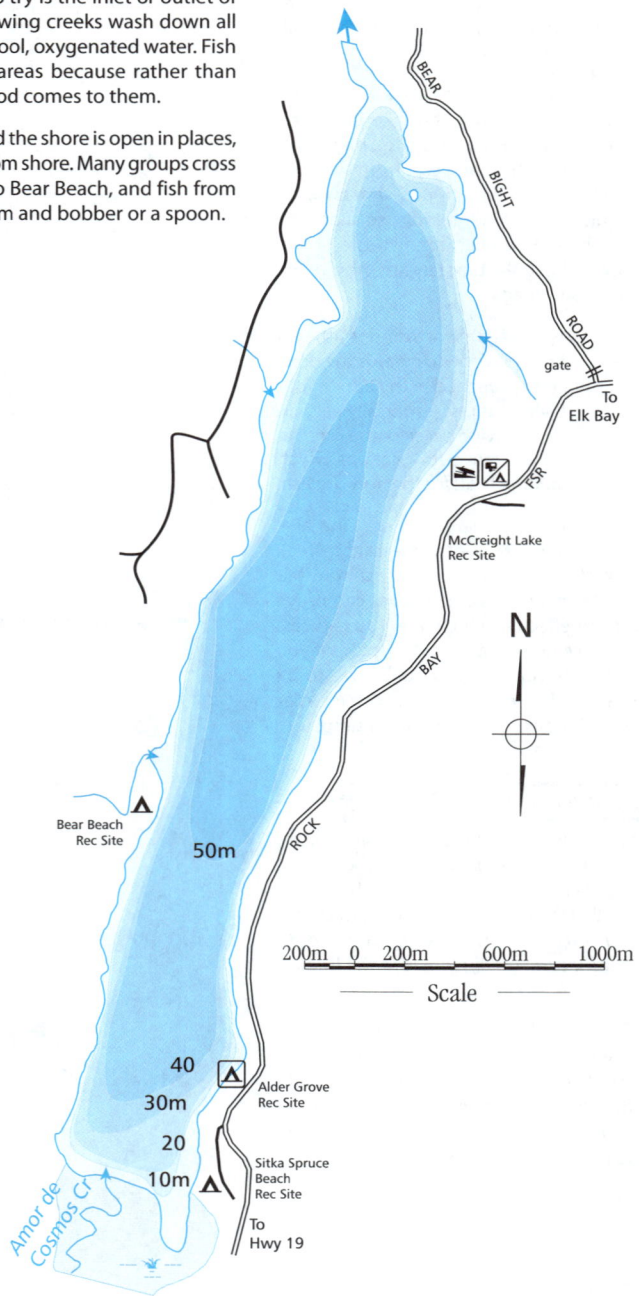

200m 0 200m 600m 1000m
— Scale —

N

© Mussio Ventures Ltd.

McKay Lake

Location: 16 km (10 mi) north of Ladysmith
Elevation: 155 m (508 ft)
Surface Area: 2.5 ha (6 ac)
Mean Depth: 3 m (10 ft)
Max Depth: 8 m (26 ft)
Way Point: 125° 17' 00" Lon - W 49° 46' 00" Lat - N

Fishing

McKay is a shallow lake, with most of lake being shoal. This means that it is a great fly-fishing lake for small stocked cutthroat to 35 cm (14 in). Specifically, it is known for its chironomid hatch, which peaks in late April or early May.

If fishing the early spring in the morning or mid-day, the best way to catch fish using a chironomid imitation is to us an intermediate sinking line or a sinking tip line. Work a brown, black or red bodied pupae imitation in 6-9 m (20-30 feet) of water such that it is within a few feet of the bottom. Slowly retrieve the fly or use a strike indicator and leave the fly just off the bottom.

In the evenings, working the fly in the surface layer of the water with a floating line and long leader is very effective. This is because as the day progresses, the insects make their way to the surface and the fish follow along. You can literally see the cruising fish. Try casting in front of the fish hoping that the fish will take your fly.

There are no restrictions on the lake that say you can't use other gear, so if you don't have a fly rod, you can always try just spincasting a small spoon, or a hook tipped with a worm.

As the summer approaches, the lake is not deep enough to withstand the summer doldrums. As a result, fishing tails off substantially and does not get better until the cooler evenings in the fall.

Shore fishing is restricted because of the marshy area surrounding the lake. The best place to fish from shore is from the floating bridge at the south end of the lake.

Facilities

There is an old sawmill at the north end of the lake where you can still see some remains. Alternatively there is a large parking area located on the west side of the lake that is ideal for camping and picnicking. From that area, the floating bridge can be found. Getting a boat into the lake can be a challenge given the marshy shoreline.

Other Options

Crystal Lake is a dark water lake located nearby to McKay Lake that has good cutthroat fishing in the spring. In particular, the chironomid hatch in April and May can be a great time to fish if you use a brown coloured pupae imitation. Try in the evenings when the stocked fish are cruising the subsurface water level in search of hatching insects. There is a small, decaying dock, a cartop boat launch next to the dock and camping nearby.

Directions

McKay Lake is found east of the Nanaimo Airport and nearby to Crystal and Timberland Lakes. Despite its very good fishing and close proximity to Nanaimo, it does not receive a lot of fishing pressure.

To reach lake, drive west on Spruston Road, which takes off from the Island Highway just north of the Haslam Creek Bridge. The first 8 km of Spruston Road is paved and then you come to an orange gate with a sign saying "Fletcher Challenge Canada-McKay Lake Division". Travel through the gate, which is usually open, and drive on McKay Lake Forest Service Road and then Branch 100. An access road leads to the parking area on the west side of the lake.

A truck is recommended to access the lake. It is best to inquire locally before planning a trip into the area, as access into this area may be closed or restricted.

Area Indicator

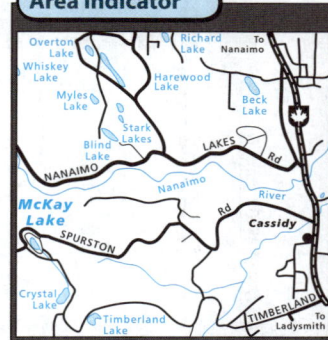

McKay Lake			
Fish Stocking Data			
Year	Species	Number	Life Stage
2009	Cutthroat Trout	500	Yearling
2008	Cutthroat Trout	500	Yearling
2007	Cutthroat Trout	500	Yearling

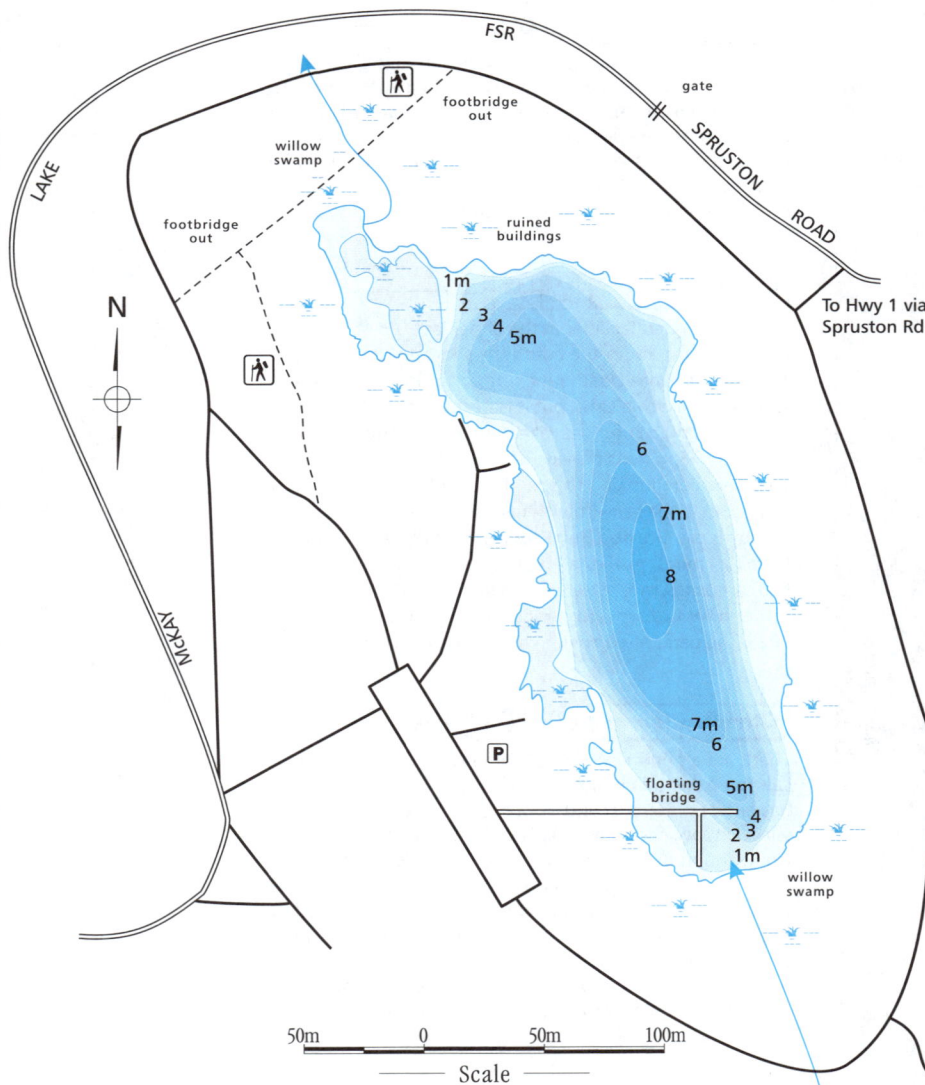

50m   0   50m   100m
Scale

Mesachie & Beaver Lakes

Beaver Lake

Elevation: 181 m (594 ft)
Surface Area: 19 ha (47 ac)
Mean Depth: 3.5 m (11.5 ft)
Max Depth: 7.5 m (16.5 ft)
Way Point: 124° 05' 00" Lon - W 48° 49' 00" Lat - N

Area Indicator

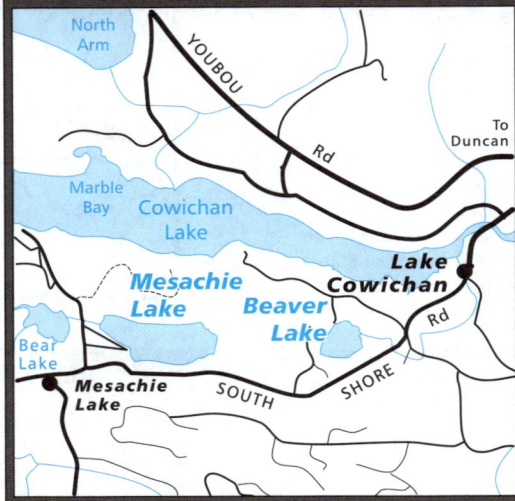

Directions

Both lakes are found near the town of Lake Cowichan, which is easily reached by driving west along Highway 18 from Duncan. At Lake Cowichan, turn south and follow the South Shore Road. Beaver Lake is 2 km (1.2 miles) from Lake Cowichan on the north side of South Shore Road, while Mesachie Lake is 3 km (1.8 miles) further along. If you reach the community of Mesachie Lake you have gone too far.

Facilities

There are limited facilities at the either lake. An abandoned railgrade runs along the southern shores of Beaver Lake. There is a private boat launch at Camp Imadene, on the shores of Mesachie Lake, but it is best to contact the camp before setting out for the lake with a boat. There is also a series of hiking trails provide access to the west end of the lake. If you are looking to spend the night, there are many campsites in the Lake Cowichan area. A nice site that is very nearby is the **Gordon Bay Provincial Park**, which is found 9 km (5.4 miles) further along the South Shore Road. It has 126 campsites, most of which can be reserved ahead of time through www.discovercamping.ca, or by calling 1-800-689-9025. The parks also provides access to Cowichan Lake.

Other Options

There are a number of great fishing lakes in the Cowichan Lake area, including, not surprisingly, Cowichan Lake itself. It is one of the largest and most popular lakes on the Island, with rainbow, cutthroat, kokanee, dollies and the odd brown trout. The trout are said to grow to 3 kg (7 lbs) but you are more likely to catch one in the 1 to 1.5 kg (3 lb) range. The kokanee tend to be very small and are usually not targeted by anglers. The best time to fish the lake is in early and late winter as well as during the spring and fall shoulder seasons. However, the lake is big enough to be produce throughout the year. The lake is written up in more detail earlier in this book.

Mesachie Lakes

Elevation: 167 m (548 ft)
Surface Area: 59 ha (146 ac)
Mean Depth: 8.5 m (28 ft)
Max Depth: 32 m (105 ft)
Way Point: 124° 06' 00" Lon - W 48° 49' 00" Lat - N

Fishing

Mesachie and Beaver Lakes are a pair of small, often overlooked lakes found southwest of the town of Lake Cowichan. They have no public facilities on their shores and have not been developed as fishing lakes. While the fishing can be hit and miss in both lakes, they are certainly worth trying if you are in the area.

Mesachie Lake is the bigger of the two, with cutthroat, rainbow, Dolly Varden and kokanee. The lake does not hold a lot of fish, and fishing can be slow. But the occasional trout to 40 cm (16 inches) can make those slow times worth the wait.

Mesachie Lake is a low elevation lake, but quite deep. Fishing gets underway early in spring, usually around April. There is an outflow stream in the northwest corner of the lake that should feature good fishing, as well as a point and bay in the southwest corner. These two locations should be the focus of your attention.

Boaters should troll a gang troll or plug like a Rapala or Flatfish around the lake just offshore from the prominent drop-off. Rainbow tend to chase after lures that are moving quite quickly. Small metallic spoons and spinners can also work well on the troll. In the early spring and later in the fall, fly-fishermen can do well working the fringes of the lake. The lake has some insect life, but is not teeming with hatches. There are occasional top-water opportunities (especially later in the evening in the early summer), but anglers should come prepared to work things like leeches, nymphs Woolly Buggers and Doc Spratleys deeper. The lake has a fair population of bait fish, and working a Muddler Minnow or streamer pattern will also work well.

Of course, spincasters can do equally well from the shore simply by casting a baited hook and bobber. As always getting on the water in a float tube or canoe will help work the lake better, but there is enough area to fish from shore.

Beaver Lake is east of Mesachie Lake and holds fair numbers of rainbow, cutthroat and Dolly Varden. Like Mesachie, fishing can begin as early as April. Unlike Mesachie, Beaver is a shallow lake, and in the summer the fishing slows nearly to a standstill. By early September, the fishing starts to pick up again

The lake is fairly hard to fish from shore, but the southwest corner of the lake is your best bet if you are restricted to the shoreline. The eastern shoreline is definitely too marshy and shallow for shore fishing. However, the best way to work the lake is from a float tube or a canoe.

The deepest part of the lake is right in the middle. Fly-fishermen should work that area, casting out towards the shoreline with a sinking line and nymph or chironomid imitation. These should be worked just off the bottom, and retrieved quite slowly. Spincasters should try a small lure tipped with a worm and a bobber. The shallow lake is difficult to troll, but people have done it. Float tube anglers will find that slowly dragging a lure behind the tube can actually improve success.

Watch for trout rising to the surface, chasing after insects after the sun is no longer hitting the lake and the wind has calmed. These are the magic hours for fly anglers. If it is a caddis hatch going on, a popular pattern is a Tom Thumb

Mesachie & Beaver Lakes

Beaver Lake

50m 0 50m 100m 150m 200m
Scale

N

2 1m
3m
4
5m

6

3m 4 4 7m
2
5m
1m

5m
4

5m 3m 3m

2

2
1m

wharf

private
property

To
Lake Cowichan

ROAD

SHORE

SOUTH

To
Mesachie Lake

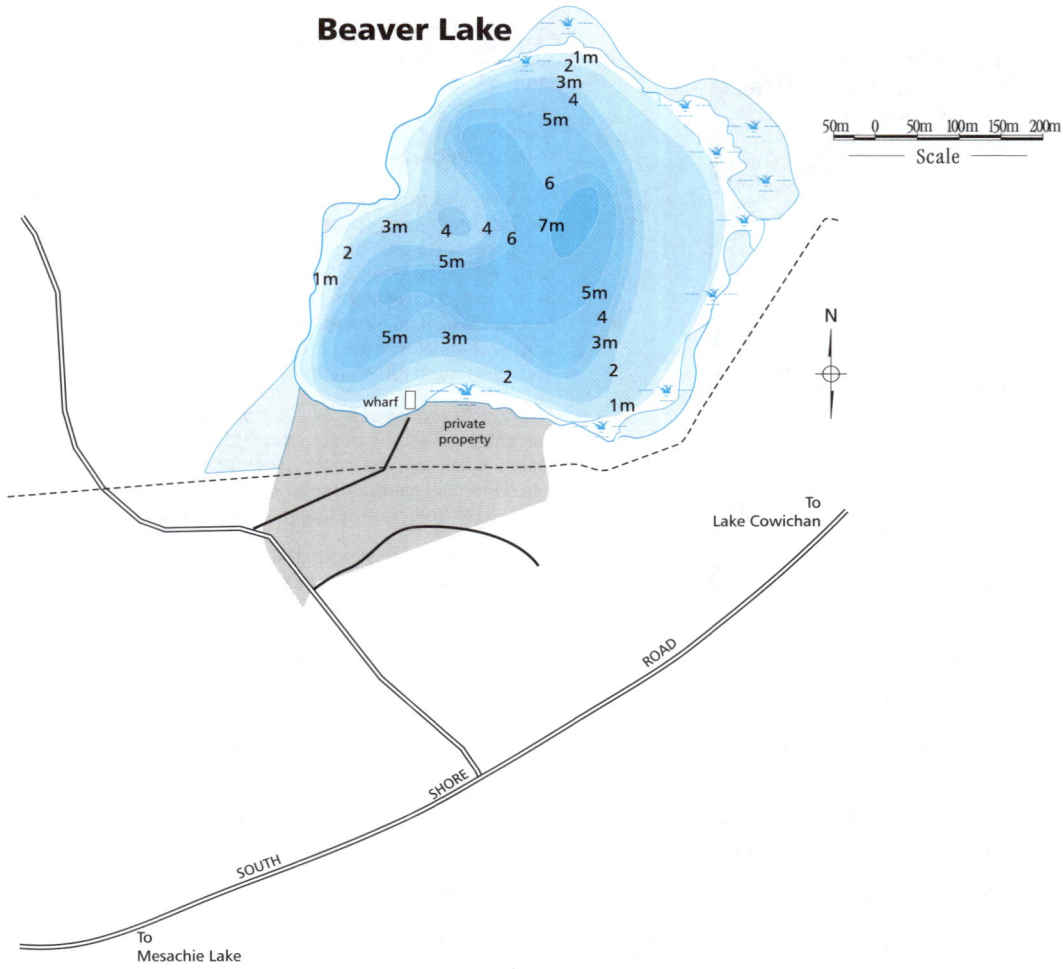

Elevation: 181 m (594 ft)
Surface Area: 19 ha (47 ac)
Mean Depth: 3.5 m (11.5 ft)
Max Depth: 7.5 m (16.5 ft)
Way Point: 124° 05' 00" Lon - W 48° 49' 00" Lat - N

Beaver Lake

Mesachie Lake

100m 0 100m 200m 300m 400m 500m
Scale

N

FOREST

ROAD

6 3
9
12m
15
18
21m

24
27m
30

3
6m

27m

30

21m 18
24
15 12m 9 6 3

3
6
18 24m
15 21
12
9m

SOUTH

abandoned

railway

SHORE

ROAD

To
Honeymoon
Bay

To
Beaver
Lake

Elevation: 167 m (548 ft)
Surface Area: 59 ha (146 ac)
Mean Depth: 8.5 m (28 ft)
Max Depth: 32 m (105 ft)
Way Point: 124° 06' 00" Lon - W 48° 49' 00" Lat - N

Mesachie Lakes

Mohun & Goose Lakes

Location: 25 km (15.5 mi) northwest of Campbell River
Elevation: 205 m (673 ft)
Surface Area: 603 ha (1,489 ac)
Mean Depth: 14 m (46 ft)
Max Depth: 43 m (141 ft)
Way Point: 125° 29′00″ Lon - W 50° 7′00″ Lat - N

Area Indicator

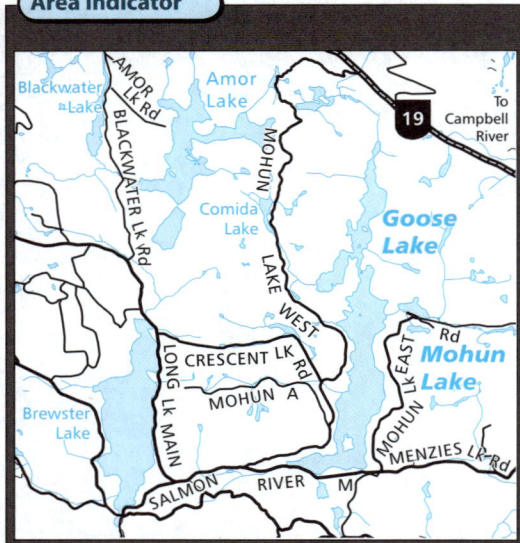

Directions

Mohun Lake is one of the main lakes in the Sayward Forest. Access to the lake is from mainline logging roads that run up both the east and the western shores of the lake. Menzies Main leaves the Island Highway (Highway 19) just north of the just north of the sawmill on Highway 19 at Menzies Bay, which in turn is about 15 km north of Campbell River. Watch for signs. From the turnoff, it is about 11 km to the Mohun Lake Recreation Site or private campsite on the south side of the lake.

Turning north on the Mohun Lake East Road will bring you to Morton Provincial Park, about halfway along the eastern shores of the lake. There is a boat launch onto Mohun Lake here as well.

Alternately, the north end of Goose/Mohun Lake is accessed by the very rough North Mohun Main, which is found about 22 km from the north end of Campbell River. Deep cross ditches make this road all but impassible beyond the 1.4km mark so it is best to walk the last 300 metres or so to the lake and Seagull Bay Recreation Site.

Facilities

Mohun Lake is part of the **Sayward Forest Canoe Route**. As a result, the lake has more developed recreation sites than most other lakes. There are water accessible sites scattered around the lake including the signature site on the large island near the south end of the lake. Other water access sites are found on either side of the narrows between the southern part of the lake and the northern, and along the eastern shores of the lake.

The **Mohun Lake Recreation Site and Morton Lake Campground** are found at the south end of the lake. The private campsite is the more developed of the two with over twenty sites and a cement boat ramp. The two site recreation site is mainly used as an access point to the canoe route. Further north, **Morton Lake Provincial Park** is found along the eastern shores of the lake. In addition to 24 campsites and a series of trails, there is a boat launch onto Mohun Lake.

Adding to the mix is the **Seagull Bay Recreation Site** at the north end of Goose Lake (or the northern extension of Mohun Lake). The small walk-in site offers little more than a place to pitch a tent.

Fishing

Mohun Lake is the longest lake in the Sayward Forest area. It is part of the Sayward Forest Canoe Route, but is equally popular with trout anglers as it is with canoeists. The lake is not stocked, at least not anymore, but it still has strong populations of rainbow and cutthroat trout.

The long and thin lake has very tight, narrow passages between the three sections of the lake. These were once bridged by logging roads and the old pilings make it a bit difficult to get from one end of the lake to the other. These narrow channels effectively divide the lake into three separate areas. In fact, the northern section of Mohun Lake is often considered its own lake, and is called **Goose Lake** on many maps (including ours). This section is again divided by a narrow channel, and the northernmost section is the smallest and shallowest, and offers good fishing early in the year.

The middle section of Mohun has plenty of structure, including bays, points, and small islands. Such structure attracts fish, making this one of the best places to fish. The southernmost section is the largest. It has one large island and one small island, and several small bays. It is the deepest section, and the fish tend to hold here during the dog days of summer.

Shoreline fishers will find that fishing is possible right from the campsite at the south end of the lake. The open shoreline begins to close in as you make your way east and west, so you only have about 1 km (0.6 miles) of accessible shoreline. Still, this is enough for most people. A simple worm and bobber set-up will do just fine, but you can try spoons, spinners and a variety of wet flies. In the evening or early morning when the fish start to rise, fly-fishers will want to switch over to dry flies.

Because of the size of the main body of the lake, this section attracts trollers, who could do worse than working a lake troll, spinner or spoon around the shores of the lake. Productive areas include the island at the south end, the bay with a feeder stream in the southwestern corner of the lake, as well the other stream about 1.5 km further along the western shore. Also working near the channel between the southern and northern section of the lake should produce well.

The northern section of the lake will attract more finesse anglers, and there is lots of structure to choose from. It would probably take a couple weeks to do this section of the lake justice.

While the fishing remains fair throughout the summer, April and May are the best time to fish here, especially if you plan on eating what you catch. Later in the year the fish begin to take on a weedy taste. While the fishing picks up again in fall, the quality of the fish (for eating) does not. If you are planning on visiting this lake after the spring, it is advised to practice catch-and-release.

Other Options

Mohun Lake is just one of dozens of lakes in the Sayward Forest. Nearby **Brewster Lake** is written up elsewhere in this book. **Amor Lake**, just west of Mohun, is not. The lake is accessed by a short portage from **Twin Lake** (itself a good fishing lake for rainbow and stocked cutthroat trout). Twin Lake, in turn is accessed from the end of Mohun Lake. To access Amor Lake by vehicle, drive west past Mohun Lake to the Long Lake Main. Turn north and follow this to the Blackwater Lake Road, and then onto the Amor Lake Road. Amor Lake holds good numbers of cutthroat, as well as some Dolly Varden.

Morton Lake, just east of Mohun, is stocked annually with cutthroat as is the small lake just to the south of Morton. Morton Lake is mostly shallow and anglers love coming here in spring, when the cutthroat rise every evening in the bay near the campground. A dry fly, small spinners or even bait and bobber set-ups all work well just before it gets dark. There is an electric motor only restriction on the lake.

Mohun & Goose Lakes

Location: 25 km (15.5 mi) northwest of Campbell River
Elevation: 205 m (673 ft)
Surface Area: 603 ha (1,489 ac)
Mean Depth: 14 m (46 ft)
Max Depth: 43 m (141 ft)
Way Point: 125° 29'00"Lon - W 50° 7'00"Lat - N

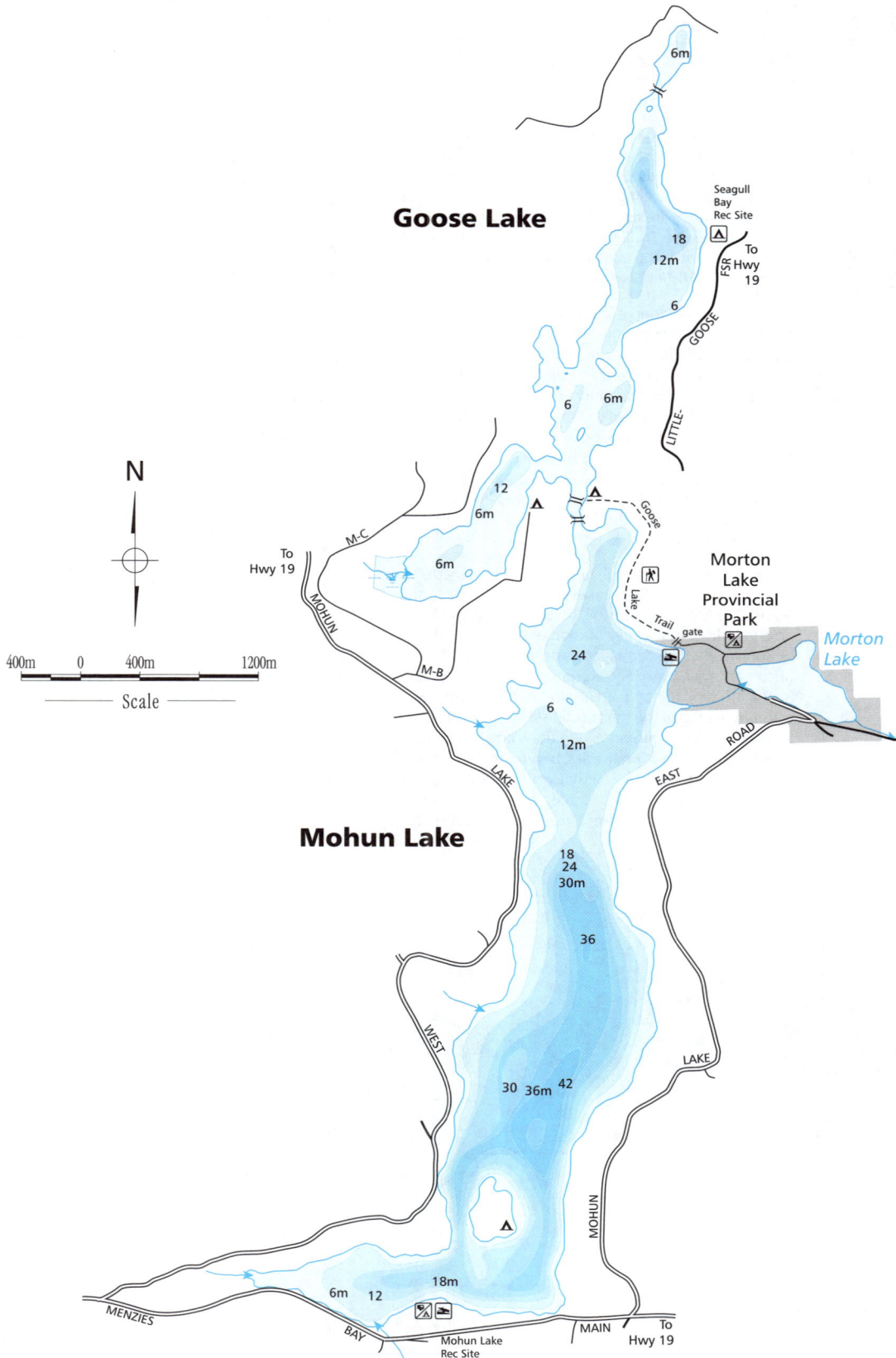

6m

Goose Lake

Seagull
Bay
Rec Site

18
12m

6

To
Hwy
19

6

6m

N

12

6m

M-C

To
Hwy
19

6m

Goose

Lake

Morton
Lake
Provincial
Park

*Morton
Lake*

gate

M-B

24

6

400m   0   400m   1200m

— Scale —

12m

Mohun Lake

18
24
30m

36

EAST

ROAD

LAKE

WEST

30 36m 42

LAKE

MOHUN

18m

6m 12

MENZIES

BAY

MAIN

To
Hwy 19

Mohun Lake
Rec Site

Location: 19 km (11.7 mi) from Gold River
Elevation: 202 m (180 ft)
Surface Area: 642 ha (59 ac)
Mean Depth: 38 m (28 ft)
Max Depth: 63 m (56 ft)
Way Point: 126° 11′ 00″Lon - W 49° 52′ 00″Lat - N

www.backroadmapbooks.com

Muchalat Lake

Area Indicator

Fishing

Muchalat Lake is a fairly big lake north of the town of Gold River. The lake holds plenty of rainbow and cutthroat that can get to 1.5 kg (3 lbs). The lake also has a few kokanee and Dolly Varden to entice anglers.

While there are occasionally big fish to be found here, the lake is better known for having fast and furious fishing for smaller rainbow and cutthroat. It is certainly possible to cast a fly here, but trolling or spincasting tends to produce better. As the fish are smaller, you should use lighter gear and smaller lures. Trolling a small spoon or gang troll should work well. The lake is deep enough to maintain a fairly decent fishery even in the heat of the summer.

The lake has a number of feeder streams that wash down food and cool, oxygenated water. Focus your efforts around these inflow streams, especially early in spring. The two main rivers are the Oktwanch, which flows in from the north, and the Muchalat, which flows in from the west, but there are many small streams that can be tested as well. Another popular place to try is near the outflow of the Muchalat River. All the water from the lake eventually flows down the Muchalat, taking along all manner of food. The fish tend to congregate around the outflow, as waiting for the food to come to them is a lot easier than going out and finding the food.

In the summer, when the fishing slows down, try trolling deeper, but not too deep. Lakes stratify into three distinct layers. The lowest depths of the lake are very cold, but hold very little in the way of food or oxygen for the fish to survive on. The top layer has plenty of food, but is uncomfortably warm for cold water species such as trout. So the fish tend to hang out just below this warm layer of water, at the top of the thermocline layer. From here, they can mount brief foraging expeditions into the shoals. It is along these transitional areas, between where the fish live and where the fish eat, that you should focus your efforts. A slow troll works, as does casting from deeper water across this transition zone, and retrieving back towards the fish.

Directions

Muchalat Lake is about 18 km northwest of Gold River along the Nimpkish Main. Take the Gold River Road north out of town. Continue over the big river and past the Head Bay Road leading to eventually cross the Muchalat River. Look for the Nimpkish Main to your left. This road divides again about 3 km later. Again, keep left. Watch for access to the Muchalat Lake Recreation Site as you make your way along the lake.

Facilities

The **Muchalat Lake Recreation Site** has recently been upgraded. In addition to 40 campsites, a boat launch and a gravel beach, there have been many improvements to the facilities and dock. A host will be on site full-time in July and August and fees are collected from mid-May until mid-September.

Float planes can also access the lake and often use the recreation site at the northeast end of the lake as a base.

Other Options

Nearby Lakes include **Upana Lake**, a small lake 17 km (10.6 miles) south of Malaspina, which has small rainbow that take easily to the fly. Also nearby is **Antler Lake**, which holds stocked rainbow trout.

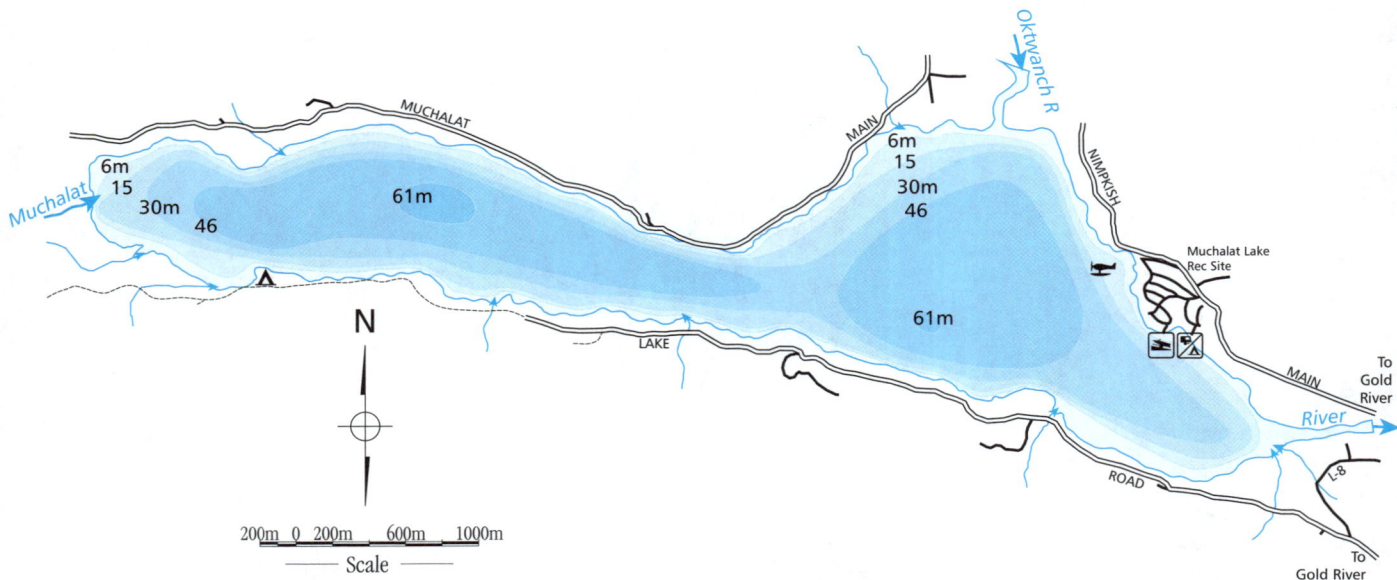

© Mussio Ventures Ltd.

Nahmint Lake

Location: 20 km (12.5 mi)southwest of Port Alberni
Elevation: 105 m (344 ft)
Surface Area: 799 ha (1,974 ac)
Max Depth: 150 m (492 ft)
Mean Depth: 79 m (259 ft)
Waypoint: 125° 03′00″ Lon - W 49° 11′00″ Lat - N

Fishing

Boasting of old growth forests, fabulous mountain views and large rainbow trout, Nahmint Lake is a wilderness lake well worth the effort to visit. Rumours of rainbow trout over 4.5 kg (10 lbs) surface every now and then. There are also cutthroat, Dolly Varden, kokanee and even steelhead in the lake. Even if the fishing is slow, the fabulous view and serene setting will help soothe the sole.

Nahmint is a long, deep lake with nice shoals and sharp drop-offs. Most anglers work the inlet and outlet areas of the Nahmint River with the former being easier to access since it is closer to the boat launch. As a salmon bearing stream, anglers are well advised to replicate salmon eggs in fall and baitfish in spring in these areas. Other trout lures like Apex and larger plugs on a downrigger are known producers. The lake is deep enough to maintain a steady fishery throughout the ice free season (April through October).

Fly anglers can also have some success on the big lake for trout. Work the shoal areas near the feeder streams with chironomids or searching patterns like Doc Spratleys earlier in the year. Later in the season, a good waterboatman hatch is reported to create a frenzy of action. Fish these patterns in the early morning or later in the day. During fall egg patterns can also be effective.

A lake troll with a Wedding Ring trolled slowly in an s-pattern is a popular method of finding kokanee. As an added bonus, smaller rainbow and cutthroat also chase down these offerings. But do note the bait ban on the lake.

Other restrictions on the lake include all trout larger than 50 cm (19.7 in) must be released, single barbless hooks and an engine power restriction of 7.5 Kw (10 hp). Please also release any steelhead caught.

Area Indicator

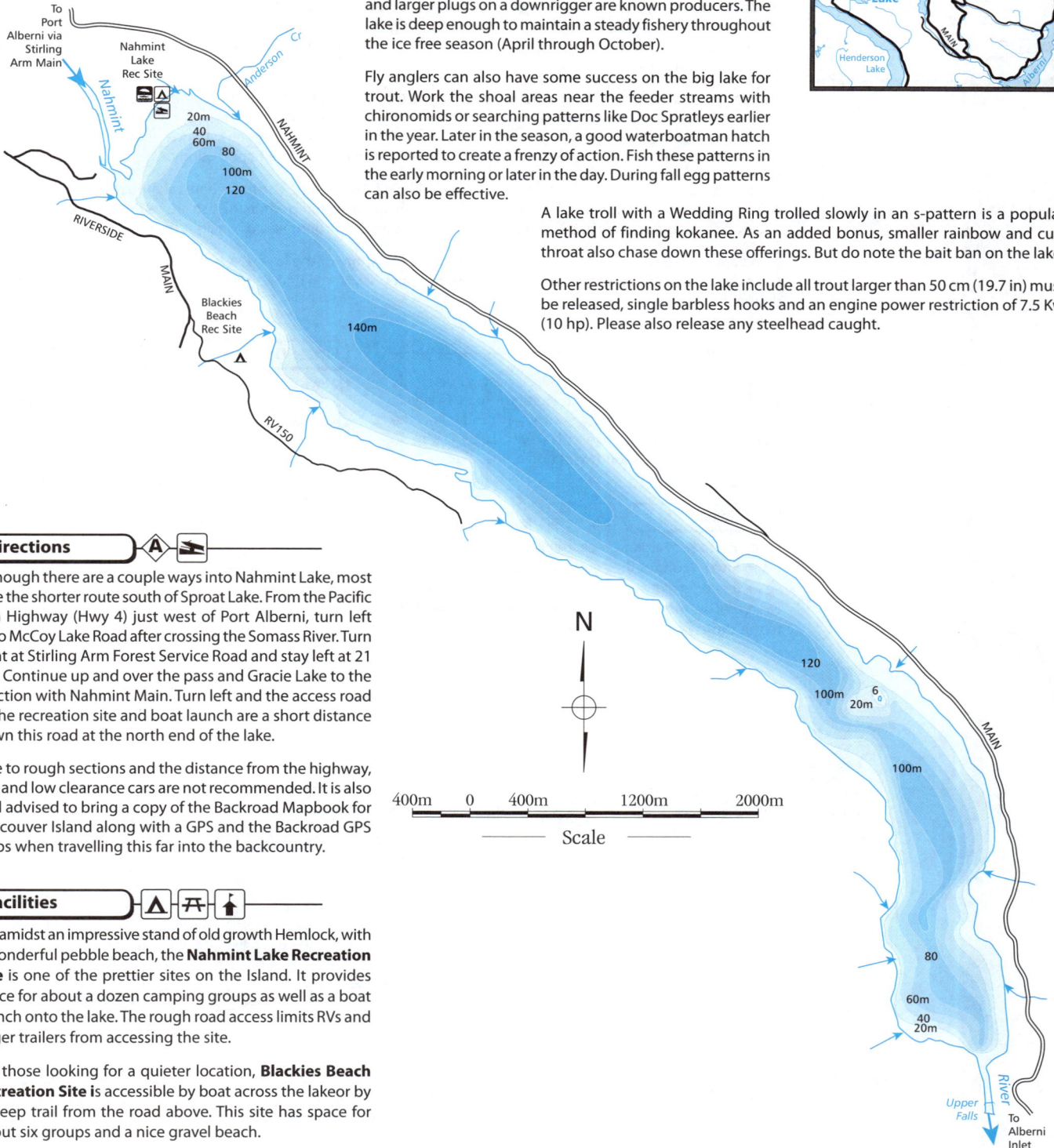

Directions

Although there are a couple ways into Nahmint Lake, most take the shorter route south of Sproat Lake. From the Pacific Rim Highway (Hwy 4) just west of Port Alberni, turn left onto McCoy Lake Road after crossing the Somass River. Turn right at Stirling Arm Forest Service Road and stay left at 21 km. Continue up and over the pass and Gracie Lake to the junction with Nahmint Main. Turn left and the access road to the recreation site and boat launch are a short distance down this road at the north end of the lake.

Due to rough sections and the distance from the highway, RVs and low clearance cars are not recommended. It is also well advised to bring a copy of the Backroad Mapbook for Vancouver Island along with a GPS and the Backroad GPS Maps when travelling this far into the backcountry.

Facilities

Set amidst an impressive stand of old growth Hemlock, with a wonderful pebble beach, the **Nahmint Lake Recreation Site** is one of the prettier sites on the Island. It provides space for about a dozen camping groups as well as a boat launch onto the lake. The rough road access limits RVs and larger trailers from accessing the site.

For those looking for a quieter location, **Blackies Beach Recreation Site i**s accessible by boat across the lakeor by a steep trail from the road above. This site has space for about six groups and a nice gravel beach.

Location: 25 km (15 miles) west of Port Hardy
Elevation: 199 m (653 ft)
Surface Area: 262 ha (647 ac)
Mean Depth: 25 m (80 ft)
Max Depth: 48.5 m (159 ft)
Way Point: 127° 51′ 00″ Lon - W   50° 42′ 00″ Lat - N

Nahwitti Lake

Area Indicator

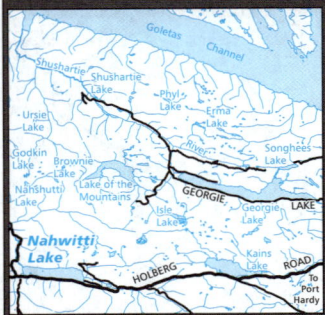

Fishing

Nahwitti Lake is one of a trio of lakes in the area that offer great cutthroat trout fishing. You would be hard pressed to decide between the three (which includes Kains and Georgie) but if pressed, many locals would choose Nahwitti as being the best. The lake is also home to Dolly Varden and kokanee.

Found near the northern tip of Vancouver Island, Nahwitti Lake is a cool, clear lake. While you still have a few kilometres to go before you hit the open ocean, it's proximity to the Pacific means two things: one, it gets lots and lots (and lots) of rain, and two, it doesn't get a lot of sun.

The two might seem to be the same, but they are not. The rain is not just there to make you miserable. All that rain tends to wash away most of the nutrients in the lake, which means that the fish that you will find here are slow growing, and generally small. On the other hand, the fact that the lake doesn't see a lot of sun means that it doesn't warm up as much in the summer. This means that even though it is a relatively low elevation lake, the fishing remains good through the summer.

All things considered, the fishing here can be pretty fast and furious for the cutthroat. The lack of food means that they will usually take most anything you throw at them, as long as it isn't too big. Spoons, spinners, flies, and even your traditional worm-on-a-hook will all produce well here. Cutthroat like pretty shiny things, so if you are finding that a realistic presentation isn't working, don't be afraid to tie on something bright and gaudy.

Anglers will also find the lake is especially popular with fly fishers, as the cutthroat here take well to flies, both wet and dry. The latter are best reserved for early morning or later in the evening when the fish are rising to the surface to feed. The fly pattern may not be important as other lakes, but we do recommend using light gear.

If you are unable to get out in a boat, access to the south shore of the lake is very good. There is a good drop off on this side of the lake allowing for some decent shore fishing, if you can find a spot where there is enough room to stand on the shore.

Directions

Nahwitti Lake is found 25 km (15 miles) west of Port Hardy on the Holberg Road. Take the Holberg Road/Granville Street exit off the Island Highway (Hwy 19) and follow the paved road past Kains Lake to Nahwitti Lake. The main access is found at the southwest end of the lake.

Facilities

Formerly called Hepler Creek, the **Nahwitti Lake Recreation Site** is found at the southwest end of the lake. It has space for about eight camping groups under an impressive canopy of old growth balsam and hemlock trees. Trails lead to the shore where it is possible to launch small boats.

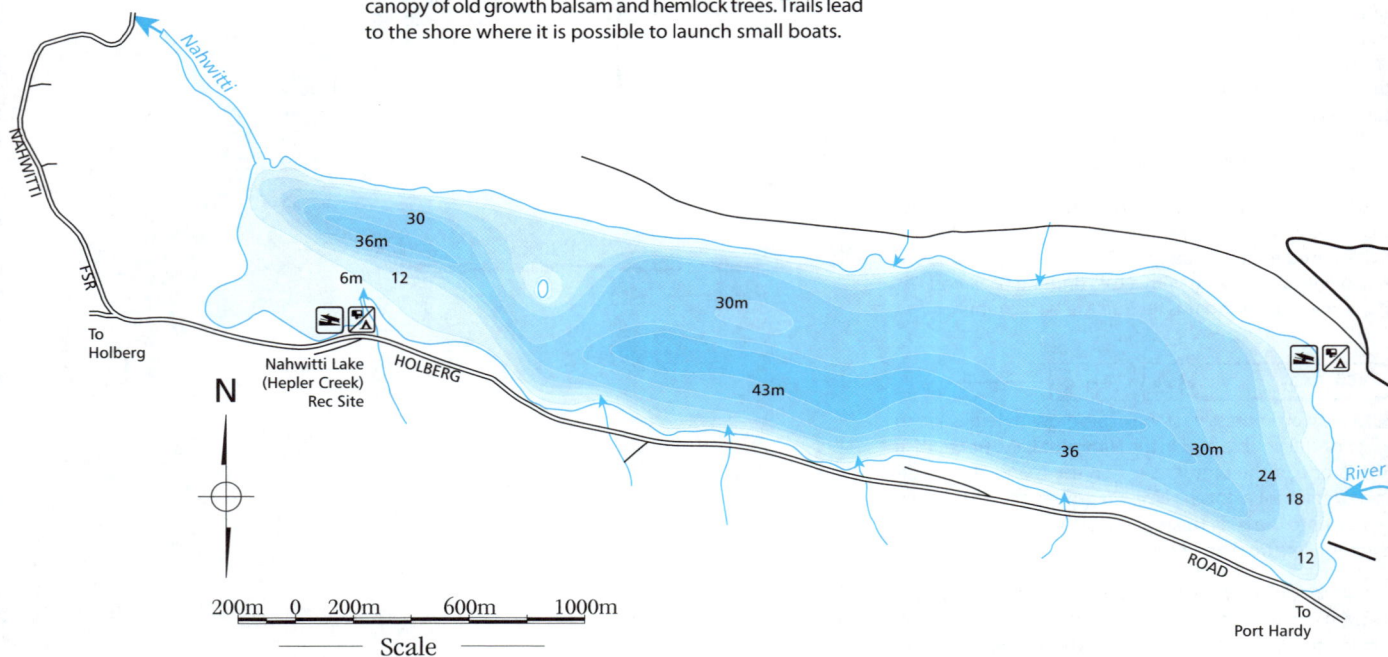

Other Options

Nahwitti is one of three great cutthroat lakes in the area. Anglers can also try their hand fishing at **Kains Lake**, which is found about 14 km (8.5 miles) west of Port Hardy at 10 km (6 miles) east of Nahwitti. It holds fair numbers of slow growing cutthroat. Due north of Kain, but accessed from a logging road a few kilometres farther east, is **Georgie Lake**. Georgie is the biggest of the three lakes, and is also popular for cutthroat.

Nahwitti Lake
(Hepler Creek)
Rec Site

To Holberg

HOLBERG

N

30
36m
6m   12
0
30m
43m
36   30m
24
18
12

River

ROAD

To Port Hardy

200m   0   200m   600m   1000m

Scale

Nanaimo Lakes

Scale
200m 0 200m 400m 600m 800m 1000m

To Nanaimo via Hwy 1

Windy Pt Rec Site

Nanaimo R

3m

First Lake

Main Gate

ROAD

RIVER

3m
6
12m 18

Old Mill Rec Site

F BRANCH

NANAIMO

N

ROAD

18
12m
6

gate

logs

gate

12m
6

18
24m

30
36m
42

F

gate

BRANCH

RIVER

NANAIMO

Second Lake

BRANCH C

Nanaimo River

To Fourth Lake

© Mussio Ventures Ltd.

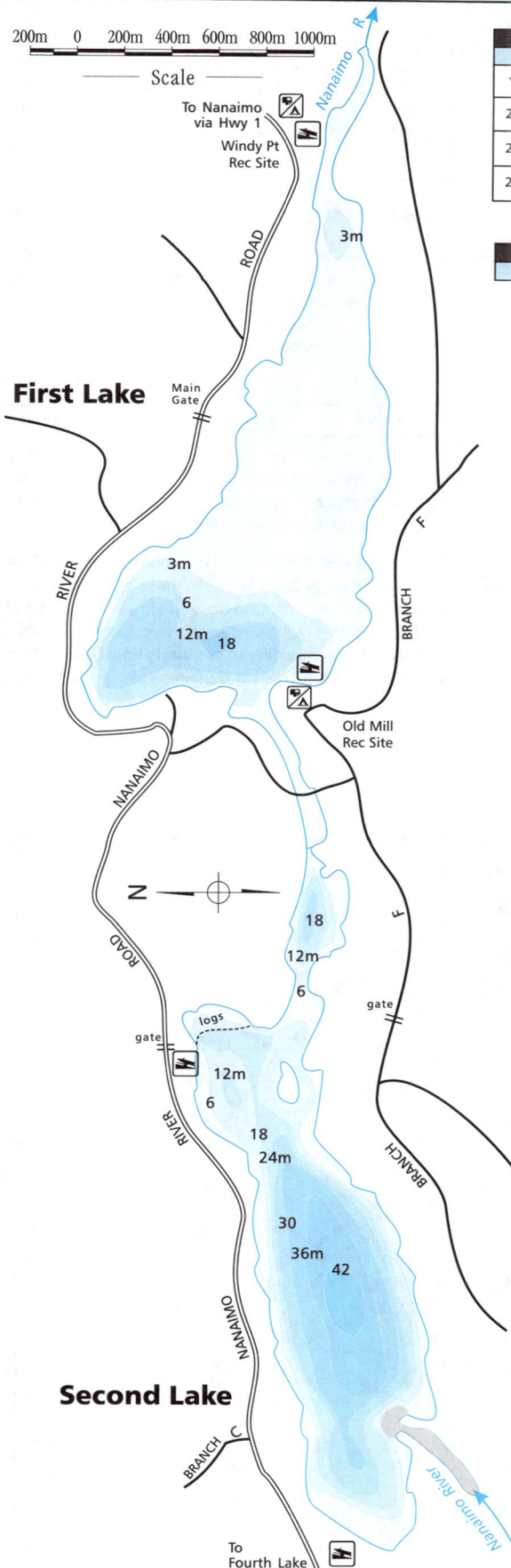

First Nanaimo Lake Fish Stocking Data			
Year	Species	Number	Life Stage
2007	Cutthroat Trout	5,000	Yearling
2006	Cutthroat Trout	5,000	Yearling
2005	Cutthroat Trout	5,000	Yearling

Second Nanaimo Lake
No Record of Stocking

Area Indicator

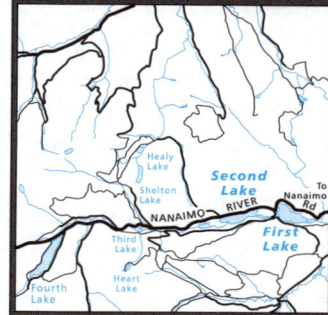

Healy Lake
Shelton Lake
Second Lake
NANAIMO RIVER
To Nanaimo Rd
First Lake
Third Lake
Heart Lake
Fourth Lake

Fishing

Southwest of Nanaimo is a series of four popular recreation lakes, stretched out along the Nanaimo River. Historically, the fishing is a little better in the Second and Fourth Lakes, but access has always been a bit of a concern. As a result the First Lake is always the busier of the set. This will continue to be the case now that the manned Timberwest gate that is found about halfway along the First Nanaimo Lake is no longer open to the public.

Both the First and Second Lakes hold good numbers of small rainbow and cutthroat trout, as well as the occasional Dolly Varden and even more occasional kokanee. A few of the trout are reported to reach 2 kg (4 lbs) in size, but catches like this are few and far between.

Similar to most low elevation, valley lakes, the fishing tends to be better between April and June and again between September and October. Of the two lakes, the First Lake is much more susceptible to the summer slow down due to the waters warming significantly. At this time, it is advised to try to line your way up the Nanaimo River to the Second Lake, which is a short distance upstream. If the water level is too low, then it is also possible to land at the launching site at the west end of the First Lake, then hike in to the Second.

The **First Lake** is extremely shallow on its east side with one small hole near the boat launch. The deeper part of the First Lake, where you should focus your fishing efforts, is at the west end of the lake where the water drops off. At that location it is possible to fish from shore. Try spincasting or fly-fishing off the drop-off at the inflow river.

The **Second Lake** is a lot deeper than the First Lake so it is better suited for trolling. Unfortunately, getting to the lake with a boat can be challenging. Fly-fishermen and spincasters can do very well by working the drop-off nearby to the inflow river or at the outflow channel between the Second and First Lake. Trollers should stick around the middle of the deeper lake.

Directions A

From Highway 1 south of Nanaimo, the paved Nanaimo River Road brings visitors to the west end of the First Lake. Look for this road or the Bungee Jumping signs on the north side of the river. It is an easy drive to the First Lake where visitors will find a recreation site that provides good access to the lake.

Driving beyond the gate on the north end of the lake, however, is currently restricted. This makes accessing the Second, Third and Fourth Lakes rather challenging. Luckily, the Second Lake can be accessed by boat or a short walk from the west end of the First Lake. Last report indicated that the gate is open to the public after May 1 each year. It is best to contact Timberwest to verify if you plan to travel beyond the First Lake.

Facilities

Camping and a boat launch are available at the west end of the First Lake at the **Windy Point Recreation Site**. The **Old Mill Recreation Site** s found along the southwest end of the lake offer 35 campsites and a boat launch. A trail links the 2 sites.

The Second Lake also provides a couple boat launch areas. Again, public access to these areas is limited.

Elevation: 198 m (650 ft)
Surface Area: 196 ha (489 ac)
Mean Depth: 4 m (13 ft)
Max Depth: 19 m (62 ft)
Way Point: 124° 9'00" Lon - W 49° 5'00" Lat - N

Second Nanaimo Lake

Elevation: 194m (636 ft)
Surface Area: 172ha (425 ac)
Mean Depth: 20 m (66 ft)
Max Depth: 44 m (144 ft)
Way Point: 124° 12'00" Lon - W 49° 05'00" Lat - N

Stream Length: 64.6 km (40.2 mi)
Geographic: 123° 52′00″Lon - W   49° 4′00″ Lat - N

Nanaimo River

Nanaimo River

Fishing

Like most of the Island's east coast rivers, the Nanaimo has been through some hard times recently. Once the east coast's second best steelhead river, steelhead returns have been very low for much of the last decade. Anglers are hoping and praying for better returns, but for now, the river is seeing very little steelhead action.

However, the river does see fair returns of Coho and Chinook, which have also remained stable but low for the last few years as well. For Coho in slack water, fly anglers use a slow sinking line, while in faster water a faster sinking line is needed. Coho will only chase moving flies. Try working with a size 4 to 8 gold or silver Muddler Minnow, Mickey Finn or beaded Woolly Bugger. Try olive colours on bright days and brighter colours on darker days. Spincasters should work spoons such as Gibbs Ironhead, or a Little Cleo with 2/0 hook by casting upstream and working through slower edges of pools.

The river also holds native cutthroat and rainbow. The cutthroat are catch and release only. Fly anglers can try using minnow patterns like the Muddler Minnow with floating line, a long leader and a weighted fly. Spincasters should try small Krocodile lures, spinners as well as worms or powerbait. Look for feeding activity and cast across the current, slightly downstream.

During the fall, cutthroat will grab salmon eggs or anything close. Attractor patterns, such as Woolly Buggers and sparkle leeches are good bets in winter when food is scarce. It is also essential to match the size and colour of the fry (in spring) or eggs (in fall) the cutthroat are chasing.

One of the best fishing holes is known as the Bore Hole. It is located near the powerlines that cross the river, although it is currently closed to fishing from here to Boulder Creek. Below Highway 19, the river is broad and open, perfect for drift fishing. There is an access point just off the highway that anglers can use.

As always, check the regulations for restrictions (both the provincial freshwater and federal tidal water) before heading out. Anglers also need to be wary of seasonal closures, location closures, and catch and release restrictions.

Directions

The lower Nanaimo River is easily accessed south of Nanaimo. It is crossed by a number of roads, including Highway 19 on the way to Duke Point Ferry, by Cedar Road, and by Highway 1 about halfway between Nanaimo and Ladysmith.

Above the highway, the river is paralleled by the paved Nanaimo River Road on its north banks. Random, often rough logging roads, lead south to the river and/or the various anglers trails. Further west, there is a recreation site on First Nanaimo Lake where the river flows into the lake. This is one of the best places to access the mid-section of the river. The upper river, however, is currently inaccessible.

Facilities

The Nanaimo River runs past one of the most heavily urbanized areas on the Island. You can find fishing retailers, restaurants, accommodations and basically whatever you want in the city of Nanaimo.

Both **Nanaimo River Regional Park** and **Morden Colliery Provincial Park** provide access to the river, but no camping facilities. They are found closer to the mouth or east of the Island Highway. Further west, there is camping and a boat launch onto the river at the **Windy Point Recreation Site**, at the east end of First Nanaimo Lake.

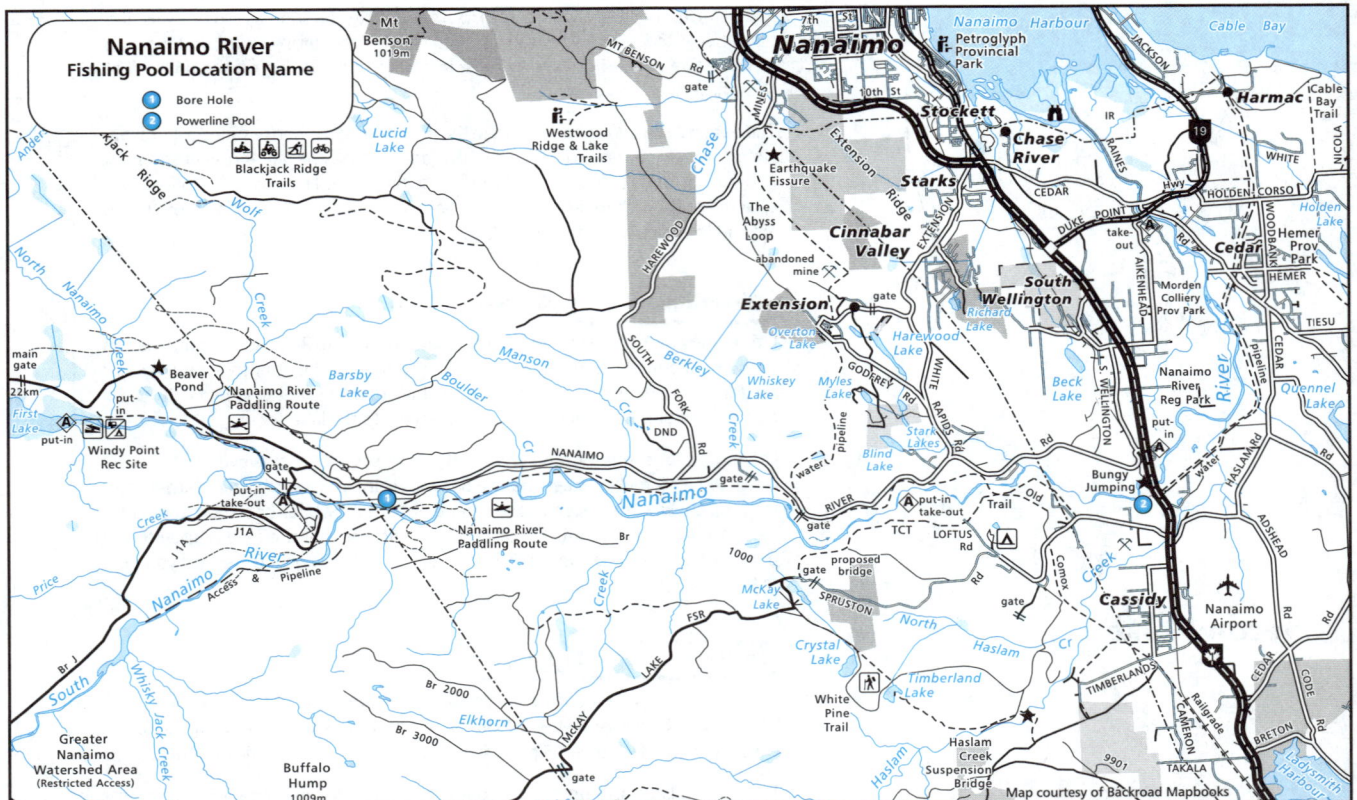

Nanaimo River
Fishing Pool Location Name
1 Bore Hole
2 Powerline Pool

Map courtesy of Backroad Mapbooks

Nitinat Lake

Location: 70 km (43.5 mi) southwest of Cowichan Lake
Elevation: 41 m (135 ft)
Surface Area: 2,748 ha (6,790 ac)
Max Depth: 205 m (673 ft)
Waypoint: 124° 40′ 00″ Lon - W 48° 48′ 00″ Lat - N

Area Indicator

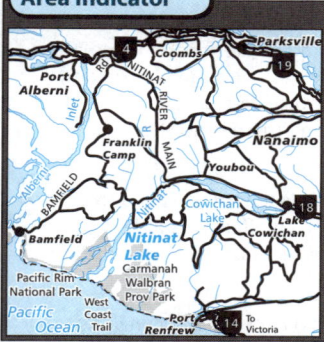

Directions A

Nitinat Lake is located on a remote stretch of land between Bamfield and Port Renfrew on the southwest coast of Vancouver Island. The lake is about 70 km southwest of Cowichan Lake or 70 km southeast of Port Alberni alongside good gravel roads. Follow Nitinat Main and South Main logging roads from the western end of Cowichan Lake or the Carmanah Main from the Bamfield Road at the old Franklin River Camp south of Port Alberni. No matter the way in, be sure to follow the signs to Nitinat village and drive through the village to the recreation site entrance at the far end.

Be wary of large, loaded logging trucks during the week.

Facilities

Services at the Village of Nitinat Lake include a small motel, restaurant, campsite, gas station and a food store operated by the Ditidaht First Nations. Camping and boat launch facilities are available at the scenic and popular **Nitinat Lake Recreation Site**. Home to 53 campsites, there is a fee to camp here.

The launch found about half way down the lake near Doobah Creek is only recommended for 4wd vehicles. Also on the lake is **Knob Point Recreation Site**. The small, secluded, boat access campsite provides good protection from the prevailing winds.

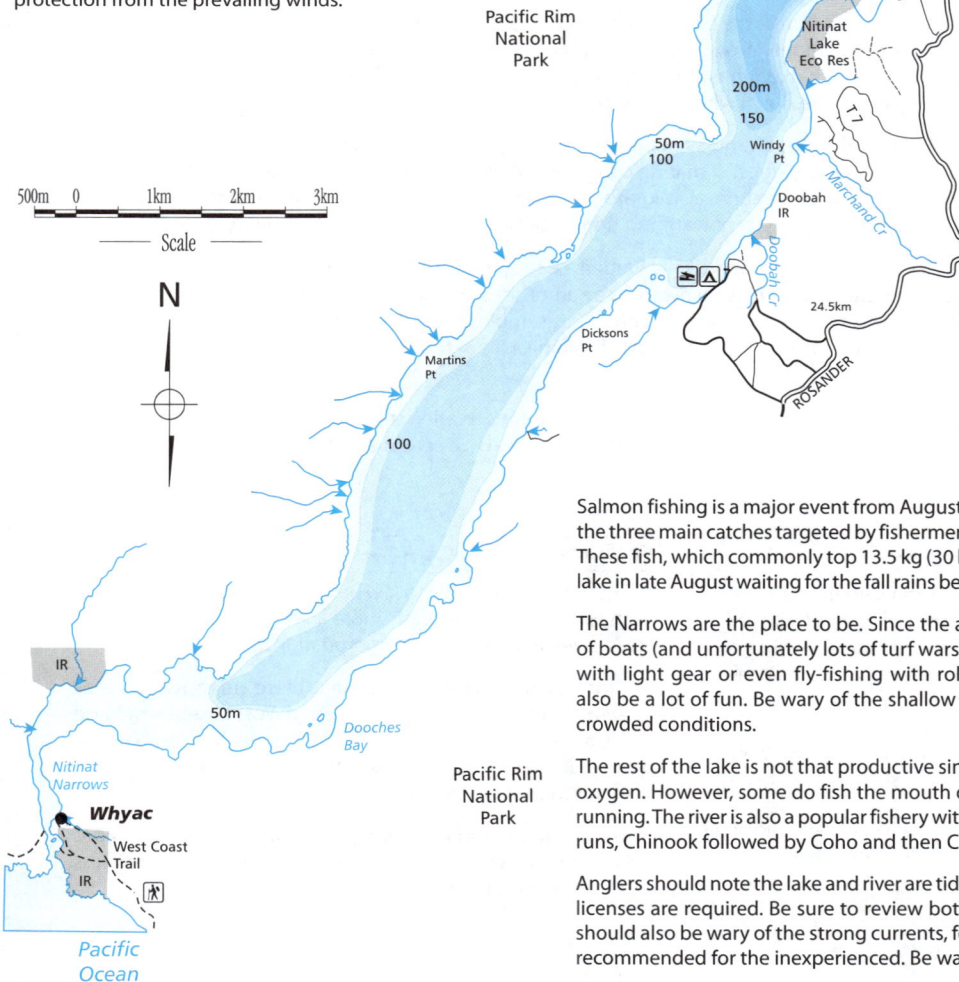

Fishing

Nitinat Lake is a beautiful tidal saltwater fjord that juts 23 kilometres inland and is joined to the Pacific Ocean via Nitinat Narrows. The lake has been named as one of the world's ten best windsurfing areas and is also a popular recreational canoe and kayaking destination with the infamous Nitinat Triangle.

Salmon fishing is a major event from August to October. Chinook, Coho and Chum salmon are the three main catches targeted by fishermen. However, most come looking for the big Chinook. These fish, which commonly top 13.5 kg (30 lbs), stage near the Narrows at the south end of the lake in late August waiting for the fall rains before heading to the north end and the Nitinat River.

The Narrows are the place to be. Since the area is so narrow and popular, there are often lots of boats (and unfortunately lots of turf wars) when the fishing is on. Most cutplug, but jigging with light gear or even fly-fishing with rolled muddlers or chartreuse Woolly Buggers can also be a lot of fun. Be wary of the shallow water (2.5 meters/8 feet deep at low tide) and the crowded conditions.

The rest of the lake is not that productive since only the shallow surface layer of the lake holds oxygen. However, some do fish the mouth of the river at the north end when the salmon are running. The river is also a popular fishery with resident cutthroat, summer and winter steelhead runs, Chinook followed by Coho and then Chum in fall.

Anglers should note the lake and river are tidal lakes and both Freshwater and Saltwater Fishing licenses are required. Be sure to review both sets of regulations before heading out. Boaters should also be wary of the strong currents, fog and wind. Venturing outside the narrows is not recommended for the inexperienced. Be wary of tidal changes!

Stream Length: 91.2 km (56.7 mi)
Geographic: 126°36′00″Lon - W   50°12′00″Lat - N

Nimpkish River

Fishing

The Nimpkish is Vancouver Island's largest river system running nearly 100 km (60 miles) in length. Adding to the sheer volume of water are the Davie and Woss Rivers, which, along with the Nimpkish, drain large lakes as the system flows into Broughton Straight 8 km east of Port McNeil. Throughout its course, the river offers a great variety of fishing opportunities. From sea-run cutthroat and salmon near the estuary to resident trout as well as both summer and winter steelhead further upstream, there is no shortage of good fishing to be found.

The upper river runs through a broad, open valley, and does not feature the same number of rapids and falls that other Island rivers do. However, many Islanders avoid it, preferring to fish lower volume, intimate streams. One of the reasons is it offers very little in the way of visual clues as to where fish might be. This is not to say the waters are not clear (most of the time), as peering over any roadside bridge will reveal what the river has to offer.

Steelheaders will find the river offers good winter steelhead fishing. From December to April the fishing above the old Duncan Bridge (near the Rona Road cut-off) can be very exciting. Another good hole is found near Woss at the junction with Gold Creek. It is reported that the fishing can be great here as late as April. Further upstream, the powerlines mark another good access point with lots of casting room and easy wading water all the way downstream to the Eagle Nest Rest Area. In addition to the standard float set-up with a Lil Corkie and worm, casting a gold wobble or Blue Fox spinner can be effective.

Cutthroat and rainbow trout can also be caught here with cutts preferring attractor flies with flash and/or beadheads. Further upstream River Main provides access to more trout water. You can drift fish here all the way to the lake. Dry fly fishing this area can be a lot of fun for rainbow.

The lower reaches are home to everything from trout to summer and winter steelhead as well as all five species of salmon. Good access is found from the Lower Nimpkish Provincial Park as well as off the highway. The clear water makes your approach a critical part of your arsenal, especially for the sockeye that like to school here.

The Nimpkish was Vancouver Island's biggest sockeye river, and fifth largest in the province. It is estimated that in the mid-1900s, the river saw over a quarter million sockeye return every year. By the year 2000, that number had dropped over 95% to about 10,000 fish.

Like most returning fish, the sockeye tend to hang out near the bottom of the river, so to have any success, you need to get your lure down. Bottom bouncing is the most common technique. A pencil lead or other weight is attached to the main line, with enough weight to bounce along the bottom but not so much that it hits and sticks. Attached a 1–2 m (3–7 ft) leader with a lure or hook and coloured wool attached to the end. This keeps the lure down where it needs to be. Try a green Spin 'n' glo, or corkie in size 12 or 14.

Other migrating fish have also suffered. Steelhead, Chinook and even Coho numbers are much less prevalent than in the past. There is a variety of factors for the poor returns. One of the biggest is marine conditions. When coastal ocean temperatures are high and saline, conditions are especially poor for juvenile sockeye survival. Migratory predators, including Pacific hake and mackerel, arrive earlier and in greater abundance in such years. With the current warming trend, the salmon returns may continue to dwindle.

Thankfully, the river also holds resident cutthroat and rainbow, Dolly Varden, sea-run cutthroat, as well as runs of chum and pink salmon. The early summer run of sockeye (as early as June) is followed by a run of sea-run cutthroat who like to feed on the eggs. At this time, anglers can have a lot of fun fishing salmon eggs or anything that resembles these. Different salmon runs treat anglers all the way until late fall when the chum dominate the fishery. These big fish can be a lot of fun to catch on fly gear and will take the most gaudy of patterns.

In addition to the standard regulations (single barbless hook, bait ban and steelhead conservation stamp), the Nimpkish River is closed to fishing above Davie River from December 1 to May 31. Anglers also need to be wary of seasonal closures and location specific closures that may be added.

Directions

The Nimpkish runs alongside the Island Highway (Highway 19) from Woss to where the highway crosses the river just east of Port McNeil. Access from the highway to the middle reaches is limited with most accessing the river between Woss and the Eagles Nest Rest Area. There are several logging road bridges that cross the river, with River Main and Nimpkish Main providing additional access to the middle reaches. Southeast of Woss, Rona Road provides good access to the upper river.

The lower Nimpkish is easily accessed by a fisherman's trail in Lower Nimpkish Park as well as from the highway itself.

Facilities

The town of Woss provides a few basics like food and gas but not much else. Port McNeill offers more amenities including fishing retailers, restaurants and accommodations.

For those looking to camp in the area, there are recreation sites at nearby Anutz Lake, Nimpkish Lake and Woss Lake that provide decent access to the lower stretches of the river. It is also possible to camp at riverside, but the steady flow of logging road traffic can deter from the experience.

Further upstream, the **Lower Nimpkish Provincial Park** provides a nice fisherman's trail. There is also a boat launch or river access at the north end of Nimpkish Lake here.

www.backroadmapbooks.com

Stream Length: 91.2 km (56.7 mi)
Geographic: 126°36'00"Lon - W   50°12'00"Lat - N

REGION 1

Nimpkish River (Mid)

Nimpkish River (Lower)

Nimpkish River

Map 1 — Mid Nimpkish River

Tlakwa

Nimpkish Lake Provincial Park

Nimpkish

Nimpkish Lake Rec Site

Steele Lake

Reserve

River

Claude Elliot Lake Prov Park

Anutz Lake

Canyon Lake Day Use Area

Reed Lake

Gold

Hwy

Little Cave Huson Reg Park

ATLUCK

Canyon Lake

OLD STEELE

put-in

NORTH

NIMPKISH

River

Eagles Nest Rest Area

Creek

Diane Lake

RELOCATION

Tsiko Lake

Nimpkish River Paddling Route

Teisum Cr

take out

Woss

Woss

19

Mukwilla Lake

Rd

Taipit

Eve

Spawning Sockeye Salmon

ISLAND

Welch Lakes

MAIN

Wolfe Lake

PINDER

Duncan Bridge

RONA

Atluck

ATLUCK Lake

Pinder

Creek

W WOSS MAIN

Rd

Rd

Helen

Creek

MAIN

Kaipit Lake

Fiddle Creek

Woss

Creek

Artlish Caves Prov Park

Cr

Mid Nimpkish River
Fishing Location Name
- ① Duncan Bridge
- ② Gold Creek Pool
- ③ Powerline Pool

Map courtesy of Backroad Mapbooks

ARTLISH

Artlish

Kaouk

River

Zeballos Lake

Woss Lake Provincial Park

Map 2 — Lower Nimpkish River

Port McNeill

Hyde Creek

Alert Bay Ecological Park

Sound

Lower Nimpkish River
Map courtesy of Backroad Mapbooks

NORTH

Alert Bay

Cormorant Channel Marine Prov Park

Broughton

Passage

CAMPBELL EAST MAIN

Gwa'ni Hatchery

BEAVER

COVE

Rd

Beaver Cove

Telegraph Cove

Strait

Nimpkish

Roselle Lake

KILPALA

Hatchery

Kokish

Robson Bite

Lower Nimpkish Provincial Park

Thiemer Lake

Iquiton River

Kaikash

NW KILPALA

ISLAND

NOMASS

Kokish

MAIN

Mudge Lake

Tsitika

KP4310

19

Cr

River

Kilpala

Ida Lake

R

Karmutzen

Bonanza

Bonanza Lake North Rec Site

MAIN

Noomas

Kinman Creek Rec Site

SOUTH

Bonanza

Lake

Rd

River

Claude Elliot Ecological Reserve

Nimpkish

MAIN

Location: 55 km (34 miles) northwest of Port Alberni
Elevation: 414m (1,358 ft.)
Surface Area: 264 ha (652 ac.)
Mean Depth: 53 m (174 ft.)
Max Depth: 81 m (266 ft.)
Way Point: 125° 20' 00" Lon - W 49° 27' 00" Lat - N

www.backroadmapbooks.com

Oshinow Lake

Area Indicator

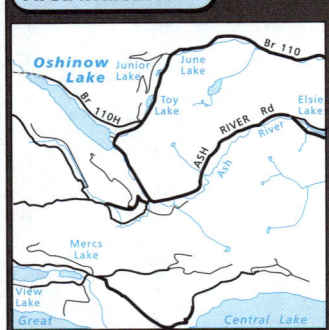

Fishing

Oshinow Lake is found within the Strathcona Provincial Park and forms part of the Ash River drainage. It is a narrow, deep lake, which gives up fish very rarely. There are rumors of some nice size trout reaching 3.5 kg (8 lbs) in size. It is the chance of hooking one of these beasts that keep people coming back for more.

Anglers looking for rainbow and cutthroat will find this lake is well suited for trolling. In addition to finding these elusive trout, anglers may find launching anything but light craft a challenge without any formal launching area. It is a fairly large lake and found fairly high in elevation. Add in the fact that it is quite deep to boot, means this lake is a good choice in the summer months when the lower elevation, shallower lakes are suffering from the summer doldrums.

Another dilemma is picking the right gear. Yes there are trophy size fish and regular catches in the 2 kg (4.5 lb) range, but most only average 25–35 cm (10–12 in) in size (less than a pound). If you are simply looking to catch fish, try using a lake troll (Willow Leaf and worm). If you are looking for bigger fish, a plug like a Rapala or Flatfish.

If you do not have a boat, the lake allows for some descent shore casting since the water drops off rapidly. If you are fly-fishing or spincasting, try around the inflow or outflow to the Ash River. Vary your presentation and the depth you are casting into until you find the right combination.

Directions

Oshinow Lake is reached by travelling on Highway 4 past Port Alberni to the Sproat Lake Provincial Park. At that point, head northwest on the Great Central Lake Road to the tiny community of Great Central where you can pick up the Ash River Road. At 6.5 km and 11.7 km stay right and at 15 km stay left. The Ash River Road will soon bring you along the northern shores of Turnbull Lake then along the southwestern shores of Elsie Lake. From there, the road continues along the Ash River and enters Strathcona Provincial Park. If there are no gates or road closures in the area, the main road should eventually bring you to the southeastern end of Oshinow Lake.

The long distance of logging road travel makes a truck with 4wd capability essential. It is also a good idea to bring along a copy of the Backroad Mapbook for Vancouver Island along with a GPS and the Backroad GPS Maps to track where you are on the often confusing logging road network.

Facilities

This remote lake offers little in the way of facilities, but visitors will find two informal camping areas along the southern end of the lake.

Other Options

In Strathcona Park, there are a couple of nearby lakes to try. **Toy Lake** is easily accessed via Branch 110 a few kilometers northeast of Oshinow Lake. The smaller lake has many small cutthroat and rainbow taken by artificial fly-fishing only in the spring or fall. Look for more details on this lake later in the book or you can venture further north to **Junior** or **June Lakes**. The lakes form part of the Ramsay Creek drainage and offers fair fishing for small rainbow and cutthroat trout.

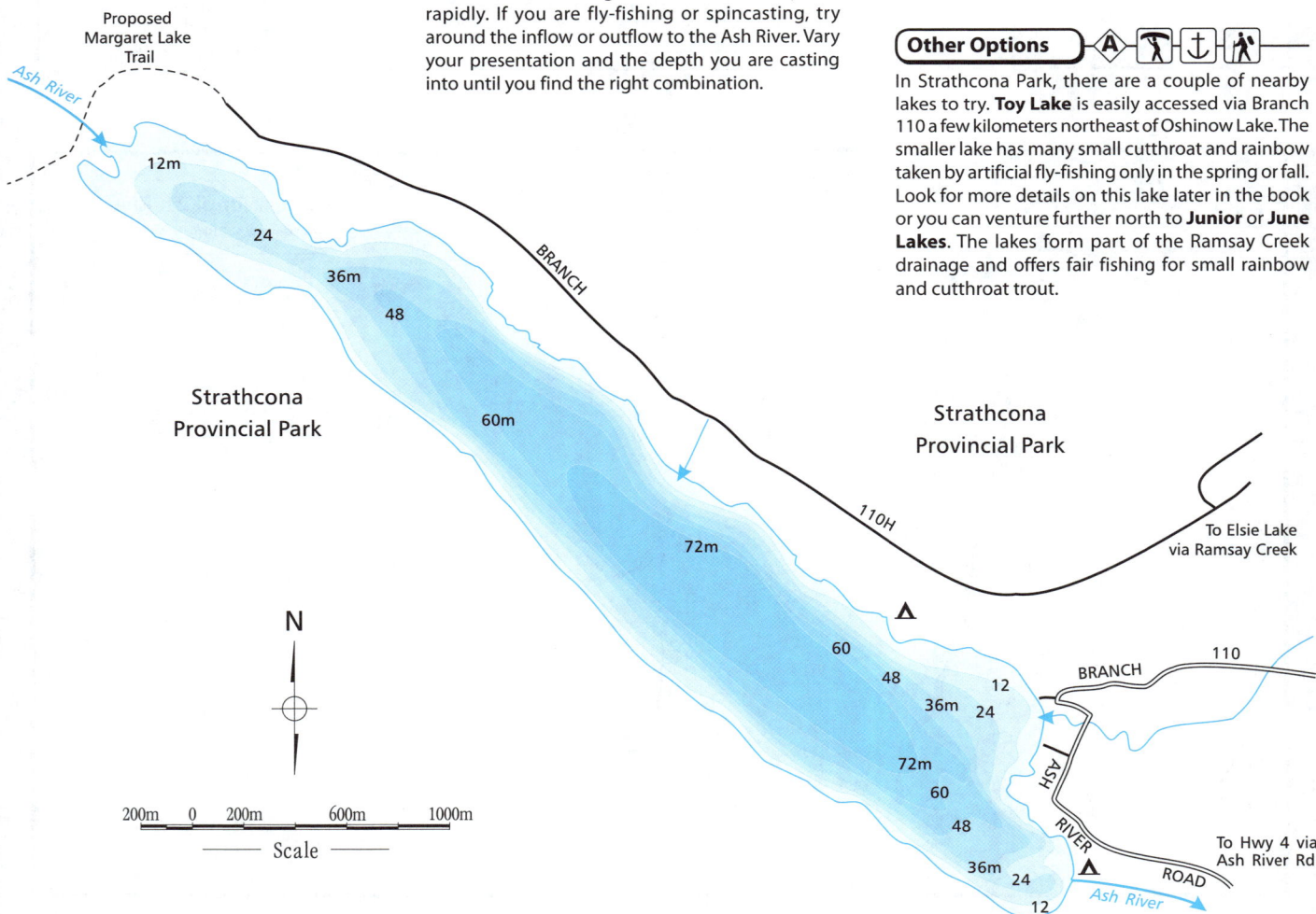

Proposed Margaret Lake Trail

Ash River

12m

24

36m

48

60m

72m

Strathcona Provincial Park

BRANCH

110H

Strathcona Provincial Park

To Elsie Lake via Ramsay Creek

BRANCH

110

60

48

12

36m

24

72m

60

48

ASH RIVER ROAD

36m

24

12

Ash River

To Hwy 4 via Ash River Rd

N

200m 0 200m 400m 600m 1000m

— Scale —

Stream Length: 47.6 km (29.6 mi)
Geographic: 125° 16'00"Lon - W   49° 53'00"Lat - N

Oyster River

Fishing

This small river flows from Pearl Lake, entering the Strait of Georgia about halfway between Campbell River and Courtenay. The real noteworthy fishery on the Oyster is sea-run cutthroat. In fact, the river is one considered of the best rivers on the Island for yellowbellies, as they are often called. Part of the Oyster's success with sea-run cutthroat is a strong hatchery program, with thousands of smolt released annually.

The small river is very popular with fly-fishermen since it has open banks and is easy to get around. However, most of the angling occurs for the sea-run cutthroat down in the estuary, or just upstream from there. The best times to fish are at sunrise and sunset, and at high tide. When the two coincide, the fishing can be amazing.

Popular fly patterns for sea-run cutthroat include patterns that imitate stonefly nymphs, juvenile needlefish or general attractor patterns like a Woolly Bugger. As a general rule, the lower the fish are in the river, the more likely they will chase after patterns that resemble baitfish. As they work their way upstream, they seem to revert back to eating insects. If you are fishing upriver, try using the nymph patterns, while fishing down in the estuary calls for a needlefish or other smolt imitators. Also, cutthroats often enter the river following salmon, and feed on the salmon eggs. Using a salmon egg pattern should also be successful upstream.

If you are not into fly fishing that is ok too. Most any form of angling can work here since the cutthroat are not very selective. Similar to above, choose lures that imitate needlefish or use salmon eggs suspended from the bottom.

In addition to sea-run cutthroat, the Oyster is also home to Pacific salmon and steelhead. But, like most of Vancouver Island's east coast rivers, the Oyster has seen better days. The runs are generally small but stable. Recent habitat work on the Oyster has also shown promise, not only for the Coho they are targeting, but also for the rest of the stocks as well. In particular, pink salmon have made a resurgence and make for a lot of fun when they school in the shallow pools near the estuary. Be sure to use light gear and if fly-fishing try drifting anything with pink in it.

Note that upstream of the Oyster's confluence with the Little Oyster River is closed from December 1 to June 30, and the river is catch-and-release only for wild trout. These regulations, as always, are subject to change. Always keep an eye open for last minute changes.

Directions

Highways 19 and 19A cross the Oyster about halfway between Campbell River and Courtenay. Smaller, side roads provide good access between the two; while a series of restricted logging roads provide access to the less productive upper reaches. Closer to the estuary, a nature trail provides good access to the north side of the river and the river mouth. You can pick this up off Regent Road.

Facilities

Those interested in camping in the area are best to try to reserve a site at popular **Miracle Beach Provincial Park**, just south from where the Oyster flows into the ocean and the Strait of Georgia. The **Oyster River Nature Park**, found near the estuary, provides a nice trail system that is frequented by anglers and birders.

Oyster River			
Fish Stocking Data			
Year	Species	Number	Life Stage
2011	Cutthroat Trout - Anadromous	9,486	Smolt

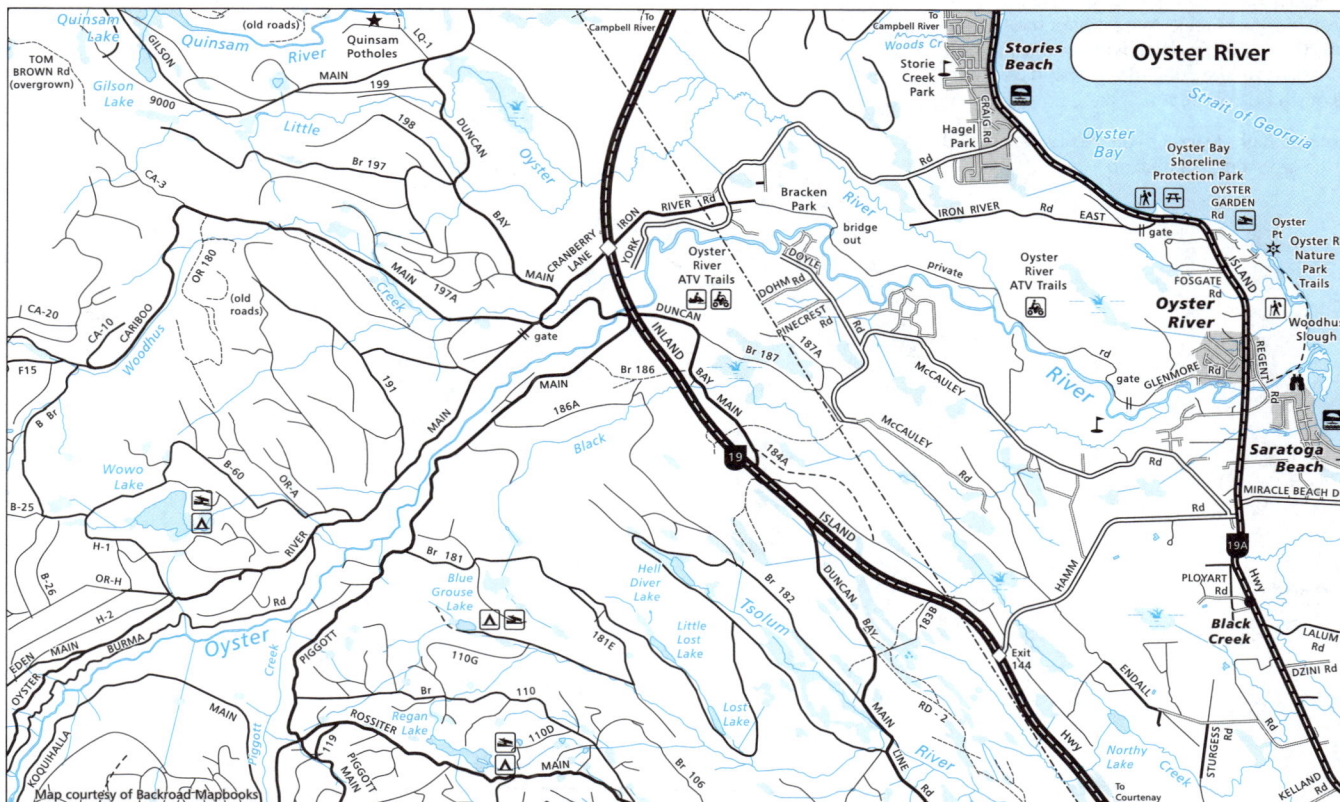

Map courtesy of Backroad Mapbooks

Location: 18 km (11 miles) east of Port Renfrew
Elevation: 67 m (220 ft)
Surface Area: 6 ha (15 ac)
Mean Depth: 2 m (7 ft)
Max Depth: 4 m (35 ft)
Way Point: 124° 12′ 00″ Lon - W   48° 36′ 00″ Lat - N

www.backroadmapbooks.com

Pixie Lake

Area Indicator

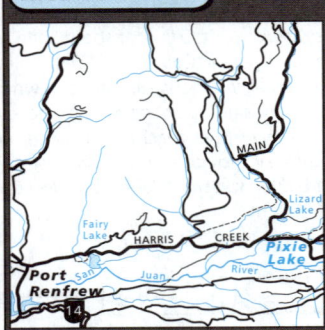

Fishing

Pixie Lake is another West Coast lake that features pretty decent fishing for small rainbow trout in a scenic setting. Although the trout are small (averaging less than 30 cm/12 inches in size), there are enough of them to provide a good spring and fall fishery.

Fly-fishing or spincasting are the preferred methods of fishing here. It is possible to launch a small boat at the lake, but given the lake's size and relatively poor opportunities for trolling, it is probably better to bring along a float tube or canoe and just spincast or fly-fish.

Still, early in the spring it is possible to troll a surface lure or fly with reasonable success, and people do, though it takes a light touch and a shallow troll to snag one of the wily rainbow that inhabit the lake. Try using a fly, like a leech, or a small spoon.

The deepest part of the lake is found in the middle of the lake. It is easy enough to cast out from shore so a small boat or float tube is not crucial, but may prove helpful. If you can get out onto the lake, work the transition areas between the shoals and the deeper areas, preferably casting from deeper water into the shallower waters and retrieving towards you. Work your presentation (be it a fly, like a Woolly Bugger, or a small spoon or...) slowly and erratically. The normal food that the fish eat does not swim at one speed in a straight line, and the more you can do to convince the fish your hook is their next meal, the better luck you will have. Try vibrating the tip of the rod to create random motion, or, for fly fishers, make short, quick strips, followed by a short pause.

The small, shallow lake is a victim of its location. While the fishing gets underway early here, by early summer the lake gets quite warm and the fish become extremely lethargic. Even if you manage to hook a fish in the summer, they will put up almost no fight. In the fall the fishing picks up again.

Directions

Pixie Lake is located east of Port Renfrew on the West Coast. It is found within the San Juan River Valley slightly north of the river.

To find the lake, head west to Port Renfrew from Victoria via the West Coast Highway (Highway 14). Once at Port Renfrew, head north crossing the San Juan River on the new Pacific Marine Road. Follow thispaved road past Fairy Lake, eventually turning right onto the Old Port Renfrew Road/Bear Creek Main at about the 16.5 km mark. This logging road leads to Lens Main, which in turn leads to the L 6000 Branch Road that skirts the north side of the small lake.

A truck or high clearance vehicle may be needed for the last stretch of this trip.

Facilities

There are no developed facilities on the lake, although camping and launching small boats is certainly possible. Most stay at nearby **San Juan River Recreation Site** where five enhanced campsites, a nice beach and even a launch onto the river are found. Another highlight of the area is the number of giant old growth trees including a giant Sitka Spruce and Douglas fir found close to the recreation site.

Other Options

On the way to Pixie Lake, you will find **Fairy Lake** via the new Pacific Marine Road. Similar to nearby **Lizard Lake**, anglers can expect descent fishing for small rainbow and cutthroat. Please refer to the sections in this book specific for those lakes. You will find a depth chart and a detailed write-up on the fishing in both those lakes.

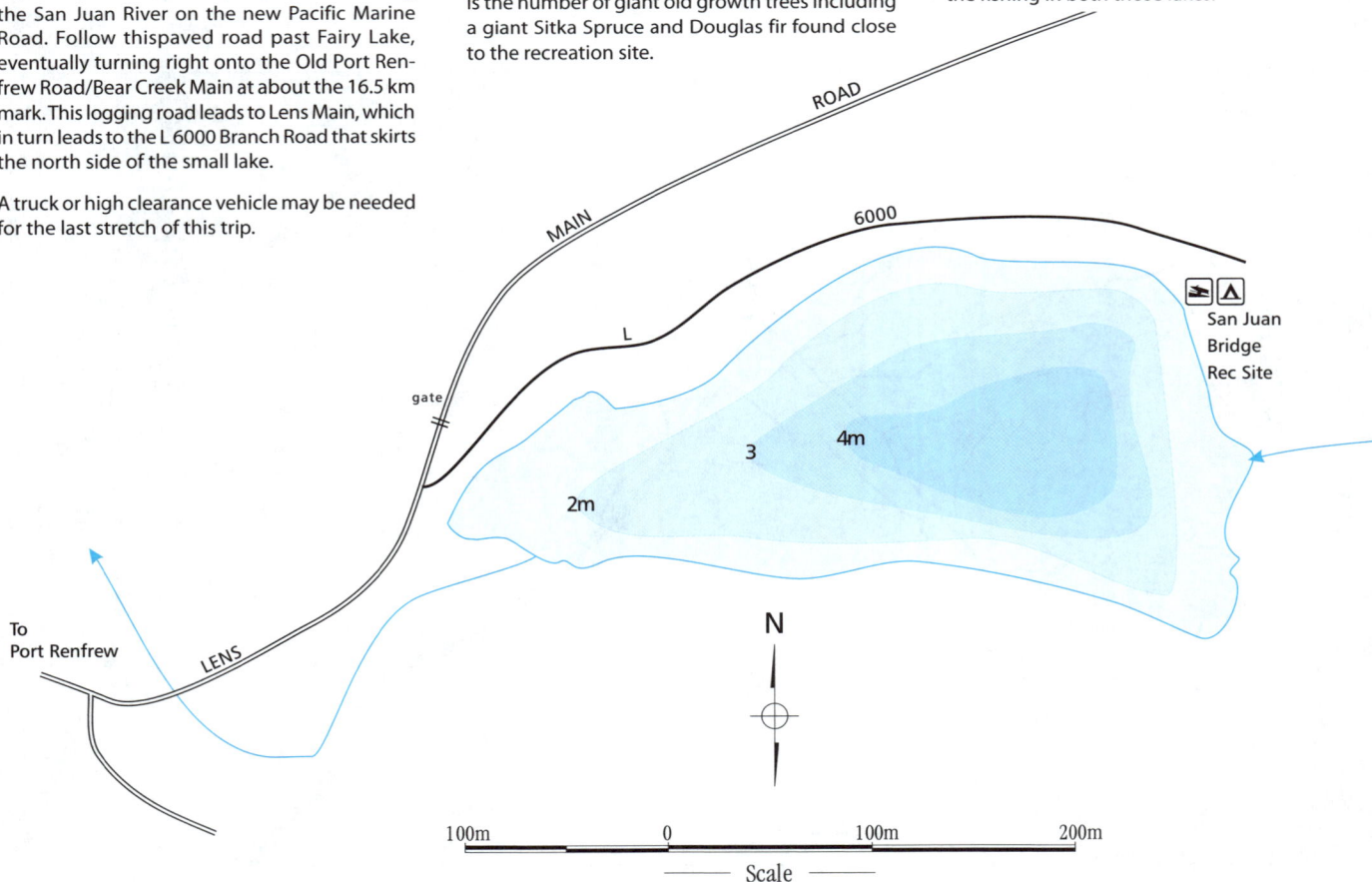

ROAD

MAIN

6000

L

gate

3

4m

2m

San Juan
Bridge
Rec Site

To
Port Renfrew

LENS

N

100m   0   100m   200m

Scale

Priest Lake

Location: 18 km (11 miles) southeast of Nanaimo
Elevation: 30m (100 ft)
Surface Area: 2.3 ha (6 ac)
Mean Depth: 5 m (16 ft)
Max Depth: 10 m (34 ft)
Way Point: 123° 46' 00" Lon - W 49° 03' 00" Lat - N

Fishing

Priest Lake is a tiny lake found on the northeastern boundary of Yellow Point Park in Nanaimo. The lake is reasonably deep for such a small lake, but it still suffers from the summer doldrums. Fishing is best here in early spring or later into fall for rainbow and cutthroat trout.

The lake is perfect for a belly boat given its small size and shallow waters. However, it is also possible to shore fish in places around the lake because the water level drops off rapidly from shore. If fishing from shore, please respect all private property.

Because the lake is found at such a low elevation, the fishing begins early in the year, often around the beginning of April. There are three areas that should draw your attention off the bat. The north and south ends of the lake feature sharp transitions between the deep water and the shallow water, which can often prove productive. Another place to try is at the mouth of the outflow stream along the northern shore of the lake.

Early in the season, anglers should work the shoals that ring the lake, as the fish will be in these areas feeding much more frequently than after the water warms up. As the season progresses, the fish begin to stay in the deeper water, making forays into the shallow shoals to search for food. Now is the time to begin to fish the drop offs. What often works the best is to set up in your belly boat in the deeper water just past the drop off, then cast into the shallows with a sinking fly. A nymph is an all-purpose fly in these situations, but if there is a hatch going on, other patterns might work better. Conversely, if a nymph is not attracting the fish, try a leech or an attractor pattern like a Carey Special.

Allow the fly to sink down to the bottom, and retrieve slowly, bouncing it along the bottom towards the drop off. Most fish are opportunists, and if they see something that looks like food coming towards them, they will strike more readily than if it is heading away from them.

Spincasters can work small spoons in a similar manner. Another option to try, especially if you don't have a belly boat and are fishing from shore, is a worm and a bobber.

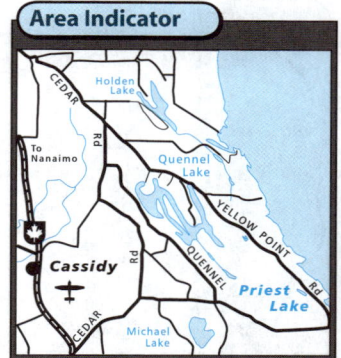

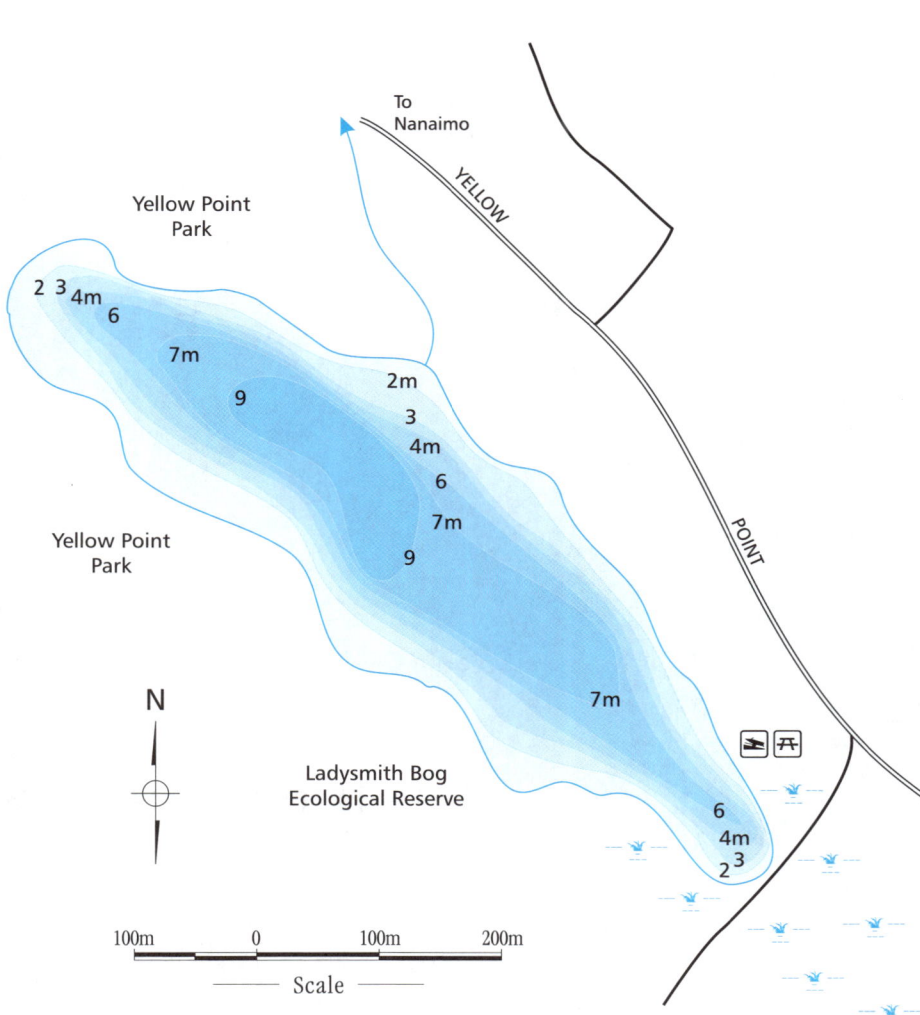

Area Indicator

Directions

Priest Lake is a tiny lake located east of the Nanaimo Airport nearby to the ocean. The lake is easily accessed by taking the Cedar Road from the Island Highway south of the airport. Cedar Road turns into Yellow Point Road, which approaches the ocean and then swings to the northwest. Priest Lake is the small lake at the northeast end of Yellow Point Park. Access is very good, with paved roads leading right by the eastern shore.

Facilities

Being part of **Yellow Point Park**, visitors will find a picnic area along with a place to launch small boats at the lake. There are private campsites in the area for those looking to overnight.

Other Options

Quennell Lake is a much bigger lake found just northwest of Priest Lake on Yellow Point Road. The lake has fair fishing for small rainbow and cutthroat which are stocked annually along with a good small-mouth bass fishery. More information, along with a depth chart, is found later in this book.

N

100m   0   100m   200m
Scale

Location: 8 km (5 mi) northwest of Victoria
Elevation: 40 m (131 ft)
Surface Area: 6 ha (15 ac)
Mean Depth: 2.5 m (8 ft)
Max Depth: 5 m (16 ft)
Way Point: 123° 28' 00" Lon - W 48° 29' 00" Lat - N

www.backroadmapbooks.com

Prior Lake

Area Indicator

Fishing

Prior Lake is a tiny little lake that is found nearby to the much more popular Thetis Lake. Although Prior receives a fair bit of fishing pressure, the Freshwater Fisheries Society of BC helps to maintain the trout fishery by stocking a few hundred cutthroat every year. As a result, the lake still offers surprisingly good fishing for small stocked cutthroat to 30 cm (12 in) in size during the spring (April to May) or fall (October). During the warmer periods, anglers will also find a growing bass population and a few sunfish.

Prior Lake is a fairly shallow lake that is just large enough to use a belly boat and casting towards shore can be quite effective. However, most anglers simply cast from the large dock area. Given the marshy shoreline and depth of the lake, shore fishing from the various trails leading to the lake is limited.

The bass, however, love hanging out in the reeds near shore, making it tough to cast for them. Tough, but not impossible. Bass fishers have come up with a variety of ways of baiting a hook with an artificial worm so as to prevent the hook from getting snagged. Some common methods include the Texas rig and the Carolina rig.

While these rigging methods keep the hook from getting snagged, they can also make it difficult to hook a fish, too, and you might find it easier to try an alternative method of fishing for bass, like jigging. This allows you to place your lure exactly where you want to, without needing as accurate of casting skills.

For fly fishers, smallmouth bass are not as likely to take a surface fly as largemouth, so use a wet fly. Unfortunately, bass like to hang out in weeds and under structure like fallen trees, and it is quite easy to lose a few flies in the process.

There are no powerboats allowed out on the small lake.

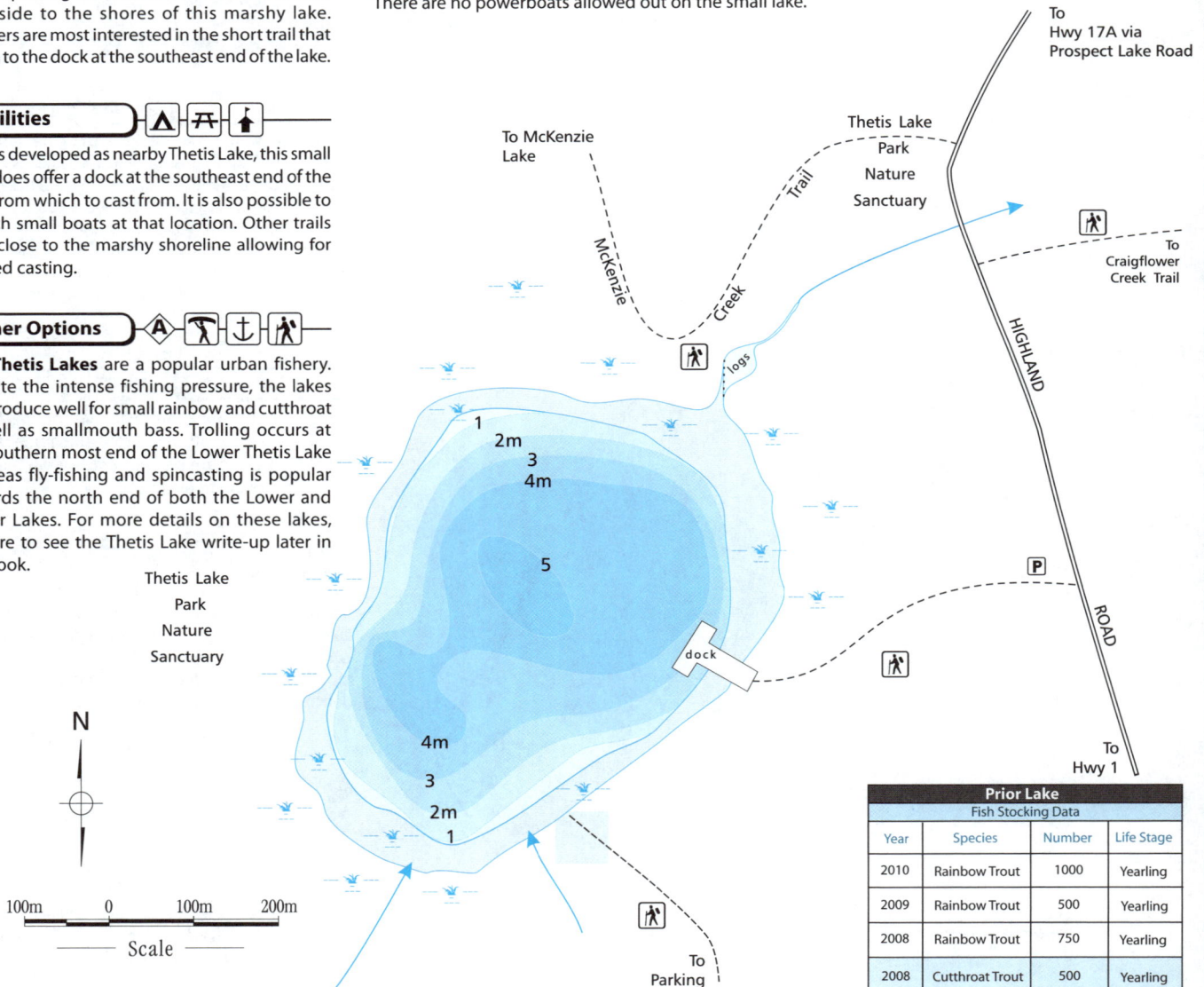

Directions

Prior Lake is located within the Thetis Lake Regional Park, but is better accessed of Highland Road. Highland Road can be found off the Island Highway (Hwy 1) near it's junction with the Sooke Highway (Hwy 14). Continue north on Highland to the parking area where a few trails lead from roadside to the shores of this marshy lake. Anglers are most interested in the short trail that leads to the dock at the southeast end of the lake.

Facilities

Not as developed as nearby Thetis Lake, this small lake does offer a dock at the southeast end of the lake from which to cast from. It is also possible to launch small boats at that location. Other trails lead close to the marshy shoreline allowing for limited casting.

Other Options

The **Thetis Lakes** are a popular urban fishery. Despite the intense fishing pressure, the lakes still produce well for small rainbow and cutthroat as well as smallmouth bass. Trolling occurs at the southern most end of the Lower Thetis Lake whereas fly-fishing and spincasting is popular towards the north end of both the Lower and Upper Lakes. For more details on these lakes, be sure to see the Thetis Lake write-up later in the book.

Prior Lake			
Fish Stocking Data			
Year	Species	Number	Life Stage
2010	Rainbow Trout	1000	Yearling
2009	Rainbow Trout	500	Yearling
2008	Rainbow Trout	750	Yearling
2008	Cutthroat Trout	500	Yearling

Prospect Lake

Location: 18 km (11 mi) northwest of Victoria
Elevation: 48 m (157 ft)
Surface Area: 60 ha (148 ac.)
Mean Depth: 7m (23 ft)
Max Depth: 14 m (46 ft)
Way Point: 123° 26′00″ Lon - W 48° 31′00″Lat - N

Fishing

Prospect Lake is a popular South Island lake located north of Victoria. The lake has a good size population of cut-throat, rainbow and smallmouth bass. In fact the Freshwater Fisheries Society of BC stocks the lake several times each year with both rainbow and cutthroat trout to help maintain the fishery. Because of its proximity to Victoria, the lake sees heavy pressure.

Being a rather rocky and deep lake, the fishing is usually better here from March to May and again in the fall. Anglers who are planning on keeping and eating the fish caught here should be aware that folks with a discriminating palate often complain that fish caught here later in the year start to take on an almost weedy or muddy taste. If you are planning on fishing here for food, consider fishing earlier in the year.

Most anglers prefer to troll the lake by working in a criss-cross pattern to work the various shore structure combined with the deeper holes near the middle of the lake. The northwest shoreline offers some nice drop-offs to work, while casting towards the rock ledges, logs and lily pads often produces exciting results.

Trout anglers can usually find success fishing   near the surface in the early morning and late into the evening. During mid-day, try fishing deep. Despite not being that fertile, there is a decent chironomid hatch. They usually appear in April when there is a spell of warmer weather, and peak in May, when other hatches start occurring. May can be an exciting time to fish since there are often multiple hatches happening at the same time. However, you may find the fish acting quite particular, and figuring out which insects the fish are feeding on can take some time.

During the summer months when the waters start to warm, smallmouth bass fishing can be good. Try casting a large attractor type fly or a plug towards the weed beds and sunken logs, or any place that offers the bass good places to hide. One of the secrets to better bass fishing is slow retrieves. The slower the better. Since bass like to hang out around weeds and fallen logs and other structure, making shorter, controlled casts is much more effective in getting your lure where you want it to be.

Directions

Located north of Victoria, Prospect Lake is easily accessed by driving the West Saanich Road (Highway 17A) to the Prospect Lake Road. Follow this road south for a short distance to access the north end of the lake at the municipal park.

Facilities

Ringed with homes, a public park and small golf course, this is a well developed lake. The best access point to the lake is at the Lakeside Park found at the northwest end of the lake. At that location, there is popular beach area from which people can hand launch small craft such as canoes or float tubes.

Alternatively, there is another launching area found at the end of Echo Drive on the east side of the lake. You can find Echo Drive off of Goward Road.

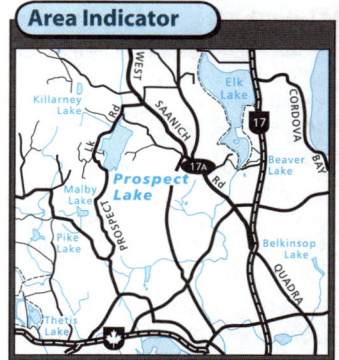

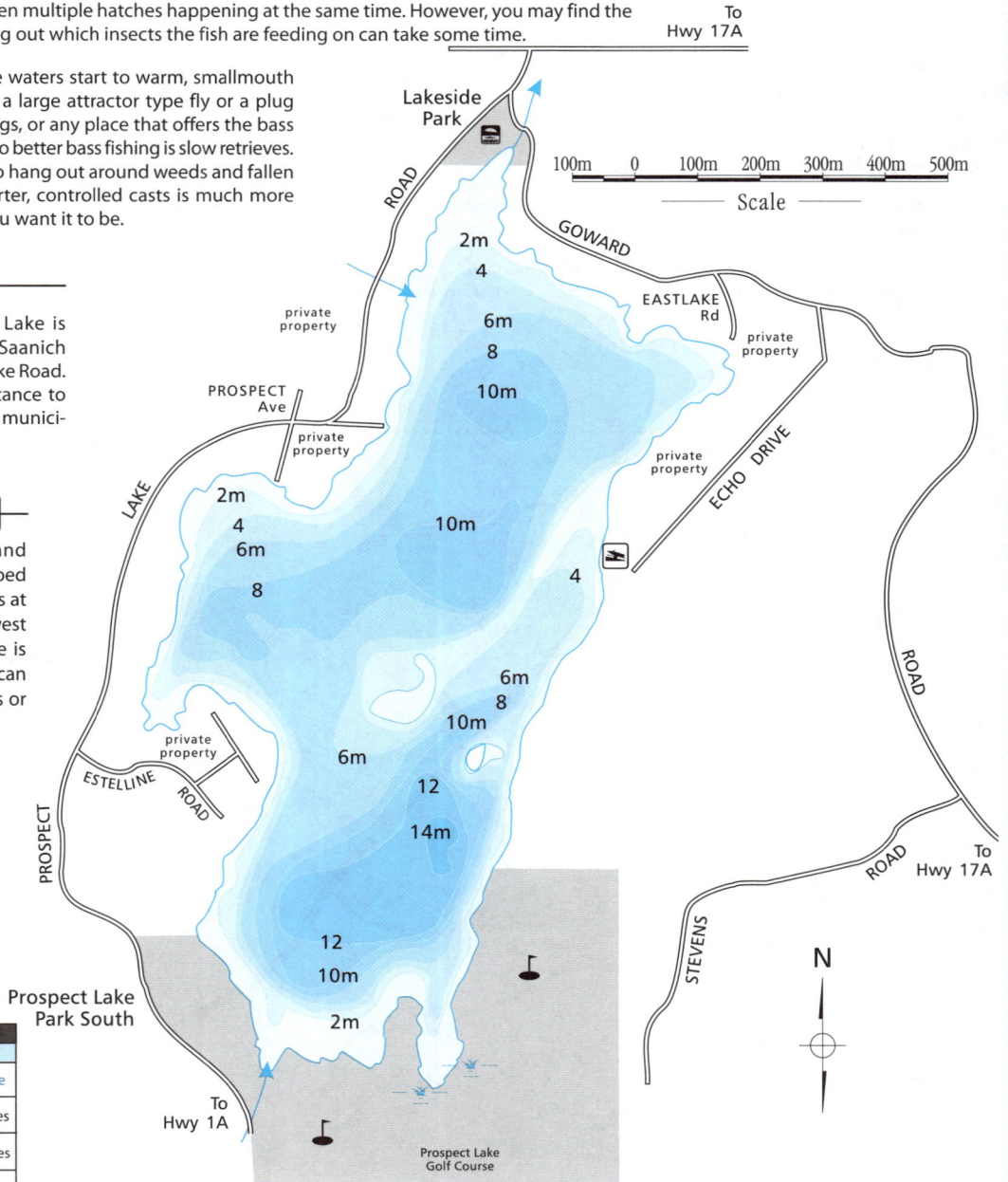

Area Indicator

Scale: 100m 0 100m 200m 300m 400m 500m

Prospect Lake Fish Stocking Data			
Year	Species	Number	Life Stage
2011	Rainbow Trout	5,000	Catchables
2010	Rainbow Trout	7,445	Catchables
2009	Rainbow Trout	9,000	Catchables

Stream Length: 28.9 km (18 mi)
Geographic: 125° 4'00"Lon - W   49° 40'00" Lat - N

Puntledge River

Fishing

Ah, the Puntledge River. Once famed in song and story as one of the best steelhead fisheries on the east coast of Vancouver Island, the Puntledge has seen its steelhead stocks collapse harder than any river on the Island. Stocks in the river are currently nearly nonexistent. There are a few fish that return each year, but counts in recent years have been less than 50 for each run.

Part of the problem is low water levels and warm water. The river is dam controlled, and the impacts from building the dams are still being felt. Still, other stocks have been doing okay, so what's up with the steelhead? Nobody is quite sure, and, while BC Government spent a lot of time and money trying to reinvigorate the stock, they had almost no success. In 2005 and 2006, the brood stock was released into the river.

Instead of swimming for the ocean, though, most of the brood stock decided to stick around the hatchery area. This has led to an interesting localized spike in steelhead numbers, but once these fish are gone, however, the river's steelhead population is in serious trouble.

It isn't all doom and gloom. The river's salmon stocks have slowly been recovering. While the DFO is still concerned over the number of returns for summer run Chinook, most other species are doing well. The numbers are low but steady, and slowly improving.

Right below the hatchery at the Rod and Gun Pool is some prime fishing territory. Other popular areas include Puntledge Park and below the Condensory Bridge, but don't rule out pools further upstream. These area areas are known to produce well for Chinook and Coho, which seem to take well to things that are green…green wool, green flies, and green spoons. The river also has a big run of chum salmon. Despite their sometime negative reputation, chum are scrappy fighters and are a great game fish to hook on the fly if you have heavy enough gear.

If that is not enough, the river even offers up some resident trout and Dolly Varden. These fish are catch and release only, but can be a lot of fun on light gear.

Not surprising, the Puntledge has a number of year-round closures with only certain areas open to fly-fishing only, as well as mandatory release of trout or char. As always check the regulations and websites for in season changes before heading out.

Directions

The Puntledge forms the boundary between Comox and Courtenay, and can be accessed, in this section, from many, many places, including Highway 19A. Condensory Road and Puntledge Park are other easily accessible locations downstream. Further upstream, the river is crossed by Highway 19 just west of Courtenay. Most of the access to the upper section is along the well developed regional park trail system.

Facilities

Most of the Puntledge's fishable waters are within a few minutes' drive of Courtenay. The upper reaches are host to the **Nymph Falls Recreation Area**, while the **Puntledge River Greenway & Park** are found in the mid-section of the river. Camping is possible at the **Cumberland Park** on the east end of Comox Lake opposite the river mouth.

Puntledge River			
Fish Stocking Data			
Year	Species	Number	Life Stage
2005	Steelhead - Winter/Summer	1,595	Adult/ Catchable
2005	Steelhead - Diploid	102,090	Smolt
2004	Steelhead - Winter/Summer	102,745	Adult/ Smolt
2004	Cutthroat Trout - Anadromous	1,960	Smolt

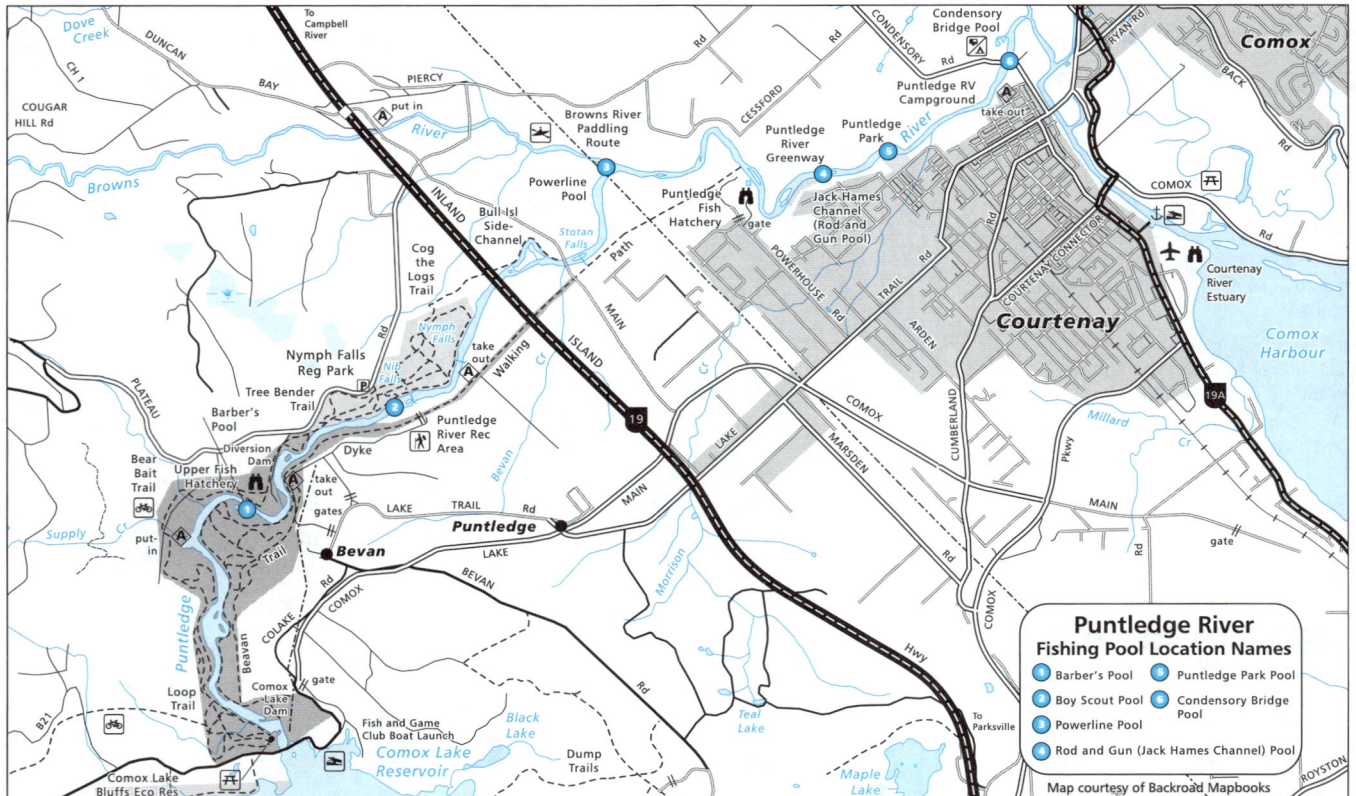

Puntledge River
Fishing Pool Location Names
1 Barber's Pool   5 Puntledge Park Pool
2 Boy Scout Pool   6 Condensory Bridge Pool
3 Powerline Pool
4 Rod and Gun (Jack Hames Channel) Pool

Map courtesy of Backroad Mapbooks

Pye Lake

Location: 42 km (26 mi) northwest of Campbell River
Elevation: 135 m (443 ft)
Surface Area: 370 ha (913 ac)
Mean Depth: 34.5 m (113 ft.)
Max Depth: 83 m (272 ft.)
Way Point: 125° 35'00" Lon - W   50° 17'00" Lat - N

Fishing

Pye Lake is a mid-sized lake located north of Campbell River that produces well for small cutthroat and bigger Dolly Varden (to 45 cm/18 in). The lake is a low elevation lake, but is quite deep. Although the spring is certainly the best time to fish here, fishing remains good through the summer since the lake does not get as warm as shallower lakes.

In the early spring, there are shallow bays at both the north and south ends of the lake, and the fish come into these bays to feed. The bay at the south end of the lake is deeper than at the north, with better structure (a deep hole and some sharp transitions between deep and shallow) and will offer good fishing for longer.

When the fish are in the shoals a shallow troll may work, but often just casting a small spinner or spoon will work better. Both Dolly Varden and cutthroat like flashy lures so don't be afraid to use the gaudiest lure to catch them. They will also take well to a fly with some sort of flash in it.

As the water warms up, the fish become more wary, moving into the deep water of the main lake. There is good structure around the ring of the lake, and in summer, you could do worse than trolling around the rim of the lake with a lake troll in about 10 m (30 ft) of water.

Cutthoat trout like to rise to a fly, and so dry fly fishing for cutthroat is a popular pursuit. However, they will take to a variety of lures and presentations, including spoons (casting or trolling) and crankbaits. If something isn't working, try another lure, another style, or another location.

Other Options

While Pye Lake has good fishing, it is often overlooked by people heading to nearby **McCreight Lake**, found just east of Pye Lake. The deep lake is best trolled for stocked cutthroat along with kokanee, rainbow and Dolly Varden. On the other side of Pye are a pair of lakes called the **Stella Lakes.** These two lakes (one big, one small) offer fair fishing for rainbow, Dolly Varden, and stocked cutthroat. Go early or later in the year for best results. More details on these lakes are provided in this book.

Facilities

There are four campsites around the lake, three on the east side, and one on the west side. If you are planning on launching a boat, there is a rustic and steep launch on the west side at the **Pye Lake Recreation Site** along with space for four vehicle units. Both **Pye Bay** and **Pye Beach Recreation Sites,** found on the other side of the lake, are nicer sites with space for about nine groups but no formal launching area. Sandwiched in between, **Pye Point Recreation Site** offers space for a couple groups and a rustic area to hand launch small boats.

Directions

Found north of the Island Highway (Hwy 19), Pye Lake is accessed by either the Pye Lake East or Pye Lake West Forest Service Roads. The access to the west side is best from the highway, about 38 km northwest of Campbell River. The recreation site is about 5.5 km down this rough logging road.

The east side is better accessed of the Rock Bay Road to the north. Look for this road branching north from the Island Highway a few kilometres past the Pye Lake West Forest Service Road. Follow the Rock Bay Road to the Pye East Forest Service Road and turn right or south. Pye Bay Recreation Site is the first of the bunch and is about 2 km from the Rock Bay Road. The nicer recreation sites and better road access is found off the east side of the lake.

Area Indicator

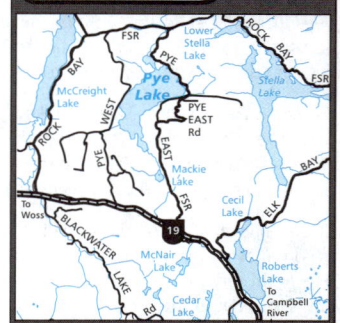

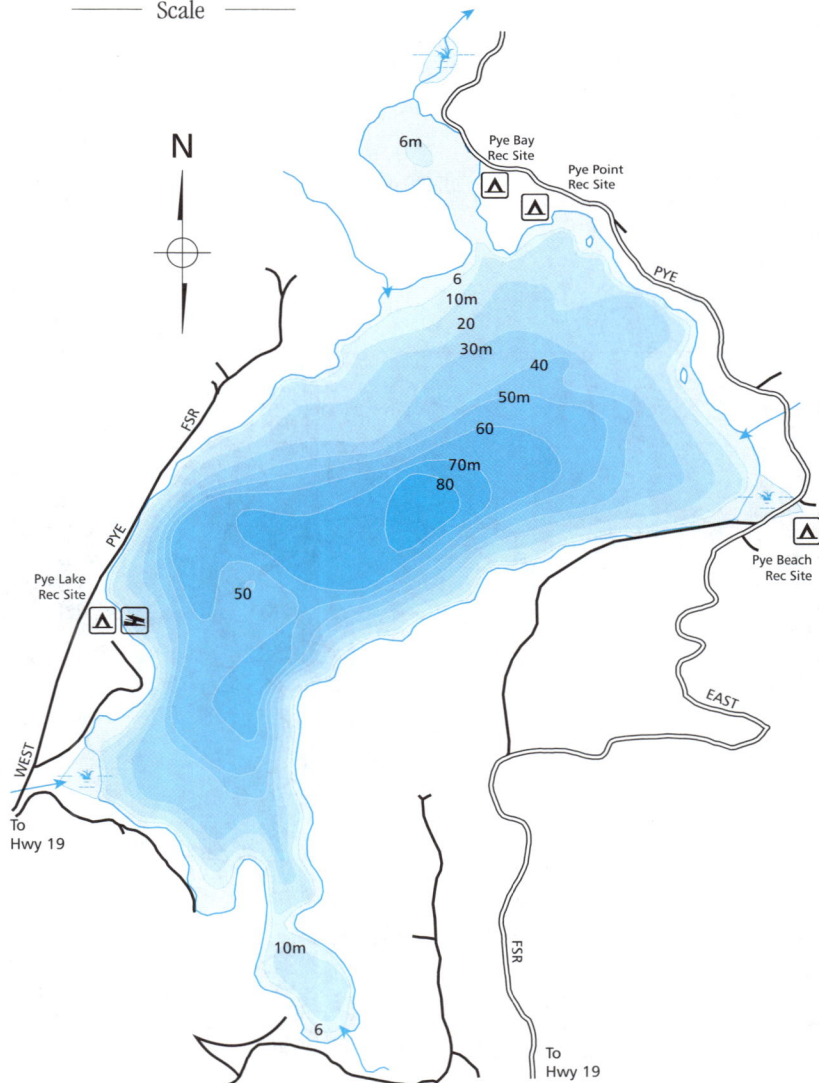

```
200m   0   200m      600m      1000m
                    Scale
```

N

6m

Pye Bay
Rec Site

Pye Point
Rec Site

PYE

6
10m
20
30m
40
50m
60
70m
80

Pye Beach
Rec Site

FSR

PYE

Pye Lake
Rec Site

50

EAST

WEST

To
Hwy 19

10m

FSR

6

To
Hwy 19

Stream Length: 16 km (9.9 mi)
Geographic: 127° 29'00"Lon - W   50° 41'00" Lat - N

www.backroadmapbooks.com

Quatse River

Fishing

The Quatse River is a low-volume, fertile river that makes its way from Quatse Lake above Coal Harbour across the northern tip of the Island to Port Hardy. It holds good numbers of hatchery fish and is a fairly popular river despite its northern position.

Recently, the river has been stocked with cutthroat in an attempt to develop this fishery. There are already a few sea-run cutthroat in the river, Dolly Varden and all five species of salmon. The hatchery stocks the river with 1.5 million pink salmon, 150,000 Coho, 125,000 chum fry and 30,000 steelhead. Returns in the last few years have been quite strong.

The river is only 10 km (6 miles) long, and the fishable length is only half of that. This makes for fishing in some rather busy quarters, especially right below the hatchery. On some days, anglers are standing nearly shoulder to shoulder here. Well, not quite, but try accessing the river at one of the bridges that cross it to avoid the crowds. The stream is not a high volume river and it is just as easy to wade to a better, or at least, less busy, location. Especially in late summer when the salmon start to run.

The river flows a deep brown, stained with tannins that leach from the decaying plant material. This makes the river about the same colour as a weak coffee, and just as easy to see through. As a result, lures and flies have to be brilliantly coloured in order to attract any attention at all. Fluorescent pinks and oranges and greens are the order of the day here. Try a Mepps Aglia in a hot pink or orange, a Roostertail in pink, or your most gaudy, garish yellow and pink wool fly.

One of the most common and most adaptable rigs for steelhead fishing is fast water bobber fishing. The basics of the rig include a weight for getting the lure to the bottom, a lure, and a bobber. The weight should be enough to keep the gear bouncing along the bottom, but not so much that it stays in one place. This gets the lure down to eye level with the fish. This is important, especially in winter (February and March) when the steelhead will only move a little to chase after food. The Quatse is a murky river, and seeing the fish is difficult at the best of times. Using a float is a visual clue as to what is happening beneath the surface.

Fly-fishers can use the same technique, just using different gear. A sinking line (sometimes augmented with an actual weight) and a strike indicator, plus a really gaudy neon fly are recommended to fly-fish the Quatse.

Directions

The Quatse can be accessed from a number of locations. The most obvious place is where the Island Highway (Highway 19) crosses the river. The easiest place to access the river, however, is from the hatchery, located south of the highway off the Coal Harbour Road. There is a pair of bridges that cross the river near the hatchery that provide alternate access points.

Facilities

Most things you need can be found in Port Hardy, including a trio of campgrounds. But if you're there for winter steelhead, it might be better to look for a motel or bed and breakfast.

The hatchery on the river is an interesting place to visit as well. It produces salmon and steelhead to help maintain these fisheries.

Quatse River			
Fish Stocking Data			
Year	Species	Number	Life Stage
2007	Steelhead - Diploid	21,575	Fry/Smolt
2006	Steelhead - Diploid	20,195	Fry/Smolt
2005	Steelhead - Diploid	25,820	Fry/Smolt

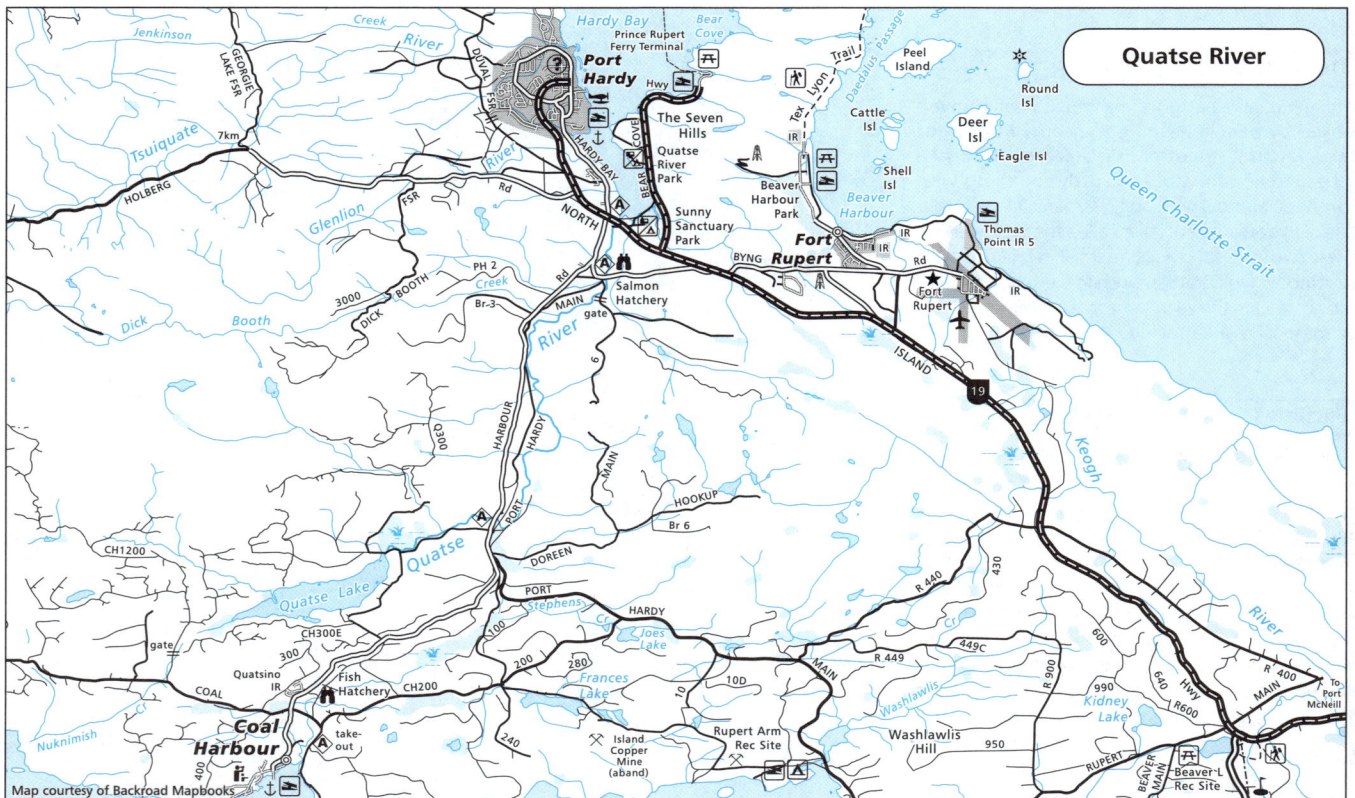

Quatse River

Map courtesy of Backroad Mapbooks

Quamichan Lake

Location: 3 km (1.8 miles) north of Duncan
Elevation: 26 m (85 ft)
Surface Area: 314 ha (776 ac)
Mean Depth: 5 m (16 ft)
Max Depth: 8 m (26 ft)
Way Point: 123° 40′ 00″ Lon - W 48° 48′ 00″ Lat - N

Fishing

Quamichan Lake offers a good fishery due in no small part to the Freshwater Fisheries Society of BC aggressive cutthroat trout stocking program that regularly supplies fish to the lake. Rainbow are also stocked on occasion and both species can provide steady action, especially during the early spring (March to May) or later in the fall. The odd fish reaches an impressive 2.5 kg (5 lbs) in size, but most are generally small.

The shallow lake is not great for trolling, although it is possible to do so, especially early in the spring with a shallow troll, before the fish move into deeper water. However, as soon as the water starts to warm up in the least, it is best to use a float tube or small boat and work the shallower fringe areas of the lake with a worm tipped lure or a damselfly or dragonfly nymph. Another alternative is to spincast or fly-fish near the outflow creek at the south end of the lake, or the inflow creek at the north end. Fishing off the dock is certainly possible, and is often practiced by youngsters, but fishing from shore is difficult as the lake is mostly surrounded by private property, trees or marshy areas.

During the summer months, the lake has a problem with an algae bloom so the lake is not worth fishing for trout. Young anglers seem to delight in the fact they can catch the brown catfish that prefer hanging around docks at this time.

Area Indicator

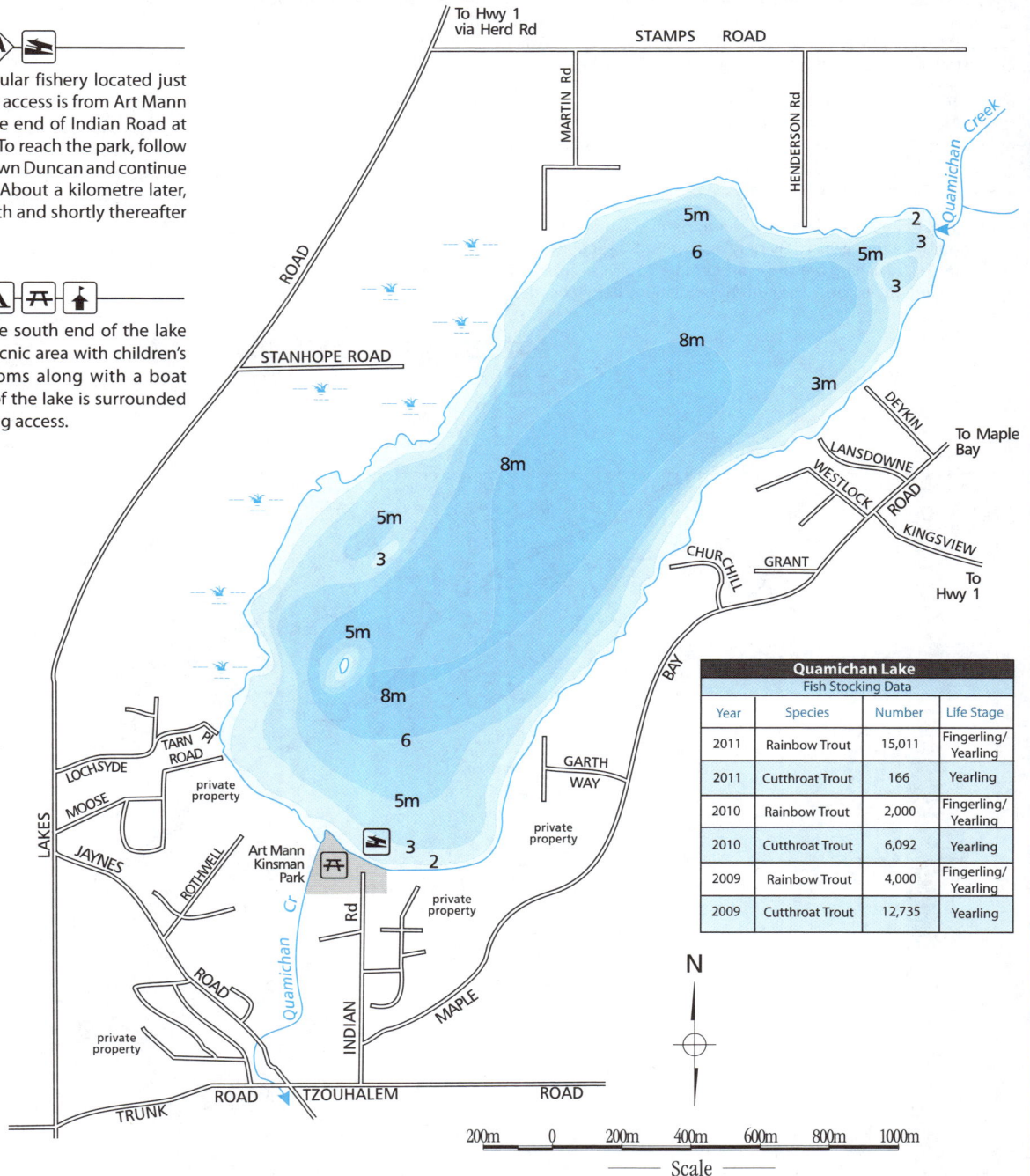

Directions

Quamichan Lake is a popular fishery located just north of Duncan. The best access is from Art Mann Park, which is found at the end of Indian Road at the south end of the lake. To reach the park, follow Trunk Road east of downtown Duncan and continue east on Tzouhalem Road. About a kilometre later, Maple Road branches north and shortly thereafter you will see Indian Road.

Facilities

The **Art Mann Park** at the south end of the lake off Indian Road offers a picnic area with children's playground and washrooms along with a boat ramp and dock. The rest of the lake is surrounded by private property limiting access.

Quamichan Lake Fish Stocking Data			
Year	Species	Number	Life Stage
2011	Rainbow Trout	15,011	Fingerling/Yearling
2011	Cutthroat Trout	166	Yearling
2010	Rainbow Trout	2,000	Fingerling/Yearling
2010	Cutthroat Trout	6,092	Yearling
2009	Rainbow Trout	4,000	Fingerling/Yearling
2009	Cutthroat Trout	12,735	Yearling

Scale: 200m 0 200m 400m 600m 800m 1000m

Big Qualicum River
Stream Length: 24.6 km (15.2 mi)
Geographic: 124° 38'00"Lon - W   49° 23'00" Lat - N

Little Qualicum River
Stream Length: 18.2 km (11.3 mi)
Geographic: 124° 32'8"Lon - W   49° 20'2" Lat - N

www.backroadmapbooks.com

Qualicum Rivers

Fishing

Like many Island Rivers, the Big Qualicum and Little Qualicum Rivers have seen better days. Salmon stocks declined precariously around the turn of the millennium, and, while returns have been better in the last few years, steelhead stocks have taken a beating in the last few years. Today, the rivers are better known as trout streams with the Big Q featuring rainbow and the Little Q brown trout.

Both rivers feature very short fishable sections. In the case of the Big Qualicum River, it is the section from Horne Lake down to Qualicum Bay. The Big Q is a dam controlled river, and access is mostly by foot upstream from the Big Qualicum Fish Hatchery parking area. Note that access is restricted below the hatchery.

In addition to runs of Coho, Chinook, and chum, the Big Q features sea-run cutthroat. However, the river is best known for having quite good fishing for resident rainbow. Stonefly, caddis and on occasion mayfly imitations can all work.

The Little Qualicum drains nearby Cameron Lake to the south of the Big Q. The Little Q is best known for its brown trout but anglers can also find a few kokanee and sea-run cutthroat near the estuary. The wily brown trout can reach nice sizes with catches in the 2 kg (4 lb) range quite common. It is best to focus in the stretch of water below the lake and above the falls using an attractor fly like the Royal Coachman.

In the 1970s, there was a stream clearing project to get rid of the debris in the Big Q that was thought to negatively effect salmon rearing habitat. It proved quite detrimental to the river's habitat. However over the last few years, there has been extensive work to add back the debris to improve habitat. This, along with building side channels and over-wintering alcoves should help re-establish the salmon and steelhead fisheries in years to come.

In an effort to maintain the fishery on these rivers, there are extensive closures and restrictions. The most notable is the artificial fly only restriction for sections of the Big Q, why the sections open on the Little Q is fly-fishing only from September 1 to November 30). These restrictions and closures are always changing, so check the current regulations before heading out.

Directions

There are four places to access the Big Q. Highways 19 and 19A cross the river west of Qualicum Beach. The third and most popular place to access the river is from the Qualicum Hatchery. To get to the hatchery, take the Horne Lake Road off the Island Highway. Watch for signs to the hatchery. If you hit the bridge over the river, you've gone too far. You have, however, found the fourth access point.

The Little Qualicum is also crossed by Highways 19 and 19A to the west of Parksville. Upstream of the Highway 19 crossing, it can also be accessed from the Little Qualicum Spawning Channel, off Melrose Road. This road is found off of Highway 4, 3.5 miles (6 km) west of Coombs. Little Qualicum Falls Park, found a few miles further along Highway 4, is another good access point.

Facilities

There is a campground at **Little Qualicum Falls Provincial Park** with 95 camping sites. Alternatively, there are a number of private campgrounds, resorts and motels throughout the area.

Big Qualicum River			
Fish Stocking Data			
Year	Species	Number	Life Stage
2004	Cutthroat Trout - Anadromous	2,280	Smolt

Little Qualicum River			
Fish Stocking Data			
Year	Species	Number	Life Stage
2007	Cutthroat Trout-Anadromous	13,155	Fry/Smolt
2006	Cutthroat Trout-Anadromous	6,070	Smolt
2005	Cutthroat Trout-Anadromous	7,665	Smolt
2005	Steelhead - Diploid	27,645	Smolt

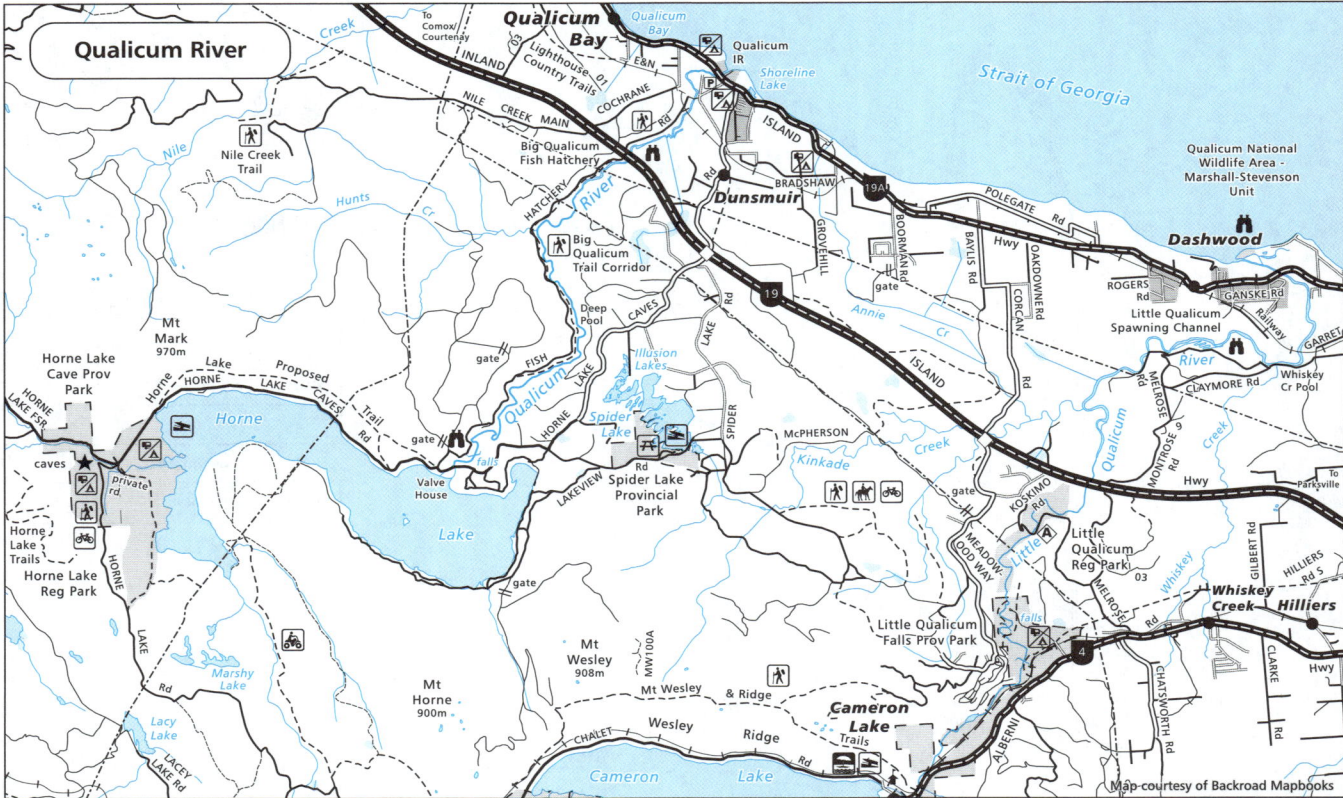

Qualicum River

Map courtesy of Backroad Mapbooks

www.backroadmapbooks.com

Quennell Lake

Location: 15 km (9 miles) southwest of Nanaimo
Elevation: 32 m (105 ft)
Surface Area: 120 ha (296 ac)
Mean Depth: 3.5 m (11 ft)
Max Depth: 7 m (23 ft)
Way Point: 123° 49′00 Lon - W   48° 05′00″ Lat - N

Fishing

One of the most productive lakes on the Island due to its slow nutrient run-off, Quennell Lake is also known as one of the best lakes on the Island for smallmouth bass. There are some big fish in this lake with reports of bass to 3 kg (7 lbs) and both rainbow and cutthroat reaching 2 kg (5 lbs). The uniquely shaped lake also has a good catfish (brown bullhead) population for the young anglers.

The shallow, low elevation lake offers some great trout fishing in the early spring or later in the fall. The rainbow are stocked annually by the Freshwater Fisheries Society of BC so the numbers are maintained despite the heavy fishing pressure at the lake. Visitors will find that the lake is made up of several long channels like bays. However, most of the action for trout will occur in the eastern most bay where the water is deeper. Shore fishing with light tackle in this eastern bay is possible, but many prefer to get out on the water to cast towards shore.

In the summer months when the trout fishing is at a standstill, the bass fishery really heats up. The bass tend to feed on chironomids, small baitfish, leeches and even tadpoles. Although using a fly that matches the local hatch may work well for trout, it doesn't really produce bass. Rather, the flies to use are attractor type patterns such as a Woolly Bugger or Werner shrimp. If spincasting, there are many different plugs such as Rapalas to use. The smaller bass tend to school together and are usually found around cover such as a sunken log, lily pad or weed bed. Unlike trout, the bass do not move much from their hiding place so you have to get your lure or fly right in close to the cover.

Area Indicator

Directions

Quennell Lake is located southeast of Nanaimo and is accessed off of Cedar Road. This road is the main access to the area and can be picked up off the Island Highway just north of the Ladysmith Harbour or off of the highway leading to Duke Point Ferry Terminal.

If coming from the south, follow Cedar Road to Yellow Point Road. This road leads east to the junction of Quennell Road, which provides access to the western end of the lake. If you are coming from the north, Cedar Road once again links to Yellow Point Road and Quennell Road. The better access from this end is off of Yellow Point Road, which runs by the eastern side of the lake. All roads are paved so a car can easily access the lake.

Facilities

Visitors will find a few informal launching areas around the lake. However, the best access is from the **Zuiderzee Campsite & Trailer Park** which offers camping, canoe or row boat rentals and a boat launch on the lake.

Other Options

To the east of Cedar Road are a few fine fishing destinations. **Holden Lake** offers a nice park and cartop boat launch along with a fairly decent year round fishery for small rainbow, cutthroat and smallmouth bass. This lake is described in more detail earlier in the book. Another option to consider is **Michael Lake**, which is located off the Doole Road. The 10 hectare lake has fair spring and fall fishing for small cutthroat and rainbow. Trolling is the preferred method of fishing, although no powerboats allowed.

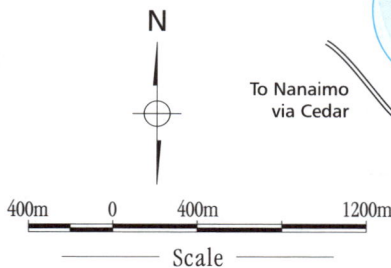

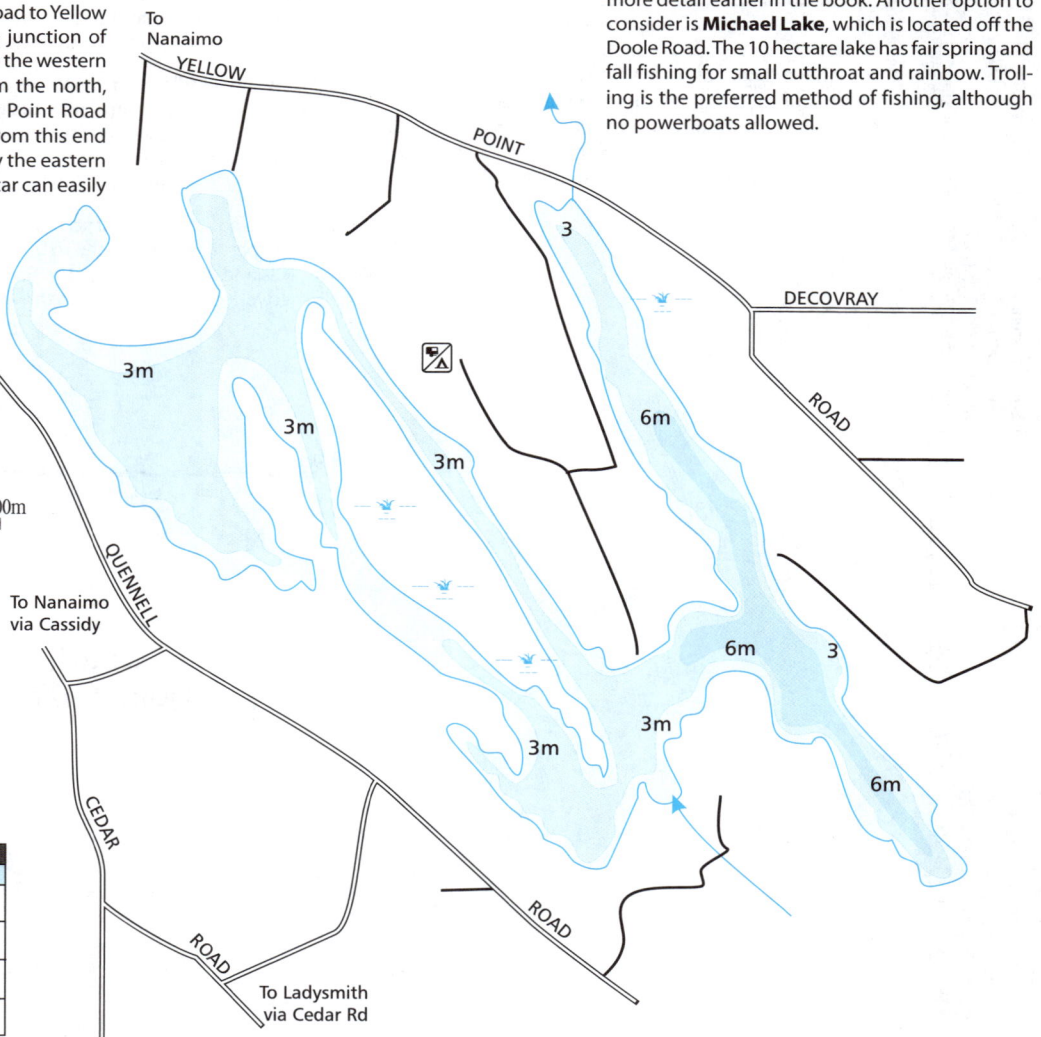

Quennell Lake			
Fish Stocking Data			
Year	Species	Number	Life Stage
2011	Rainbow Trout	5,000	Yearling
2010	Rainbow Trout	5,000	Yearling
2009	Rainbow Trout	5,500	Yearling

© Mussio Ventures Ltd.

Quinsam Lake

Elevation: 179 m (587 ft)
Surface Area: 117 ha (289 ac)
Mean Depth: 7.6 m (25 ft)
Max Depth: 22 m (72 ft)
Way Point: 125° 23' 00" Lon - W 49° 57' 00" Lat - N

Middle Quinsam Lake

Elevation: 179 m (587 ft)
Surface Area: 117 ha (289 ac)
Mean Depth: 7.6 m (25 ft)
Max Depth: 22 m (72 ft)
Way Point: 125° 29' 00" Lon - W 49° 55' 00" Lat - N

Upper Quinsam Lake

Elevation: 369 m (1210 ft)
Surface Area: 505.8 ha
Mean Depth: 13.1 m (43 ft)
Max Depth: 48 m (157 ft)
Way Point: 123° 33' 00" Lon - W 49° 53' 00" Lat - N

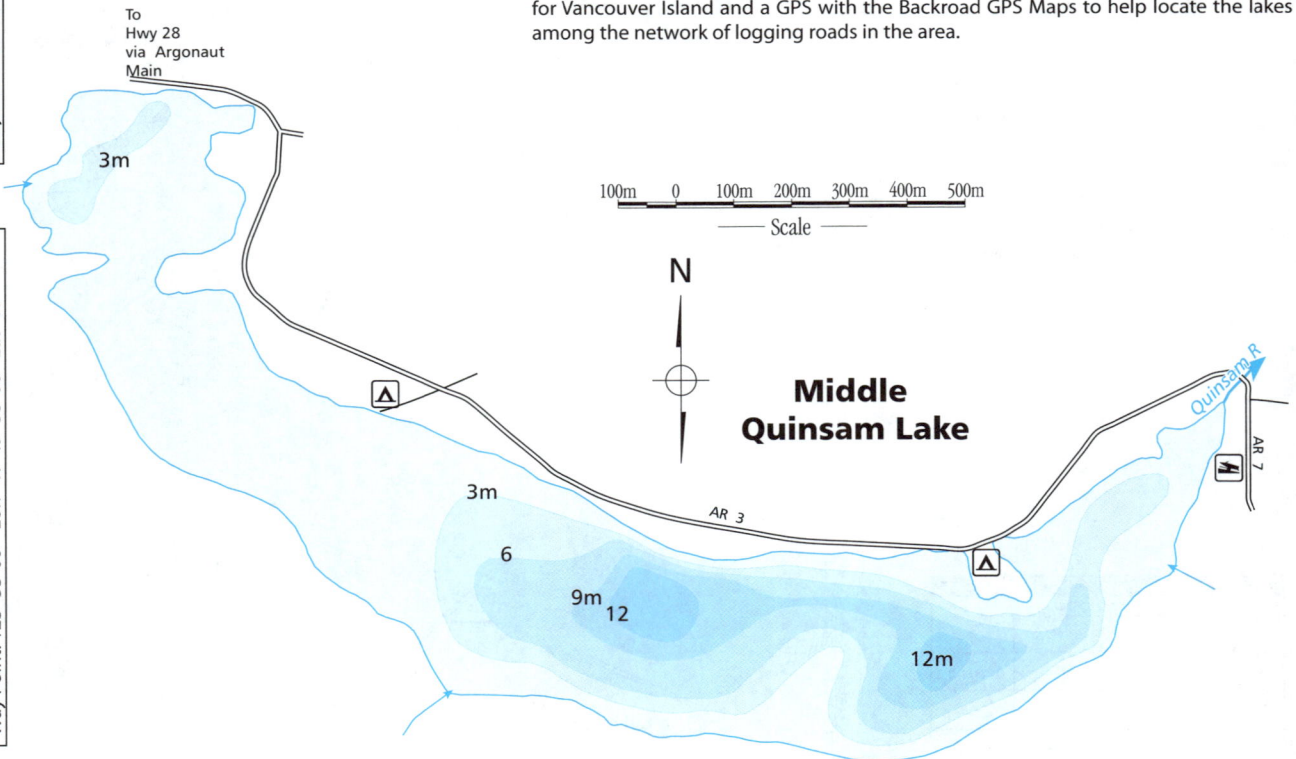

Area Indicator

Fishing

The trio of lakes that make up the Quinsam Lakes are found on the Quinsam River southwest of Campbell River. While the lakes all bear the same name, they are spread out over a couple dozen kilometres, far enough that they all feature a slightly different fishery.

Quinsam Lake is the closest to Campbell River, and is found at the end of Gilson Main. The lake has good fishing for rainbow, cutthroat and Dolly Varden. Shore fishing is certainly possible, but there is a rough boat launch, and getting out onto the lake might prove more productive. Focus your efforts around the inflow and outflow of the Quinsam River at the northwest and southeast ends of the lake respectively. It is best fished in spring and fall.

Middle Quinsam Lake is the smallest of the bunch. It is reached by truck off Argonaut Main and offers good fly-fishing using nymph patterns near the weed beds. There are also a number of good hatches on the lake to look for. Although it is possible to fish from the shore, fishing is much more productive if you can get out onto the water.

Upper Quinsam Lake is the biggest and deepest of the three and found at the end of the Argonaut Main. The size of the lake combined with the higher elevation means that the fishing gets underway a little later in the season. Things don't slow down too much during the summer so this lake is your best alternative when other lakes in the area are suffering from the summer doldrums. Trolling works well on this lake, while shore fishing is limited.

Also attached to Upper Quinsam is the much smaller **Wokas Lake**. The lake is surprisingly deep and offers a similar fishery to the bigger lake.

Facilities

While there are no officially developed facilities on any of the lakes, there are former recreation sites that provide rustic campsites and launches on all. Look for these sites on the western side of Quinsam, the northeast side of Middle Quinsam and the eastern side of Upper Quinsam. The nicest boat launch of the three is found on Upper Quinsam.

Directions

To get to **Quinsam Lake**, take the Gold River Highway (Highway 28) to Duncan Bay Main. Turn left onto Gilson Main, and follow this road to the western side of the lake.

To get to **Upper** and **Middle Quinsam Lakes**, watch for the Elk River Main, just past Echo Lake. Follow this road to Argonaut Main, which leads south. Middle Qunisam is found off the rough AR3 side road, while Upper Quinsam is found a little further along Argonaut Main. When the road begins to stray away from the lake, watch for a turnoff towards the lake. This brings you down to an informal camping and launch area.

At the time of writing, it is unclear if access to these lakes will remain open to the public. If the gates are open, it is well advised to bring a truck a copy of the Backroad Mapbook for Vancouver Island and a GPS with the Backroad GPS Maps to help locate the lakes among the network of logging roads in the area.

To Hwy 28 via Argonaut Main

3m

100m 0 100m 200m 300m 400m 500m
Scale

N

Middle Quinsam Lake

3m

3m

6

9m 12

12m

Quinsam R

AR 7

AR 3

Quinsam Lakes

Quinsam Lake

To Hwy 28

3
6m
9 12
15m
18
21

21

18m
12

9m

6m

3

GILSON

AR 6-1

MAIN

Q130

Wokas Lake

EYE-2

6

30

35m

MAIN

To Hwy 28

Upper Quinsam Lake

35
30
25

20m

15m

20

15

25m

10
6

30

35m

QUINSAM

ARGONAUT

30 45m

N

Elevation: 179 m (587 ft)
Surface Area: 117 ha (289 ac)
Mean Depth: 7.6 m (25 ft)
Max Depth: 22 m (72 ft)
Way Point: 125° 23' 00" Lon - W 49° 57' 00" Lat - N

Quinsam Lake

Elevation: 179 m (587 ft)
Surface Area: 117 ha (289 ac)
Mean Depth: 7.6 m (25 ft)
Max Depth: 22 m (72 ft)
Way Point: 125° 29' 00" Lon - W 49° 55' 00" Lat - N

Middle Quinsam Lake

Elevation: 369 m (1210 ft)
Surface Area: 505.8 ha
Mean Depth: 13.1 m (43 ft)
Max Depth: 48 m (157 ft)
Way Point: 123° 33' 00" Lon - W 49° 53' 00" Lat - N

Upper Quinsam Lake

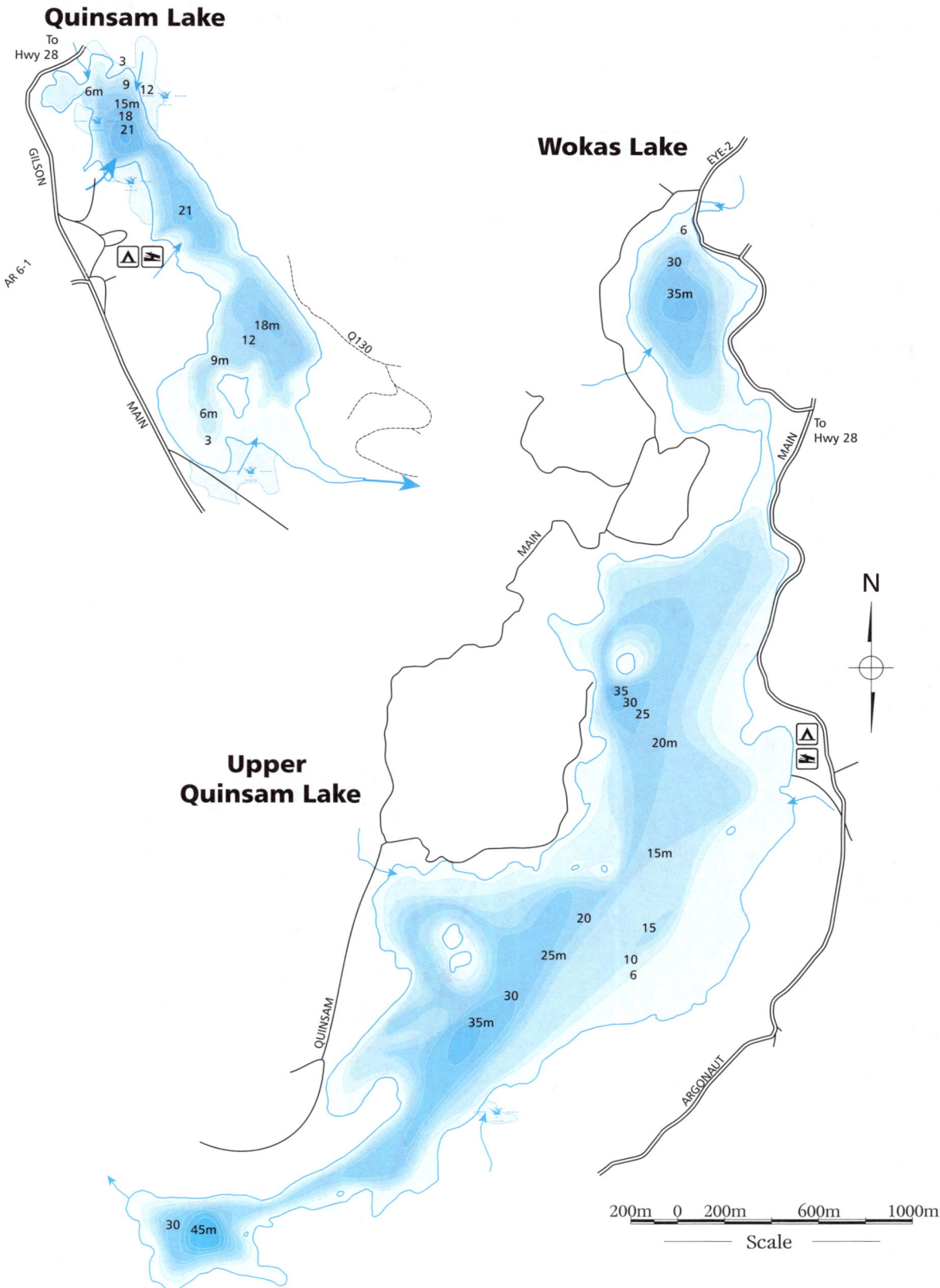

200m 0 200m 600m 1000m

Scale

Location: 25 km (15.5 mi) northwest of Campbell River
Elevation: 160 m (525 ft)
Surface Area: 161 ha (398 ac)
Mean Depth: 25m (82 ft)
Max Depth: 53 m (174 ft)
Way Point: 125° 32′ 00″ Lon - W 50° 13′ 00″ Lat - N

www.backroadmapbooks.com

Roberts Lake

Area Indicator

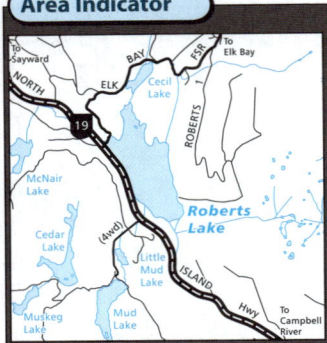

Directions

Roberts Lake is located immediately beside the Island Hwy (Highway 19), 25 km (15 mi) northwest of Campbell River. Access is excellent on a paved road.

Facilities

There is a sandy beach at the pullout along the highway. Many anglers carry a boat down to the beach to launch. It is also possible to camp at this site if you do not mind the highway traffic and the short walk down to the beach. Alternatively, cottages are available for rent at **Roberts Lake Resort**.

Roberts Lake Fish Stocking Data			
Year	Species	Number	Life Stage
2007	Rainbow Trout	3,000	Yearling
2007	Cutthroat Trout	3,000	Yearling
2006	Rainbow Trout	3,000	Yearling
2006	Cutthroat Trout	3,000	Yearling

Fishing

Located just off the Island Highway, Roberts Lake is easy to get to. As a result, the lake is extremely popular for swimming, windsurfing and fishing, especially with anglers out of nearby Campbell River. Fortunately, the Freshwater Fishery Society of BC keeps the lake well stocked. In fact, Roberts Lake is one of the heaviest-stocked lakes on the island, seeing 3,000 rainbows and 3,000 cutthroat added to its population every year. You will also find some Dolly Varden, but in much smaller numbers.

Fishing is fairly consistent through the spring, summer and fall, although it does drop off slightly in summer. There are literally hundreds of options in spoons, spinners or plugs that can be trolled or cast. Flatfish, Hotshots or Kwikfish are the three most common trout plugs used in BC. Silver, black/silver speckled, and fluorescent fire are great colours to have in the tackle box at all times. These plugs, or one of the many variations of spoons or spinners trolled 30–60 cm (12–24 in) behind a lake troll, will usually produce well.

Fly fishers will find the chironomid/midge hatch typically begins in March or April and can remain strong through May. Mayfly hatches start in mid April, followed by the caddisfly/sedge hatch in mid-May. If there is no telltale evidence of a hatch, use a fly pattern that imitates the nymph stages of one of the invertebrates that are an available food source all year long.

The best fishing areas are the shoals, near the drop-off, where the fish are likely to be feeding on nymphs or leeches. Fishing from the shore is also possible, although the best places to try are on the opposite side of the lake from both the road and the boat launch.

Roberts Lake has seasonal regulations that include a bait ban, single barbless hook restrictions and no trout/char over 50 cm (20 in) from November 1 to April 30.

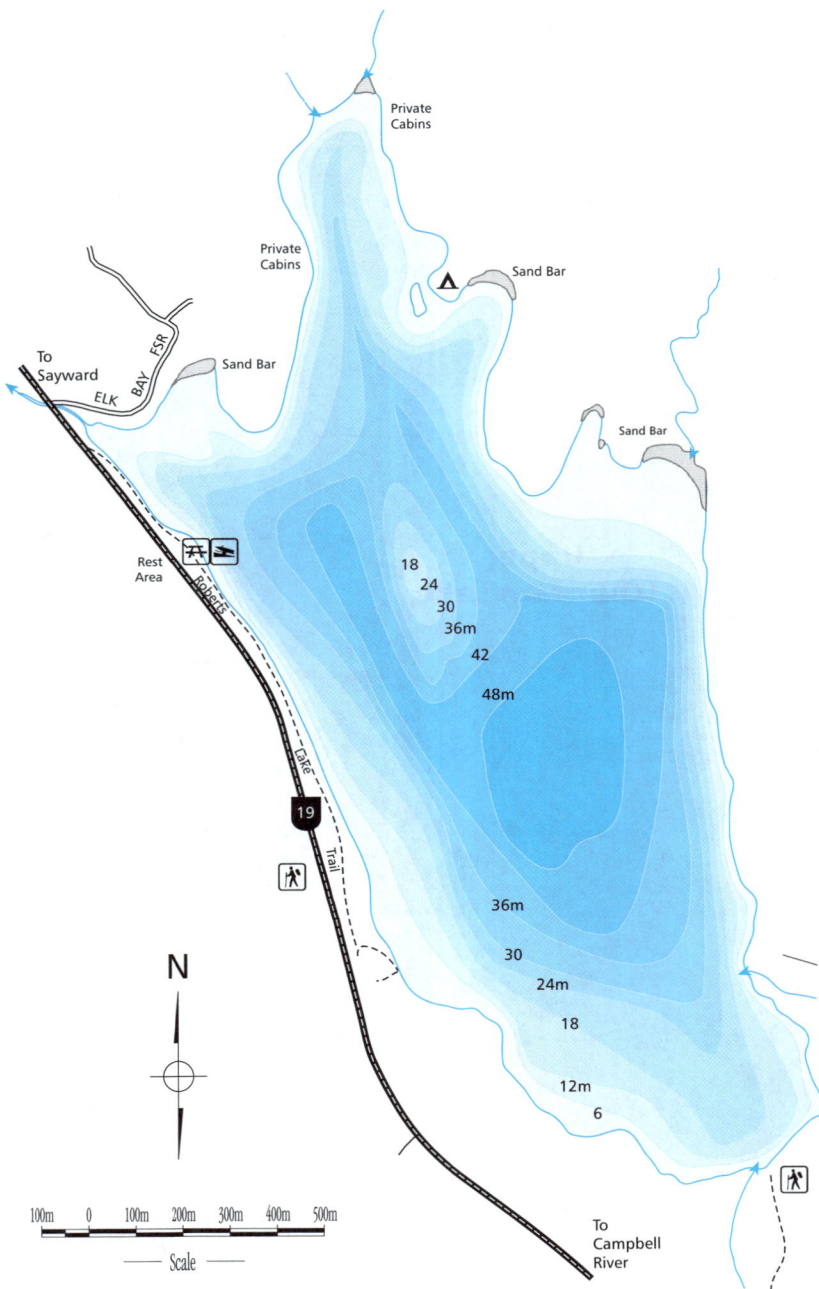

© Mussio Ventures Ltd.

Rooney Lake

Location: 28 km (17.4 mi) west of Sayward
Elevation: 239 m (784 ft)
Surface Area: 15.5 ha (38 ac)
Mean Depth: 7 m (23 ft)
Max Depth: 22 m (72 ft)
Way Point: 126° 09′ 00″ Lon - W   50° 21′ 00″ Lat - N

Fishing

Rooney Lake is a small lake found next to Highway 19, 28 km west of Sayward. The lake is home to a population of cutthroat trout, which were last stocked in 2002. Since that time, the population has been left to its own devices, and, by all accounts, it has been thriving.

Part of that has to do with the fact that the lake has strict regulations for angling. It is managed as a fly-fishing only lake, with a barbless hook restriction and a bait ban as well. This not only helps the fish population, but it should also help the lake produce bigger trout in the future.

Visitors will also find that the lake holds a native population of brown trout and a few larger Dolly Varden that are known to reach 1.5 kg (3 lbs) in size. The brown trout fishery is quite unique for Vancouver Island and there is a one brown trout per day limit to help maintain this fishery.

As the lake has been set aside for fly-fishing only, your choice of gear here is limited. As always, your goal is to match the hatch, or at least offer the fish a chance to eat something that they're interested in. The chironomid/midge hatch typically begins in March or April and can remain strong through May. Mayfly hatches start in mid April, followed by the caddisfly/sedge hatch in mid-May.

While not technically a hatch, another good time to go is when the winged black ants start getting blown off course and into the lakes during warmer periods. If you time it right, these ants can create a flurry of topwater activity. While jumping fish will make any angler excited, it is best to look for subtler rises or rings in the water. Smaller fish tend to jump, while the larger, smarter ones feed with stealth. A good pair of polarized glasses will help you spot fish or underwater structure. Note that the fish are usually lethargic for a few days after the winged ant feast, as the ant's hard exoskeletons are hard to digest. At these times the fishing will be very slow.

When there is no apparent hatch (say, during the fall), the trout usually will go for the usual: leeches, nymphs and attractors like the Doc Spratly or the Woolly Bugger.

The small, relatively low elevation lake is not very deep, as a result fishing tends to slow down nearly to a standstill in the heat of summer. The best time to go is spring or fall.

Directions

The lake is found next to Highway 19, 28 km (15 miles) west of Sayward. The lake can be accessed directly off the highway, or by following a short logging road around to the north side of the lake, where you will find an informal launching area.

Facilities

There is a former recreation site on the north side of the lake, across from the highway. In addition to the rustic boat launch, you will also find a place to camp, too. A few kilometres farther west is the **Montague Creek Recreation Site** offers a more formal camping area.

Area Indicator

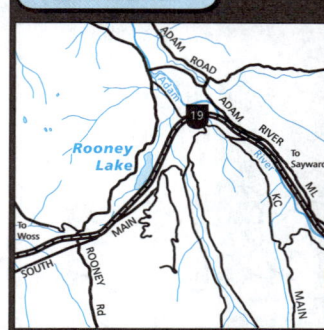

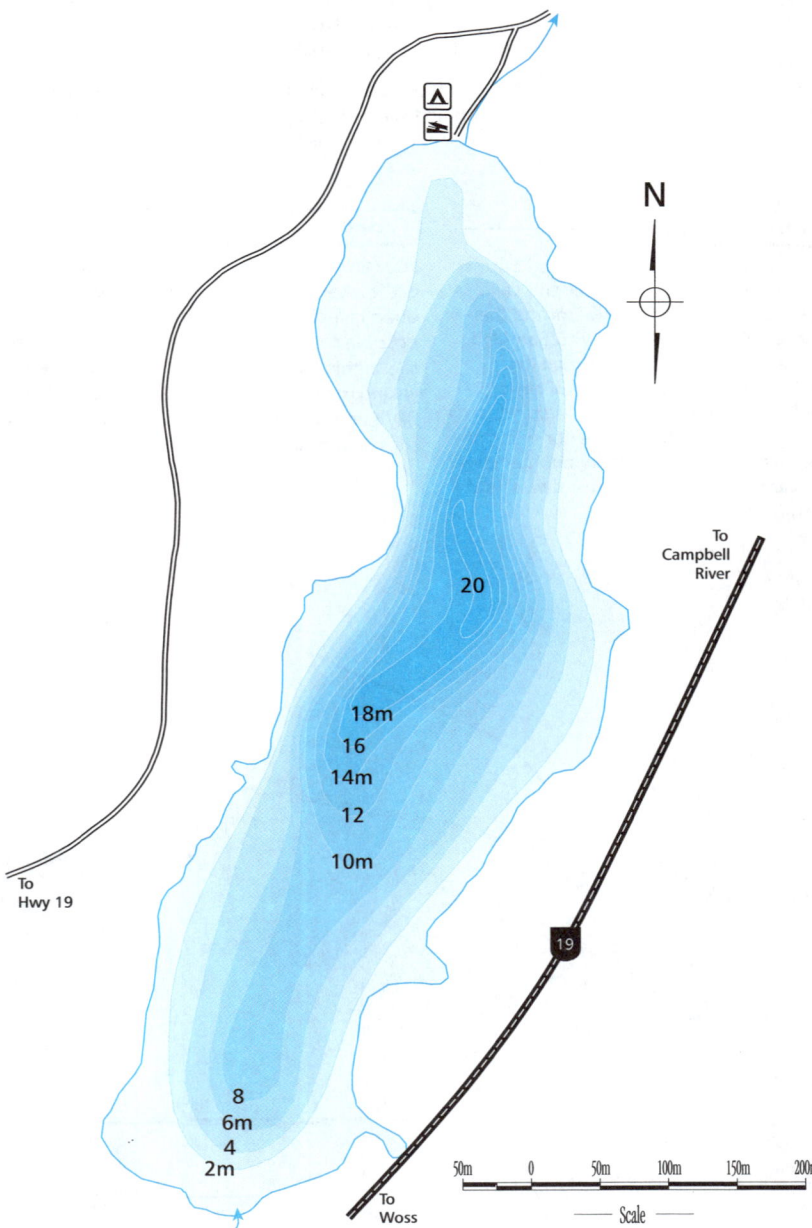

Location: 10 km (6 mi) east of Bamfield
Elevation: 137 m (449 ft)
Surface Area: 13 ha (32 ac)
Mean Depth: 6 m (20 ft)
Max Depth: 11 m (36 ft)
Way Point: 124° 59′00″ Lon - W   48° 49′00″ Lat - N

Rosseau Lake

Rosseau Lake

Area Indicator

Fishing

Rosseau Lake is located off the Central South Main near the quaint town of Bamfield on the West Coast of Vancouver Island. The lake sees relatively light fishing pressure. As a result fishing can be good for small rainbow and cutthroat that average 20–25 cm (8–10 in) in size. There are also some small kokanee and smallmouth bass.

The lake lies in a low elevation valley. This, in combination with its proximity to the ocean, means that the fishing season gets underway as early as March. The season lasts well into fall. Because the lake is on the west coast of the Island, it does not warm up as much as other lakes. While fishing does slow a bit during the summer, it remains more active than other lakes further east.

In spring, fly fishers will be served by trying to match the hatch, starting with the chironomid/midge hatch, which typically begins in March or April and can remain strong through May. Mayfly hatches start in mid April, followed by the caddisfly/sedge hatch in mid-May.

When the trout fishing slows down in summer, the bass fishing begins to pick up. Smallmouth like to hang out where they can hide underneath logs and stumps or rock outcroppings. They take well to common flies like Carey Specials, Woolly Buggers, Doc Spratleys, shrimp, leaches or nymphs.

In fall, the trout fishing picks back up, as the fish begin preparing for the winter. Nymphs and leeches work well at this time, as do standard attractors like the Carey Special and the Doc Spratley. Fishing with bigger flies tends to work well, as the fish are trying to get as much food as possible while expending as little energy as possible.

The lake is deep enough to be trolled with reasonable success. Shore fishing is also possible around most of the lake, but fishing from a belly boat or cartopper with light tackle usually is much more exciting. In particular, try near the overflow of the Pachena River at the west end.

Directions

Rosseau Lake is located off the Central South Main nearby to Frederick and Pachena Lakes. To reach the lake, drive to Port Alberni and then follow the signs pointing the way to Bamfield. The Bamfield Road is a long bumpy road that can be driven by a car. After about 65 km of bone jarring road, look for the Central South Main, which branches from the main road at the north end of Frederick Lake. Follow that road for another few kilometers and you will reach the northwest end of Rosseau Lake.

Facilities

You can launch a small boat off the northern shore of the lake via Central South Main. There is no developed camping area at the lake, but it is certainly possible to camp at roadside if you do not mind the logging truck activity. Alternatively, if you're willing to make the trip into Bamfield, the Pachena Bay Campground is considered one of the nicest sites on the island.

Other Options

Along the Bamfield Road nearby to Bamfield are **Frederick** and **Pachena Lakes**.

Rainbow and cutthroat make up the bulk of the action, although Pachena also offers a few Dolly Varden. Look for more details on these lakes earlier in the book.

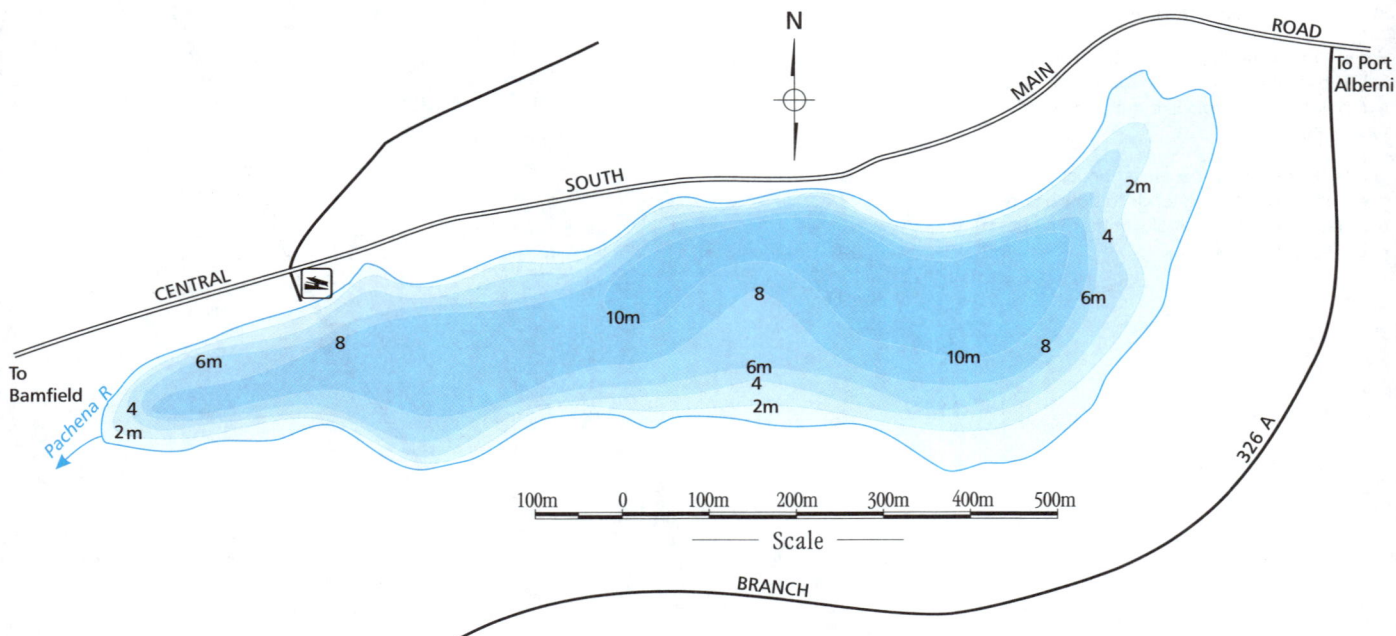

Scale

Round Lake

Location: 16 km (10 mi) west of Nanaimo west of Sayward
Elevation: 310 m (1017 ft)
Surface Area: 3.7 ha (9 ac)
Mean Depth: 4.6 m (15 ft)
Max Depth: 10 m (33 ft)
Way Point: 124° 09' 00" Lon - W   49° 12' 00" Lat - N

Fishing

Round Lake is relatively remote lake located in the hills to the west of Nanaimo. It is low enough in elevation to offer an early season fishery for small rainbow and cutthroat. The lake is only 10 m (33 ft) deep so the water warms in the summer months resulting in slow fishing. As a result, try in April to early June and again in September to October for best success.

The lake is a very promising fly-fishing lake due to the extensive shoals. It is best to work along the southern and eastern shores where the shoals are more pronounced. During brighter periods, the fish hang out in the transition zones between deep water before cruising into the shallower water to eat. Casting a fly that matches the hatch into these areas can result in a nice trout. Searching patterns will work when there are no hatches, especially in the fall.

Shore anglers will find this lake almost impossible to tackle. The north and the south shores are extremely marshy, while the western shore is littered with snags and other debris. The eastern shore is all but inaccessible except by boat, and if you have one of those, why not just fish from it? Of course, a float tube will work, too, as will anything that allows you to get out onto the water. Casting flies, bait and a bobber or small spinners all work as long as you cast from the deeper areas of the lake into the shallows.

The lake is also deep enough to troll, so long as you stay out past the drop-off and do not fish too deep. Remember, the western shores of the lake are filled with all manner of snags and debris to snap your line and the northern shore is rather shallow.

Area Indicator

Directions

Found in the hills to the west of Nanaimo, visitors are well advised to bring a truck to reach the lake. The best access is found from Doumont Road, which is found at the north of Nanaimo off of the Inland Island Highway (Highway 19). To find Doumont Road, look for the Hammond Bay Interchange and then head east a short distance to Metral Road before driving south. Within a kilometer, turn right and you will be on Doumont Road, which links with Weigles Road. Within another 6 kilometers, you will come to a "T" intersection. Head north and soon you will be at the west end of Round Lake.

Note that access into this area may be closed or restricted. It is best to enquire locally before planning a trip into the area.

Facilities

There are no developed facilities at the lake. It is possible to launch a small boat where the road leads along the western shores of the lake. Nearby Nanaimo and Lantzville are thriving communities that offer all amenities including retailers, camping areas, hotels and motels.

Other Options

Round Lake is nearby to **Boomerang Lake, Cattle Lake, Blackjack Lake** and **Kidney Lake**. All these lakes have good numbers of trout caught by spin-casting or fly-fishing. Boomerang and Blackjack Lakes are written up in greater detail earlier in this book.

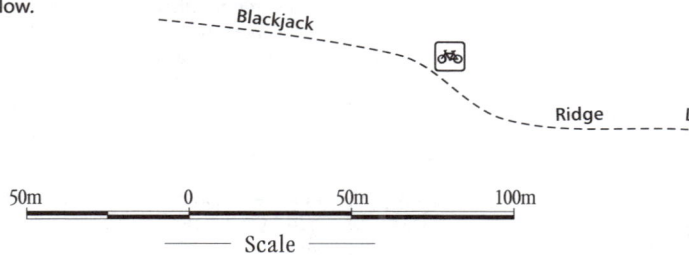

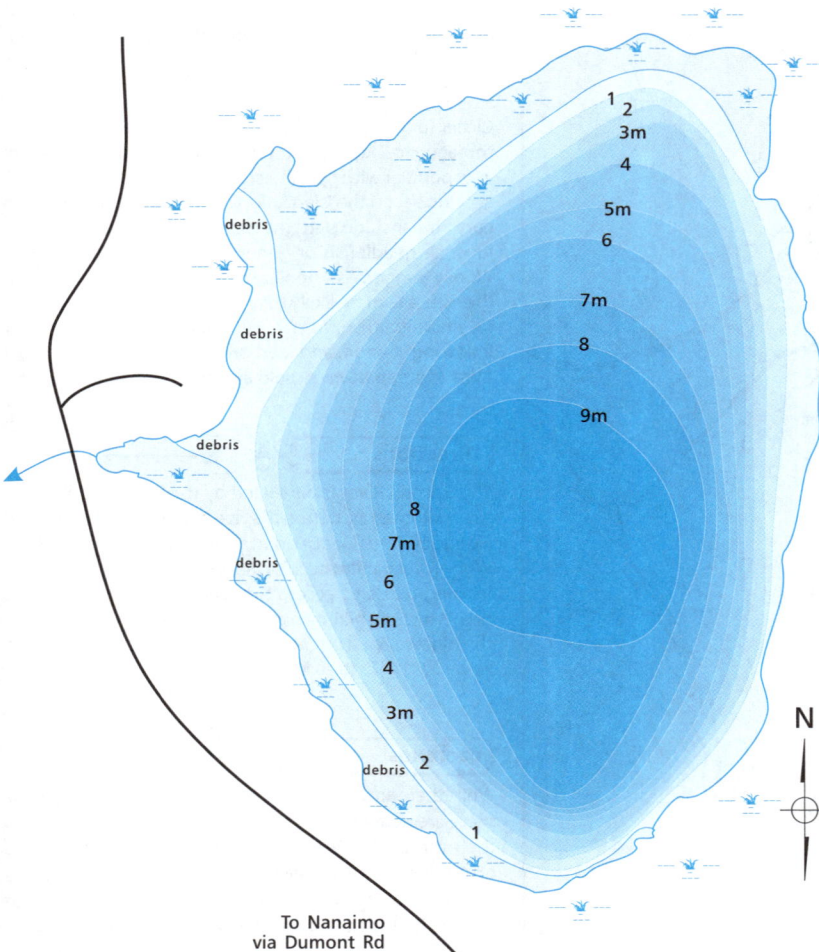

Round Lake			
Fish Stocking Data			
Year	Species	Number	Life Stage
2007	Cutthroat Trout	500	Yearling
2006	Cutthroat Trout	500	Yearling
2005	Cutthroat Trout	500	Yearling

Stream Length: 87.6 km (54.5 mi)
Geographic: 125° 54′00″Lon - W   50° 18′00″Lat - N

Salmon River

Salmon River

1. Garbage Can Pool
2. Boards Pit Pool
3. White River Pool
4. Salmon River Estuary

Map courtesy of Backroad Mapbooks

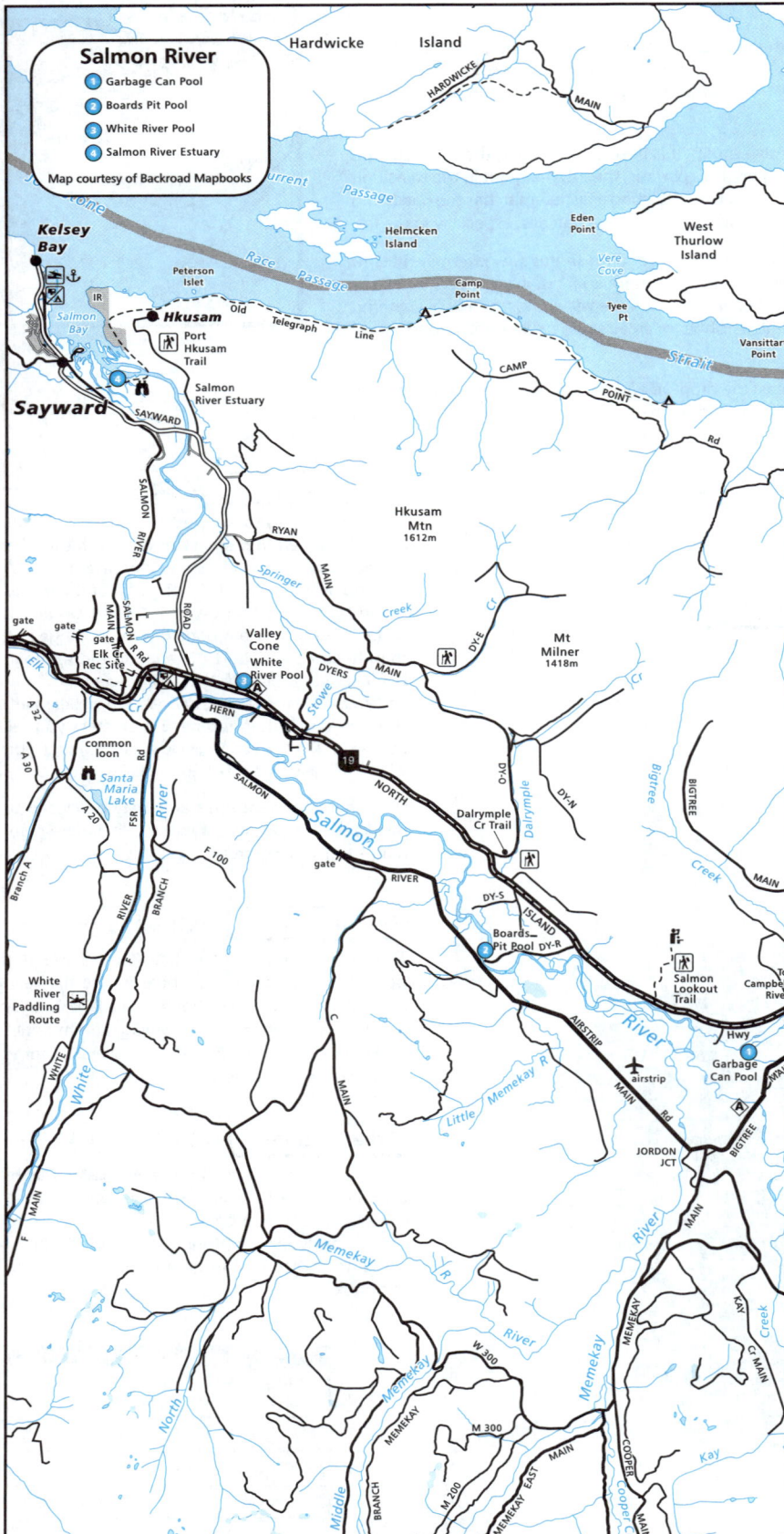

Fishing

Fed by the Memekay and White Rivers, the Salmon River is one of the best performing rivers on the east coast of Vancouver Island for steelhead. In addition to summer and winter steelhead, the river has rainbow trout and Dolly Varden in the upper reaches along with one of the best runs of sea-run cutthroat on the Island. The river also features runs of all five species of salmon, including good runs of Coho and pinks. Despite these acclaims and close proximity to the highway, the river sees very light fishing pressure.

Historically, the Salmon was one of the best steelhead streams on the Island. While it has never had the same returns as other rivers, the fish were the biggest you would find. The river was also one of the first to experience habitat enhancement, dating back to the mid-1970s. And while it hasn't been perfect, the river has fared better compared to others on the east coast of the Island. One of the most successful elements of habitat restoration has been fertilizing a 30 km section of the river to replace the nutrients lost with the decline in returning salmon (and their carcasses). More recently, side channels have been developed in the watershed to improve over-winter survival of steelhead and Coho juvenile.

Still, steelhead returns are all over the map, with a few good years, followed by a few bad years. The last few years (2006-2007) have been good years. Fishing has been decent and there are still steelhead over 9 kg (20 lbs) being caught. The Garbage Cans Pool, at the junction of Bigtree Creek, is a good place to look for steelhead. Further downstream, the junction with the White River is a popular fly-fishing pool.

Closer to the mouth of the river, you will find sea-run cutthroat up to 2 kg (4 lbs), especially in the estuary. These are very popular with fly-fishers, and remain one of the strongest stocks on the Island. Popular fly patterns for sea-run cutthroat include patterns that imitate stonefly nymphs, juvenile needlefish or general attractor patterns like a Woolly Bugger. As a general rule, the lower the fish are in the river, the more likely they will chase after patterns that resemble baitfish. Also, cutthroats often enter the river following salmon, and feed on the salmon eggs. Using a salmon egg pattern should also be successful upstream.

Directions

The Salmon River is paralleled by the Island Highway for a few kilometres, before the river turns north to Sayward along Sayward Road. A good access point is at the Salmon/White River confluence. Further upstream there are several logging roads to access the river from. Popular access points include hiking in to the Bigtree Creek estuary from the highway pull out at the 54 km to Campbell River sign as well as off Bigtree Main near Jordan Junction.

Facilities

While there are a variety of facilities in the town of Sayward, there are no recreation sites or parks with facilities along the river itself. There is rustic campground at Elk Creek, north of the Sayward junction near the Salmon River. There are a number of campgrounds in and around Sayward as well, including the **Fisherboy Park RV Campground.**

San Juan River

Fishing

The San Juan River is a lazy river along the west coast of Vancouver Island, best accessed from Port Renfrew. Its main tributary is the Harris Creek, a popular fishing stream in its own right. The streams are best known for their steelhead fishing, with both a summer and a winter run.

Summer run steelhead are a different beast than winter run steelhead. Summer run steelhead enter the San Juan well before it is time to spawn. As a result, they are often more interested in eating than in partaking in ichthyologic intercourse. Winter run steelhead, on the other hand, are more interested in spawning. So anglers need different techniques when fishing for either. Summer steelhead will actually chase flies like a steelhead bee, a stone fly nymph, or lures like a Gooey Bob when they go floating past. In the winter, what you present is almost meaningless as long as you drop it within a few inches of the steelhead's nose. And whether the fish strike out of hunger or annoyance is a matter of some debate. In the summer, you can watch the steelhead give chase to a well presented lure, and you can see more clearly when the fish takes the lure, meaning you have a better chance of setting the hook. Regardless, it is the fight that is the thing, and steelhead, whether winter or summer, will put up one heck of a battle.

During the fall, anglers will find a strong return of Chinook, followed by Coho in October and November. The Coho fishery on also quite popular since returns are usually good. In fact, the San Juan and Harris system is one of only two river systems on the west coast of Vancouver Island with returns of over 5,000 fish, on average. And the fish are unusually large; the biggest Coho pulled out of the Harris weighed in at over 13.5 m (30 lbs). And there are occasional catch and keep openings on the river; call DFO Victoria at (250) 363-3252 for current openings.

When there are no runs happening, anglers can try their hand at catching some of the river's resident cutthroat, which take well to flies like a Royal Coachman. The cutts are most plentiful in the lower reaches of the river.

Floating the river is quite popular. Many people put in at either the bridge on Harris Creek or the bridge over the San Juan, and float down to Fairy Lake. A shuttle is needed for this trip. Popular fishing holes include the 11 Mile Hole on the Harris, which is popular for lure casters, and the 13 Mile Hole, which is popular for fly-fishers. On the San Juan, the two most popular places to fish are the bridge near town, and the San Juan Bridge Recreation Site.

Anglers should note the river is closed to fishing above the Fleet River.

Directions

The San Juan River flows into Port San Juan at Port Renfrew. Access to the river's estuary is from the Gordon River Main Bridge or from Highway 14. The upper reaches of the river can be accessed from the new Pacific Marine Road. This paved road links Port Renfrew with Lake Cowichan providing good access to the middle stretch of river.

Accessing the upper reaches is best off the Old Port Renfrew Road, which branches east of the Pacific Marine Road. This road also accesses the San Juan River Recreation Site, a popular access point.

Facilities

There is camping at the various recreation sites along the Pacific Marine Road. The most popular are **Fairy Lake** and the **San Juan River Recreation Sites.** Alternatively, there are private campsites, motels and restaurants along with most other amenities in the quaint town of Port Renfrew.

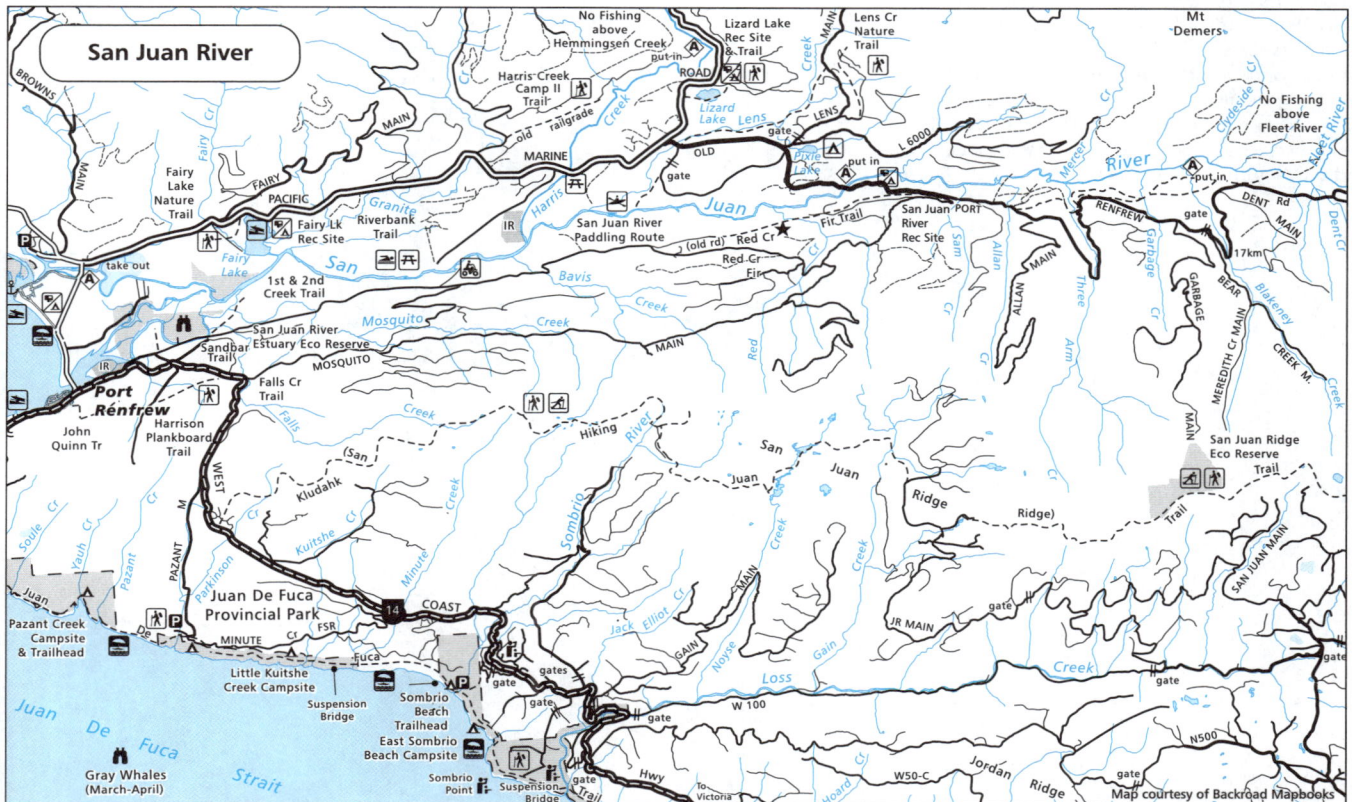

San Juan River map

Location: 31.5 km (20 miles) northeast of Bamfield
Elevation: 41 m (135 ft)
Surface Area: 133 ha (329 ac)
Mean Depth: 15 m (49 ft)
Max Depth: 29 m (95 ft)
Way Point: 124° 53' 00"W Lat - W   48° 54' 00" Lat - N

Sarita Lake

Area Indicator

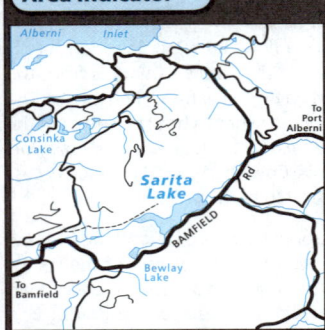

Fishing

Sarita Lake is located northeast of Bamfield next to the Bamfield Road. The fairly big, low elevation lake offers good fishing for small cutthroat, rainbow, Dolly Varden and kokanee from April to October. Due to it's location on the cooler west side of the Island, fishing remains relatively steady even in the warmer summer months.

The lake is well suited for trolling; the trick is to get a boat of any size on the lake now that the recreation site is permanently closed. Luckily the lake is deep enough and drops off quickly enough to allow for easy shore fishing. Casting almost any small spinner or spoon with some bait (worms are preferred) can prove successful. Favorites are the Panther Martin (silver or black), black Mepps or Blue Fox. As for lures, the Deadly Dick with worms is a classic, but small Dick Nite, Flatfish or Kwikfish also work well. Try casting along the shore or towards a fallen log, weed bed or drop-off. Use the countdown method to find where the fish are holding. With each cast, count a little longer until you find the strike zone.

The better places to cast from shore are near the old launch site at the southeast end of the lake and at the point across from this washed out area. You will need to cross the Sarita River to get to that point.

Due to its size, the lake is not a great float tube lake. It is better to launch a canoe or pontoon boat and beetle over to the inflow creeks, the outflow and/or inflow to the Sarita River. You will achieve the best results by casting towards shore at drop-offs and towards weed beds or deadfalls.

Directions

Sarita Lake is located northeast of Bamfield on the West Coast of Vancouver Island. The lake is found next to the busy Bamfield Road. To reach the lake, drive to Port Alberni and then follow the signs pointing the way to Bamfield. The Bamfield Road is a long bumpy road that can be driven by a car. After about 49 km of bone jarring road, Sarita Lake sneaks up on the west side of the road.

Facilities

In the winter of 2008, the former Sarita Lake Recreation Site was destroyed by a storm, forcing the Ministry of Tourism, Sports and the Arts to close the site permanently. There was a boat launch there, but it is no longer accessible. Towards the south end, there is a picnic area and informal place to camp that is still open. There is no boat launch here, but it is possible to hand launch small craft.

Other Options

Further along the Bamfield Road closer to Bamfield are **Frederick** and **Pachena Lakes**. Primarily rainbow and cutthroat lakes, Pachena also offers a few Dolly Varden. Look for more details on these lakes earlier in the book. Another option to consider is the **Sarita River**. There are a couple falls along the river that block migration, but it is a good place to find sea-run cutthroat trout in the lower reaches, resident cutthroat in the upper, and a fair return of winter steelhead.

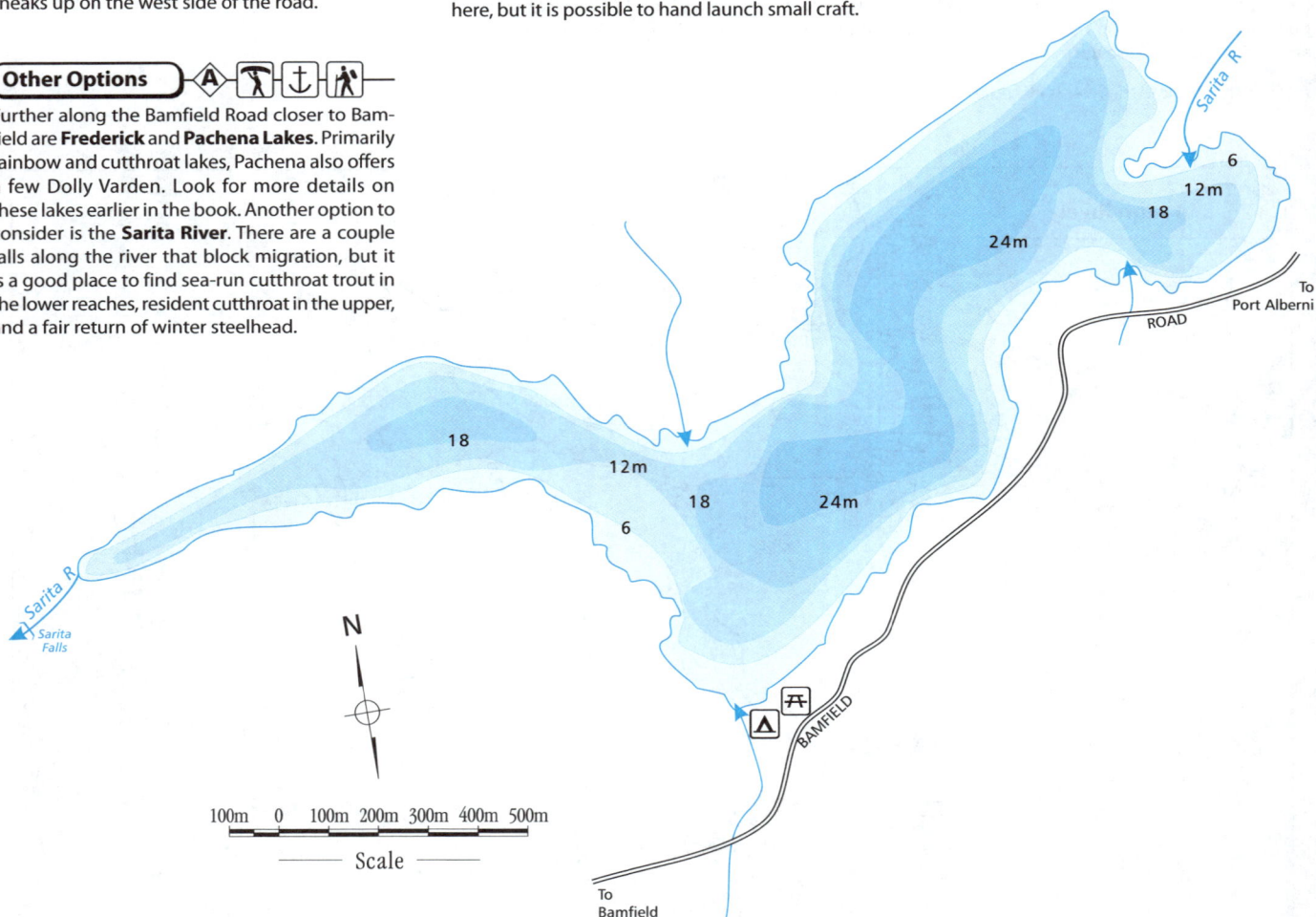

N

100m   0   100m   200m   300m   400m   500m

Scale

To Bamfield

Sarita R

6
12m
18
24m

To Port Alberni

ROAD

18
12m
18
6
24m

BAMFIELD

Sarita R

Sarita Falls

Shawnigan Lake

Location: 16 km (10 mi) south of Duncan
Elevation: 118 m (387 ft)
Surface Area: 537 ha (1,326 ac)
Mean Depth: 12 m (39 ft)
Max Depth: 50 m (164 ft)
Way Point: 123° 38' 00" Lon - W   48° 38' 00" Lat - N

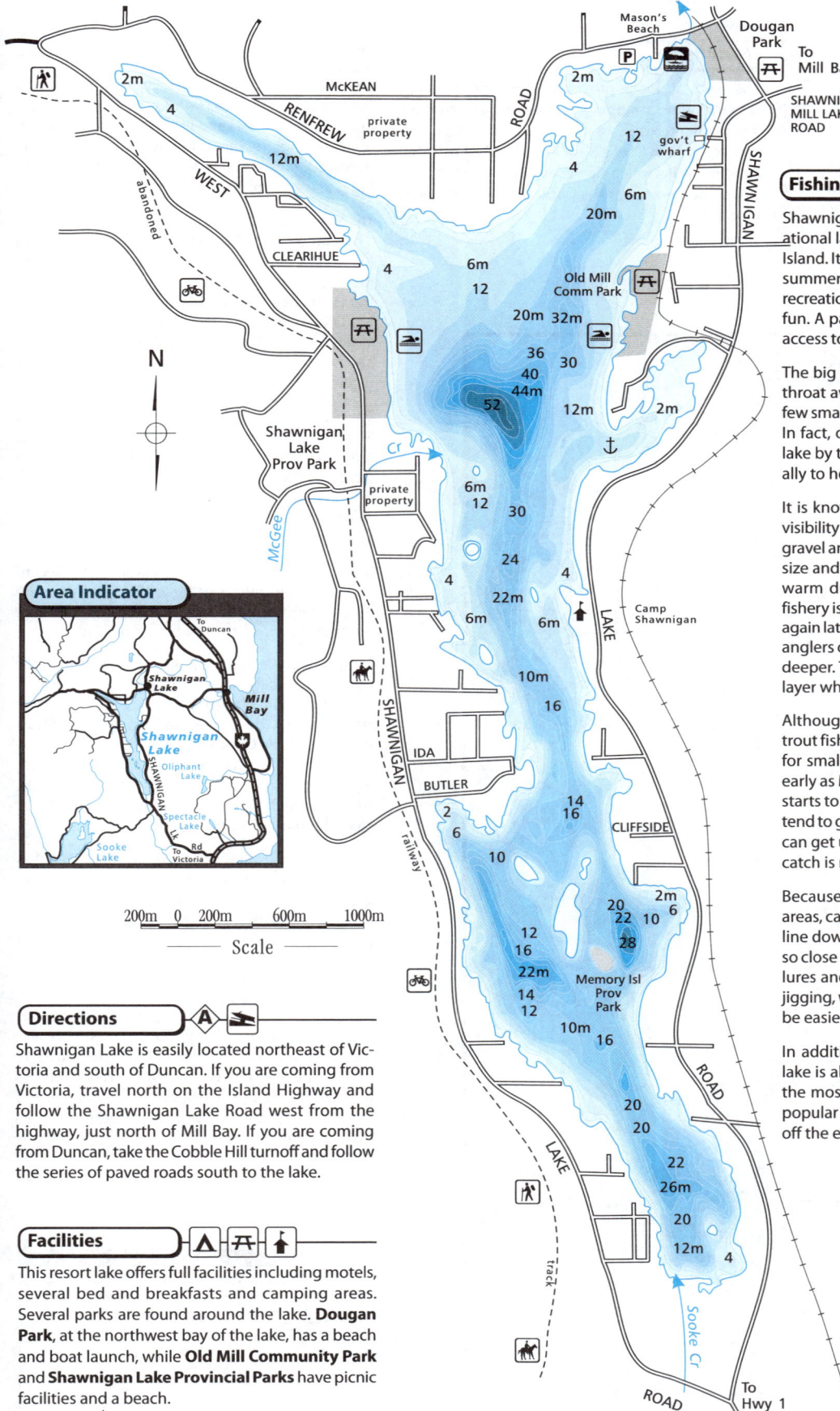

Map Labels

McKEAN
RENFREW
private property
WEST
abandoned
CLEARIHUE
Mason's Beach
P
Dougan Park
To Mill Bay
SHAWNIGAN-MILL LAKE ROAD
gov't wharf
Old Mill Comm Park
N
Shawnigan Lake Prov Park
Cr
McGee
private property
SHAWNIGAN
Camp Shawnigan
Lake
IDA
BUTLER
railway
CLIFFSIDE
Memory Isl Prov Park
ROAD
LAKE
track
Sooke Cr
ROAD
To Hwy 1

Depth markings: 2m, 4, 12m, 4, 12, 4, 6m, 12, 4, 20m, 32m, 36, 40, 44m, 52, 30, 12m, 2m, 6m, 12, 30, 24, 22m, 6m, 6m, 10m, 16, 14, 16, 2, 6, 10, 12, 16, 22m, 14, 12, 10m, 16, 20, 22, 10, 28, 2m, 6, 20, 20, 22, 26m, 20, 12m, 4, 2m, 12, 6m, 20m, 2m, 6m

Area Indicator

To Duncan
Shawnigan Lake
Mill Bay
Shawnigan Lake
Oliphant Lake
SHAWNIGAN
Spectacle Lake
Rd
Sooke Lake
To Victoria

Scale

200m 0 200m 600m 1000m
Scale

Directions

A

Shawnigan Lake is easily located northeast of Victoria and south of Duncan. If you are coming from Victoria, travel north on the Island Highway and follow the Shawnigan Lake Road west from the highway, just north of Mill Bay. If you are coming from Duncan, take the Cobble Hill turnoff and follow the series of paved roads south to the lake.

Facilities

This resort lake offers full facilities including motels, several bed and breakfasts and camping areas. Several parks are found around the lake. **Dougan Park**, at the northwest bay of the lake, has a beach and boat launch, while **Old Mill Community Park** and **Shawnigan Lake Provincial Parks** have picnic facilities and a beach.

Fishing

Shawnigan Lake is one of the more beautiful recreational lakes found on the East Coast of Vancouver Island. It is also one of the most popular. During the summer months, anglers will share the water with recreational boaters, jetskiers and others out having fun. A paved road circles the lake, providing good access to the many cabins and facilities on the lake.

The big lake has fair numbers of rainbow and cutthroat averaging 40 cm (16 in) in size along with a few small kokanee, whitefish and smallmouth bass. In fact, over 30,000 rainbow are dumped into this lake by the Freshwater Fishery Society of BC annually to help maintain the trout fishery.

It is known as a clear lake, with 3–5 m (8-15 ft) of visibility being the norm. The bottom is mostly sand, gravel and rock, with sparse weed cover. Despite it's size and impressive depths, the lake still gets fairly warm during the summer. This means the trout fishery is best during the spring (March to June) and again later in the fall (September to October). Ardent anglers can still find trout in the summer by trolling deeper. The trick is to find the cooler thermocline layer where the trout prefer to hang out.

Although the summer months are fairly slow for trout fishing, this is the best time of the year to look for smallmouth bass. The bass can start to bite as early as March and can be lured away until the lake starts to cool again in fall. Later in the year, the bass tend to go for plugs like a trout coloured X-Rap. Bass can get up to almost 3.5 kg (7 lbs), but the average catch is much smaller.

Because bass like to hang out in well-protected areas, casting for bass is an art, as you must lay your line down close enough to attact the bass, but not so close as to get snagged. Bass also like soft plastic lures and artifical worms. The latter works well for jigging, which is fairly effective and should prove to be easier on your lures than casting.

In addition to the above-mentioned species, the lake is also home to a few yellow perch. While not the most popular game fish, they are tasty, and a popular target for young anglers. Jigging for perch off the end of a dock can be a real treat.

Shawnigan Lake Fish Stocking Data			
Year	Species	Number	Life Stage
2011	Rainbow Trout	11,851	Fry - Catchables
2010	Rainbow Trout	41,392	Fry - Catchables
2009	Rainbow Trout	33,279	Fry - Catchables

Sooke River

Sooke River

Directions

A

Sooke is located west of Victoria on Highway 14. The highway crosses the Sooke River near where the river flows into the harbour. Just east of the river, Sooke River Road leaves the highway and follows the river north to Sooke Potholes Provincial Park. Phillips Road parallels the west side of the river. To reach the upper reaches, continue north from the potholes on the Galloping Goose Recreation Trail that follows the former railway as far as the ghost town of Leechtown.

Facilities

The town of Sooke provides all amenities necessary including shopping, restaurants and motels. If you are interested in camping, there is a private campground at Sooke River Flats. **Sooke Potholes Provincial Park** is a day-use only park that provides good access and a popular swimming hole in summer.

Fishing

The Sooke River is a pretty, short river that drains Sooke Lake into Sooke Harbour. Despite the river's proximity to Victoria and impressive hatchery program, fishing pressure is not as heavy as might be expected. River anglers are often drawn north to big name streams like the Campbell or the Gold.

The Sooke Salmon Enhancement Society operates a hatchery on the Sooke River, releasing up to five hundred thousand Chinook salmon plus two hundred thousand Coho salmon and twelve to fifteen thousand Steelhead each year. In addition to these impressive numbers, the river has a small run of sockeye, as well as small populations of resident and sea-run cutthroat and resident rainbow that receive little attention.

That's the good news. Now the bad. Returns for the 2006 and 2007 seasons to the Sooke were dismal, forcing the cancellation of the 2008 Chinook Fishing Derby. In 2006, only 300 Chinook were counted in the river and in 2007 that number dropped to 150. The factors for the low returns are many, but it all adds up to terrible fishing for salmon.

Steelhead in the river are faring little better. Recent counts of returning steelhead have been around 50 returning fish annually. Although small, these numbers have been stable for the last few years.

Fly-fishing is the most popular means of fishing the Sooke, especially since there is a fly-fishing only restriction below the falls from September 1 to November 30. This is the peak season for salmon, in particular the Coho and chum runs, which show up in late October and run through to November. Fly-anglers don't mind as all since both species take well presented flies. The open banks with lots of space for back casting are an added bonus.

There is a no-fishing zone around the Sooke Potholes (a popular recreation area). It is possible to access the river below the potholes, but few people do. Instead, the river is best accessed from the west, from Phillips Road, and most of the fishing takes place in a stretch across from the Sun River Estates. There is a riverside trail here that allows anglers good access to the river.

On top of the hatchery work, Sooke Salmon Enhancement Society is looking to open up more salmon spawning areas to improve returns. The falls at Sooke Potholes present a barrier to spawning and they are looking into adding a fish ladder to open up habitat above the falls.

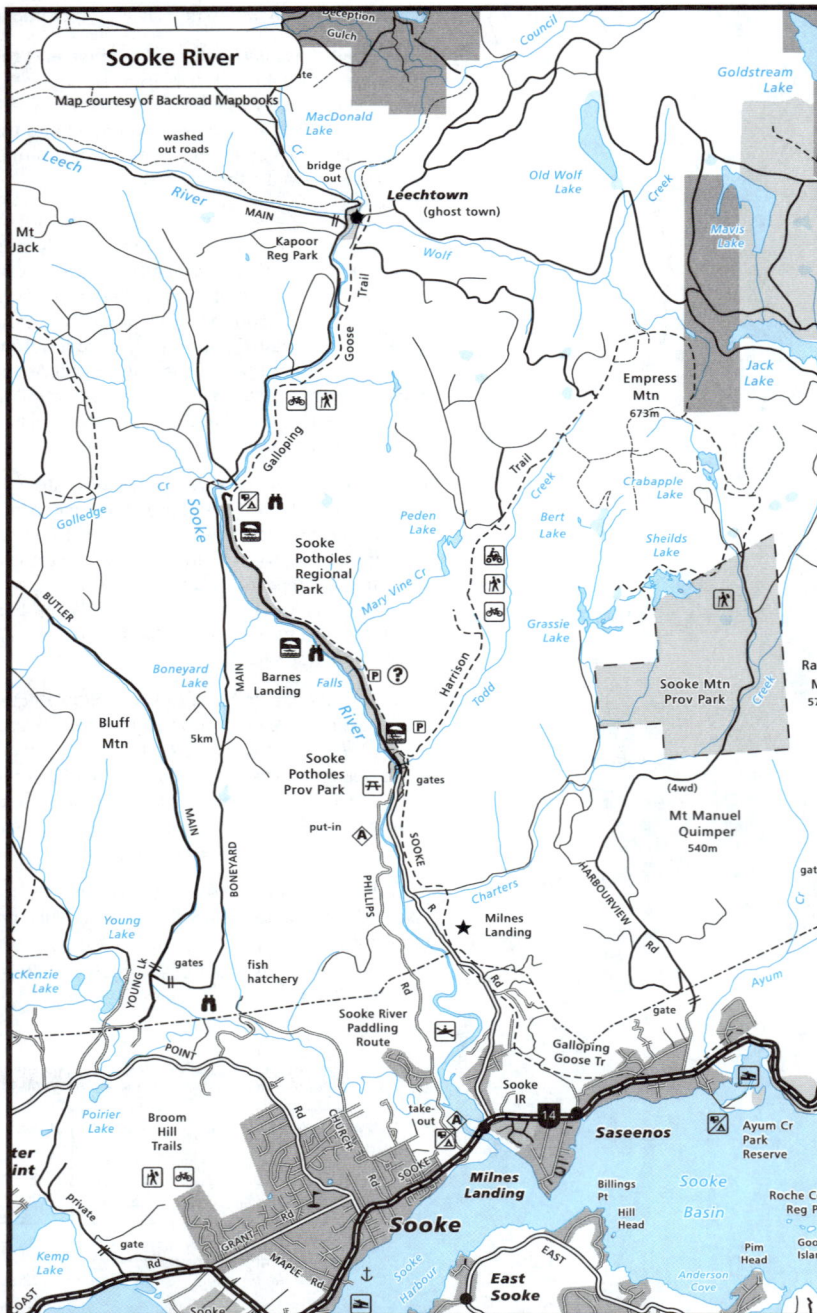

Map

Sooke River

Map courtesy of Backroad Mapbooks

Sooke River			
Fish Stocking Data			
Year	Species	Number	Life Stage
2007	Steelhead - Diploid	11,800	Fry
2006	Steelhead - Diploid	5,800	Fry
2005	Steelhead - Diploid	8,000	Fry

Somenos Lake

Location: 2 km (1.2 mi) northeast of Duncan
Elevation: 5 m (16 ft)
Surface Area: 101 ha (249 ac)
Mean Depth: 4 m (13 ft)
Max Depth: 7 m (23 ft)
Way Point: 123°42'00" Lon - W   48° 48'00"Lat - N

Fishing

Stocked annually by the Freshwater Fishery Society of BC, Somenos is a popular lake found close to the small city of Duncan. Both rainbow and, to a lesser degree, cutthroat are stocked and provide for decent fishing for average size trout. However, many come here in pursuit of the rare brown trout.

Because of its proximity to Duncan, the lake is beginning to be urbanized, and new properties are springing up around it. Fortunately, the same marshy area that makes shore casting difficult also makes waterfront development difficult, too, and so the houses remain at a short distance…for now.

The lake is best suited for spincasting or fly-fishing in March to early May after the hatches have started, but before the algae bloom begins. Being only 7 metres (24 ft) deep, the lake is best fished from the water since the marshy area that surrounds the lake makes shore fishing somewhat difficult. Try casting from the boat towards the weed-covered shallows. You can also troll a surface lure or fly when the hatches are slower and the fish are harder to find.

Somenos Lake is one of a few lakes in the southern portion of Vancouver Island where you will find brown trout. These fish are very difficult to catch, as they are suspicious of anything unnatural. In fact, brown trout are the most discriminating of all the trout species, making it one of the most prized catches. Spincasters will find browns all but ignore spoons and spinners and plugs, except in the early spring when food is scarce.

Browns will often eat only one kind of insect, even if there is a variety available, so careful observation is necessary. When in doubt, error on the size of caution and choose a smaller fly. If you are not having much luck, try a smaller tippet, because the fish might be able to see the one you're currently using. Placing your cast gently in the right place will go a long way towards success. Also, make sure you are not casting a shadow near the trout. In a perfect world, you would fish from shore into the sun, but shore fishing here is difficult. Using a wet fly is often more successful than a dry fly, as the fish can be spooked by the movement of the line on the surface of the water. Browns tend to favour nymphs, but again, you need to pick the right nymph to match what the trout are eating at the time.

Facilities

Somenos Lake is home to a wildlife reserve for wintering waterfowl that protects some of the marshy shoreline. Anglers will find a good boat launch on the western shores of the lake at the end of Drinkwater Road, but need to be wary of private property that is encroaching on the lake.

Other Options

Quamichan Lake is a nearby alternative that offers a good early season fishery for stocked rainbow and cutthroat trout. Look for more details on this lake earlier in the book.

Directions

Somenos is a popular South Island lake. It is found just northeast of Duncan and is easily accessed by car.

The main access to the lake is Drinkwater Road, which leads from the Island Highway north of Duncan. Alternatively, Inverarity Road off Wicks Road provides access to the eastern shoreline.

Area Indicator

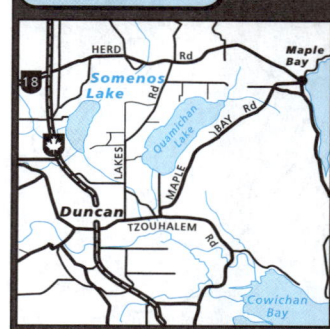

100m 0   100m 200m 300m 400m 500m
Scale

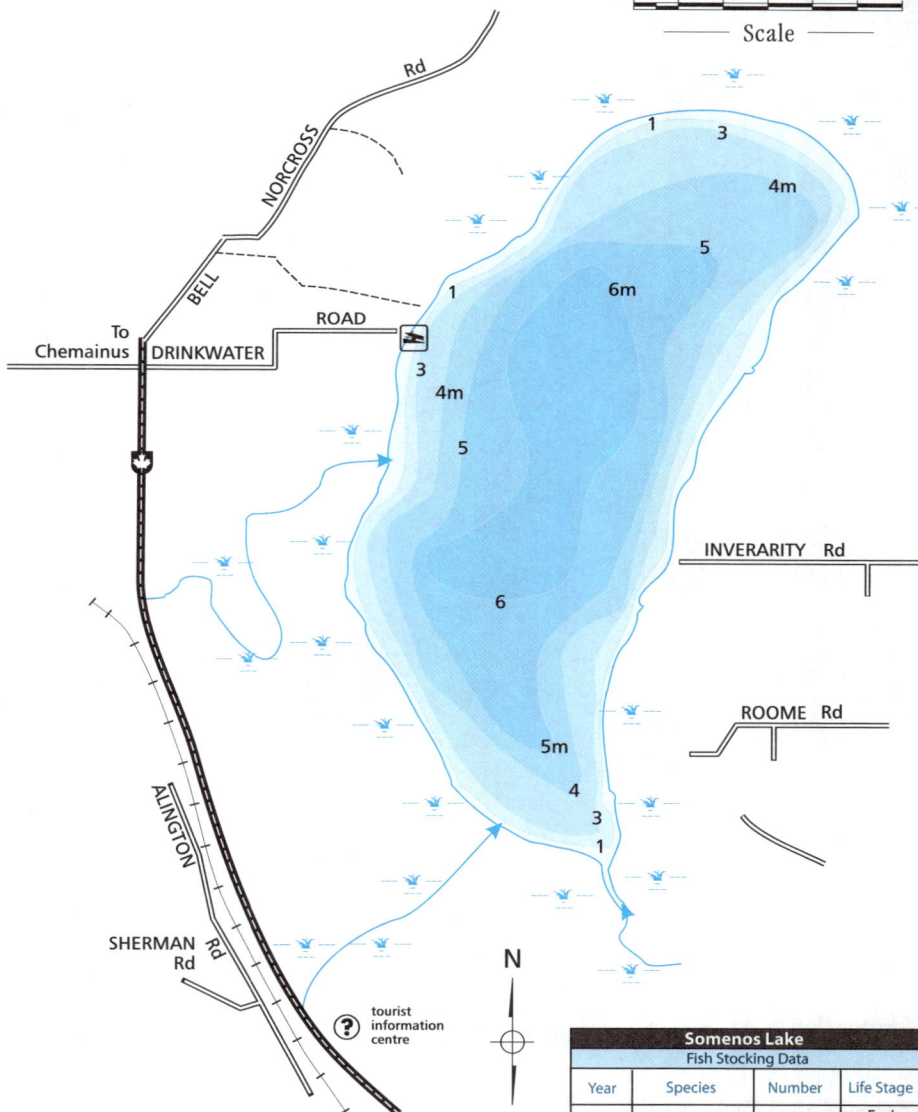

| Somenos Lake | | | |
Fish Stocking Data			
Year	Species	Number	Life Stage
2011	Rainbow Trout	10,500	Fry/Catchables
2010	Rainbow Trout	500	Yearling
2010	Cutthroat Trout	4,000	Yearling
2009	Rainbow Trout	3,500	Yearling
2009	Cutthroat Trout	2,292	Yearling

Location: 30 km (19 mi) northwest of Victoria
Elevation: 379 m (1,243 ft)
Surface Area: 4 ha (10 ac)
Mean Depth: 2 m (7 ft)
Max Depth: 7 m (23 ft)
Way Point: 123° 34' 00" Lon - W   48° 34' 00" Lat - N

www.backroadmapbooks.com

Spectacle Lake

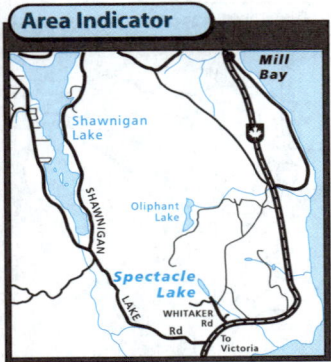

Area Indicator

Mill Bay

Shawnigan Lake

Oliphant Lake

Spectacle Lake

SHAWNIGAN LAKE

WHITAKER Rd

To Victoria

Directions

Spectacle Lake is found north of Victoria off the Island Highway (Highway 1) near the infamous Malahat Summit. Look for the Spectacle Lake Park sign and turn west off of the highway on Whitaker Road, which leads to Spectacle Lake Road. Access is easy since the road is paved and signed.

To Oliphant Lake

Spectacle Lake Provincial Park

2
3m
4
5m
6
5m
4
3m
2
1m

5m
4
6
3m
2
1m

Spectacle Lake Provincial Park

Spectacle

Cr.

WHITTAKER

To Hwy 1 via Whittaker Rd

N

Fishing

Spectacle Lake is so named because the lake looks like a pair of eyeglasses. (A grossly deformed pair, certainly, but still, if you squint and turn your head just so…).

It is a tiny lake, but is no less special, as it is the only place on the Island that holds eastern brook trout. They can get to 40 cm (16 in) in size, but most of the ones caught here are small. Fishing is best at ice-off in the fall when the fish are spawning. Casting an attractor type fly or a small lure like a Deadly Dick tipped with a worm can be effective. Unfortunately, the lake also holds smallmouth bass. These aggressive fish were introduced illegally and have been negatively impacting the trout fishing. Reports of anglers catching brookies here are becoming fewer and fewer.

The lake also holds rainbow trout, which are stocked on an as-needed basis by the Freshwater Fisheries Society of BC at a catchable size. Bring a canoe or a float tube and try spincasting a small spoon or spinner from deep water to shallow. Flies will also work well, either by matching the hatch or by using your favourite attractor pattern.

As with other Island lakes, the chironomid (midge) hatch on Spectacle begins in March or April and usually lasts through May. Prior to or during early hatches, the larval stage of chironomids (bloodworms) will be targeted by trout. April brings mayfly hatches followed by the caddisfly (sedge) hatch in mid-May. April through to early June produces many opportunities for nymph and dry fly fishing on this small lake.

Rainbow anglers use a variety of methods: casting or trolling flies, spinning with small lures, trolling with lake trolls and worms, and still-fishing with powerbait or worms. Small spoons, plugs (Flatfish and Kwikfish in a Cracked Frog or White Coach Dog pattern) are other good choices for trolling. Fishing for trout is best during the spring and fall, as the lake tends to warm up in the summer.

Smallmouth bass anglers report success with crankbaits, spinner baits, powerbaits or soft plastics in protected areas along the shore. In deeper water, try deep running crankbaits or soft plastics.

Facilities

The lake is found in beautiful **Spectacle Lake Provincial Park**, a day-use park that is a popular destination for swimming and picnicking in the summer. There is parking is at the southeast end of the lake, but you will have to carry boats or small craft about 100 metres (300 feet) to the lake if you plan on getting out onto the water. The park also offers an easy one-hour walk around the lake via the Spectacle Lake Loop. Along the trail, there are several areas that you can cast from shore.

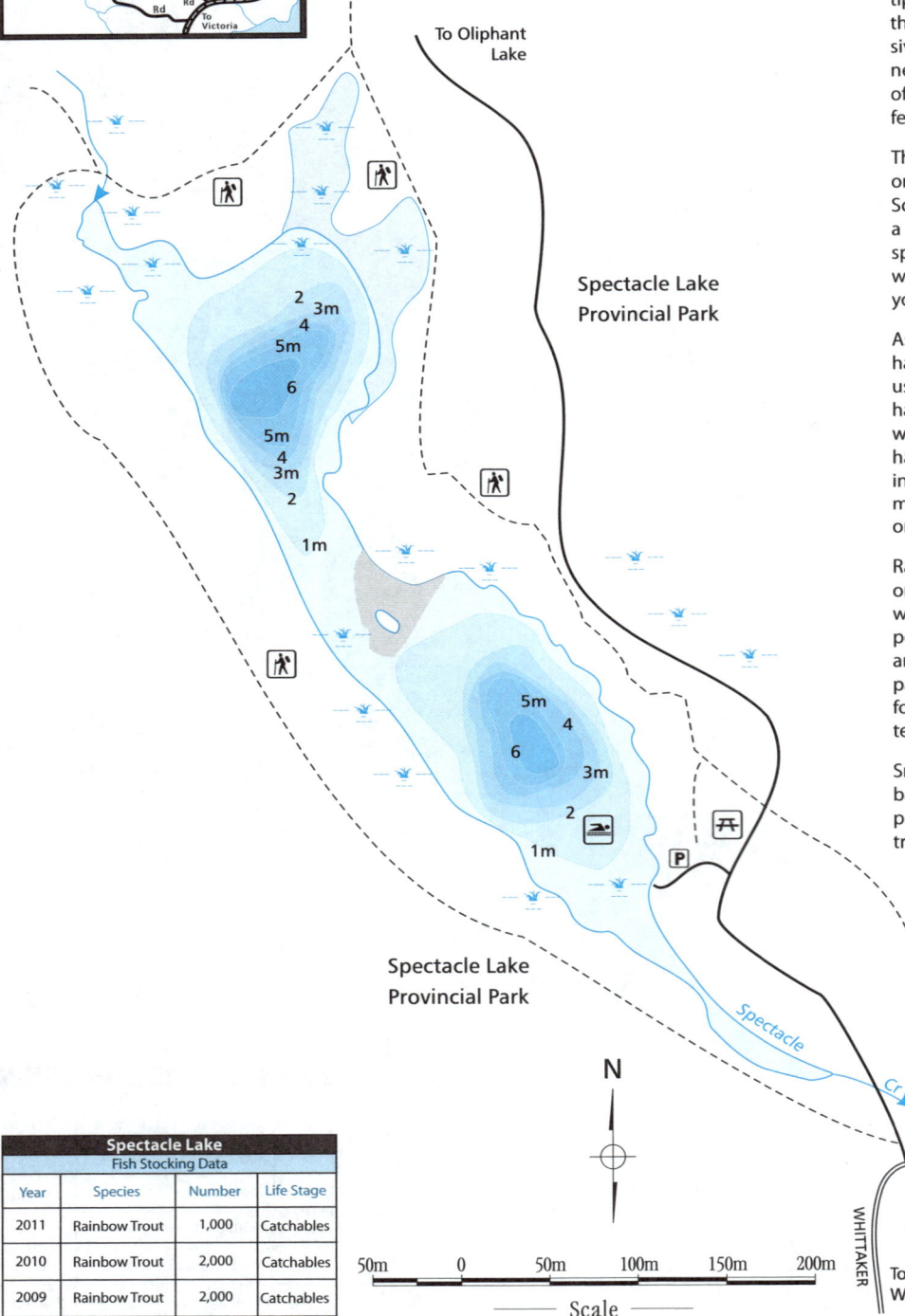

Spectacle Lake			
Fish Stocking Data			
Year	Species	Number	Life Stage
2011	Rainbow Trout	1,000	Catchables
2010	Rainbow Trout	2,000	Catchables
2009	Rainbow Trout	2,000	Catchables

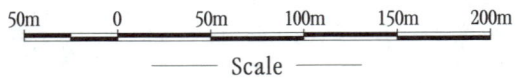

50m   0   50m   100m   150m   200m

Scale

Spider Lake

Location: 16 km (10 mi) west of Qualicum
Elevation: 140 m (459 ft)
Surface Area: 44 ha (109 ac)
Mean Depth: 4 m (13 ft)
Max Depth: 13 m (43 ft)
Way Point: 124° 37' 00"Lon - W   49° 20' 00" Lat - N

Fishing

Spider Lake has many arms (or legs, if you will), formed by winding inlets and secluded bays. When viewed from above, it's easy to see where the lake gets its name. The lake also has and a series of small islands, which offer great habitat for the stocked rainbow as well as smallmouth bass that have been here since 1923.

The rainbow average over 30 cm (12 in) in length and regularly reach 1.5 (3 lbs) in size. The larger trout are best caught on a deep troll with light tackle or trolling an artificial fly with a fast, full-sink line. Exceptions are during the chironomid, mayfly and sedge hatches that usually occur from April to June. During this time, anglers can target fish in the shallower shoal areas. Olive mini leeches with some sparkle tied in, or green bodied seal Woolly Buggers with an orange grizzly hackle do well on the fly. A needlefish spoon tipped with baited and trolled slowly also produces good results. The best time to trout fish is in April and again in the fall. By May to June, the focus of the good fishing swings to the smallmouth bass.

Into the summer months when the trout fishing is at a stand still, the bass fishery is very good. The bass stay around cover such as a sunken log, lily pad or weed bed and can grow to 2.5 kg (5 lbs). They do not move out from their hiding place in search of food so you have to get your plug or fly right next to the cover to get a bite. As a result, many people lose many lures trying to attract bass. A popular option is to jig for the bass. Of course, casting poppers, crankbaits, soft plastics or large flies are the mainstay of the bass angler.

No powerboats are allowed at the lake, but anglers will find several good spots to fish from shore. Still fishing with natural or artificial baits can be effective for both trout and bass. Try working your lure along the shoreline where fallen trees provide excellent habitat.

Facilities

Spider Lake Provincial Park is a day-use park offering a nice picnic area and beach along with a good place to launch a small boat near the main parking lot. Visitors will also find nice walking trails in this area, which is only open from May through October. A smaller day-use area, open year-round, can be found off Lakeview Road less than a kilometre before the main park entrance. Small craft can also be launched from this location.

Nearby Horne Lake offers camping.

Directions

Spider Lake is a popular fishery located to the east of Horne Lake. From the Inland Island Highway (Highway 19), take the Horne Lake exit west. You will need to turn south almost immediately and follow the signs to Spider Lake Park on the paved road. When the pavement ends, there is a short section of gravel. Watch for the lake on your right.

Area Indicator

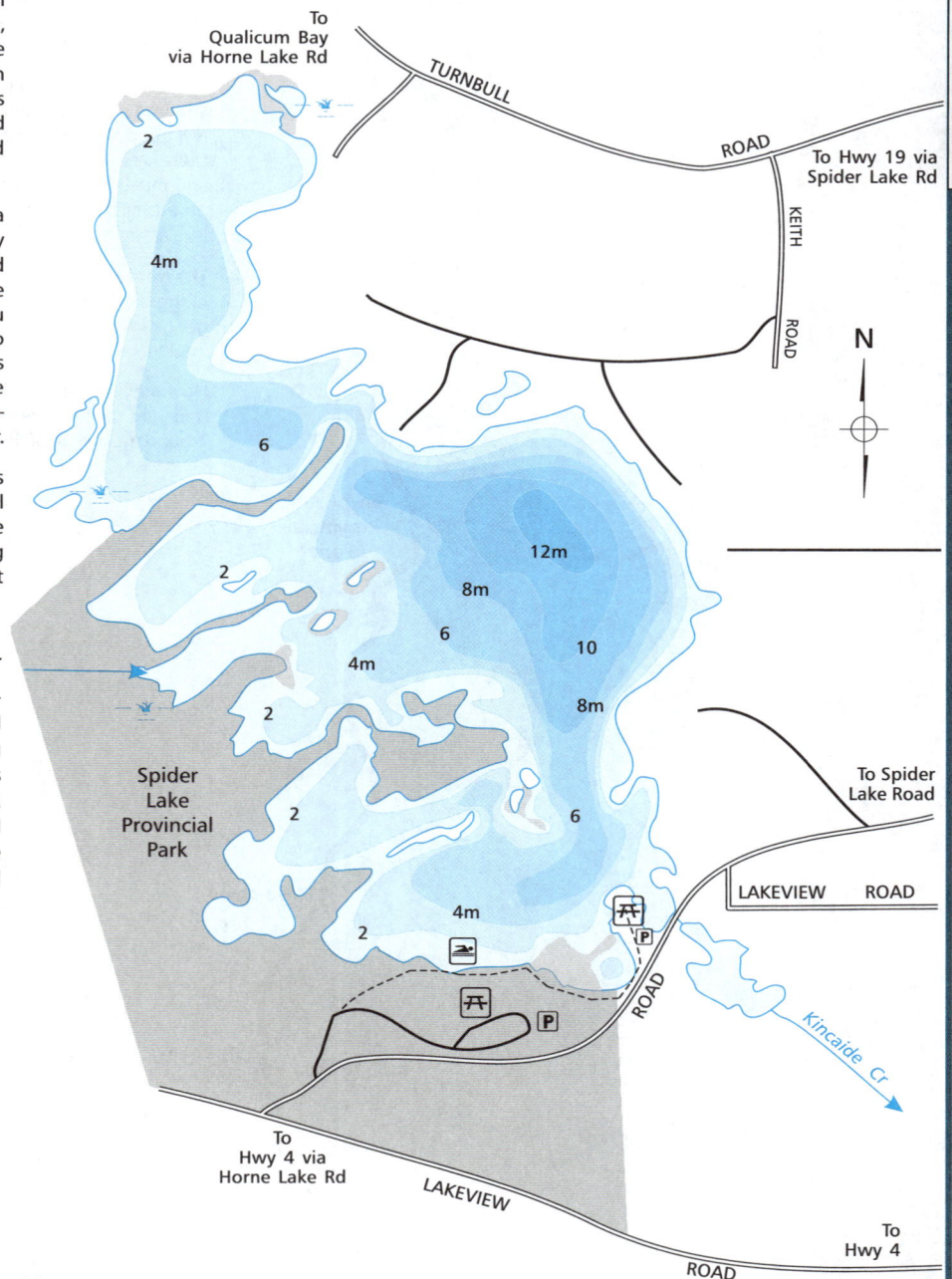

Scale: 100m 0 100m 200m 300m 400m 500m

Spider Lake			
Fish Stocking Data			
Year	Species	Number	Life Stage
2011	Rainbow Trout	4,000	Yearling/Catchables
2010	Rainbow Trout	8,500	Yearling/Catchables
2010	Steelhead	5,540	Yearling
2009	Rainbow Trout	5,500	Yearling/Catchables
2009	Steelhead	12,321	Yearling

Location: 16 km (10 mi) west of Port Alberni
Elevation: 32 m (105 ft)
Surface Area: 3,775 ha (9,324 ac)
Mean Depth: 74 m (243 ft)
Max Depth: 195 m (640 ft)
Way Point: 125° 00' 00" Lon - W 49° 16' 00" Lat - N

www.backroadmapbooks.com

Sproat Lake

Area Indicator

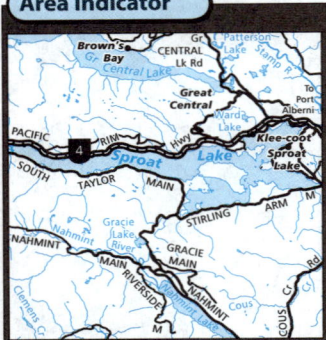

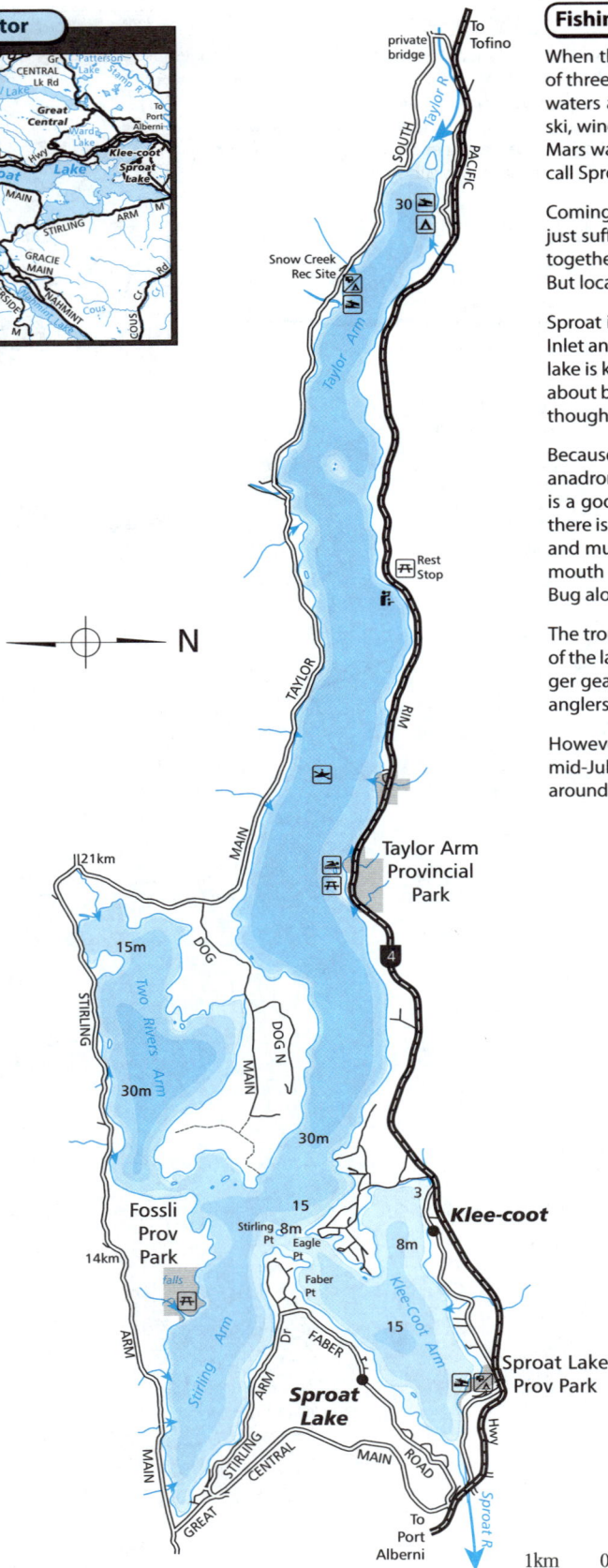

Fishing

When the topic of Sproat Lake comes up, people's minds usually go to one of three things. The first is recreation; the lake is surrounded by cottages, the waters are plied by houseboats, and people come here in droves to water ski, windsurf, or just hang out on the beach. The second thing is the Martin Mars water bombers. These are the world's largest water bombers, and they call Sproat Lake home.

Coming in a distant third is fishing. Not because fishing is bad as such. It just suffers from its proximity to Barkley Sound and the Alberni Inlet, which together make up some of the greatest saltwater salmon fishing areas in BC. But local anglers do not mind the crowds zooming by.

Sproat is a big lake, only about 10 km (6 miles) from the end of the Alberni Inlet and Port Alberni. It has clean water, with visibility up to 10 m (30 ft). The lake is known for its rainbow and cutthroat trout fishing, and the great thing about big lakes is they grow big fish. Here, they will grow over 4.5 kg (10 lbs), though these are rare catches indeed.

Because of its proximity to the Alberni Inlet, the lake also sees large runs of anadromous fish, including three species of salmon. In April and May, there is a good steelhead fishery in the lake. From mid-January to mid-February, there is even a winter run of steelhead. Winter steelhead are much less active and much less interested in food, but people have good luck fishing at the mouth of the Sproat River. Try working a weighted stonefly or size 10 Glo Bug along the bottom.

The trout seem to hang out in the Two Rivers arm in spring and fall. Because of the lake's size, it is best fished on the troll during these times, and downrigger gear is recommended. Try trolling a lake troll and a Flatfish or worm. Fly anglers can try leech or minnow patterns.

However, it's not all about trolling. During the summer, starting around mid-July, the sockeye start to return to the Taylor River, and the trout gather around the mouth of the river, waiting for the inevitable wash of sockeye eggs.

Directions

Sproat Lake is a big lake that lies alongside Highway 4 west of Port Alberni en route to Tofino. The highway follows the northern shore of the lake its entire length. It is only 13 km (7.6 miles) from Port Alberni to Sproat Lake Provincial Park, which is one of the best places to access the lake. The Stirling Main/Taylor Arm Main roads provide good access to the south side of the lake.

Facilities

Sproat Lake is dotted with cabins and cottages, and renting houseboats on the big lake is quite popular. There are three provincial parks on the shores of the lake. **Fossli** and **Taylor Arm** are both day-use parks with no boat launch. Fishing from shore is possible, as is hand launching a boat.

However, the most popular place to launch a boat, as well as to stay, is at **Sproat Lake Provincial Park.** The park has two separate campgrounds, one on either side of the highway (the lower campground is closer to the lake, and is much more popular). Some of the 59 campsites can be reserved through www.discovercamping.ca.

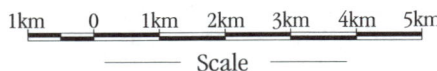

Stamp-Somas & Sproat Rivers

Fishing

The Somas River is the name given to the super-river that is formed when the Stamp River and the Sproat River join. Over half of all the steelhead caught on Vancouver Island come from these rivers. That speaks to the sheer number of steelhead found in these waters, as well as the extreme popularity of fishing these rivers.

Indeed, these two rivers have some of the best river fishing on the entire Island. And while Campbell River might call itself "Salmon Capital of BC", the folks in Port Alberni know that it isn't polite to boast. This system is BC's third most productive steelhead stream.

More and more people discover this amazing river system, which is not only the biggest steelhead river on the Island, but is also features some of the best returns for Chinook, too. And because the steelhead and salmon return at the same time in summer, there is a perfect storm for anglers.

While the river is best known for steelhead and Chinook, there are also strong returns of Coho. The Robertson Creek Hatchery, to which much of the success of the returns on this river are credited, was originally started to introduce pink salmon into the river system. The pinks didn't take, and the hatchery switched over to augmenting the three main runs on the river to help offset the heavy fishing pressure they receive.

Of the two, the Stamp River receives the most attention for Steelhead. Winter steelhead begin to arrive in November, while the big runs begin to arrive in December and don't let up until March. Summer steelhead begin to arrive in late June, and fishing remains strong until October. Spinners such as the Blue Fox can be a lot of fun at this time.

Due to private property and area closures, especially downstream and along the Sproat, there are only a few places to access the river. Don't expect to have the area all to yourself, but if you have waders focus on areas like the Stamp River Falls. Most steelhead hold below the falls. Unfortunately this popular pool is closed for most of the season, but is open for winter steelheading. There are some good places above the falls, too, like Money's Pool (named after General Noel Money, and made famous by Roderick Haig-Brown).

Drift fishing is another common method along the rivers. Make sure you don't go over Stamp Falls and watch for closures during the peak runs and private property in the lower reaches.

It should be noted that returns were down in 2007. But the hatchery program and close monitoring of the fishery should help to keep this fishery strong and steady.

Directions

The rivers are found in the Alberni Valley, about an hour and a half drive from either Victoria or Nanaimo. The Somas flows into the Alberni Inlet along Port Alberni's western edge. Highway 4 parallels the river for a ways, and access to the Stamp River is from a variety of roads that head north from the highway or south off Beaver Creek Road.

Facilities

The Somas River is easily accessed from Port Alberni, where you will find all services including fishing retailers, accommodations and restaurants. Folks fishing the Stamp River often base camp at **Stamp River Provincial Park**. The campground is open year round and offers 23 campsites and good river access including a nice trail to access popular fishing holes. Reservations through Discover Camping or BC Parks are recommended if visiting during the summer.

Stamp/Somass River			
Fish Stocking Data			
Year	Species	Number	Life Stage
2007	Steelhead - Winter/Summer	100,225	Smolt
2006	Steelhead - Diploid	90,350	Smolt
2005	Steelhead - Diploid	79,390	Smolt

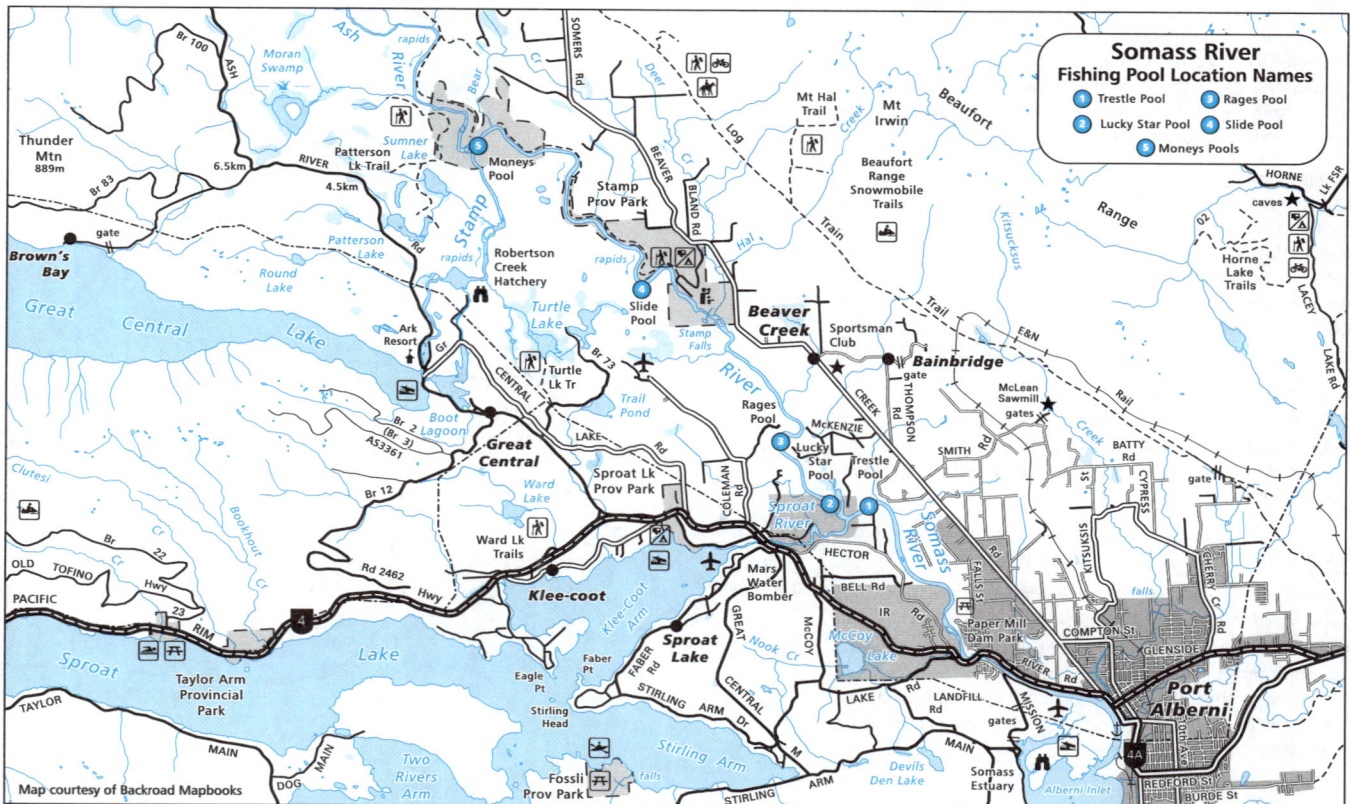

Map courtesy of Backroad Mapbooks

Location: 3.5 km (2.2 mi) north of Ganges
Elevation: 195 m (640 ft)
Surface Area: 195 ha (482 ac)
Max Depth: 16.7 m (55 ft)
Waypoint: 123° 32′00″ Lon - W 48° 52′00″ Lat - N

St. Mary Lake

Area Indicator

Directions A

Getting to St. Mary Lake requires getting to Salts Spring Island, which is serviced regularly by BC Ferries. From Victoria the ferry takes you to the Long Harbour Terminal. Follow the Long Harbour Road to Upper Ganges Road and turn left. Turn right at the next stop sign on Lower Ganges Road, which turns into North End Road. This road runs north along the east side of the lake. Public access is found at the north end off Lang Road at the community park.

Fro Crofton on Vancouver Island, the ferry takes you to the Vesuvius Ferry Terminal. Follow Vesuvius Bay Road to the North End/Lower Ganges Road junction and directions described above.

St. Mary Lake Fish Stocking Data			
Year	Species	Number	Life Stage
2011	Rainbow Trout	4,000	Yearling
2011	Cutthroat Trout	1,500	Yearling
2010	Rainbow Trout	5,232	Yearling
2010	Cutthroat Trout	1,500	Yearling
2009	Rainbow Trout	5,000	Yearling
2009	Cutthroat Trout	2,500	Yearling

Fishing

Although the Gulf Islands are not known for their freshwater fishing, St. Mary Lake on Salt Spring Island is a notable exception. The lake provides excellent fishing between April and October for a variety of sportfish including stocked cutthroat and rainbow trout as well as perch. However, it is the abundant and large smallmouth bass that attracts anglers from far. Bass in the 4 kg (9 lb) range are reported here.

Smallmouth bass are an introduced species that have thrived in the wide shoals and contoured bottom of the lake. More recently, man-made tire reefs have been made to assist in the development of the bass. These aggressive fish spend their spring months in the shallow parts of the lake where they spawn. At this time, they will strike most top water lures. The trick is to cast near or into the reeds and retrieve rapidly. From late spring until early fall, bass migrate into the depth of the lake and are best caught using plastic baits such as tube baits or grubs suspended near structure.

Trout fishing is known to be good in spring and fall when the water is cooler. There is a prolific chironomid hatch early in the year, while searching patterns like leeches and Carey Specials are also popular with the fly-fishing crowd. During the warmer months, troll deeper. The trout can be aggressive too and have been known to take bigger baits and flies.

Another introduced species in St. Mary Lake is yellow perch. These fish are usually quite small (in the 15–20 cm/6–8 in range) and like to hang out around the reeds, floating docks and any submerged structure. These fish are easy to catch with a bait and bobber combination and are often a favourite with young anglers looking for some fast action. Catching them by fly-fishing is also possible. A micro-leech tied onto a thin leader and floating line is deadly when stripped in the shallows.

Surrounded by private property there are only limited spots to fish from shore. It is best to use a small, electric motor only boat and cast towards shore when targeting both bass and trout. Also note the other restrictions such as seasonal closures on bass.

Facilities

St. Mary Lake has seen some development on the north and west sides of the lake. Farm land on the south shore and the steeper east side limit development there. Visitors will find a small community park with a beach and lake access for small cartop boats at the north end. Those looking to stay in the area will find cottage and boat rentals with **St Mary Lake Resort** or **Lakeside Gardens Resort.**

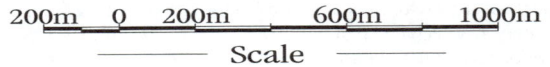

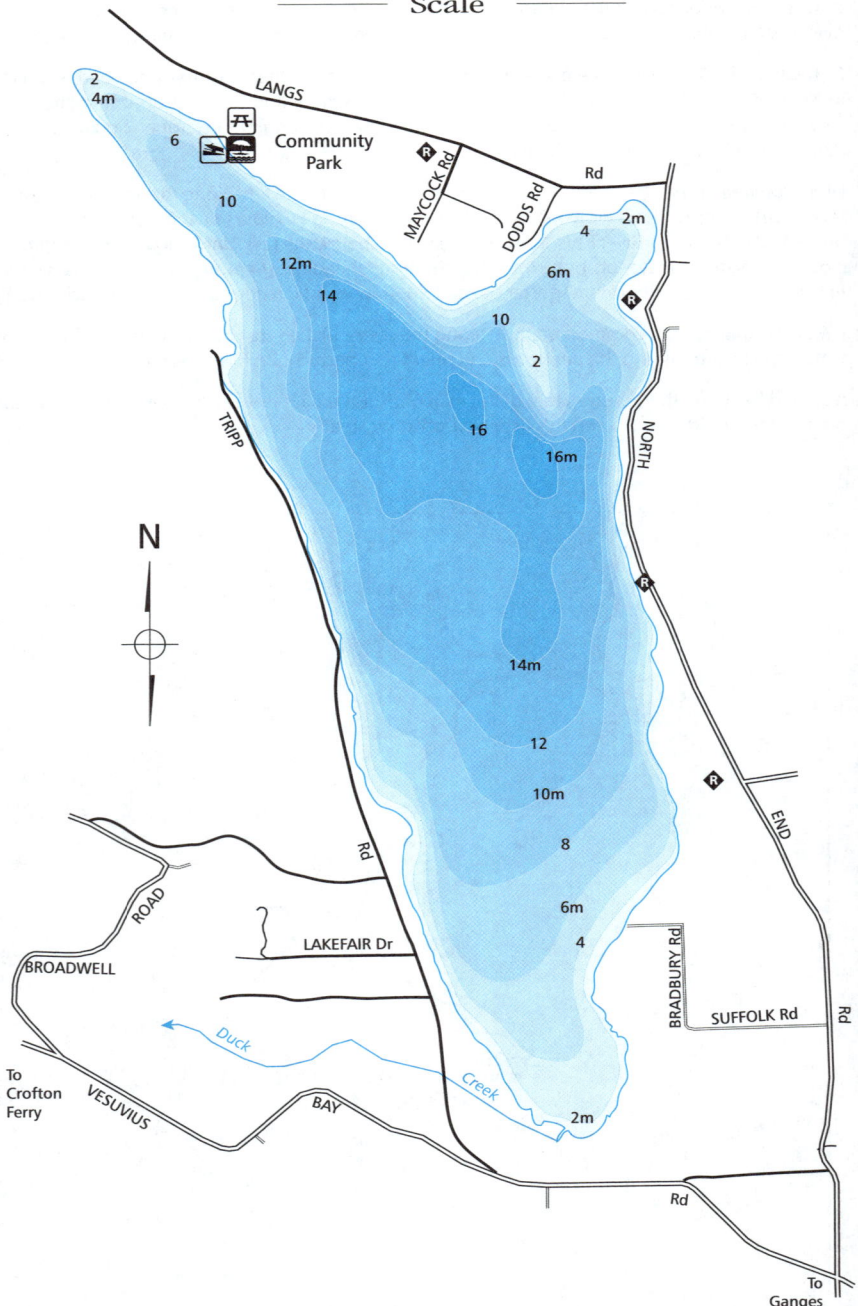

200m 0 200m 600m 1000m
Scale

Stella Lake

Location: 40 km (25 mi) northwest of Campbell River
Elevation: 130 m (427 ft)
Surface Area: 423 ha (1,045 ac)
Mean Depth: 19 m (62 ft)
Max Depth: 43 m (141 ft)
Way Point: 125° 31' 00" Lon - W   50° 17' 00" Lat - N

Fishing

Stella Lake is the first in a trio of good fishing lakes found north of Campbell River, along with nearby Pye and McCreight Lakes. It is noted for its clear water, its mostly untouched wilderness setting and its good fishing for stocked cutthroat as well as some kokanee.

In fact, Stella Lake is one of the heaviest stocked cutthroat lakes on the Island, with 10,000 cutthroat being deposited into the lake annually by the Freshwater Fisheries Society of BC. This means angling gold for the local anglers. While it doesn't offer up the same monster cutthroat as nearby McCreight, the fishing is usually very consistent.

Stella is a deep, low elevation lake. While the spring is certainly the best time to fish here, fishing remains good through the summer since the lake does not get as warm as shallower lakes.

In the early spring, there are bays at both the north, south and east ends of the lake, and the fish come into these bays to feed. As the water warms up, the fish become more wary, moving into the deep water of the main lake. The lake has plenty of structure, with a couple of islands, and lots of nooks and crannies along the shoreline. In summer, you could do worse than trolling around the rim of the lake with a lake troll in about 10 m (30 ft). In the spring and into fall, the fish will be in shallower water, so adjust your troll accordingly. Locals tend to focus their efforts along the northwest arm of the lake.

When the fish are in the shoals a shallow troll may work, but often just casting a small spinner or spoon will work better. Cutthroat like flashy flies and lures, so don't be afraid to use the gaudiest lure to catch them. They will also take well to a fly. There is good structure around the ring of the lake and dry fly-fishing for cutthroat is a popular pursuit. However, they will take to a variety of lures and presentations, including spoons and crankbaits. If something isn't working, try another lure, another style, or another location.

Facilities

There are a few recreation sites on the shores of Stella Lake that are accessed off of the Rock Bay Forest Road. As you are travelling northwest, the first site you will come across is the **Stella Bay Recreation Site**. This is a very small site with space for maybe two groups and limited turn around space for bigger units. The second, **Stella Beach Recreation Site** is found a few kilometres down the lake. It is much bigger than the last, with space for 14 groups. The site is noted for its sandy beaches. Both sites have cartop boat launches. Further along there is also the **Stella Lake North Recreation Site**, which is a single unit site and a nearby launching site for smaller boats.

Other Options

Lower Stella Lake lies to the northwest and is also stocked with cutthroat every other year. There are also rumors of kokanee in the smaller lake.

Directions

Stella Lake is found north of Campbell River off the Rock Bay Forest Service Road. From the bridge over Campbell River, it is 32 km to the Elk Bay turn off, which is just past Roberts Lake. Follow the Elk Bay Road for about 11 km until you see the Rock Bay Road on your left. Follow this road for about 3 km to find the more popular Stella Beach Recreation Site.

Those hauling trailers are well advised to return to the highway by following the Rock Bay Road northwest to avoid the big hill on the Elk Bay Road.

Area Indicator

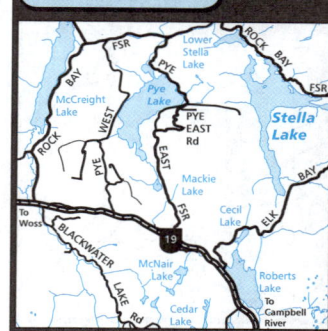

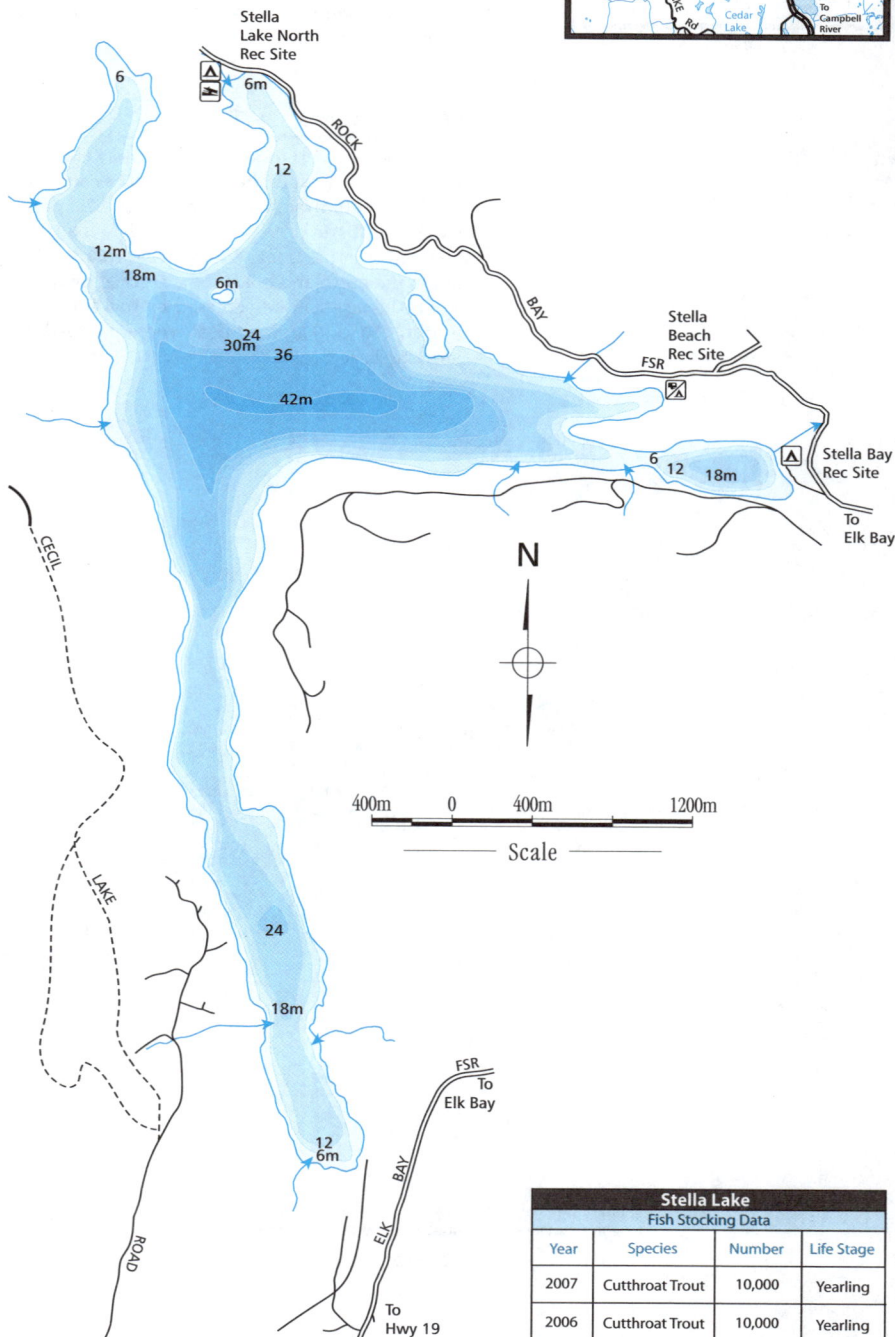

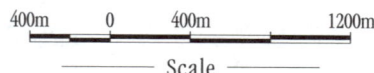

Stella Lake / Fish Stocking Data

Year	Species	Number	Life Stage
2007	Cutthroat Trout	10,000	Yearling
2006	Cutthroat Trout	10,000	Yearling
2005	Cutthroat Trout	10,000	Yearling

Location: 5 km (3 mi) south of Ladysmith
Elevation: 360 m (1,181 ft)
Surface Area: 18 ha (44.5 ac)
Mean Depth: 8.5 m (28 ft)
Max Depth: 26 m (85 ft)
Way Point: 123° 49' 00" Lon - W   48° 57' 00" Lat - N

Stocking Lake

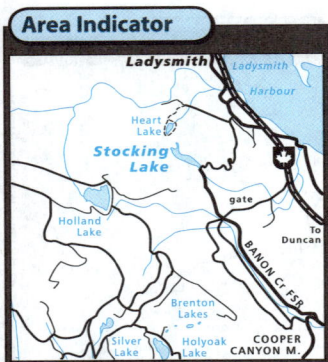

Area Indicator

Ladysmith
Ladysmith Harbour
Heart Lake
Stocking Lake
Holland Lake
gate
To Duncan
BANON Cr FSR
Brenton Lakes
Silver Lake
Holyoak Lake
COOPER CANYON M.

Directions

Stocking Lake is located south of Ladysmith. Look for the Davis Road exit off of the Island Highway and follow this road to a small side road that leads to an old logging road that winds up the hill to the lake. As with most logging roads on the south end of the Island, gates can pop up anytime and vehicle access may be closed.

Facilities

There are no facilities at the lake. It is possible to launch a small boat at the lake and to camp at roadside.

Other Options

To the southeast of Stocking Lake is **Fuller Lake**. The lake is located next to the Island Highway and has small numbers of rainbow that can reach an impressive 3 kg (6 lbs) in size. Look for more details on this lake earlier in the book. Alternatively, **Heart Lake** lies to the north and holds some stocked rainbow trout. The lake can be accessed by trail from the Branch 200 logging road near where the road to Stocking Lake begins.

Fishing

Stocking Lake is a small lake found just south of Ladysmith. Because of its proximity to Ladysmith (and Nanaimo and Duncan), and ease of access off the Island Highway, it sees a fair amount of pressure from area anglers. However, the difficult to find and sometimes rough road access is enough of a deterrent for people without a 4wd vehicle to keep the hoards away.

Despite the name, Stocking Lake is not stocked. Or at least, not anymore. For a few years in the 1980s it was stocked with rainbow trout, but these days, the population is self-sustaining. Despite this, the fish aren't big, averaging 20-25 cm (8–10 inches) in size, but there are quite a few of them.

The relatively small lake is quite deep and well suited to trolling. But with such small fish, your gear needs to be small, too. Rainbow tend to chase spoons with metal finishes, like a Luhr Jensen chrome/blue, or chrome/green, or a Little Cleo with gold or nickel patterns. These are best trolled at a medium to fast speed to simulate a minnow swimming through the water. Fly anglers can use a minnow pattern, like a Muddler Minnow, a leech, or a general attractor like a Carey Special. Start closer to shore, targeting the drop-off areas. If you are not finding the holding area, work your way out to deeper water until you find where the rainbow are hiding. If casting, use the countdown method to figure out the depth the fish are holding at.

Shore fishing is possible as the water drops off rapidly from shore. Spincasters can use small spoons, or they can try a bobber and bait, usually a worm. In the spring fly fishers should watch for the hatches, but when there's nothing happening, a leech or a Carey Special are always reliable fall-back patterns.

The low elevation lake is best fished in April to June and again from September to October. If you do come in summer, try working the deeper parts of the lake.

No powerboats are allowed at the lake.

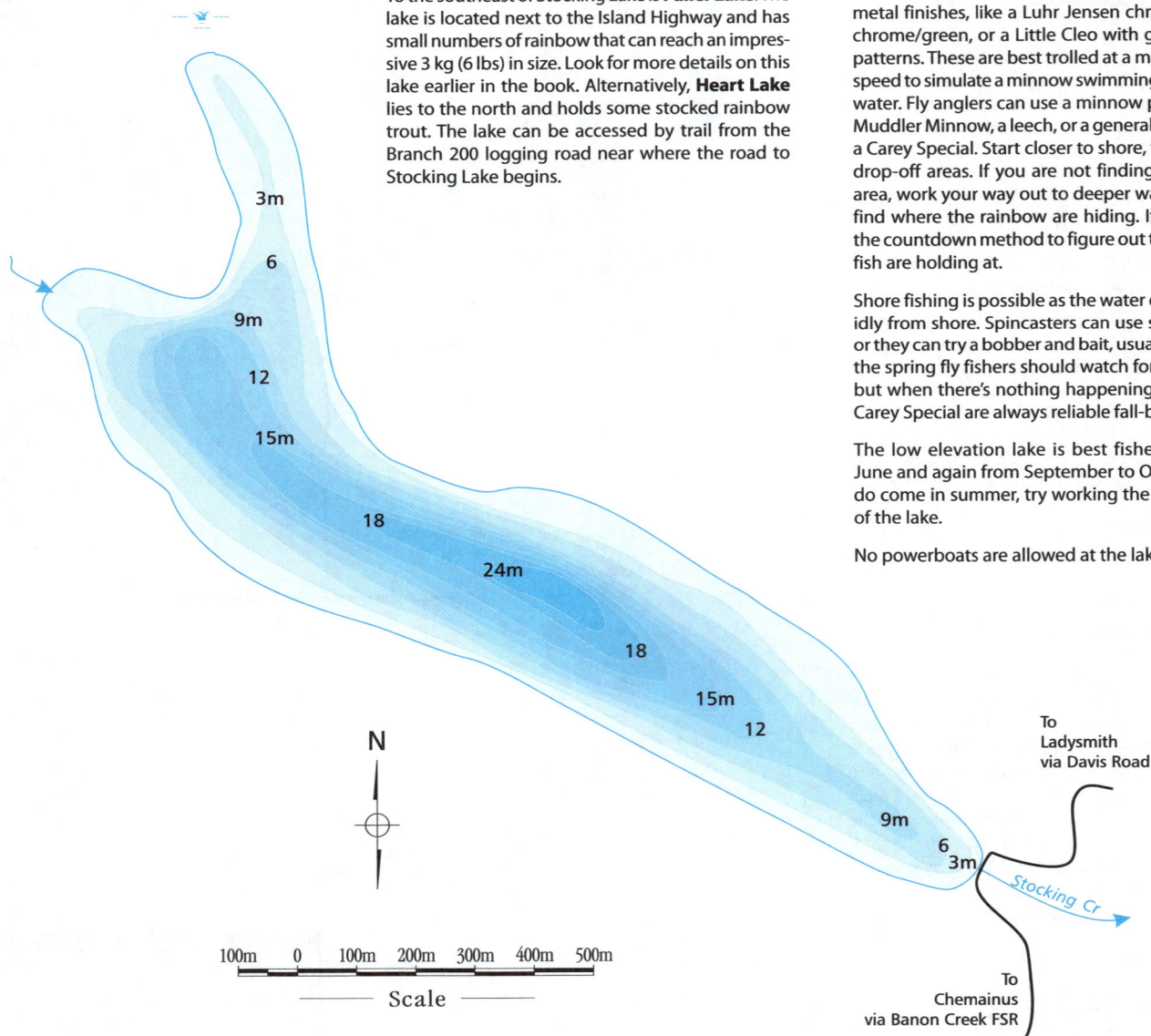

3m
6
9m
12
15m
18
24m
18
15m
12
9m
6
3m
Stocking Cr
To Ladysmith via Davis Road
To Chemainus via Banon Creek FSR

N

100m 0 100m 200m 300m 400m 500m
Scale

© Mussio Ventures Ltd.

Thetis Lakes

Location: 8 km (5 mi) northwest of Victoria
Elevation: 60 m (197 ft)
Surface Area: 36 ha (89 ac)
Mean Depth: 4 m (13 ft)
Max Depth: 9m (30 ft)
Way Point: 123° 28' 00" Lon - W   48° 28' 00"Lat - N

Fishing

Collectively known as Thetis Lake, there are actually two lakes here, Upper and Lower Thetis Lakes, which are connected by a short channel. The lakes are located in a regional conservation area, which was established in 1958 as Canada's first nature sanctuary. The pretty 835 hectare park is located on the fringes of Victoria, and is popular with paddlers, swimmers, hikers, naturalists, and, of course, anglers.

Because of its proximity to Victoria, the lake sees heavy pressure throughout the year, but the Freshwater Fisheries Society of BC stocks Thetis several times a year with catchable size rainbow trout. Cutthroats were stocked in the recent past and are still present in fair numbers. Both species prefer cool water and are active from March into June and again in the fall. Anglers will also find a good population of smallmouth bass.

Bass anglers net excellent results with crankbaits, spinner baits, powerbaits or soft plastics in protected areas along the shore. Look for any sort of structure, such as fallen logs or weeds. In deeper water, deep-running crankbaits or soft plastics are generally reliable.

Because bass like to hang out close to structure, casting for them is an art, and losing hooks is almost a certainty. There are two common ways around this. The first is the Texas rig, which works really well in weeds. The other option is to skip casting, and just jig a spoon or some other lure.

Most any trout fishing method will work for the indiscriminate rainbow. Small chrome, orange, brass or silver spoons work well, while Flatfish or Kwikfish are considered good choices for trolling. Try one of these in the rainbow or silver patterns. When the lake warms up, the trout are deep. Try using your lure with a lake troll or additional sinkers to get down to the deeper water. Although the trout are generally small, the odd 35 cm (14 in) beauty is caught.

Fly-fishing for trout is most productive in the spring through to early June during the chironomid (midge) and caddisfly (sedge) hatches, and again in the fall when the weather cools down. During chironomid hatches try a No. 12 black with silver or red rib. General fly patterns such as pheasant tail nymph, half-back and Doc Spratleys can be effectively used to match hatches for mayfly, damselfly, dragonfly and caddisfly.

Adding to the mix are perch and even brown bullhead (also known as catfish). Both are relatively easy to catch making them a good fish to introduce youngsters too. Pretty well all you need is a small hook and some bait. Adding a bobber to this set up will help to cast out from shore.

Area Indicator

Thetis Lake Fish Stocking Data

Year	Species	Number	Life Stage
2011	Rainbow Trout	2,000	Catchables
2010	Rainbow Trout	3,000	Catchables
2009	Rainbow Trout	3,000	Catchables

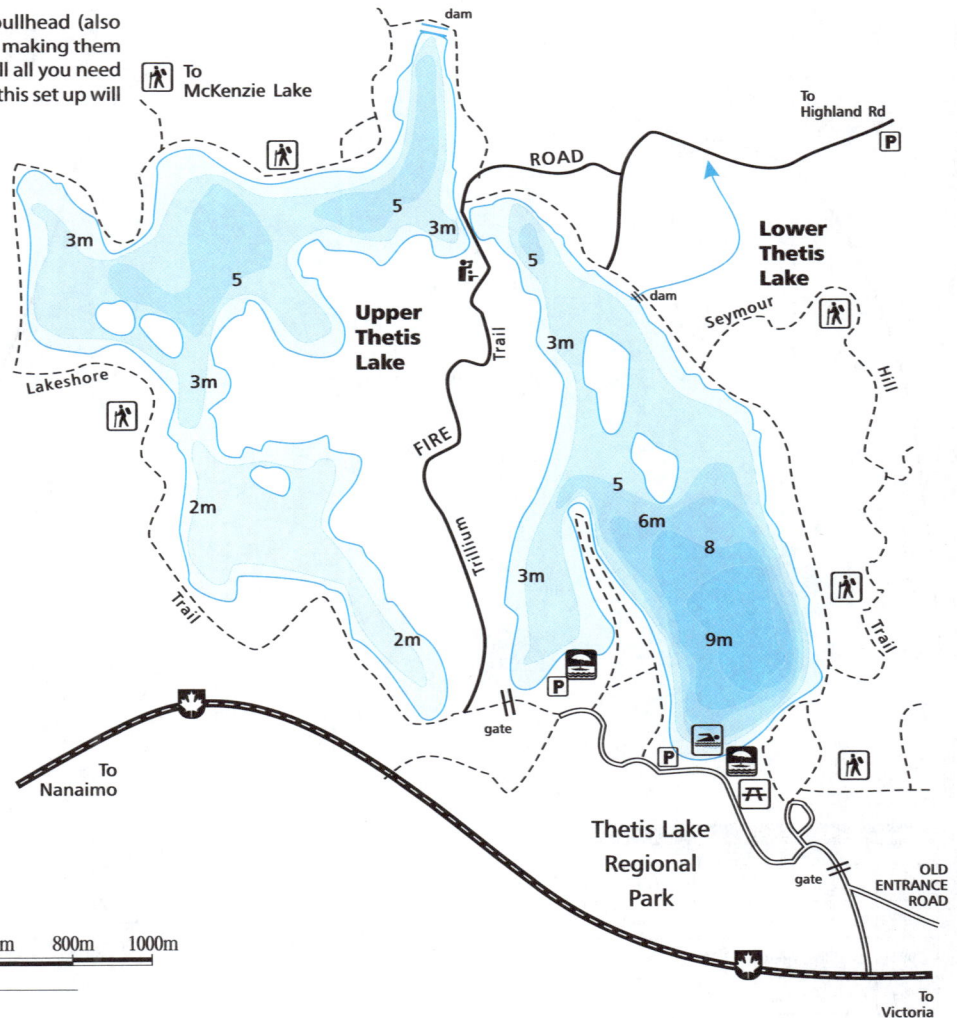

Directions

Located about 8 km (5 mi) northwest of Victoria, these lakes are found nearby to the Island Highway (Highway 1). Take the Colwood Exit and follow the Old Island Highway to Six Mile Road. A right here leads to the park entrance. Signs direct the way.

Facilities

Thetis Lake Regional Park is a very popular park that features a well developed trail system, sandy beaches and a variety of amenities. Anglers can hand launch canoes or small boats from the beach area, or hike around the lake to look for interesting places to stop and cast your line. If the water level is high enough, it is possible to navigate your way from the northwest end of Lower Thetis to Upper Thetis.

© Mussio Ventures Ltd.

Timberland Lake

Location: 14 km (8.7 mi) south of Nanaimo
Elevation: 219 m (719 ft)
Surface Area: 5.5 ha (13.5 ac)
Mean Depth: 5m (16 ft)
Max Depth: 12 m (39 ft)
Way Point: 123° 56' 00" Lon - W   49° 02' 00"Lat - N

Timberland Lake

Area Indicator

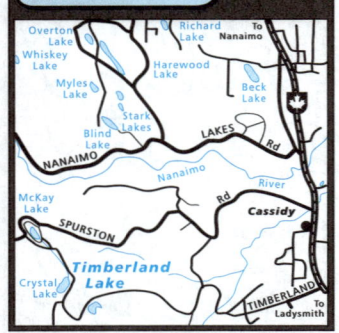

Directions

Similar to most backcountry south Island lakes, access into this area may be closed or restricted. It is best to inquire locally before planning a trip into the area.

To reach lake, follow Spruston Road west, which leaves the Island Highway (Highway 1) just north of the airport after crossing the Haslam Creek Bridge. The first few kilometres of Spruston Road is paved and then you come to an old orange gate with a sign saying "Fletcher Challenge Canada-McKay Lake Division". Travel through the gate (which is usually open) and take an immediate left. It is three kilometers to Timberland Lake on a gravel logging road.

A truck is recommended to reach the lake.

Facilities

Timberland Lake has a few lakeshore camping sites as well as a cartop boat launch and a large parking area. A good footpath, part of which makes up a tiny portion of the Trans Canada Trail, accesses the lake. In fact, visitors are encouraged to visit the Haslam Creek Suspension Bridge, which is found a short distance to the southeast of the lake.

Fishing

Despite its proximity to Nanaimo, this small, quiet lake is not usually very busy. It has good fishing for cutthroat to 30 cm (12 in) which are stocked regularly as yearlings. Fly-fishing or spincasting are most productive particularly throughout the spring (March to June) and fall (September to October).

The lake is known as a good chironomid lake. The insect begins to hatch as early as March when there is a spell of warmer weather. However, the best time to fish the chironomid hatch is in April and May. If fishing in the morning or mid-day, the best way to catch fish using a chironomid imitation is to us an intermediate sinking line or a sinking tip line. Work a brown, black or red bodied pupae imitation in 6-9 m (20-30 feet) of water such that it is within a few feet of the bottom. Slowly retrieve the fly or use a strike indicator and leave the fly just off the bottom.

In the evenings, working the fly in the surface layer of the water with a floating line and long leader is very effective. This is because as the day progresses, the insects make their way to the surface and the fish follow along. You can literally see the cruising fish. Try casting in front of the fish hoping that the fish will take your fly.

As the summer approaches, the lake is not deep enough to withstand the summer doldrums. As a result, fishing tails off substantially and does not get better until the cooler evenings in the fall.

Other Options

Crystal Lake is a dark water lake located nearby to Timberland Lake. Like Timberland Lake, Crystal Lake has good cutthroat fishing in the spring for generally larger cutthroat (up to 40 cm/15 in). In particular, the chironomid hatch in April and May can be a great time to fish if you use a brown coloured pupae imitation. Try in the evenings when the fish are cruising the subsurface water level in search of hatching insects. There is a small, decaying dock, a cartop boat launch next to the dock and camping nearby. The cutthroat are stocked regularly.

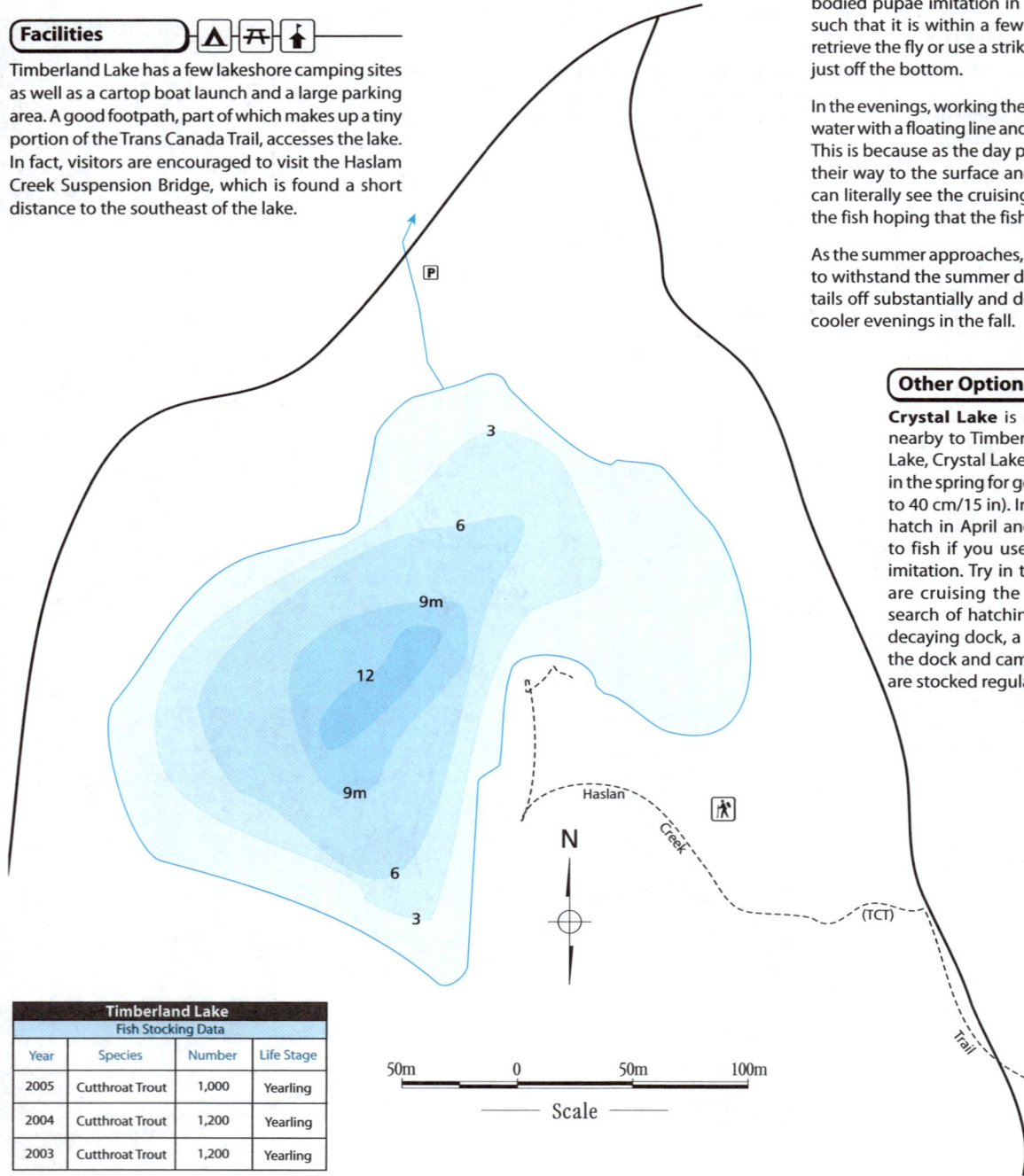

Timberland Lake Fish Stocking Data			
Year	Species	Number	Life Stage
2005	Cutthroat Trout	1,000	Yearling
2004	Cutthroat Trout	1,200	Yearling
2003	Cutthroat Trout	1,200	Yearling

50m   0   50m   100m

Scale

N

Haslam Creek

Trail

(TCT)

3
6
9m
12
9m
6
3

Toy Lake

Location: 50 km (31 miles) northwest of Port Alberni
Elevation: 484 m (1,588 ft)
Surface Area: 10 ha (25 ac)
Mean Depth: 2m (7 ft)
Max Depth: 5m (16 ft)
Way Point: 126° 16' 00"Lon - W   49° 27' 00" Lat - N

Fishing

The name of the lake might lead one to imagine that this is an easy lake to fish, like child's play. One would be wrong. Toy Lake can be a challenging place to fish, especially without a belly boat. On the other hand, the 10 hectare lake is managed as a fly-fishing only fishery to help increase the chances of catching bigger cutthroat.

Fly anglers like to visit this lake during the early spring and later in the fall when the water is cooler. However, getting here too early in the year can be a challenge due to its remote location. The small lake also warms up in the summer creating a slower fishery and is susceptible to winterkill. To help maintain the fish stock, cutthroat are stocked every second year by the Freshwater Fisheries Society of BC.

The lake is nearly impossible to fish from shore, so a cartop boat or a float tube is mandatory. However, the lake is also tough to troll because it is so shallow. It is possible to drag a standard attractor pattern like a Carey Special or Doc Spratley close to the surface, but easier just to pick your place and cast towards shore, again, using a standard attractor. The lake has extensive shoals towards the south end, which can be productive early in spring, and a fairly nice drop-off at the north end, which will be more productive later on. Remember to match the hatch for better success.

Facilities

Despite resting in the southeastern confines of **Strathcona Provincial Park**, there are no developed facilities at the lake. As with most remote lakes, it is possible to launch a cartopper at the lake as well as camp at roadside. An old dock is found on the eastern shore that can be used by brave fly casters.

Other Options

There are three other lakes in the area that can be tried if the fish are not biting at Toy Lake, **Junior** and **June Lake** are north of Toy Lake on Branch 110, and offer small rainbow and cutthroat that are relatively easy to catch. **Oshinow Lake** is the bigger lake found off the Ash River Road southwest of Toy Lake. It has slightly bigger rainbow and cutthroat which are usually caught by trolling. Look for details on this lake earlier in the book.

Directions

Toy Lake is found within Strathcona Provincial Park nearby to Oshinow Lake and the Ash River. The lake is reached by travelling on Highway 4 past Port Alberni to the tiny community of Great Central where you can pick up the Ash River Road. At 6.5 km and 11.7 km stay right and at 15 km stay left. The Ash River Road will soon bring you along the northern shores of Turnbull Lake then along the southwestern shores of Elsie Lake. From there, the road continues along the Ash River and enters Strathcona Provincial Park. The main road should eventually bring you to the southeastern end of Oshinow Lake before swinging northeast to Toy Lake.

However, road access can change since the Ash River Main travels through private property. Be sure to inquire locally before planning a trip into the area. The long distance of logging road travel also makes a truck with 4wd capability essential. It is also a good idea to bring along a copy of the Backroad Mapbook for Vancouver Island along with a GPS and Backroad GPS Maps to track where you are on the often confusing logging road network.

Area Indicator

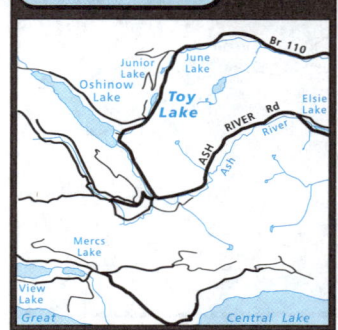

Toy Lake — Fish Stocking Data

Year	Species	Number	Life Stage
2007	Cutthroat Trout	1,000	Fry
2005	Cutthroat Trout	1,100	Fry
2003	Cutthroat Trout	1,000	Fry

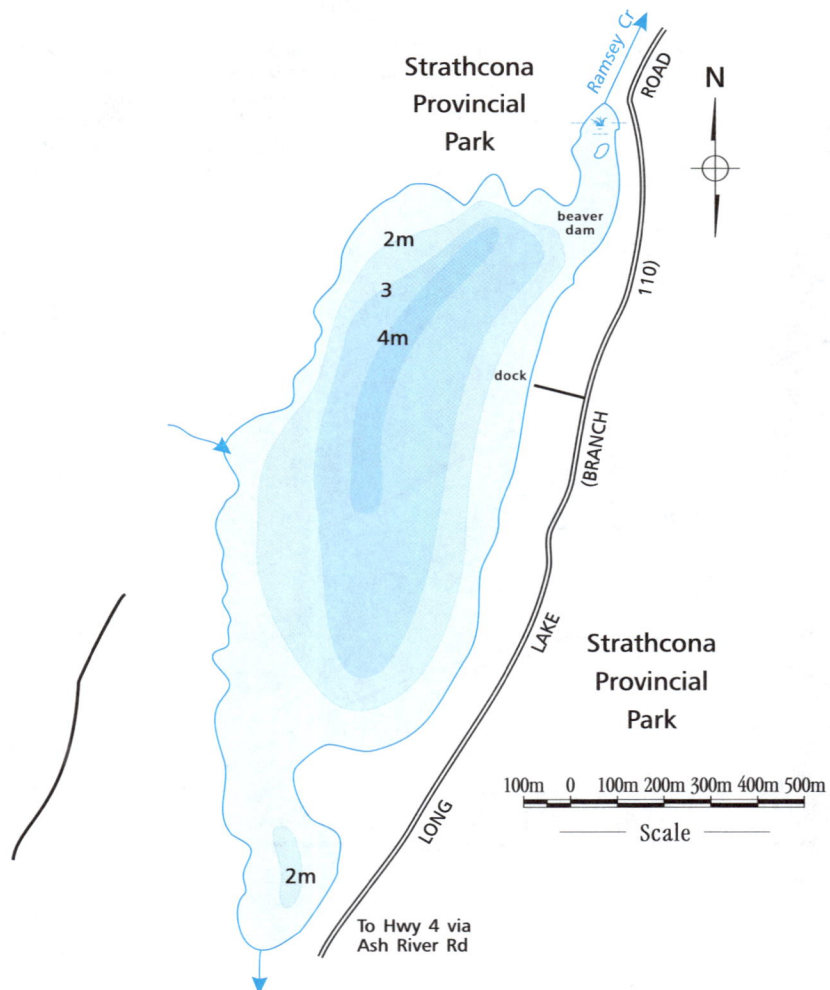

Location: 30 km (18.6 mi) northwest of Port Alberni
Elevation: 265 m (869 ft)
Surface Area: 23 ha (57 ac)
Mean Depth: 4 m (13 ft)
Max Depth: 12 m (39 ft)
Way Point: 125° 06′ 00″ Lon - W   49 °25 ′ 00″ Lat - N

Turnbull Lake

Area Indicator

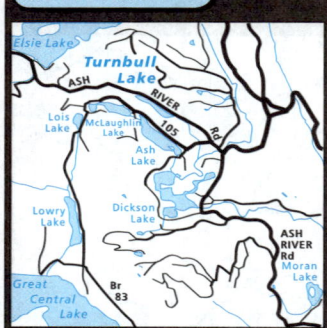

Turnbull Lake
Fish Stocking Data

Year	Species	Number	Life Stage
2008	Cutthroat Trout	500	Yearling
2006	Cutthroat Trout	500	Yearling

Fishing

Turnbull Lake is a long, thin lake located alongside the Ash River Road north of Great Central Lake. It is one of a bunch of lakes found in the Ash Valley that offer good fishing for small rainbow and cutthroat trout.

The lake has an expansive shoal at the east end, while the west end is much deeper. Since the lake is a low elevation lake, and not terribly deep, the water tends to warm in the summer months. The best fishing happens during the early spring (April to May) and late fall (October). At that time, you should do well for small rainbow and cutthroat in the 20-30 cm (8-12 in) range plus a few Dolly Varden to 2 kg (5 lbs).

The lake is difficult to troll unless you stay near the west end and do not troll too deep. Given the lake's depth, or lack of it, shore fishing is fairly difficult, too, but you can try from a few places along the northern shore. As usual, it is best to get out onto the water in a canoe or float tube. In addition to the west end of the lake where the water is deepest and the transition zone from deep to shallow is most pronounced, you could also try just southwest of the island at the east end of the lake.

The cutthroat are fairly aggressive. Fly fishers should try a Muddler Minnow in gold or silver, a Wool Head Sculpin in spring or similar streamer type patterns. Spincasters can try bait fishing, or use small lures like a Panther Martin or Mepps spinner. Trollers need to use light gear, but lake trolls without much weight can be effective.

Directions

Turnbull Lake is one of several lakes north of Great Central Lake and south of Elsie Lake. Similar to the others, road access may be closed or restricted. It is best to inquire locally before planning a trip into the area.

The lake is reached by travelling on Highway 4 past Port Alberni to the Sproat Lake Provincial Park. Turn northwest on the Great Central Lake Road to the tiny community of Great Central on the northern shores of Boat Lagoon. From there, head northwest along the Ash River Road. At 6.5 km and 11.7 km stay right and at 15 km stay left. The Ash River Road will bring you along the northern shores of the lake. The route is clearly shown in the Backroad Mapbook for Vancouver Island and is best travelled in a truck.

Facilities

There are no developed facilities at the lake, but it is possible to launch small craft from the main road. It is also possible to camp near the lakeshore.

Other Options

Off the Ash River Road, there are a number of other lakes, all with small rainbow and cutthroat. **Dickson Lake** is the first of the series and perhaps the most versatile. **Ash** and **McLaughlin Lakes** are better trolled. All three can be fished throughout the open water season. Look for depth charts and more detailed fishing tips on these lakes earlier in this book.

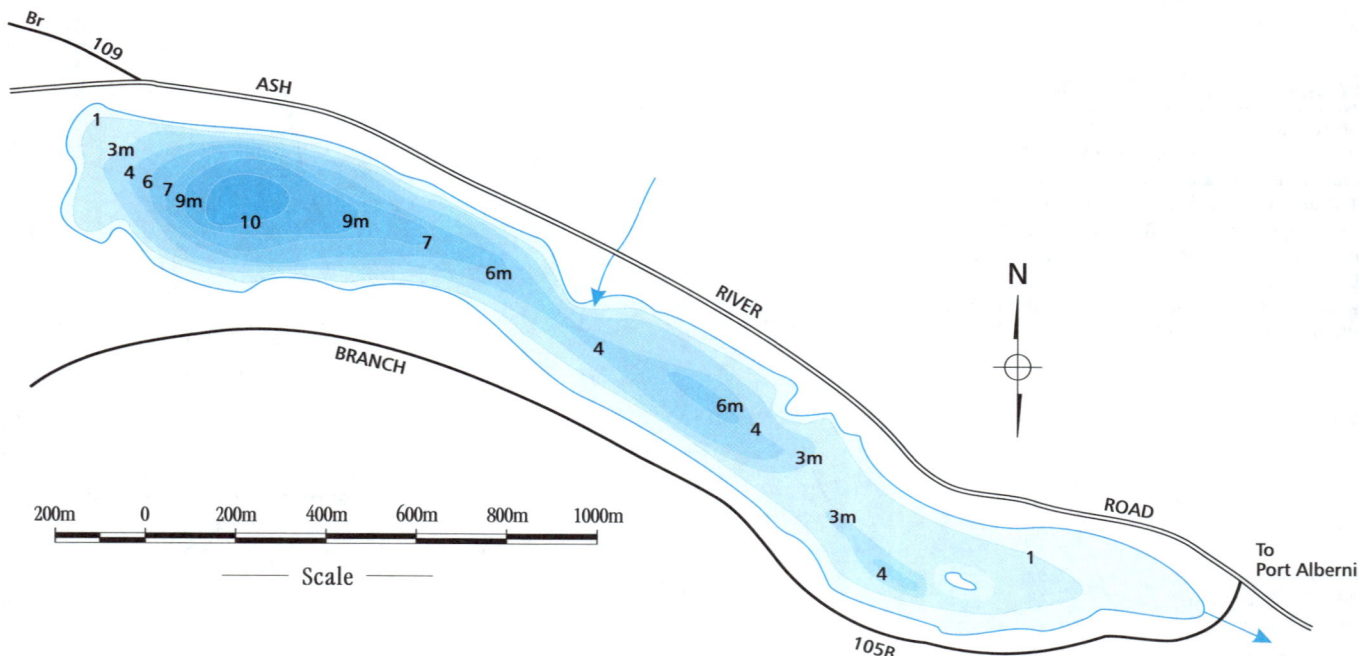

Turtle Lake

Location: 16 km (10 mi) northwest of Port Alberni
Elevation: 83 m (272 ft)
Surface Area: 16 ha (40 ac)
Mean Depth: 4.5 m (15 ft)
Max Depth: 10 m (33 ft)
Way Point: 124° 57' 00" Lon - W   49° 19' 00" Lat - N

Fishing

Turtle Lake is a hike-in lake located northwest of Port Alberni in the Great Central Lake area. Fortunately, the hike in is only 1.3 km (0.8 miles), but that's enough to keep the hordes away. The lake is still busy but is stocked annually (sometimes twice a year) with cutthroat to keep up with the fishing pressure. Visitors will also find this is a popular bird watching location and home to over wintering populations of swans and loons.

The low elevation lake is best fished in the early spring and again in the late fall to avoid the warm water months of the summertime. There are extensive shoals at the northwest end. In fact, it is nearly impossible to shore fish here outside of the first few weeks of spring, as the lake drops off so slowly. If you are desperate and without a float tube, you might be able to hit the drop-off from a slight point along the southwest shore of the lake, but most people who fish here do so from on the water, moving about 50 metres (150 ft) or more offshore for the best results. The lake drops off fairly steadily from all sides, so there are no pronounced transition zones that can be worked. Try positioning yourself in deeper waters and casting towards the shoals.

Spincasters can try a small lure tipped with a worm, or maybe a small spoon. Fly fishers will have the best results with wet flies such as a Doc Spratley. The most common method of fishing the Doc Spratley is on a troll with a full sink line in 2-5 m (8-15 ft) of water, with a 9 foot tapered leader of four to six pound test, close to the bottom. Your fly should hit bottom occasionally when fishing the fly properly.

Although it is possible to troll with a float tube, another popular method is the long retrieve. This involves casting the fly as far as you can, then kick backwards, stripping the line off the reel until you run out of line or lake. Then, slowly strip the line back in.

Other Options

Around the end of Great Central Lake are several other small lakes to try. **Trail Pond** is located less than a kilometer from the Turtle Lake trailhead on Branch 73 and offers decent numbers of small trout. **Patterson Lake** is found just off the Ash River Road and has fair numbers of small cutthroat caught during the spring and fall. A rustic boat launch can be used to get on the lake.

Directions

Turtle Lake is one of several small lakes in the Great Central Lake area. It is accessed by travelling on Highway 4 past Port Alberni to the Sproat Lake Provincial Park. At that point, head northwest on the Great Central Lake Road and look for the Branch 73 of the north side of the main road. Take Branch 73 and less than a kilometer from the junction when you just pass the powerline, you will see the trailhead to Turtle Lake on the north side of the road. Park here and begin the short hike to the south end of Turtle Lake.

Facilities

There are no developed facilities at the lake. If you want to overnight at the lake, bring a small tent and there are several openings where you can pitch the tent nearby to the lake.

Area Indicator

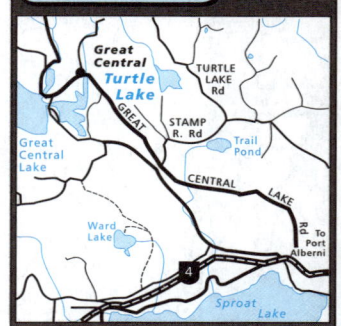

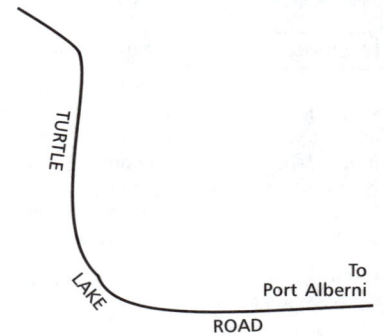

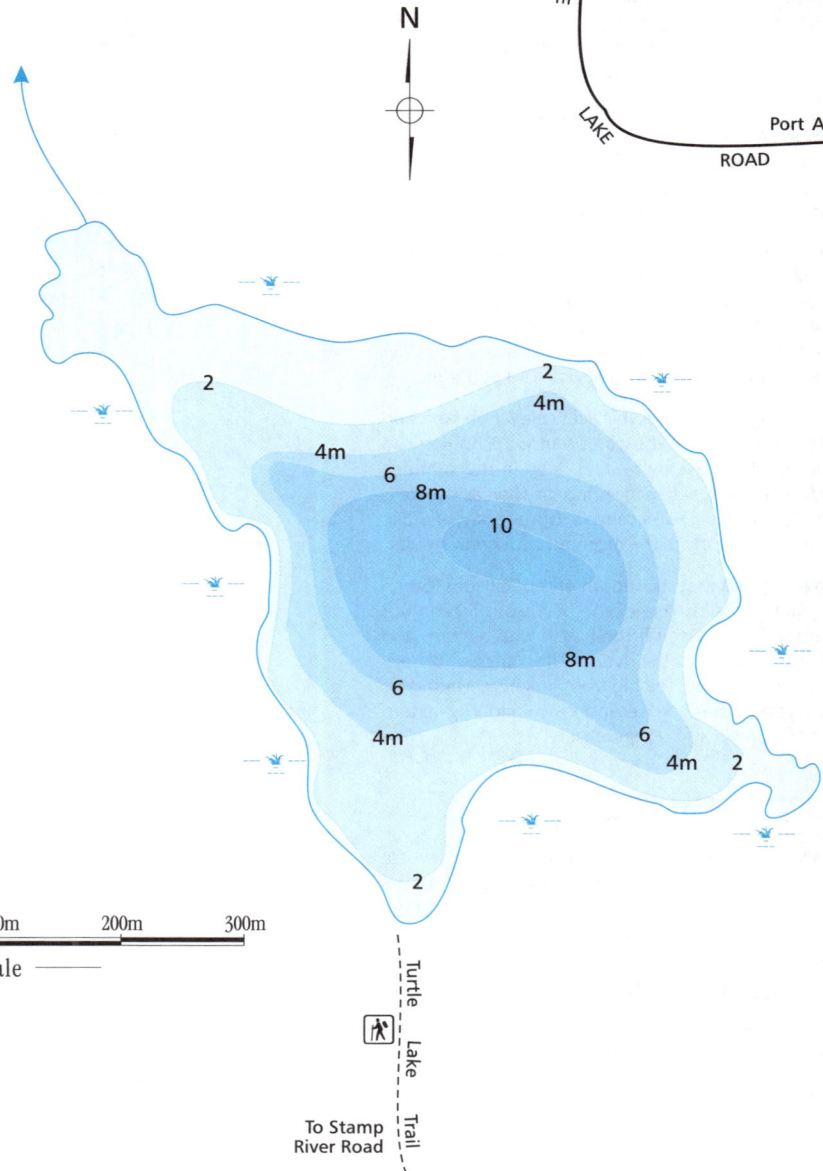

Turtle Lake			
Fish Stocking Data			
Year	Species	Number	Life Stage
2011	Cutthroat Trout	500	Yearling
2010	Cutthroat Trout	500	Yearling
2009	Cutthroat Trout	1,000	Yearling

Location: 60 km (40 mi) southwest of Port Hardy
Elevation: 97 m (318 ft)
Surface Area: 1,576 ha (3,893 ac)
Mean Depth: 43 m (141 ft)
Max Depth: 110 m (361 ft)
Way Point: 127°22'00" Lon - W   20° 21'00" Lat - N

www.backroadmapbooks.com

Victoria Lake

Area Indicator

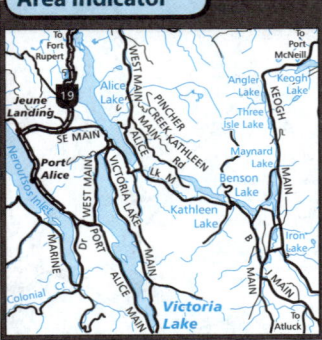

Fishing

If you are only going to fish one lake on the north island, say the locals, don't fish this one. But scratch a little deeper and you will start hearing stories of monster trout lurking in the depths of Victoria abound. People tell of 8 lb test being snapped like string, and pulling out a 5 kg (10 lb) rainbow is not uncommon. No, don't fish here, the locals say, because we want it all to ourselves.

Unfortunately for them, the secret is out. Located near the town of Port Alice, Victoria Lake is a large lake that holds the aforementioned trophy rainbow (although catches in the 2.5 kg/5 lb range are much more common), good-sized cutthroat trout, and the occasional Dolly Varden.

Trolling a plug or spoon is usually the most productive method. While there are a lot of options, a simple black Flatfish F4 or F5 is the most reliable. Troll closer to shore at the break of day, and move farther offshore as the day warms up. It is also recommended to use slightly heavier gear than normal, in case you do hook a 10 pounder.

While it is a large, deep lake, it is a low elevation lake, and the fishing cools down as the water warms up. Anglers can still have good success by trolling deep in the summer, but the fish are most active in spring (as soon as the ice is off until May) and fall. Folks camp at Spruce Bay, and fish the sheltered bay early in the morning with great results.

It is also rumoured that the mouth of the Teihsum (Green River) is quite possibly one of the best trout fishing hot spots on the island. Fish off the beach with a worm and bobber at the mouth of the river, or drop anchor just off-shore and do the same. The big trout lurk here waiting for fry to come down the river. Presenting a minnow fly pattern in gold or silver will also do quite well.

Facilities

Victoria Lake Recreation Site is one of the larger day-use sites on the island. There is a boat launch and a dock, as well as a large, sandy beach. It is found on the west side of the lake. On the east side of the lake is **Spruce Bay Recreation Site**, a beautiful site with boat launch, a beach and space for about five groups to camp.

There are a number of private, boat-accessed cabins around the lake. Please respect private property in the area.

Directions

Victoria Lake is located 5 km east of the small town of Port Alice and there are a number of main logging roads that access it. From the Port Alice Highway, continue south past the pulp mill and find the Port Alice Lake Main. This road leads northeast, eventually splitting near the west side of the lake and the popular Victoria Lake Recreation Site. There is also a rough boat launch a bit further south on the mainline.

To access the east side of the lake, the SE Main can be picked up off the Port Alice Highway near Jeune Landing. This good logging road takes you past Alice Lake and the Link River Park. Continue over the Benson River and turn right on Victoria Lake Main. This road eventually leads to the Spruce Bay Recreation Site, where you will find a boat launch and a campsite.

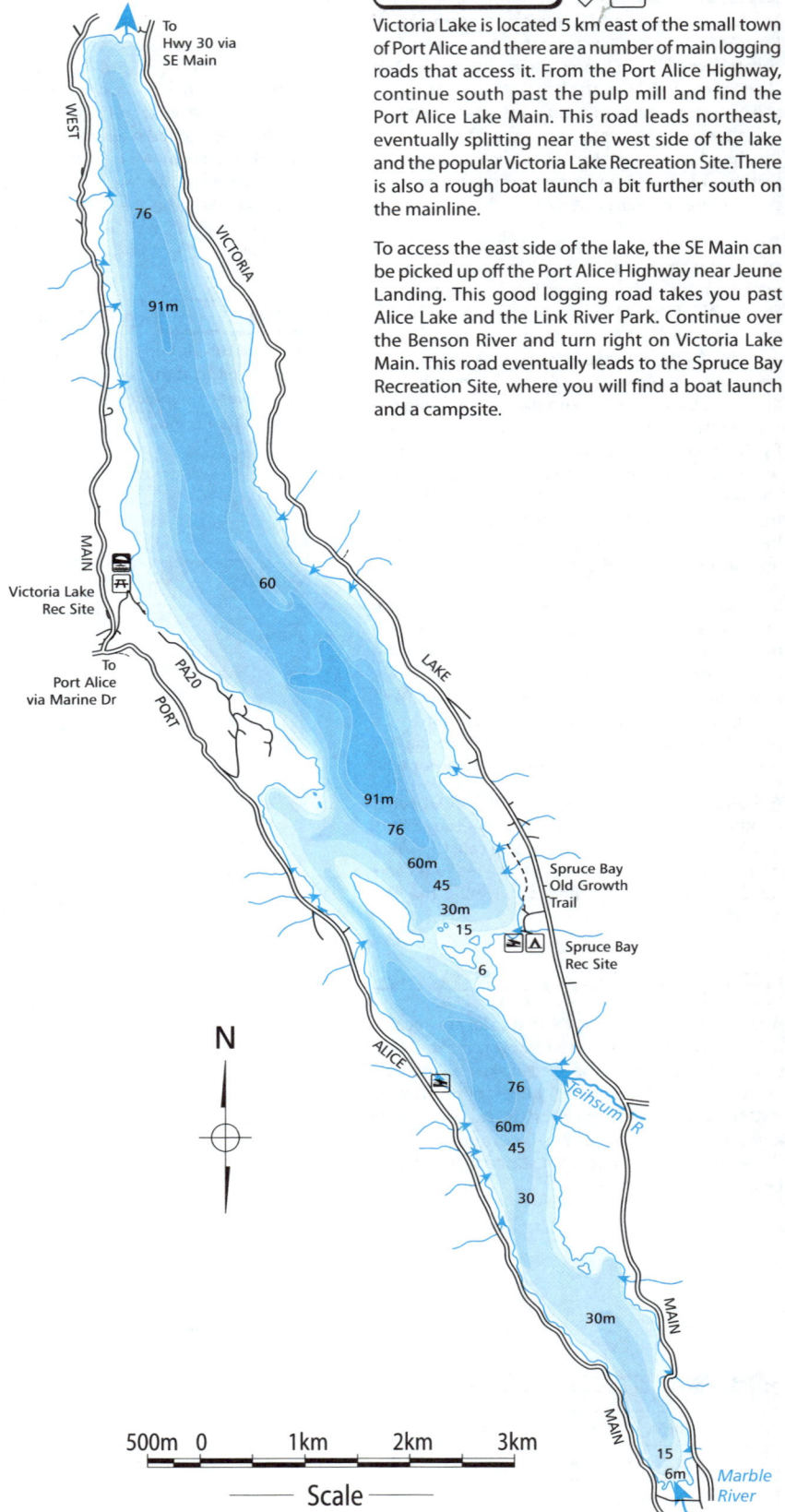

To Hwy 30 via SE Main

WEST MAIN

VICTORIA

76

91m

Victoria Lake Rec Site

To Port Alice via Marine Dr

PA20

PORT

60

LAKE

91m
76
60m
45
30m
15
6

Spruce Bay Old Growth Trail

Spruce Bay Rec Site

N

ALICE

76
60m
45
30

Teihsum R

MAIN

30m

MAIN

15
6m

Marble River

500m 0   1km   2km   3km

Scale

Westwood Lake

Location: 5 km (3 mi) west of Nanaimo
Elevation: 164 m (538 ft)
Surface Area: 63 ha (156 ac)
Mean Depth: 4m (13 ft)
Max Depth: 7m (23 ft)
Way Point: 124° 0'00"Lon - W   49° 09'00" Lat - N

Fishing

Westwood Lake is a sanctuary for a diversity of wildlife above the water's surface, and a generous population of hard-fighting rainbow trout, cutthroat trout and smallmouth bass below. Catchable rainbow trout are released into Westwood Lake each year by the Freshwater Fisheries Society of BC. For the young angler, pumpkinseed sunfish are also present.

The lake is located in a well-developed municipal park and is a popular destination for fishing, as well as hiking, swimming, mountain biking, birding and paddling. The 7 km (4 mi) trail around Westwood Lake is the jumping off point for a myriad of trails that wind over the rugged Westwood Ridges and climb to the top of towering Mount Benson. A trail map is located in the parking lot.

Many Westwood anglers cast spinners or spoons, and the lake offers a number of locations along the shore to cast out and try your luck. There are many excellent lures available for targeting trout. The Gibbs Silvex, Mepps Black Fury, Blue Fox, Panther Martin Gold and Bangtail are some of the more common spinners available at most tackle suppliers. An equal number of effective spoons are also available. Similar to spinners, they can be cast or trolled. Local tackle shops in Nanaimo can provide great tips for success on Westwood.

Fly fishers can have success throughout most of the year. Anglers can target hatches of chironomids, mayflies, caddisflies, dragonflies or damselfly throughout various times of the year. When no hatch is visible, general search or attractor patterns made to imitate the nymph stage of several invertebrate groups are usually effective. These patterns include Spratleys, Woolly Buggers, halfbacks, fullbacks and Careys. Having these patterns in a few colour and size combinations will produce results almost anytime throughout the season. The best fly-fishing areas are the shoals where the fish move in to feed on insects. The peak times of the year are April to June, and September through October, although Westwood can be fished year round.

When the lake warms up, the trout move off the shoals to deeper water. Deep trolling can produce success at these times of the year. Also in warm summer weather, when the trout become less active and move to deeper water, many anglers turn their attention to fishing for smallmouth bass. In the mornings and evenings, bass anglers find surface lures perform relatively well. In shallow waters, crankbaits, spinner baits, powerbaits or soft plastics produce good results in protected areas along the shore. In deeper water, try deep-running crankbaits or soft plastics.

Area Indicator

Westwood Lake
Fish Stocking Data

Year	Species	Number	Life Stage
2011	Rainbow Trout	3,500	Catchables
2010	Rainbow Trout	6,500	Catchables
2009	Rainbow Trout	22,000	Catchables

Directions

Access is via Jingle Pot Road and Westwood Road, 5 km (3 mi) west of Nanaimo city centre. The main park access point and boat launch is found at the end of Westwood Road.

Facilities

Westwood Lake Municipal Park is situated on the northern shores of the lake. It is a municipal park with a nice picnic site and beach as well as a good boat launch. Camping is available at nearby Westwood Lake R.V. Park.

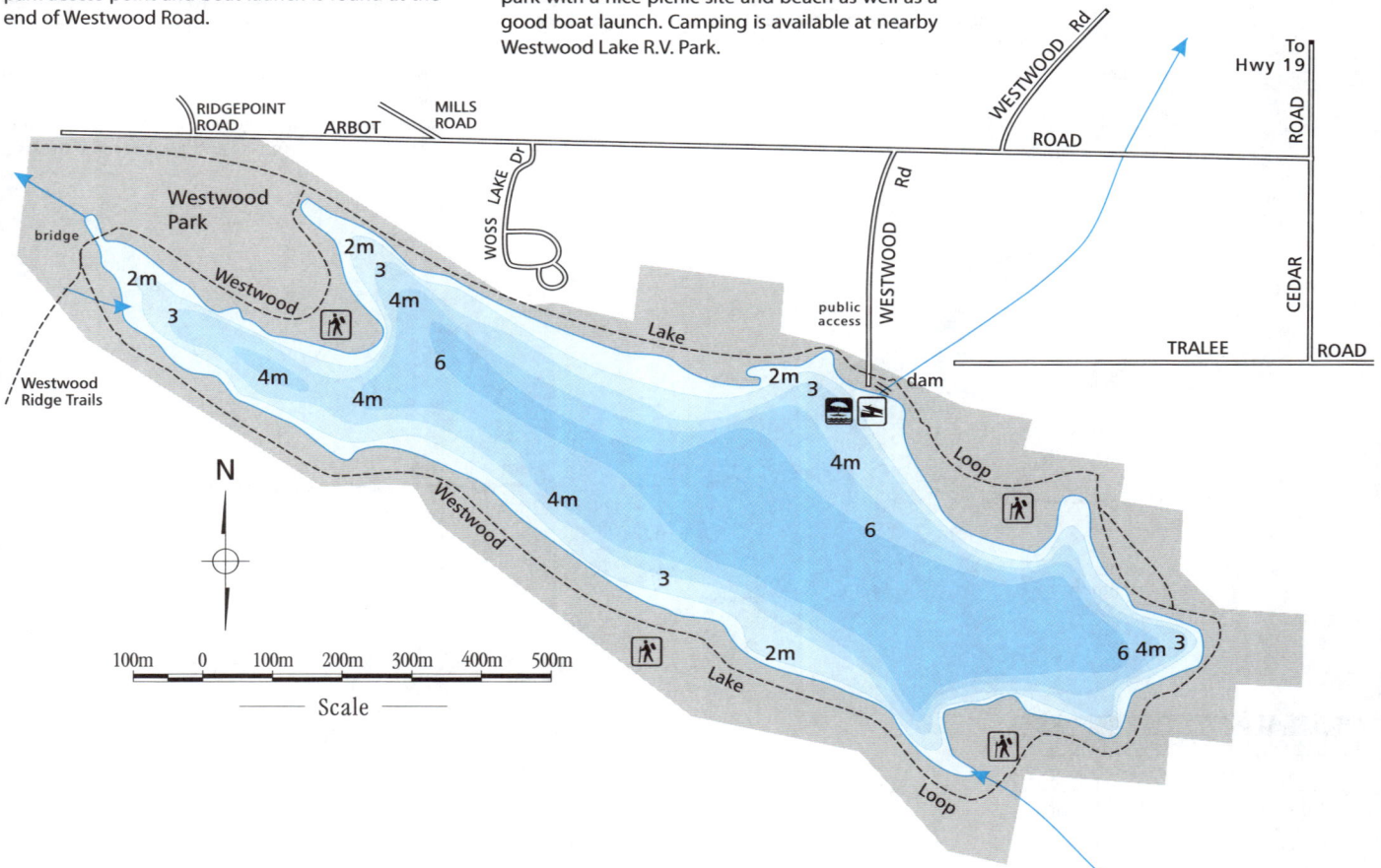

Location: 16 km (9.8 mi) northwest of Courtenay
Elevation: 191 m (627 ft)
Surface Area: 156 ha (385 ac)
Mean Depth: 13 m (43 ft)
Max Depth: 39 m (128 ft)
Way Point: 125° 10'00"Lon - W   49° 45'00" Lat - N

www.backroadmapbooks.com

Wolf Lake

Area Indicator

Fishing

Wolf Lake is a medium sized East Coast lake that offers good fishing for small rainbow and cutthroat during the peak fishing seasons of spring and fall. To help maintain the fishery, the Freshwater Fisheries Society of BC stocks the lake annually with cutthroat. There are rumours of a few Dolly Varden here as well. Fish that reach 35 cm (14 in) in size are not uncommon here.

Wolf Lake is a long, thin and deep lake. This means that trolling a lake troll is one of the most effective ways to find fish in the lake. A lake troll is one of the most effective set ups since the small flashers help attract fish and the spinner helps entice the fish into striking. Other popular trolling lures include Krocodiles, Kwikfish, Flatfish or Dick Nite spoons.

Spincasting and fly-fishing from a boat or from shore is certainly possible. Any small spinner tipped with a worm is a good choice. For fly-fishermen, try a nymph or chironomid pattern on a sinking line. Good places to work are at the estuaries of any one of the many small streams that flow into the lake.

The lake is deep, but it is at a fairly low elevation, meaning that the fishing slows down in summer. The fish are still active, but they tend to stick to the depths, and finding where they are hiding can be tricky. Fishing a deep troll during these times is your best bet.

There are informal boat launches found at both ends of the lake, but if you don't have a boat, your best bet is to hike in from the Duncan Bay Main road along one of the streams that flow into the lake. This is because the extensive shoals, especially around the southern launch, do not allow much opportunity to fish from shore.

Directions

Wolf Lake is found about 16 km northwest of Courtenay off of the Duncan Bay Main Road. To reach the lake, follow the Inland Island Highway north towards Campbell River and take the Mount Washington exit west. About 2 km later, the Duncan Bay Main courses northwest, eventually running along the western side of the lake. A short trail leads down to the lake.

You can also reach the lake from the north via the Duncan Bay Main. From the highway, take the Cranberry Lane exit west. This road soon meets the Duncan Bay Main, which continues south over the Oyster River and up and over the highway a couple times before eventually running alongside the west side of Wolf Lake.

Facilities

Wolf Lake has an undeveloped campsite and cartop boat launch at the southeast end of the lake. An informal picnic area and a cartop boat launch are also found at the northwest corner of the lake.

Other Options

Regan Lake is found to the northwest of Wolf Lake. Drive past Wolf Lake on the Duncan Bay Main heading northwest. At the 16 km mark, take the left branch called the Rossiter Main. That road continues northwest to the lake. Regan Lake is a 20 hectare lake with fair numbers of cutthroat and rainbow averaging 35 cm (14 in). Fishing is the best in the spring and fall primarily by fly-fishing or spincasting. There is a rustic campsite and launch area at the lake.

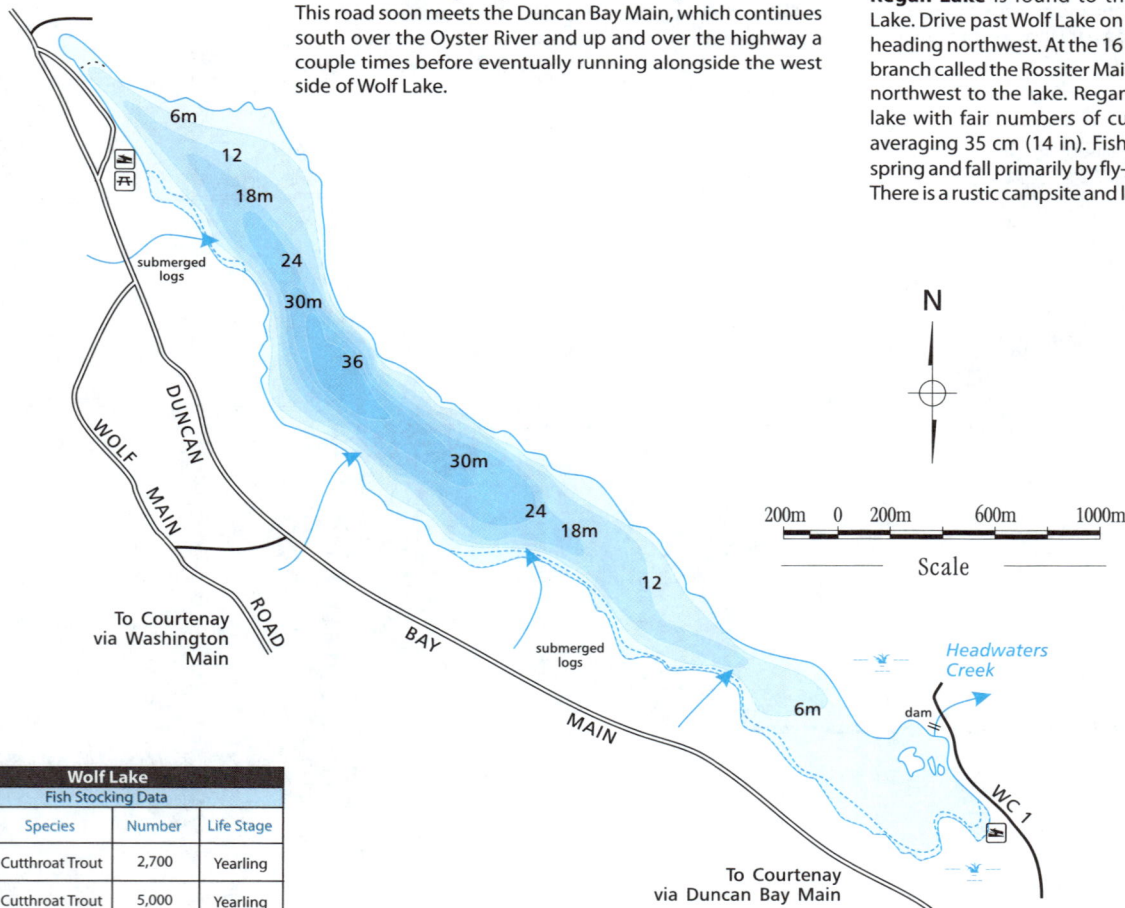

Wolf Lake Fish Stocking Data			
Year	Species	Number	Life Stage
2011	Cutthroat Trout	2,700	Yearling
2006	Cutthroat Trout	5,000	Yearling

Woss Lake

Location: 5 km (3 mi) south of Woss
Elevation: 147 m (482 ft)
Surface Area: 1,366 ha (3,374 ac)
Mean Depth: 65 m (213 ft)
Max Depth: 155 m (506 ft)
Way Point: 126° 36′ 00″ Lon - W   50° 09′ 00″ Lat - N

Directions

Getting to Woss Lake is relatively easy, although it makes for a long trip from larger centres like Victoria. The tiny settlement of Woss lays just south of Highway 19 as it makes its way from Campbell River to Port McNeill. From town, there are signs that point the way south over the Nimpkish River to the lake.

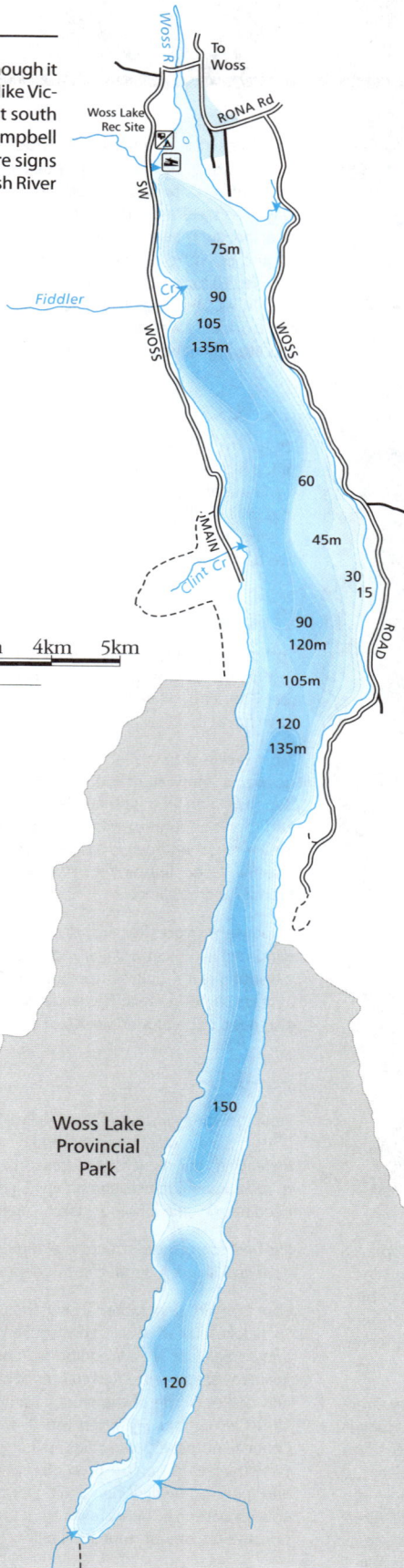

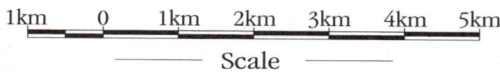

Area Indicator

N

1km 0 1km 2km 3km 4km 5km
Scale

To Woss
RONA Rd
Woss Lake Rec Site
Woss Rd
SW
WOSS Cr
Fiddler
75m
90
105
135m
WOSS
60
45m
30
15
90
120m
105m
120
135m
MAIN
Clint Cr
ROAD
Woss Lake Provincial Park
150
120

Fishing

Woss Lake is a large lake easily accessed by car just south of the settlement of Woss. The lake is dominated by Rugged Mountain and the glaciers and snowfields of its north-facing slopes. The seldom visited 6,634 hectare Woss Lake Provincial Park protects the south end of the lake.

The lake offers some great fishing early in the season, right after ice off. At this time, trolling produces fair numbers of small cutthroat, rainbow and Dolly Varden. Like most big lakes, trolling is the most productive method of fishing. And a black Flatfish, size F4 or F5, with a bit of silver glitter works really well, as does a blue and silver Flatfish. Lake trolls are also common on the lake.

Locals say there are two places to focus your efforts, one at either end of the lake. At the north end of the lake, next to the forest service site, the Woss River flows out of the lake. You can bring a boat, get out onto the water and troll this area. But it's easy enough just to cast off the end of the dock and have great success. Small spinners, Flatfish or even a worm and bobber are effective. This is also a good place to try your luck with a fly.

If the campsite end is too crowded for you, pack your gear and head for the south end of the lake. You will need a reasonable sized boat but if you can get down to the far end of the lake, look for an unnamed creek that flows out of the mountains from the east. There is a sandbar at the mouth of the creek, which is a great place to stop and have a picnic. This is a spectacular location and you're almost guaranteed to see wildlife, most likely elk. You're also almost guaranteed to catch a fish here, as this is one of the bigger feeder streams into the lake. Fry come down the stream and into the lake, where larger fish await them. You can do your part in helping protect these helpless fry by catching a few of these bigger fish. Try trolling just off the drop-off here, or if you prefer, drop an anchor and cast from there.

In between, there are a few places that you will also find along the big lake that are more promising than others. In particular, work the mouths of the many streams that flow into the lake. Some produce better than others. The trick is to find the bigger streams that tend to wash food (fry, bugs, etc.) into the lake. It is also a good idea to look for structure in your depth finder as you cruise the lake.

Facilities

Woss Lake Provincial Park protects the south end of Woss Lake, but it is not road accessible, and has no developed facilities. Instead, most people who come here stay at the **Woss Lake Recreation Site** at the north end of the lake. The site features a 24 unit campsite, a sandy beach and a boat launch. There is also a wharf to moor boats to.

© Mussio Ventures Ltd.

In addition to the tips under each fish species, we have provided more tips and techniques below. This section is designed to give you a better understanding of the various types of fishing styles as well as a much more elaborate breakdown on fly-fishing. Whether new to the sport of fishing or a Wiley veteran, we recommend reading through this section to pick a few tricks. We also recommend stopping in at the local tackle shop before heading out. They are the ones that know the local tricks and what has been producing well recently.

SPINCASTING ROD

PLUG   **SPINNER**

SPOON   **LURE**

LAKE TROLL

Bait (Still) Fishing

Probably the simplest way to catch fish and introduce young people or novice anglers to sport fishing is by a technique known as still fishing. When still fishing from the shore or a boat, the angler casts out and waits for a bite. Still fishing can be done with or without the use of float. Floats (bobbers) can be attached to the line so the baited hook stays suspended in the water. The depth can be adjusted by simply sliding the float up or down the line.

Casting just beyond the drop-off or around shoreline structure is very effective. In smaller lakes, a one metre (3 to 5 ft) leader with a size 8-12 hook is recommended. Weights should be avoided if possible, as they tend to scare off the fish. If you do need a weight, use 1-3 small split shot weights at least 30 cm (12 in) above the hook. Most fish tend to bite on worms and a single egg or roe. Other effective baits include maggots and shrimp meat or krill. Alternatively, artificial bait such as powerbait comes in a variety of colours, scents and shapes. The trick is to use the lightest line and smallest hook possible.

Jigging

Jigging can be an effective method of fishing if you can find where the fish are congregating. Jigging is a popular method of fishing though the ice in winter, although it is also widely used for bass fishing throughout the open water season as well as steelhead fishing on the rivers. Jigging is essentially sitting in a prime location, such as near underwater structure and working a jig head and body up and down to entice strikes. Outside of the traditional jig head and (where permitted) bait set up, you will also see anglers jigging spoons and other similar type lures. The great thing about jigging is that when the fish are in the area it can work very well, while the downfall obviously is that if the fish are not there, you literally have to wait for them to show up.

Ice Fishing

Ice fishing is limited on the Island. Many low elevation lakes do not ice up, and many high elevation lakes are not accessible. However, there are a few options to try. Generally speaking, ice fishing is possible from the end of December through to early March as long as the ice is safe. Jigging a small spoon or other attractant lure up and down has become one of the most popular fishing methods since live bait is not permitted in BC.

Spincasting

Spincasting is another popular and effective fishing method for all types of water. Essentially, spincasting is the process of casting a line from a rod with a spinning reel. The set up is quite simple making it easy for anyone to learn how to fish and have fun at it.

Most tackle shops offer good reel and rod combinations. It is recommended to go with a lightweight rod and 8-pound test or lighter, but this can vary obviously depending on what you are fishing for. The key is to have line light enough to cast and tough enough to withstand trolling and landing some fairly large fish. A good idea is to get an open face reel with removable spools. One spool could have light line (6 lb test or lighter) for small lakes and another have heavier line (8 lb or higher) for rivers and trolling.

If you want to go after big salmon or steelhead, a longer 10.5-foot rod with a level-wind reel is typical. Smaller rods will work for sockeye and pink. For most species, 12-pound test should suffice, but if you want to land those big Chinook you will need at least 30-pound test. The leader should be slightly smaller than mainline. Swivels also need to be bigger, size 10 or 8 should do.

Trolling

Trolling is the mainstay of bigger lakes, but also a popular alternative for many smaller lakes. It is a popular fishing method because you are able to cover large areas of water, increasing your chances of success on a lake. Ideally you should use a longer, stiffer rod than traditional spincasting set ups. Eight-pound test is okay for small lakes but you will need heavier line for bigger lakes, especially if using a downrigger.

It is best to troll near structure, along the drop-off or near a mid-lake shallow, such as a sunken island. A depth chart or depth finder will help you pinpoint these locations.

Lake trolls are popular because of their effectiveness and ease of use on both big and small lakes. These usually consist of a Willow Leaf or Ford Fender with a short leader and a small lure like a Wedding Ring or similar along with bait where allowed. There are many shapes, sizes and colours of lures that have proven effective trolling for trout and dollies. Some of the most common trolling lures include Flatfish, Krocodile or Little Cleo spoons. Fly fishers usually troll a leech pattern, particularly in murky water. Other all purpose trolling flies are Carey Specials, Woolly Buggers, and Doc Spratleys. Work the area just off the drop-off in a figure-eight pattern to vary the direction, depth and speed of the fly. When trolling for cutthroat, try a silver Muddler Minnow or other baitfish patterns. There are many shapes, sizes and colours of lures that have proven effective trolling for trout and dollies.

Fishing Tips & Techniques

On larger lakes, trolling for rainbow is very effective. Concentrate on points, inflow creeks or bays. In the fall or winter, troll a streamer type fly pattern like a bucktail quickly behind the boat. As the water warms, try an Apex, Lyman plug or flasher with a hoochie in the 10-30 m (30-90 ft) depth for bigger fish. For deep trolling, downriggers with the aid of a heavy weight will enable you to troll your lure deep enough to find holding areas. Alternatively, led core line or similar set-ups allow you to get your presentation down deeper without having to use downrigging equipment.

Fly-Fishing Equipment

Basically, there are three parts to a fly-fishing outfit: the rod, the reel and the line. Rods come in a variety of lengths and weights, depending on your size and the size of the species you intend to fish. As an example, a 9 ft, 6-weight rod would be an ideal set up for everything from trout to salmon up to about 5 kg (11 lb) in size. Longer rods are helpful in casting and helping manipulate flies into position on streams, especially on rivers and streams.

To handle bigger fish, fly anglers need a much heavier rod such as an 8 or 9-weight rod. For big Chinook, use an 11-weight rod. Many experienced fly anglers will have at least two if not three or more rods of different size and weight in order to maximize their fishing experience. Essentially, a smaller size and weight rod would be used for fishing small trout or panfish, while the longer heavier rod would be used on rivers for big salmon or northern pike.

When picking up a fly reel, the vast majority of reels (or any that are worth buying) will be weighted similar to the way rods are weighted. The reels are actually made to fit the appropriated rod. The difference in the weights of reels is mainly the size of the reel, since larger rods will be loaded with thicker line; therefore, the reel has to be a little larger to hold the increased line size. Also, the reel itself is often physically weighted to suit the rod weight so that the casting motion is balanced properly when casting your fly line.

When fly-fishing lakes, it is necessary to have a floating line in addition to a medium or fast sinking line. The floating line presents dry flies, as well as sub-surface wet flies. Dry line can also work well with weighted wet flies. However, a more popular subsurface option is using sink tip line, which is a combination of sinking and floating line where just the end of the fly line sinks. This type of line has a number of advantages, one being the ability to present subsurface flies while retaining the visibility of the fly line on the surface. This helps dramatically in spotting strikes, especially when fishing for trout. One of the best times to surface fish is during the mayfly and caddis hatches, however, trout usually prefer streamers and subsurface flies since they are very reluctant to strike the top of the water.

Medium sinking lines are ideal for fishing wet flies such as nymphs or chironomid pupae near the bottom. The medium sinking line offers the best control when attempting to fish a specific depth. If you do not have a medium sinking line, you can use a longer leader with some weight on your dry line. With a properly weighted fly or leader, this method can produce similar results. This type of presentation is ideal for working a particular depth, such as along a drop-off or along weed beds. Dragonfly, damselfly and even leech patterns can be worked quite effectively this way.

Fast sinking lines are ideal for trolling. If you are not familiar with the lake, trolling a fly is a good way to start. This allows you to cover a lot of distance searching for the ideal spot on the lake. Also, trolling is most effective on lakes with a low population of fish or during the summer doldrums. Woolly Buggers, streamers and leeches are all good all purpose trolling flies. Work the area just off the drop-off in a figure-eight pattern to vary the direction, depth and speed of the fly.

Regardless of which line you run with, you will also need backing and leader. The backing is designed to fill up the spool, as well as to act as reserve for when that steelhead goes for a 100 metre dash. Most people keep 100–150 metres of backing on their reel. The leader is a thinner monofilament line that attaches to the thick fly line to the fly. Leaders have a thicker butt that tapers to a thin tippet.

Fly-fishing is easily the most popular or at least most talked about fishing method of fishing in BC. It is also the hardest technique to master. Perhaps it is the challenge that attracts so many people to devote so much time. Or maybe it is the fact that once you have caught a fish on fly gear, everything else pales in comparison. Whether it is a small trout or an acrobatic salmon, the shear excitement of landing a fish with fly-fishing gear is exhilarating.

FLY FISHING ROD

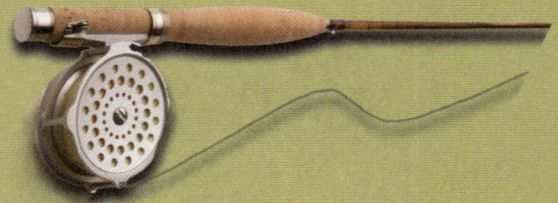

BEAD-HEAD NYMPH

CAREY SPECIAL

CHIRONOMID

DOC SPRATELY

Flies

There are numerous books on fly-fishing techniques and how to choose the best fly for the particular season; however, it is really quite simple. Match the hatch! What you want to do is use a fly that most approximates the insect or baitfish on which the sportfish are feeding.

To determine this, spend some time observing the aquatic insects at the lake and try to determine what the fish are rising to and how the insects are moving in the water. If you can not see the adult insect on the water surface then try using a small fine net to scoop up the insects. Once you have discovered what type of insect the fish are feeding on, you should try to determine how the insect moves in the water so you can imitate it. For example, is the adult insect sitting motionless on the water or is it rapidly flapping its wings?

DRAGON NYMPH

ELK HAIR CADDIS

BEAVERTAIL LEACH

MUDDLER MINNOW

SILI SCUD

MAYFLY

MAYFLY RIG

STREAMER

WOOLLY BUGGER

Here is a list of recommended flies to include in your fly box. By no means is this exhaustive, but rather a good base to work from:

Bead Head Nymph is a variation of the halfback or pheasant tail nymph patterns, but is often a little more versatile. The fly is already weighted so it can be fished easily in streams and lakes with either sinking or floating line. The bead head also is an attractant that often glistens in the water attracting attention of predatory fish.

Carey Special is versatile enough to be used in both lakes and streams. Try size 4-8 for trout or 6-12 for salmon in red, green or brown. One of the most popular lake patterns in BC, it is a great searching pattern that can simulate many insects, including dragonfly, mayfly and caddis nymphs, as well as leeches. Smaller flies using a simple strip retrieve with sinking line is best in lakes, while moving water requires a bigger fly that is drifted with quicker strips.

Chironomid (Midge) has quickly become one of the most important flies in the fly box of a BC lake angler. Chironomids can be found in every lake in the BC and varies in size and colour depending on the lake and time of year. The fly must always be worked very slowly in the part of the water column that depends on what stage of the main hatch is taking place. The big hatches are mainly in the spring, although they are present all year round.

Doc Spratley is a general-purpose fly that can imitate most insects and a number of leeches. Perhaps the most popular fly in BC, the large sizes can imitate the dragonfly or damselfly nymphs, while smaller versions are like chironomid pupae. Black is the most versatile, but red, green and brown work, too. Depending on what you want to imitate dictates the method of presenting this fly. If you are looking to imitate a dragonfly nymph, stripping the fly in a consistent manner would be appropriate. On the other hand if you are looking to imitate a smaller nymph pattern, a shorter stripping retrieve may be required.

Dragon and Damselfly Nymphs vary in size and colour. Since they are found everywhere, they should certainly be part of every fly box. There are literally dozens of patterns that are used throughout the province and your best bet to know what works is to inquire locally before you head out. These nymphs are often worked deep and even off bottom for cruising trout.

Elk Hair Caddis is a specific caddis imitation fly that revolutionized top water caddis fly fishing. Depending on the time of year your presentations will vary with this type of fly. In the early part of the season, hatching caddis will often flap along the surface attempting to break away. Therefore, your presentation should imitate this. Later in the season when caddis are laying eggs, they will literally smack the water and trout will pounce on them. They key is to be observant of the hatch and what the flies are doing.

Leeches are a definite must in every fly box since they are found in virtually all lakes in BC. Leech patterns are versatile and great for searching lakes. At times, this is all trout are feeding on. Even if they are feeding on something else, they will rarely pass up a well-presented leech.

Mayfly patterns vary dramatically in size and colour. During a hatch, trout can sometimes be so picky that they will literally pass up your mayfly if it is a size or two too small or a wrong colour. However, the mayfly hatch is a big part of the open water season and a good variety of this fly is needed in your box, especially early in the season.

Muddler Minnow imitates a minnow in distress and is the ideal meal for a wide variety of fish. In general, larger fish seem to like bigger presentations of this fly. The fly is mainly worked below the surface although some anglers have been known to put floatant on them and work them on or just below the top of the water for big aggressive fish.

Scud (Shrimp) patterns, similar to chironomids, vary greatly in size and colour depending on the lake. A good rule of thumb is to use whatever colour the lake bottom is. Working the fly needs patience. It should be allowed to sink close to the bottom and retrieved with slow short strips followed by a short pause. Working closer to shore is better, since shrimp are most often found frolicking here.

Streamer is a good versatile pattern for all sportfish species as it imitates baitfish or larger meals that most sportfish thrive on. This fly can be of almost any size and colour, but the key is that it should have a long sleek profile in the water and is used to fish subsurface. While you will see bright coloured streamer patterns out there, typically you are looking for a pattern that imitates baitfish.

Tom Thumb is one of the more popular dry flies in British Columbia. Size is very important to match the current hatch, especially if surface fishing. While the fly can imitate a number of different insects, it is most commonly used as a caddis imitation.

Woolly Bugger is a good versatile pattern for cutthroat, salmon, steelhead and trout. This fly imitates larger meals such as a baitfish or leeches and can be effective in both streams and lakes. While the most popular colours are olive and black, other colours and variations, such as a bead head or Egg Sucking Leech, can create a unique fly for that unique situation.

Fishing Tips & Techniques

Fishing Small Lakes

On smaller Island lakes, the predominant fish species are rainbow, brook and cutthroat trout. If you are looking for more success and less size on your day out on the water, small lakes are a good bet as there is less water to cover. Fishing near structure such as logs and weeds, shoals or at the edge of a drop-off produces the best results. Food sources also congregate around weeds and inflow or outflow streams and in the thermocline. The thermocline is the area of the lake between the warm surface water and the cold water. Concentrate your efforts in these areas to improve your chances of angling success.

A good way to explore a new lake is to use searching type lures or flies and work them near the subsurface structures. Along with your depth chart map, it is a good bet to invest in a depth finder. Depth finders can give even more detail to the underwater structure that maps simply cannot provide. Another tool that can help when fishing lakes or streams is a good pair of polarized glasses. Polarized lenses will help you spot fish or underwater structure that may not show up on a map or depth finder.

A universal set up that will attract all species is a lake troll with a short leader and a Wedding Ring or similar with bait. Flatfish, Krocodile or Little Cleo spoons are trolled, while fly fishers usually troll a leech pattern, particularly in murky water. Other all purpose trolling flies are Carey Specials, Woolly Buggers, and Doc Spratleys. Work the area just off the drop-off in a figure-eight pattern to vary the direction, depth and speed of the fly. When trolling for cutthroat, try a silver Muddler Minnow or other baitfish patterns.

If you are fishing from shore, try casting along the shore or towards a fallen log, weed bed or drop-off. Use the countdown method to find where the fish are holding. With each cast, count a little longer until you find the strike zone. Casting almost any small spinner or spoon with some bait (worms are preferred) can prove successful, but watch for bait restrictions. Favorites are the Panther Martin, Mepps or Blue Fox. As for lures, a Deadly Dick, small Dick Nite, Flatfish or Kwikfish also work well. Fly anglers must vary their presentation with the season by paying attention to the current hatches.

As the water warms up and the fishing slows during the late spring, move to a higher elevation lake. By continually moving to higher elevations you can continue to fish the first few weeks of prime time period right until the lakes begin to cool down in the fall. And as the water gets too cold up high, begin moving down to the lower elevations. Most of the high elevation walk-in lakes offer good fly-fishing during their limited season, which lasts from late June until October. Another nice thing about these lakes is the fish are more active when the light penetrates the water. This makes an 11 o'clock arrival a good thing. If the water is murky, you might as well move on, as the lake is experiencing turnover and the fish will rarely bite.

Fishing Bigger Lakes

Big lakes can be intimidating. This is where the map comes in really handy. Study your map for structure and devise a game plan prior to arrival. Once at your spot, use your depth finder to hone in on those really unique structure areas and work them hard before heading on to another area.

Here Trolling for rainbow is very effective. Concentrate around creek or river mouths. Fish seem to hold around the drop-offs in these areas because of the large amount of feed available. Drop-offs near cliffs or rock walls are also good areas to focus your efforts. In spring, fall or winter, troll a streamer type fly pattern quickly behind the boat so they skim off the surface can produce some big trout. Muddler Minnows, Polar Bear or bucktails are popular choices. As the water warms, try an Apex, Lyman plug or flasher with a hoochie in the 10-30 m (30-90 ft) depth. For deep trolling, downriggers with the aid of a heavy weight will enable you to troll your lure deep enough to find holding areas.

If fishing from shore, working the drop-off around creek mouths is your best bet. Bait balls (a large cluster of worms or eggs and a hook) can be fantastic for Dolly Varden and sometimes rainbow. During the summer a float with a grasshopper can also land you a nice trout.

Fishing Streams & Rivers

Rivers and streams can be a challenge to fish, but at the same time they offer other opportunities that lakes do not. Most notably, hot spots in rivers can be very easy to find as they are often at the bottom of a small waterfall, or the slack water next to the fast water. The main problem with bigger rivers is getting your presentation out far enough from shore to where the fish are holding. The easiest way to overcome this problem is to use a boat if possible. This way you can find seams and pools where fish are holding and get your presentation to where the fish are instead of fighting the

The Island hatches generally maintain the same pattern starting with chironomid/midge hatches in early March to mid-July followed by dragonfly nymphs from early May to the end of September. Damselflies emerge mid-June to mid-August and the caddisfly/sedge hatch takes flight mid-June to the end of August. Leech and halfback nymph patterns are usually successful all year long.

March:
· All chironomid stages
· Shrimp
· Leeches

April:
· All chironomid stages
· Mayfly nymph
· Shrimp
· Leeches

May:
· All chironomid stages
· Mayfly nymph
· Dragonfly nymph
· Shrimp
· Leeches

June:
· All chironomid stages
· Mayfly nymph
· Damselfly nymph
· Dragonfly nymph
· Shrimp
· Leeches

July:
· Damselfly nymph
· Dragonfly nymph
· Caddisfly/Sedge
· Terrestrials
· Shrimp
· Leeches

August:
· Damselfly nymph
· Dragonfly nymph
· Caddisfly/Sedge
· Terrestrials
· Shrimp
· Leeches

September:
· All chironomid stages
· Dragonfly nymph
· Water boatman
· Shrimp
· Leeches

October:
· All chironomid stages
· Water boatman
· Shrimp
· Leeches
· Water boatman

current with your cast from shore. You can also access some of the more remote areas that shore anglers are not fishing to find some of the more productive holes.

Of course getting a boat onto smaller streams is often not possible. In these cases, a good set of waiters and river shoes can make a big difference in being able to get to the good holes. To work these streams effectively, you need to sneak up on holes to avoid being detected by trout. Work every pocket, pool or seam no matter the size. Some of the biggest fish are hiding in the most unlikely places.

Salmon, steelhead, sea run cutthroat and Dolly Varden are the main sportfish pursued by Island river anglers. Specific techniques for each species are found earlier in this book.

Please Note: There are regulations imposed for many of the lakes and streams in order to preserve the quality of the resource. Always check the regulations before fishing!

Releasing Fish - The Gentle Way

There is a growing trend among anglers to catch and release, unharmed, a part of their allowable catch. As well, more restrictive regulations on specific waters can severly limit the angler's allowable harvest.

A fish that appears unharmed may not survive if carelessly handled, so please abide by the following:

1- Play and release fish as rapidly as possible. A fish played for too long may not recover.

2- **Keep the fish in the water as much as possible.** A fish out of water is suffocating. Internal injuries and scale loss is much more likely to occur when out of water.

3- Rolling fish onto their backs (while still in the water) may reduce the amount they struggle, therefore minimizing stress, etc.

4- Carry needle-nose pliers. Grab the bend or round portion of the hook with your pliers, twist pliers upside down, and the hook will dislodge. Be quick, but gentle. **Single barbless hooks are recommended**, if not already stipulated in the regulations.

5- Any legal fish that is deeply hooked. Hooked around the gills or bleeding should be retained as part of your quota. **If the fish cannot be retained legally, you can improve its chances for survival by cutting the leader and releasing it with the hook left in.**

6- If a net is used for landing your catch, it should have fine mesh and a knotless webbing to protect fish from abrasion and possbile injury.

7- **If you must handle the fish, do so with your bare, wet hands (not with gloves).** Keep your fingers out of the gills, and don't squeeze the fish or cause scales to be lost or damaged. It is best to leave fish in the water for photos. If you must lift a fish then provide support by cradling one hand behind the front fins and your other hand just forward of the tail fin. Minimize the time out of the water, then hold the fish in the water to recover. If fishing in a river, point the fish upstream while reviving it. When the fish begins to struggle and swim normally, let it go.

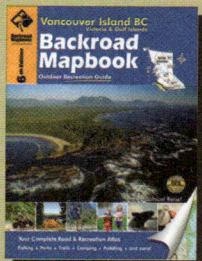

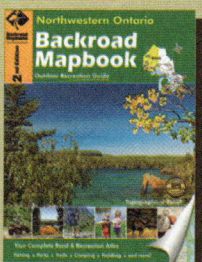

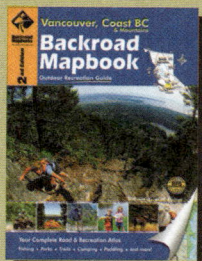

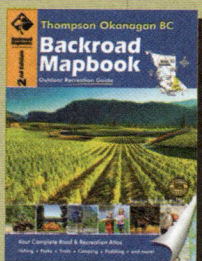

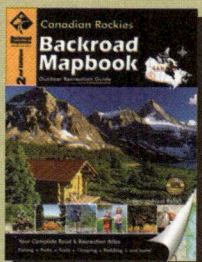

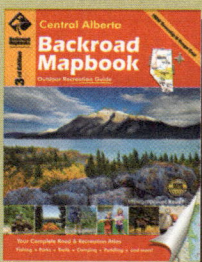

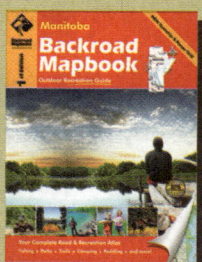

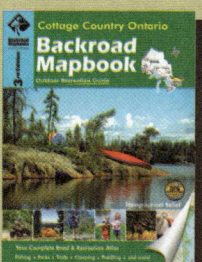

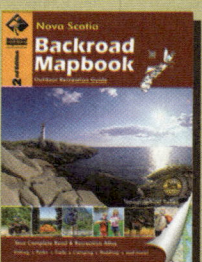

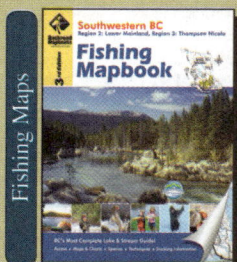

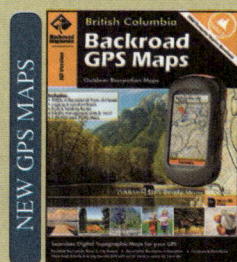

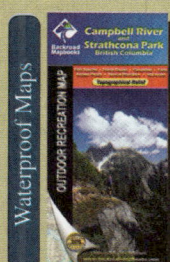

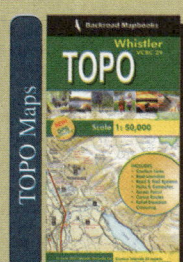

Index

Important Numbers

Fish and Wildlife

General

B.C Forest Services

Parks

Advertisers